1974

P9-CKR-733

To maman
and her
garden

YIELDS IN CANNED OR FROZEN PRODUCE

(Since the legal weight of a bushel of fruits or vegetables differs between States, the weights given below are average; the yields are approximate.)

Fruits	Fresh	Quarts Canned	Pints Frozen
Apples	1 bu. (48 lbs.)	16–20	32–40
Apricots.	1 bu. (50 lbs.)	20–24	62–74
Berries (not strawberries). . .	24-qt. crate	12–18	32–36
Cherries, as picked.	1 bu. (56 lbs.)	22–32	36–44
Peaches	1 bu. (48 lbs.)	18–24	32–48
Pears	1 bu. (50 lbs.)	20–25	40–50
Plums	1 bu. (56 lbs.)	24–30	38–56
Strawberries	24-qt. crate	12–16	38
Tomatoes	1 bu. (53 lbs.)	15–20	———
Vegetables			
Asparagus.	1 bu. (45 lbs.)	11	15–22
Beans, Lima, in pods	1 bu. (32 lbs.)	6–8	12–16
Beans, snap/green/wax . . .	1 bu. (30 lbs.)	15–20	30–45
Beets, without tops	1 bu. (52 lbs.)	17–20	35–42
Broccoli	25-lb. crate	———	24
Carrots, without tops	1 bu. (50 lbs.)	16–20	32–40
Corn, sweet, in husks	1 bu. (35 lbs.)	8–9	14–17
Peas, green, in pods	1 bu. (30 lbs.)	5–10	12–15
Pumpkin	50 lbs.	15	34
Spinach	1 bu. (18 lbs.)	6–9	12–18
Squash, summer	1 bu. (40 lbs.)	16–20	32–40
Sweet potatoes	1 bu. (55 lbs.)	18–22	34–38

PROCESSING ADJUSTMENTS FOR ALTITUDE

Because atmospheric pressure at altitudes 1,000 feet or more above sea level affects processing either in a Boiling-Water Bath or a Pressure Canner, it is necessary to make the following adjustments to ensure the right results. For the B-W Bath you add minutes to processing time— how much, depending on whether the original time required is 20 minutes or less, or more than 20 minutes. For the Pressure method you add pounds—at the same progression regardless of whether the original pressure called for is 5 or 10 (the most-used pressure) or 15 pounds.

TO B-W BATH ADD:		ALTITUDE	FOR PRESSURE, PROCESS AT:		
If 20 mins. or less	*If over 20 mins.*	*(Feet)*	*If 5 lbs.*	*If 10 lbs.*	*If 15 lbs.*
1 min.	2 mins.	1,000	5½ lbs.	10½ lbs.	15½ lbs.
2 mins.	4 mins.	2,000	6 lbs.	11 lbs.	16 lbs.
3 mins.	6 mins.	3,000	6½ lbs.	11½ lbs.	16½ lbs.
4 mins.	8 mins.	4,000	7 lbs.	12 lbs.	17 lbs.
5 mins.	10 mins.	5,000	7½ lbs.	12½ lbs.	17½ lbs.
6 mins.	12 mins.	6,000	8 lbs.	13 lbs.	18 lbs.
7 mins.	14 mins.	7,000	8½ lbs.	13½ lbs.	18½ lbs.
8 mins.	16 mins.	8,000	9 lbs.	14 lbs.	19 lbs.
9 mins.	18 mins.	9,000	9½ lbs.	14½ lbs.	19½ lbs.
10 mins.	20 mins.	10,000	10 lbs.	15 lbs.	20 lbs.

Putting Food By

This book is for

John Hutchens, who said to write it, and
"P.R." who helped it so, and

all the people everywhere who want the
happiness of putting food by safely for their
families and knowing what's in it.

Putting Food By

RUTH HERTZBERG

BEATRICE VAUGHAN

JANET GREENE

The Stephen Greene Press
Brattleboro, Vermont 05301

ACKNOWLEDGMENTS

For firsthand learned-by-successful-doing information, the authors are grateful to all the anonymous dedicated people in federal- and provincial- and state-run projects in the United States and Canada who are constantly researching better and safer ways to handle our food; and to Guy Brunton, master of old and new building; Mary Scott Buntin and Mary Lou Williamson of the Consumer Service of the Ball Corporation; Robert Carpenter and Kenneth Carpenter, pharmacologists; Lona B. Chatterton, expert router of queries to the Extension Service; William H. Darrow, Jr., apple-grower and -storer; Val Dubal, D.V.M., of the Vermont Department of Agriculture; Jane Keely of the Good Housekeeping Institute; Merrill Lawrence of Lawrence's Smokehouse; Shirley Knight Morris of Burns & MacEachern Limited, Ontario, Canada; Alexis Nason, geologist; Walter Needham, author of *A Book of Country Things;* Samuel R. Ogden, countryman and organic gardener; Ronald Rood, naturalist; and, for their help in dealing with maverick questions and problems, Jon Anderson, Mildred M. Dupell, Thure Hertzberg, Hazel D. Howard, Ann C. Johnson, Nancy Lent, Ethel R. May and Alice B. Robinson.

All photographs and drawings not otherwise credited are from the U.S. Department of Agriculture. The exceptions are: drawings on pages 9 and 10—John Devaney; photograph on page 14, left—Rowe Automatic Can Sealer; drawings on pages 6, 169, 190, 226, 227, 248, 275, 281, 314, 317—Norman Rogers.

Library of Congress Catalog Card Number: 71-188897
International Standard Book Numbers: 0-8289-0163-5 (*paper*)
0-8289-0164-3 (*cloth*)

74 75 76 77 78 79 9 8 7 6 5 4

Contents

What "Putting By" Is

To "put by" is an early nineteenth-century way of saying to save something you don't have to use now, against the time when you'll need it. You still hear it today from old-time country people, and applied to food it embraces canning, freezing, preserve-making, drying, curing, wintering-over in a root cellar, and a handful of maverick methods like rendering lard and even making soap from scrap fats.

Putting food by is prudence, and it's involvement. It's also a meaningful return to old simplicities and skills. Above all, it is deeply satisfying. We know what is added to food we put by for our families. And we have a direct return for effort—which has become a luxury in these times of remote and deviously routed forces.

My contribution to this book has been to agree with John Hutchens's suggestion to do it, and then to have the gumption to enlist Ruth D. Hertzberg for it. She spent fifteen years as a County Agent in Home Economics with the Vermont Extension Service, where she worked continually in the field with young people in communes, student families in towns, and older experienced housewives, all of whom turned to her for better ways of using their food resources. She also taught Peace Corps volunteers in training the best ways to use and preserve food in places as far apart as the Chilean Andes and Equatorial Africa.

For this book she has drawn on firsthand experience as well as on the great body of information available from the United States Department of Agriculture and the Food and Drug Administration, from state Extension Services and from many highly regarded sources not government-sponsored. Together we asked Beatrice Vaughan to supply old-time recipes for preserves and for cooking food that's been put by.

As completely as we can, throughout we give the basic reasons that make each food-handling method work safely. Our stress is always on safety—protection against spoilage that makes the result of one's effort unfit or even dangerous to eat—because we believe that a newcomer to putting by food can always keep track of the *How* for any process if the *Why* is handy and clear. It was good, during all the digging and conferring, to watch the safety principles apply to such a wide variety of procedures as this book describes.

Feasibility, on the other hand, we feel to be a matter for individual decision. We comment sometimes on whether one kind of treatment gives a notably more usable product than another one does, but generally we assume that each householder must decide which preserving method to use. There are several titles dealing with nutrition in the list of references on the endpapers, and we recommend them.

Finally, I turned occasionally to people whose unfailing good sense and experience I needed in amplifying a point from time to time. The generosity and wisdom are theirs: the interpretations, however faulty, are my own.

Janet Greene

Canning

Canning is a comparatively recent way to put food by—only freezing, with its offshoot of freeze-drying, is newer—and canning is the means most often used in North America for preserving perishable foodstuffs safely at home.

For its effectiveness, canning relies on sterilization and the exclusion of air. Both these functions are accomplished by heat, which destroys the things in the food that cause spoilage, and drives air out of the contents and seals them completely from any outside contamination during storage.

Two factors determine how much heat is needed, and how long to apply it.

One factor is the kind of substance or organisms that cause spoilage or even dangerous toxicity in canned food which is held in storage.

The other factor is the natural or added acid in the food itself, because this acid aids in controlling the spoilers that attack the food.

In order to turn out SAFE home-canned products, we always consider HEAT, TIME and FOOD TYPE in deciding which of the several canning methods to use.

Finally, when our foods are canned, we must store them in a dry, cool, dark place. For even when they are adequately processed, they will lose Vitamin C, carotene, thiamine, riboflavin and niacin at temperatures above 50 degrees Fahrenheit; and light hastens oxidation of fats and oils, destroys fat-soluble and light-sensitive vitamins, and fades the color of the food.

TEMPERATURE vs. SPOILAGE

Four kinds of things cause spoilage in preserved food: *enzymes,* which are naturally occurring substances that help to promote organic changes in plant and animal tissues; and three types of micro-organisms—*molds, yeasts* and *bacteria*—which are present in the soil, water and air.

The growth, production and destruction of all four are affected by heat.

1

NO CHEMICAL PRESERVATIVES

Several chemical preservatives in prescribed amounts are allowed by the U.S. Food and Drug Administration to be added to food canned commercially, but we do not include them in the specific instructions that follow later.

The only things we do include—*and they are optional*—are: sugar or other natural sweeteners in fruits, to hold the flavor; small amounts of ascorbic acid (Vitamin C), as an anti-oxidant; and small amounts of plain table salt, for seasoning in vegetables and various meats.

CONTROLLING THE ACTION OF ENZYMES

The enzymes themselves in organic matter don't hurt us (quite the contrary), but their *action* is reversible: they can turn around and cause decomposition—hence changing the flavor, texture and color of food, and making it unappetizing. Their action is slowed down by cold, increases most quickly between around 85 and 120 degrees Fahrenheit, and begins to be destroyed at about 140 F. Therefore if food is heated thoroughly at well above 140 F., either by precooking or by an adequate heat-canning process, enzymes are no longer a factor in spoilage.

CONTROLLING THE ACTION OF MOLDS

Molds are microscopic fungi whose dry spores (seeds) alight on food and start growing silken threads that become mats of fuzz. Many molds are innocent—indeed, they're responsible for the highly prized veining in "blue" cheese—but others are unpleasant in cooked fruits and tomatoes and jellies and preserves, which they make musty and distasteful. Molds are alive but don't grow below 32 degrees Fahrenheit; start to grow above freezing, with maximum acceleration between 50 and 100 F.; taper off to inactivity beginning at *c.* 120, and the growing cells are destroyed with increasing speed from 140 until they reach 190 F.

But even though the growing cells of mold *in* a food are done for, fresh spores can reach it before it is sealed, or can get inside containers that are unsterilized or imperfectly sealed; and there—unless the capped container is subjected to killing heat or inactivating cold—they start growing brand-new mold.

2

CONTROLLING THE ACTION OF YEASTS

The micro-organisms we call yeasts are also fungi grown from spores, and they cause fermentation—which is delightful in beer, necessary in sauerkraut, and horrid in applesauce. As with molds, severe cold holds them inactive, 50 to 100 F. hurries their growth, and 140 to 190 F. destroys them. And they too can contaminate sterilized food that's handled carelessly or sealed imperfectly.

CONTROLLING THE ACTION OF BACTERIA

Bacteria also are present in soil and water, and their spores, too, can be carried by the air. But bacteria are often far tougher than molds and yeasts are: certain ones actually thrive in heat that kills these fungi (creating recognizable "flat-sour" spoilage as they grow); and in some foods there can exist bacteria or bacteria spores which make hidden toxins that will be destroyed in a reasonable time only if the food is canned at 240 to 250 degrees Fahrenheit—*at least 28 degrees higher than the boiling temperature for water, and obtainable only under pressure.*

Without reveling in horrors, it is enough to mention that, of the disease-causing bacteria we're concerned with in canning food at home, the most fragile are members of the genus Salmonella, which includes typhoid fever—and which are transmitted by pets, rodents, insects and human beings, in addition to existing in our soil, water and air. Salmonellae live in frozen food, are relatively inactive up to 45 F., and are killed when held at 140 F., with destruction much quicker at higher temperatures.

More heat-resistant are the transmittable bacteria that cause "staph" poisoning, the *Staphlococcus aureus* whose growth makes a toxin that is destroyed only by many hours of boiling or 30 minutes at 240 F., although the growth of the bacteria themselves is checked if the food is kept above 140 F. or below 40 F. Thus "staph" germs are halted in their tracks fairly easily at temperatures that kill Salmonellae, but the poison they make merely by growing takes a very long time at boiling, or a much higher temperature (240 F.), more briefly, to destroy.

Toughest and most dangerous is *Clostridium botulinum,* which causes botulism, a fairly rare disease—but one that the USDA Research Service listed in December 1971 as 65 percent fatal. Also called Botulinus, it grows in certain moist foods *in the absence of oxygen—*

which means that it can thrive in an airless, sealed container of these foods—and its extremely heat-resistant spores continue to produce the deadly toxin for some time after the growing cells are killed at *c.* 190 F. Botulinus is inactive when frozen, although it survives.

It takes more than 6 hours of steady boiling to kill the spores; depending on the food, this translates into around 100 minutes at 240 F. However, the toxin allowed to form in the stored containers as a result of under-processing can be destroyed by briskly boiling the food for 15 to 20 minutes before it is eaten.

> *Note:* Two of the best presentations we've seen on preventing spoilage are simple ones. The first is the USDA Consumer Service *Home and Garden Bulletin No. 162, Keeping Food Safe to Eat,* 25 cents* from the Superintendent of Documents, U.S. Government Printing Office, Washington, D.C. 20402—or maybe your Home Ec County Agent can give you a copy. The other, formerly a separate pamphlet, is now incorporated in shorter form in the *Ball Blue Book,* New Revised Edition 29, from Ball Brothers Company, Muncie, Indiana 47302, and costing 50 cents.*

*Both prices @ January 1974: ask your County Agent if they've changed.

ENTER *pH*—THE ACIDITY FACTOR

The strength of the acid in various foods determines to a great extent which of the spoilage micro-organisms each food can harbor: therefore acidity is a built-in direction that tells us at what temperature, and for how long, a particular food must be heat-processed to destroy these spoilers within it, and make it safe to eat. (Heat alone, not natural acidity, controls the action of enzymes.)

Acid strength is measured on the *pH Scale*, which starts with strongest acid at 1 and declines to strongest alkali at 14, with the Neutral point at 7, where the food is considered neither acid nor alkaline. The following grouping is enough for our discussion now.

The strong-acid foods

The strongest-acid food we deal with in canning is *pickles,* which have a large amount of acid added in the form of vinegar.

Less strong, but still highly acid, are, in descending order, the foods with natural acidity: rhubarb, green gooseberries, cranberries, plums, apricots, apples, "soft" berries (blackberries, raspberries, etc.), pie (sour) cherries, peaches, kraut (fermented cabbage or turnip), sweet cherries, pears and tomatoes. (Often these foods are referred to for simplicity's sake merely as "acid," since their flavor is noticeably sharp; but they are classed as *strong-acid*.)

Molds thrive in stronger acid than yeasts do, as a rule, but both flourish on fruits and tomatoes and some vinegared foods. No dangerous bacteria that we're concerned with in canning prefer the more strongly acid foods at the top of the list just given, but several which are destroyed at 190 F. do grow in the lower range of strong-acid foods.

FOODS IN THE STRONG-ACID CLASS ALLOW GROWTH OF MOLDS, YEASTS AND SOME DANGEROUS HEAT-SENSITIVE BACTERIA, BUT THEY DO NOT FOSTER GROWTH OF HEAT-*RESISTANT* BACTERIA.

The low-acid/nonacid foods

Except for the vinegared things and fruits and tomatoes, above, all the other foods we meet in home-canning are low on the acid-strength scale —and many of them are so low as to have no acid at all. Such *low-acid* foods are, in roughly descending order of protective acidity: okra, peppers, pumpkin and squash, carrots, cabbage, turnips, beets, snap/ green/string beans, greens (spinach and other leaf vegetables), potatoes (sweet or white), asparagus, cauliflower, Lima and other shell beans. Peas are nearly on the Neutral line, corn *is* Neutral, and lye hominy actually crosses over to alkaline.

Classed with all natural vegetables—and all are low-acid to nonacid (tomatoes being really a fruit)—are *meats, poultry, seafood and dairy products, all of which are NONACID*.

In addition to the expectable molds, yeasts, and heat-sensitive bacteria, low-acid and nonacid foods invite the growth of dangerous heat-resistant bacteria, and, in certain conditions, the growth of toxin-producing organisms that thrive without air. Therefore:

LOW-ACID/NONACID FOODS ARE LIKELY TO FOSTER GROWTH OF DANGEROUS HEAT-*RESISTANT* AND ANAEROBIC BACTERIA, AND ALSO CONTAIN OTHER SPOILAGE MICRO-ORGANISMS.

HEAT + ACIDITY = SAFETY

Combining (1) the temperatures that control life and growth of spoilage micro-organisms with (2) the *pH* acidity factor of the foods that are particularly hospitable to certain spoilers, gives the conscientious home-canner this rule to go by: *It is safe to can strong-acid foods at 212 F. in a Boiling-Water Bath, but low-acid/nonacid foods must be canned at 240 F.–a temperature possible only in a Pressure Canner at 10 pounds' pressure–if they are to be safe.*

Processing times vary according to acidity and density of the food concerned. Adequate temperature and length of processing time are given in the specific instructions for individual foods.

> **Before tasting canned low-acid food—vegetables, meat, poultry, seafood—boil it hard for 15 minutes to destroy any hidden toxins (corn and greens require 20 minutes). If it looks spoiled or foams or has an off-odor during boiling, destroy it completely so it can't be eaten by people or animals.**

TEMPERATURE vs. THE SPOILERS
(Degrees Fahrenheit)

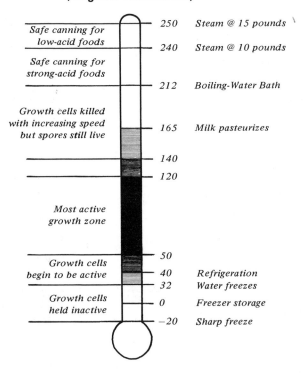

	250	*Steam @ 15 pounds*
Safe canning for low-acid foods	240	*Steam @ 10 pounds*
Safe canning for strong-acid foods		
	212	*Boiling-Water Bath*
Growth cells killed with increasing speed but spores still live	165	*Milk pasteurizes*
	140	
	120	
Most active growth zone		
	50	
Growth cells begin to be active	40	*Refrigeration*
	32	*Water freezes*
Growth cells held inactive	0	*Freezer storage*
	−20	*Sharp freeze*

EQUIPMENT FOR CANNING AND PRESERVE-MAKING

If your canning is merely occasional—just a batch of tomatoes, say, or a bit of jelly or a favorite relish—your regular kitchen utensils will be adequate. Spend money for big specialized items only when you're serious about volume canning, and want or need to process lots of several kinds of foods. Or join a few friends in sharing the cost, and use, of such equipment.

Essential:

> Water-bath canner for processing strong-acid foods
> Steam-pressure canner for processing low-acid foods
> 6- to 8-quart kettle for precooking food or making jelly
> 6- to 8-quart enameled kettle for making pickles
> Jars or "tin" cans in prime condition, with lids/sealers/gaskets
>   ditto
> Sealing machine (hand operated), if you're using cans
> Alarm clock, for timing long processing
> Pencil-shaped glass food thermometer (you'll need it if you're
>   a serious canner, or are using cans)
> Shallow pans (dishpans will do)
> Wire basket or cheesecloth to hold foods for blanching
> Ladle or dipper
> Perforated ladle or long-handled slotted spoon, for removing
>   food from kettle
> Wide-mouth funnel for filling jars
> Jar-lifter
> Sieve or strainer, for puréeing
> Colander, for draining
> Large measuring cups
> Muslin bag, for straining juices
> Plenty of clean, dry potholders, dish cloths and towels

Nice, but not absolutely necessary:

> Long-handled fork
> Household scales
> Food mill, for puréeing (a blender's the ultimate in luxury)
> Large trays
> Minute-timer with warning bell (more accurate than an alarm
>   clock, and particularly good for short processing periods)

ABOUT JARS AND CANS

Either glass jars or metal cans may be used for putting food by.

Anything that is canned in metal may also be canned in glass, but there are several foods which should be canned only in glass (the individual instructions will tell you).

Except for doing meat and poultry, canning in metal cans requires one step more than canning in jars does.

Jars show off their contents and hence are a requisite for exhibiting your canning skill at the county fair. Jars of food must be stored in a cool, dry, dark place—dark, so the contents won't fade.

Cans keep light away from the contents, but they too must be stored in a cool, dry place. But they also stack better than glass jars do.

Jars are easier to buy than are cans and the machine for sealing them: supermarkets and neighborhood hardware and farm supply stores get jars in well before the canning season gets in full swing. The Summer catalogs (usually out in the middle of spring) of the leading mail-order companies list cans and can-sealers, etc. Most hardware stores will special-order cans and sealers for you.

THE EMPTIES

With all these considerations in mind, each beginning canner must make up her own mind whether to go in for jars or for cans (since it wouldn't make much sense for the average householder to lay out the initial expenditure for both).

There's one more thing, though: storing emptied jars *versus* heaving emptied cans.

If she has the place to store jars filled with food, there's usually nothing to keep her from storing emptied jars alongside them as she goes through the year.

But maybe she has a sanitary landfill waiting near by for her empty cans. Or a recycling station.

Many accomplished home-canners prefer cans to jars because they have mastered the techniques required, and like cans for their light-proof and storing virtues. Also, community-canning projects—such as those sponsored by the government during the Depression of the 1930's and into World War II—seem to favor cans over jars.

The types of jars

Although the modern jars come in ½-pints, pints, 1½-pints, quarts and ½-gallons, with only several exceptions the measurements and processing times for specific foods given later involve only pints and quarts, either straight-sided (i.e., without a shoulder that impedes dumping the contents), or regular (wide or standard mouth); *but we give no data for ½-gallons: dense low-acid foods don't process well in them.* If some modern jars are O.K. for freezing, their carton will say so.

BUT DON'T USE THESE:

(1) Containers you bought food in (like baby-food jars, etc.) —once opened, their lids never seal fully again. Or (2) very old canning jars—whose metal fittings may have lost the gimp needed for a perfect seal (and anyway the jars may have bona fide antique value!).

OLD-STYLE BAILED JARS

There are many bail/wire-clamp jars still in use. Sometimes called "Lightning" type, these·have an all-glass lid which is cushioned on the jar by a separate rubber ring, and the whole thing is held in place during processing by the longer hoop of the two-piece wire clamp. When the jars are removed from the canner after processing, the shorter spring-section of the clamp is snapped down on the shoulder of the jar to complete the seal. (This is the action referred to in individual instructions as *"complete seals if necessary."*)

OLD-STYLE SCREW-TOP (MASON) JARS

There are a number of these still around too. "Mason" no longer means the maker (who patented them in 1858)—it designates that the top is screwed on, not held with bails.

One variety has a porcelain-lined zinc cap which is screwed down on a separate rubber ring that acts as a sealing cushion. (The *zinc* here could cause exposure to cadmium, although the cap is lined with porcelain. Henry A Schroeder, M.D., calls cadmium "our most insidious pollutant—mammals have not learned to handle it; an industrial contaminant, always found with zinc." Dr. Schroeder is founder and director of the Trace Element Laboratory and author of *Pollution, Profits & Progress.*)

The other type of old-style Mason jars has a flat glass lid which lies on a separate rubber ring, and is held down by a threaded metal band that screws on.

With both these types of old-style jar, you screw down the lid/band completely, then loosen it ¼ inch (to allow space for air to be forced out during processing) before putting it in the canner. When these jars are removed from the canner after processing, you tighten the lids/bands completely again. (This is the action referred to in individual instructions as "*complete seals if necessary.*")

MODERN SELF-SEALING (MASON) JARS

These have a flat metal lid (called a "dome" lid, for some reason) with a rubber-like sealing compound around the edge where it meets the rim of the jar; the lid is held in place with a metal screw band. The band is *screwed down completely* before the filled jar goes in the canner (there's enough give in the lid to let air escape during processing).

And don't give them an inquisitive tightening after the jar is processed: the seal has automatically completed itself, and indeed you could *break the seal* by trying to tighten it further.

After the jar has cooled for 12 hours or more, you may remove the band and use it on another jar: the flat lid has been sealed on to the jar. You *NEVER re-use the flat lids.*

Fittings for the jars

FOR BAIL-TYPE LIGHTNINGS

Only the fresh separate rubbers, for either regular or wide-mouth jars of this type, are sold these days (unless a few boxes of glass lids have remained in stock in a neighborhood store, or you find them at an auction of household goods).

NEVER use old, stale jar rubbers, or re-use rubbers. Whether they're stale from hanging around or have been used before, they have lost their gimp and *will not give a perfect seal.*

And some of the wire bails are so old and tired that they don't hold the lid down tightly enough. *Please* don't go in for makeshift tightening by bending the wires or padding the lids.

FITTINGS FOR OLD-STYLE MASONS

Again, the only fittings you're likely to find in the stores are the fresh rubbers which you'll use (only once) with the lids you have on hand. Or, write to the manufacturer to learn where you may buy zinc screw-caps or glass-tops-with-bands.

FITTINGS FOR MODERN SELF-SEALING MASONS

The flat "dome" lids and their screw bands may be bought combined, or the flat lids may be bought separately.

Since you never re-use the flat lids, whose sealing compound has lost its original muscle, you'll use fresh lids for each canning session. If you run out of bands, you'll have to buy them with lids included in the package.

General handling for jars

Check carefully any held-over jars and their fittings which you plan to use again, and discard any with weak bails and nicked rims, and throw away chipped or imperfect lids and bands. Also, don't forget to check all the new jars and their fittings. *And note "Don't Use" on page 9.*

CLEANING/STERILIZING

All jars and lids must be washed before each use, but only those which are processed below 212 F. need be sterilized (this means sterilizing for Open-Kettle, *Hot*-Water Bath, and for the rare Cold-Water method; in Boiling-Water Bath and Pressure Canner the containers sterilize along with the contents).

Wash jars and lids with soap and hot water, scald-rinse in boiling water; and, if they're to be filled right away with boiling-hot foods, let them keep hot in the hot rinse water while they wait. If you wash them long ahead of time, drain them dry, put on their lids to keep their insides clean, and warm them before filling with boiling food (so they'll be sure not to crack).

Sterilize *clean jars and glass or porcelain lids* by covering them with water and boiling them for 10 minutes; let them wait in the sterilizing water to keep hot until you fill them. You must *not boil rubbers and self-sealing lids with gaskets:* this hurts their ability to seal; instead, put them in a bowl, cover them with briskly boiling water and let them stand in it until you're ready to use them.

LOADING/UNLOADING JARS FROM THE CANNER

Don't put cold jars of food into very hot water; don't fill a canner with jars of boiling-hot food and then slosh cold water into the canner. Don't clunk filled jars against each other—especially if they're filled with boiling-hot food.

After processing, take care that you don't knock the jars against each other as you unload them. Set them on a rack, a wooden surface, or one padded with cloth or newspaper, and be sure it's not in a draft of cold air. Complete seals if necessary.

COOLING JARS

Jars must cool slowly and undisturbed. Let them sit on their draft-free surface for 12 hours before you test the seals; then wipe, label, and store the jars in a cool, dark place.

The types of cans

The containers called "tin cans" aren't made of tin: they're usually made from reclaimed scrap metal and are merely coated with tin inside and outside. This tin coating is satisfactory for use with most foods. These are called *plain* cans.

But certain deeply colored, acid foods will fade when they come in long contact with plain tin coating, so for them there is a can with an inner coating of special acid-resistant enamel that prevents such bleaching of the food. This is called an *R-enamel* can.

Then we have still other foods that discolor the inside tin coating —perhaps because some of them are high in sulfur, and act on the tin the way eggs tarnish silver; or because some are so low in acid as to nudge or straddle the Neutral line. Although there's no record of any damage to these foods from tin coating, there's a can for them that is lined with *C-enamel.*

A leading manufacturer of cans for home-canning says that we may use *plain* cans and *C-enamel* cans *interchangeably,* with the sole detriment that sometimes the insides of plain cans will be discolored.

Note: Although there are many sizes of canned foods on supermarket shelves, the cans used in putting by food at home are: *No. 2*—which holds about 2½ cups; and *No. 2½*—which holds about 3½ cups. (The difference in measure between No. 2 and pints, and No. 2½ and quarts accounts in part for the difference in processing time given for jars and cans.)

WHAT FOODS TO CAN IN WHICH

Throughout the individual instructions we've included the type of can— plain, R-enamel or C-enamel—to use if you use cans at all.

However, here's a rule-of-thumb to go by if you're canning a food we don't go into:

R-enamel. Think of "R" as standing for "red" and you'll have the general idea: beets, all red berries and their juices, cherries and grapes and their juices, plums, pumpkins and winter squash, rhubarb and sauerkraut (which is very acid).

C-enamel. Think of "C" as standing for "corn" (which has no acid) and for "cauliflower" (whose typically strong flavor indicates sulfur) and you get: corn—and hominy, very low-acid Lima and other light-colored shell beans (and, combined with corn, succotash); cauliflower—and things with such related taste as plain cabbage, Brussels sprouts, broccoli, turnips and rutabagas; plus onions, seafood and tripe.

Plain. This is the catch-all, and may take these foods, as well as others: most fruits, tomatoes, meats, poultry, greens, peas, and green/snap/string/wax beans, and certain made dishes (like baked beans, etc.).

If you're canning Mixed vegetables, use *C-enamel for preference* if one or more of the ingredients would go in C-enamel by itself.

Remember, though, that the heavens won't fall if you mix up *plain* and *C-enamel.* Nor will "red" acid foods be bad if they're not canned in *R-enamel*: they just won't have their full color.

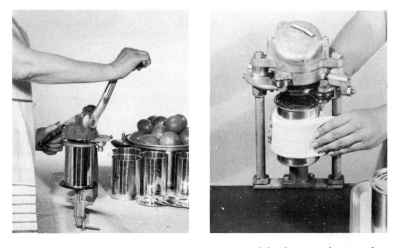

Two types of can-sealers, with the one at right in actual operation (the dry cloth pad helps in handling cans full of food at 170 F.).

The extra step in using cans

As with jars and their lids, cans and their lids must be scrupulously clean.

As with putting lids on jars, you put the lids on cans—and crimp them with the sealing machine tightly enough to seal them. (Check the can-sealer by adjusting it to fit the size of can, then partly fill a can with water, seal it, and drop it in a kettle of boiling water for a few seconds.

If air bubbles rise from around the sealed rim of the can, you do not have a good seal so adjust the sealer again.)

IT'S CALLED "EXHAUSTING"

There is an extra intermediate step, though, that must be taken when you put food by in cans.

Food in cans must be *hot* (170 F. is the minimum temperature given) *before cans are sealed.* This heat drives out any air in the tissues of the food, and any air in the canning liquid (plus any air trapped in packing the food in the can) and thus gives you a good vacuum in the can when it's processed. Also, food is less likely to discolor or change flavor if all the air is driven out of it by preheating.

Food *packed raw* must be heated in the open can to a minimum of 170 F., and food *packed hot* (precooked) must be raised back to 170 F., if necessary, before the can is sealed with little or no headroom. See "Raw Pack and Hot Pack" for general details of the two methods of packing jars/cans.

This heating-to-170-F.-process is called *exhausting.* To do it, place filled, open cans on a rack in a kettle and add water up to about 2 inches below the tops of the cans. Cover the kettle, bring the water to boiling, and boil until a food thermometer stuck deep into the center of a can has reached the desired 170 F.

Then, as you take each can from the kettle, check it to see if the level of food and processing liquid are still at the right heights in it, carefully wipe the can rim free of any food that might have spilled over (bits of food or fat will prevent a good seal)—and put on the lid and crimp it on completely with the can-sealer. Add the can to the rest in the processing canner, and process the load for the required time.

COOLING THE CANS

Unlike jars, which must be allowed to cool gradually after they leave the canner (or else they'll break), cans *must be cooled quickly* to stop their contents from cooking further.

Fill your sink or any other large vessel with very cold water and drop processed cans into it. Change the water to hasten the cooling. Remove cans when you're able to handle them comfortably and let them dry.

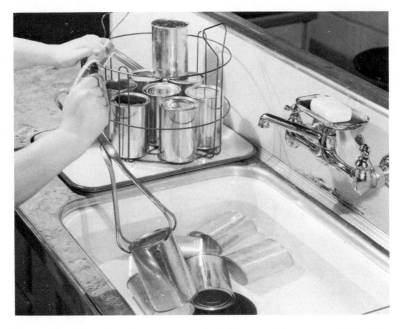

Use a jar-lifter to drop processed hot cans into very cold water.

Checking the seals

Jars get a perfect seal by means of the vacuum created as processing drives air from the food within them, and, after the seals are "completed" by tightening non-self-sealing lids, the vacuum is increased as the contents cools and shrinks.

Snapping down bails or re-screwing down lids on old-style Mason jars does not *make* the seal: it merely holds the lids in place while the food cools.

Cans, however, have a perfect seal before they go into the canner—provided that they're properly filled and exhausted and their lids are crimped on tightly by the can-sealer.

FOR JARS

Let jars stand upright and undisturbed for 12 hours before you check them.

Jars with separate rubber rings (bailed or old-style Mason types). Tilt the jar in your hands and watch for rising bubbles in its contents, or for moisture around the rim. Moisture or bubbles rising to the top mean a poor seal.

Jars with flat metal lids (modern Mason type). If the "dome" in the center of the lid is down or stays down when pressed, the jar is sealed. (Sometimes you'll even hear the "domes" snap down as the jars are cooling.)

FOR CANS

Allow cans to finish cooling undisturbed overnight. Then check them for bulging ends or seepage at the seams, either of which means an imperfect seal.

WHAT TO DO WHEN SEALS AREN'T PERFECT

If you see that the seal is not perfect within 24 hours after canning the food, open the container at once and re-process the food. Or serve it.

But if you find an imperfect seal after the jar/can has been *stored*, discard the contents without tasting it. And dispose of it in such a way that it can't be eaten by animals or human beings.

IF THE SEALS ARE O.K., LABEL AND STORE

Label each jar/can with the name of the food and the date it was put by (dated, because you'll want to serve first the foods that have been longer in storage).

GOOD SEALS ARE ALMOST CERTAIN IF—

1. All jars/cans and their covers are in perfect condition when used.
2. Complete cleanliness is maintained throughout preparation, packing and capping the containers.
3. Jars/cans are filled to the proper level with food at the required temperature, and are processed for a time long enough to create the condition that makes and holds a seal.

RAW PACK AND HOT PACK

Before they go in the Pressure Canner or Boiling-Water Bath, many fruits, vegetables and meats can be packed in their containers *either raw* (sometimes also designated as "cold") *or hot.* The food is trimmed, cleaned, peeled, cut up, etc., in the same manner for both packs; the liquid in the containers is virtually always hot to start with; the seasoning—in the form of salt or sugar sirup—is added just before processing either pack; and in both packs the containers are handled identically after being processed and cooled.

So, where you have a choice, the pack you use is up to you. Here are the general considerations.

RAW PACK

Foods of relatively low density tend to hold their shape better if they are packed raw, because they are handled less (this is particularly noticeable with tomatoes, for example).

Boiling water or sirup is added to the raw foods that require added liquid for processing.

Jars of raw-packed food must start their processing treatment in hot, *not boiling,* water; otherwise they may crack.

Processing time is usually longer for raw-packed foods canned in a Boiling-Water Bath—especially for the denser ones.

HOT PACK

Food that is precooked a little or almost fully is made more pliable, and so permits a more solid pack. Foods differ in the amount of preheating they need, though: spinach is merely wilted before it's packed, but green string beans boil for 5 minutes.

In a Boiling-Water Bath, hot-packed food requires less processing time, being thoroughly hot beforehand. This is assuming that you're hewing the line drawn by the experts, and are using the B-W Bath *only* for acid vegetables and fruits, which take a relatively moderate processing time at 212 F.

There is usually no difference in the time required for Pressure Canning raw-packed and hot-packed foods: by the time you start counting—at 240 F.—raw-packed food has become as hot as if it had been packed hot to begin with. (One of the interesting exceptions is summer squash, which needs longer Pressure Canning for hot pack than for raw, because the precooked squash is much denser in the container than the crisp raw pieces are.)

Pressure-processing will condense this Raw pack of summer squash a great deal, even after it's tamped down and given generous headroom.

LEAVING HEADROOM

In packing jars of food that will be processed in a Hot-Water Bath, Boiling-Water Bath or Pressure Canner, there must be some leeway left between the lid and the top of the food or its liquid. This space— called *headroom* in the instructions that follow later—allows for expansion of solids or the bubbling-up of liquid during processing. Without it, some of the contents would be forced out with the air, thus leaving a deposit of food on sealing surfaces, and ruining the seal.

Too much headroom may cause food at the top to discolor—*and* could even prevent a seal, unless processing time were long enough to exhaust all the excess amount of air.

The right headroom for each food and its processing liquid is specified in individual instructions.

No headroom is needed for fruits canned by Open-Kettle (q.v.), but if Open-Kettle is to be followed with a few minutes in a B-W Bath to ensure the seal, leave appropriate headroom when filling the jars.

Cans generally require no headroom between liquid and lid: all air is driven out in the exhausting step, and the lids are sealed on, before the cans are processed.

Three kinds of headroom: left, for chicken packed Raw in a jar, and exhausted; below, 1 inch left above boiling water added to Raw-packed summer squash; and right, ¼ inch for whole-kernel corn packed Hot in cans, with boiling precooking liquid added right up to the brim.

The Canning Methods

THE *WHY* OF PRESSURE CANNING

Processing under pressure allows the contents of jars/cans to reach higher-than-boiling temperatures—228 F. at 5 pounds, 240 F. at 10 pounds, 250 F. at 15 pounds—thereby destroying the tough bacteria spores in low-acid foods, discussed on pages 5–6.

A Pressure Canner—don't confuse it with a plain *steamer*, which peaks at 212 F.—is a big edition of the pressure saucepan you may already own. It's usually made of cast aluminum. At this writing, one described as of 8-quart capacity (meaning loose contents though: it actually holds only 4 1-quart jars) costs around $30; 16-quart models (in jars really 7 quarts or 16 pints) are about $40; bigger ones taking 4 ½-gallons or 18 pint jars can be harder to find, and cost comparably more. But we suggest you avoid ½-gallons: see "Types of Jars" on page 9—and they don't fit in the average canner anyway.

It may make economic sense to buy a Pressure Canner if you plant a good-sized garden or can get lots of fresh produce cheaply in season, and have surplus meat to put by. But if your family is small and you have just a few surplus foodstuffs to store, maybe your answer is freezing (discussed later on).

Borrowing?—usually not feasible. But something that is: Go shares with thoroughly compatible friends in buying a large one (estimating the size carefully beforehand) and pool the group's resources and energies for canning bees, along the lines of the successful community canning projects sponsored by the WPA during the Depression of the 1930's. Such bees are equally practical for young families on tight budgets in cities and for communes in the country. Perhaps the best source of information for organizing a really big group operation is the Home Economics department of your state university. Its records can go back much further than your County Agent's do, and therefore it can describe procedures (and pitfalls) under actual working conditions when these centers flourished years ago.

Note: If you are buying, check the depth of its innards with the top on, because you may want it to double as a Boiling-Water Bath canner from time to time—and the B-W Bath requires several extra inches of headroom above the tops of the jars/cans.

The anatomy of a Pressure Canner

The base, or kettle, is covered with a tight-fitting lid that contains the controls. The lid is fastened down with clamps or a system of inter-locking ridges and grooves. It may or may not have a rubber gasket to ensure a tight seal.

Controls consist of: (1) a pressure gauge—usually a dial type; (2) a vent that lets air and steam exhaust before the processing period begins, and is closed with a weight or petcock to start raising pressure, and (3) a safety valve or plug that will blow off excess steam if the pressure gets too high for safety.

The canner also will have a shallow removable rack to keep jars/cans from touching the kettle bottom, or a strong wire basket that serves as a rack and lets you lift all the containers out in one fell swoop when processing is completed.

Caring for a Pressure Canner

First, read the instruction book that comes with it.

Next, clean the canner according to directions, to remove any factory dust or gunk. Use hot sudsy water for the kettle, avoiding strong cleansers or scouring powders. Do *not* immerse the lid in water: instead, wipe it clean with a soapy cloth, and follow with a clean damp one to remove the soap.

Check the openings of the vent, safety valve and pressure gauge to make sure they're unclogged and clean. Take a small sharp-pointed tool (like a large darning needle or a bodkin) to the openings if they need it; clean the vent by drawing a narrow strip of cloth through it.

Be sure the rims of kettle and lid are smoothly clean, so they'll make a perfectly tight seal.

At the start of each canning season—or more often if you put up large quantities—the dial pressure gauge should be checked for accuracy against a master gauge. You can find out from the manufacturer where to send it; the information may even be in his instruction book. Or you can perhaps save time by calling your county Agricultural Extension Service offices to see if they have equipment right there to do it. If they have, they may be able to check it for you. But please unscrew the gauge at home—carefully, so the threads don't strip—and bring it in by itself: the Extension Service people have wrestled with more than their share of lids and cranky screws.

You need a new gauge if yours is 5 pounds or more off an accurate reading in either direction.

The gauge is not likely to be this far off, though. So for lesser variations adjust your pressure as follows for food that is to be processed at 10 pounds (the pressure most often required):

If the gauge reads high by 1 pound—process at 11 pounds; by 2 pounds—process at 12; by 3 pounds—process at 13; by 4 pounds—process at 14.

If it reads low by 1 pound—process at 9; by 2 pounds—process at 8; by 3 pounds—process at 7; by 4 pounds—process at 6.

Note: Just because the dial may rest at 2 pounds pressure when the canner is not in use does not necessarily mean that the gauge is either simply 2 pounds high or is uniformly 2 pounds off throughout its scale. So have it checked.

THE PRESSURE CANNER AT WORK

Here are the mechanics of using a Pressure Canner. How jars/cans are filled will be taken up in the individual instructions for processing each food.

WATER IN—

Put at least 2 inches of boiling water in the thoroughly clean canner. If you know that your canner leaks steam slightly when the vent is closed, have an extra inch or so of water to ensure that the canner will not boil dry and warp during processing time.

START IT HEATING—

Place the uncovered kettle over heat high enough to raise the pressure quickly after the lid is clamped on. (See how to estimate this heat in the box "Leary of Pressure Canners?")

COVER ON TIGHT—

Put the lid in position, matching arrows or other indicators. Turn tightening knobs, bands or clamps to fasten the closure evenly and so snug that no steam will escape around the rim.

MANAGE THE CONTROLS—

Know and follow the manufacturer's instructions: techniques for processing vary slightly with the different makes and models.

For canners with a *dial-faced gauge,* leave the vent open until steam has issued from it in a strong, steady stream—7 minutes for a canner that holds 7 or 8 quart jars, and at least 10 minutes for the larger ones. Then close the vent with a weighted cap or petcock and let pressure rise inside until the gauge registers a little less than the desired number of pounds. Lower heat under the kettle and, when the gauge registers the exact poundage you want, adjust the heat again to keep pressure steady at the correct poundage. Constant pressure is important: liquid is drawn from the jars if the pressure is allowed to fluctuate.

For canners with older-style *weighted gauges* (which are harder to follow than a dial is), allow steam to flow in a steady stream through the vent for 7 or 10 minutes (depending on the size of the canner, as above). Then set the gauge on the vent, and carry on as for a canner with a dial-faced gauge—but of course keeping track of the frequency of the jiggles as the maker's instructions say to.

Two "musts" first and last—time carefully, and lift the lid this way.

WATCH THE CLOCK—

Count the processing time from the moment pressure reaches the correct level for the food being canned. *Be accurate:* at this high temperature even a few minutes too much can severely overcook the food.

LET OFF STEAM—

At the end of the required processing time turn off the heat or remove the canner from the stove. It's heavy and hot, so take care.

If you're using *glass jars,* let the canner cool until the pressure drops back to Zero. Then open the vent very slowly.

CAUTION: If the vent is opened suddenly or before the pressure inside the canner has dropped to Zero, liquid will be pulled from jars, or the sudden change in pressure may break them.

If you're using *tin cans,* the pressure does not need to fall to Zero. Open the vent gradually as soon as processing time is passed, so as to let steam escape slowly.

LIFT THE LID—

Never remove the lid until after steam has stopped coming from the vent.

Open lid clamps or fastenings.

Lift the back rim of the cover first, tilting it to direct remaining heat and steam *away* from you.

TAKE OUT JARS OR CANS—

If the canner does not have a basket which can be lifted out bodily, use a jar-lifter and *dry* potholders (wet ones get unbearably hot in a wink) to remove jars/cans. Complete the seal if necessary.

Stand jars/cans—with space between—away from drafts on a wood surface, or one padded with cloth or paper.

Test the seal when containers are completely cooled.

Summarizing: Pressure Canners are nothing to be afraid of if you treat them with respect. Don't try short cuts or hearsay innovations. Do follow the manufacturer's directions exactly. Much research by government and private agencies has determined the best techniques for using pressure canners. They are fully described in the instruction book that comes with each model.

> **Before tasting canned low-acid food, boil it hard for 15 minutes to destroy any hidden toxins (corn and greens require 20 minutes). If it looks spoiled or foams or has an off-odor during boiling, destroy it completely so it can't be eaten by people or animals.**

LEARY OF PRESSURE CANNERS?

If you're a beginner, and fearful, prepare the canner and take it through a practice run on your stove before processing any food in it. Thus:

Put a couple of inches of water in it, secure the cover, and put it on heat; exhaust the air until you have a steady flow of steam through the vent. Close the vent and watch the gauge until it reaches 10 pounds pressure (the pressure used most often in canning), and hold it there—fiddling with the heat under the canner to determine how much is needed to hold a steady 10 pounds—for at least five minutes, to get the feel of it. Then slide the canner off heat, let pressure fall back to Zero, open the vent to release any last gasp of steam, and remove the cover, tilting it away from you.

You've done it! Now you'll know what to expect, and you know you can boss the beast.

Modern quart jars of fruit, ready to start a B-W Bath.

WHAT THE BOILING-WATER BATH DOES—

Because the temperature in the center of containers of food processed by the B-W Bath never exceeds 212 degrees Fahrenheit. it is SUITABLE ONLY FOR STRONG-ACID FOODS—tomatoes, fruits, and vinegared things. With such foods, it does these things if it's used correctly:

(1) Kills bacteria, yeasts and molds that cannot live at 212 F., the temperature reached in the middle of the contents of jars/cans processed by this method.

(2) Drives out air in the food and processing liquid, as well as any air trapped in the container during packing—because air can prevent a perfect seal and permit spoilage.

(3) Seals the *jars*. (The *cans* are sealed by your hand before they go into the bath—which then brings the food to the required 212 degrees and holds it there for the necessary length of time.)

> *Important:* In order to fulfill its function right, the B-W Bath must be kept at a full rolling boil for the time stipulated to process the food with the boiling water constantly covering the tops of the containers by at least 2 inches.

DIRE WARNING DEPARTMENT

Although canning manuals of thirty and forty years ago still sanctioned processing low-acid vegetables (and meats and seafood!) in the Boiling-Water Bath—

And though the occasional homemaker (trained in the days when a pressure canner was a newfangled gadget too way-out for widespread use) may still get away with doing green beans and corn and meats and suchlike in the old wash boiler—

—canning these things this way could almost be called "How All the Family Can Play Russian Roulette Without Actually Trying."

Even back then, the experts felt that it was chancy to can low-acid foods in a water bath, but the best advice they could offer the housewife was to process for 3 to 6 *hours* in continuously boiling water. Today's research into spoilage and toxicity has shown conclusively, however, that 240 to 250 degrees Fahrenheit is the minimum processing temperature for low-acid foods: and therefore all up-to-date information stipulates that they be done *only in a Pressure Canner* (and for a pretty long time at that).

The Boiling-Water Bath canner

People with long memories recall the covered copper wash-boiler filled with jars of orchard and garden goodness boiling merrily on the family range.

Those oblong boilers that covered two burners or the length of the firebox on the kitchen stove are now collectors' items. Today we buy our water-bath canner. It is a round kettle, usually made of enameled ware, and deep enough to hold the jars on a shallow rack with space above for water to cover them by 2 inches *plus* room to boil actively (in all, a minimum depth of 12 inches for one layer of quart jars). The cost is modest and the kettle makes a splendid lobster cooker between canning duties.

The canner must have a rack to hold the jars away from the bottom of the kettle; it may be made of wooden slats, wire or some perforated material. Some canners have wire baskets.

Of course the kettle has a cover.

Any kettle that is deep enough may be used as a B-W canner. Your pressure canner, with lid *not locked* and vent open (and pressure therefore nil), will do—provided it allows enough headroom over the jars/cans. Or you can lock the lid, thus raising pressure to 1 pound even with the vent left open, and process fruits and tomatoes in water only as high as the neck of the jars for the full B-W Bath time.

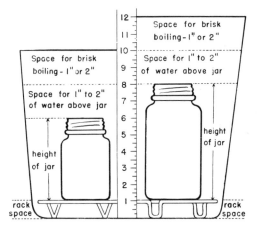

Boiling water must circulate freely below, around, above the food.

How to use the B-W Bath

Put the canner on the stove with water to the halfway mark and the rack in the bottom. Start heating.

Prepare each food either by Hot Pack or Raw Pack, and according to its individual instructions.

Fill clean jars/cans to the recommended point for enough clearance under their lids. (Containers will sterilize as food processes.)

Adjust the lids. At this point some kinds of jars need to be partially sealed, while others should be completely sealed. (See the section "About Jars and Tin Cans.")

Use your jar-lifter to lower jars/cans into the hot water. Keep them apart and away from the side of the canner to allow good circulation of the boiling water around them.

Put jars holding raw food into the *not yet boiling* water (lest, being cooler, they crack). If the food in the jars is already very hot, the jars are put into boiling water without fear of breakage. Cans are already hot from exhausting.

Add enough more boiling water to the kettle to bring the level

2 inches above the tops of jars/cans. Pop on the cover and count processing time from the minute the water begins to boil hard. The directions for individual foods stipulate processing times.

When time is up, remove jars/cans from the bath. See "About Jars and Cans" for completing seals, cooling and storing jars/cans.

HOT-WATER BATH (PASTEURIZATION)

We have bent over backwards in referring to the *Boiling*-Water Bath because it's necessary to distinguish clearly between the B-W—which maintains a real boil at 212 F.—and the *simmering* Hot-Water version at 180, 185 or 190 F., and which is a form of pasteurizing.

The Hot-Water Bath is recommended over the B-W for canning sweet fruit juices, whose flavor is impaired by a true boil; and it is recommended *only for sweet fruit juices.* Despite the casual swapping of these terms in some older manuals, the processes themselves are not interchangeable.

Specific temperatures and processing times are given under "Fruit Juices" in the blow-by-blow procedures for canning particular fruits.

OPEN-KETTLE CANNING

What we now call Open-Kettle canning is used only with jars and is the method whereby: (1) sterilized, hot jars (with their covers ditto) are filled with (2) boiling-hot *acid* foods—usually those having a high content of added sugar and/or vinegar—and (3) the covers are put on immediately, so that (4) the steam in the contents condenses as the jar cools, shrinking to form the vacuum that completes the seal between jar and cover.

It was Nicolas Appert, a Frenchman, who discovered that the elimination of air from cooked foods prevents spoilage (but he didn't know why); commercial canning, based on his principle, was started in 1830. The "why" was solved by Louis Pasteur, who determined that the exclusion of air from processed foods is vital to their preservation because air carries the living organisms—molds, yeasts and bacteria—which cause otherwise safely cooked foods to spoil.

Later it was established that the temperatures reached in the Open-Kettle method *are not hot enough for low-acid and nonacid foods.*

Another drawback: the food is exposed to possible contamination by airborne spoilage organisms during transfer from kettle to jar.

Food suitable for Open-Kettle canning

Jellies, jams, marmalades, conserves and preserves (sugar has some pre-servative quality in high concentration) and cooked relishes or pickles with a high vinegar content can be canned by Open-Kettle, *except in warm climates or where storage conditions are poor*—i.e., above 50 F. and humid. Here a finishing Boiling-Water Bath is in order.

Although some of our older folks still can applesauce, tomatoes and peaches by Open-Kettle, the latter two foods do not hold their shape as well as when canned in the B-W Bath. And for all of them there is a greater chance of imperfect seals, and of mold, etc., developing inside the jars during storage.

How to can by Open-Kettle

First, plan to handle only small batches of suitable food at a time, otherwise it will cool off as it waits while you fill and cap many jars —and cooled food doesn't seal right. Also plan to have your jars and lids sterilized and piping hot when the food is ready (see how to sterilize jars and lids on page 11).

Prepare any suitable food, add the sugar and/or vinegar that is called for, and heat the mixture slowly until any sugar is dissolved; then boil it until the "done" stage is reached. This boiling will (or should) exhaust the air naturally present in food tissue.

Using sterile utensils, ladle the boiling food and its liquid im-mediately into each hot sterile jar *to 7/8 full.* Just as quickly, run a sterile knife-blade or spatula down and around the inside of the jar to eliminate any air trapped in packing.

Carefully finish filling the jar to 1/8 inch of the top; wipe its sealing edge with a clean wet cloth to remove any food particles that can prevent a perfect seal. Now clap the cover on the filled jar, and close the lid all the way. Set the filled jar aside to complete its seal as it cools. Cap each jar the minute it is filled, before turning to another one.

Next day, when the jars are totally cooled, check them carefully for possible leaks (which show that the seal is faulty). Remove the food

Open-Kettle peaches going into hot sterile jars.

from any jars that don't pass muster and reprocess it by bringing it to a boil and putting it in freshly sterilized containers; cap, cool, check, then store. Proper storage (see page 31) is a must for foods canned by Open-Kettle.

> *Note:* You always risk some spoilage with this method, even if all sealing edges were sound and clean, and the food was hot enough when put in the jars, and the lids were tightened well. Still, if you have only a small amount of *some* acid foods to put by, Open-Kettle will do—provided your storage is right.
>
> Store them at the front of your shelves, though. And keep an eye on them: their storage life is comparatively short.

MAVERICK CANNING METHODS

Now and again unusual ways of processing home-canned food crop up or are revived from an old cookbook, and some of them are adequate within their limits and some of them would give the health and safety councils fits.

What about Oven-canning?

'Way back in the 1920's, when housewives didn't know not to, process-ing canned food in the oven enjoyed a certain vogue. Even today, with all the accumulated research that's been recorded about the causes of food spoilage (and with the many Boiling-Water Bath and Pressure canners that are easily gettable), Oven-canning continues to surface.

And despite our original warning against Oven-canning when this book first came out, we still get queries from people who remember that their mothers or grandmothers did can food in the oven, or from people who have run across this method in the folklore of homemaking.

WE'LL LAY IT ON THE LINE

It's significant that none of the old directions we've collected includes canning low-acid foods in the oven—an omission to be thankful for.

In addition, it's impossible, from their welter of haphazard how-to, to formulate a rule-of-thumb for safe and sensible Oven-canning of even strong-acid food like fruits.

The only concession our old manuals made to the hairiness of Oven-canning was to murmur that setting the jars of fruit in a pan would keep boiled-over juices from messing up the oven. But not one word in any of them warned of the hazards to the product of faulty oven gauges or fluctuating temperature, or of the recovery time necessary after heat was spilled when the jars were put in to be processed.

THE TROUBLES WHEN WE TRIED IT

Liquid from the jars escaped into the dry oven air, and the fruit at the top of the jars discolored.

Some jars exploded during processing, or as cool air hit them when we opened the oven door to take them out. Others just cracked or erupted.

After cooling, many seals were imperfect because juice had bubbled out, leaving food particles lodged between jar and lid.

SO RELY ON THE GOOD OLD B-W BATH

Canning fruit in a well-managed Boiling-Water Bath (1) takes less time and less fuel; (2) is far less dangerous to be around; (3) ensures a safer, better-textured and handsomer product, and (4) promises a better seal.

Note: With the recent introduction of microwave ovens for the home, the question of Oven-canning has cropped up anew. We can reply only that there has not been enough research reported to convince us that a microwave oven will prevent the faults in the product which we object to about Oven-canning in general—plus other faults in the product that could stem from the unique character of the microwave process.

What about Steamer-canning?

Steamer-canning, *NOT to be confused with Pressure Canning,* is another method we've seen discussed in the aged manuals that are being turned to nowadays for their otherwise good ideas for making simple, tasty and inexpensive meals.

In its brief and long-gone heyday, Steamer-canning had to be restricted to processing strong-acid foods like fruit and tomatoes, for the method relies on steam generated in a special tank affair and allowed to circulate around the jars on racks inside it.

TOO MOOT FOR COMFORT

Obviously the key to Steamer-canning is maintaining a strong flow of steam kept at a constant 212 F. And even when the method was fairly popular, apparently there were reservations about the reliability of the steam's force and temperature: the most nearly explicit of our old cookbooks says to add substantial time "per rack" (whatever this stipulation actually means) to the processing time required for jars of the same food in a Boiling-Water Bath.

FEASIBILITY: NIL

Few steam canners designed for the job produce a steady flow of steam hot enough: letting jars of food putter along in a gentle vapor simply cannot result in a product safe from spoilage.

As for trying to use a clam-steamer or a regular water-bath kettle for Steamer-canning—*Don't!*

Cold-Water canning

There is an old-fashioned way of canning raw rhubarb, cranberries and green gooseberries that works if its limitations are observed (and it's *not the same as the Raw Pack* preliminary to processing, discussed earlier).

Use jars that have rubber seals and screw caps or lids held with bails. Fill sterilized jars with picked-over, washed, perfect berries (rhubarb is cut in 1-inch lengths, but not peeled). Next, run cold drinking water into a scrupulously clean and scalded pail to a level some 6 inches above the height of the jars. Then fill the jars of fruit to overflowing with cold drinking water and submerge them—still open—in the pail and, *under water,* cap them tightly. Store immediately in a cool place.

THE LIMITATIONS

Fruit/berries canned this way should be strongly acid, and be tough-skinned and firm, so they don't break down readily during storage. Old-time country housewives used to can fresh lemons this way when they could get a supply fairly cheaply in February or March.

Because there's no heat processing anywhere along the line, you must wash the fruit well and sterilize utensils and jars. If you're leary of your water you can always boil it in advance (cooling it well before canning with it)—but then so much boiled water would be needed for canning by this method that you're off easier, and better, using a Boiling-Water Bath in the first place.

Fruits and berries that are Cold-Water canned require really cool storage; having no added sugar to retard freezing, though, they should not get below 32 F.

Remember that the seal is not a perfect one, and that some air remains in the tissues of the food: therefore it can't store as long as properly heat-processed food does.

USING THE FRUIT

If you're going to stew the fruit with sugar for dessert, drain off the canning water and boil it down to at least ½ its volume before adding the fruit and sugaring to taste.

If you're making a pie or tart, etc., as with fresh fruit, discard the water.

Canning Fruits

Use firm, just-ripe fruit and berries for canning: if even a shade over the hill they're likely to float to the top of the jar. As for all raw materials suggested for putting by, use quality produce that is absolutely fresh, and can it as soon as possible. If you have to hold it over, keep it refrigerated.

It used to be that Open-Kettle (above) was the routine method for canning fruits, berries and juices, and the homemaker simply made allowance for a "normal" amount of spoiling. Then she discovered that Raw or Hot pack plus a short time in a Boiling-Water Bath equaled a more satisfying product with a safer seal—and therefore it stored a lot better.

So the individual procedures that follow use the B-W Bath (or the pasteurizing Hot-Water Bath for juices). But if you find a tempting old-time rule that relies on Open-Kettle, here's a rule-of-thumb for including the B-W Bath:

Prepare and cook it by the Open-Kettle method described in the old recipe, and, when it's cooked enough, pack the fruit boiling hot in clean jars with the hot liquid, leaving ½ inch of headroom. Adjust lids, and process in a B-W Bath (212 F.)—pints for 10 minutes, quarts for 15 minutes. Remove jars; complete seals if necessary.

In cans? Better not try to translate Open-Kettle in terms of cans. The old-fashioned rules didn't mention cans, so it's best to stick to jars only, here.

If you prefer cans for the procedures that follow, you will be using R-enamel cans for virtually all the berries and a few of the fruits to keep the contents from bleaching. (See "About Jars and Cans.")

To prevent air pockets

The Boiling-Water Bath can be relied on to drive out air trapped during packing—except in two cases. One may occur when whole firm berries or chunky pieces of fruit are done by Open-Kettle, with only a brief finish in a B-W Bath to ensure the seal. The other may happen when

SUGAR SIRUPS FOR CANNING FRUITS

Sugar is not necessary to prevent spoilage of correctly processed fruit: it is added to help retain texture, flavor and color. (It does aid preservation, though, when used in the very high concentrations common for jellies and jams, etc.) Most fruits are canned with a sugar sirup to suit the sweetness of the fruit and the family's taste.

Roughly, estimate ½ to ¾ cup of sirup for each pint or No. 2 can, and increase the allowance proportionately for larger containers.

To make sirup, mix sugar with water in the proportions given below; heat sugar and water together until sugar is dissolved, skimming if necessary.

Water and/or Juice	*Sugar*	*Yield*
4 cups	2 cups	5 cups *thin* sirup
4 cups	3 cups	5½ cups *medium* sirup
4 cups	4 3/4 cups	6½ cups *heavy* sirup

Substitutions: Juice may be used for part or all the water, as desired. Prepare it by crushing sound, fully ripe and juicy fruit that has been set aside for the purpose. Bring it to simmering over low heat for several minutes, stirring gently; strain the hot pulp through a jelly bag.

Raw sugar (which is semi-refined) may be substituted for white sugar in proportions to taste, but its sweetening power differs slightly from that of white sugar, and it will darken the fruit and tend to change its flavor. Probably it should be reserved for fruits with strong flavor and dark juice.

Light corn sirup or mild-flavored honey may be substituted for up to ½ the white sugar called for in the table above. Top grade maple syrup is usually too hard to come by to be used for routine canning, and anyway should take the place of only ¼ the sugar because of its pronounced flavor.

Sorghum and molasses are too overpowering on their own to be satisfactory in canning fruit.

peach halves, say, are fitted cut side down in jars in a Raw pack, and any air held in the cavities cannot find its way out even in a standard B-W Bath.

In both cases, run a sterilized knife or spatula gently around the inside of the jar to release the air before you adjust the lids for processing. But don't move the knife through the middle of the contents: this actually creates air pockets.

You can also put ½ cup of hot packing liquid in the bottom of the jar first, and pack the fruit as usual; then adjust the lids and process.

Cans do not need the knife/spatula treatment, because air is driven out when the open filled cans are exhausted to 170 F. before sealing.

To prevent canned fruit from discoloring

Certain fruits darken in the air while they're being prepared for canning; several may darken during storage; and all jars of red fruits and berries and juices lose color if exposed to light.

Apples, apricots, peaches and pears discolor in air. Either coat the cut pieces well as you go along with a solution of 1 teaspoon crystalline ascorbic acid (Vitamin C, the safe and best anti-oxidant) to each 1 cup water; OR drop the pieces in a solution of 2 tablespoons salt and 2 tablespoons vinegar for each 1 gallon of cold water—but not for longer than 20 minutes, lest nutrients leach out too much—then rinse and drain the pieces well before packing the Raw or Hot way.

Optional: to prevent their darkening while in the containers, add ¼ teaspoon Vitamin C to each 1 quart during packing—IF they haven't been treated with ascorbic acid as they were being prepared. (See more about ascorbic acid under Freezing Fruits, Drying, and Curing Meats.)

If your cool storage space is not completely dark, prevent bleaching in the light by wrapping each jar in newspaper or stash it in the carton the jars came in.

And remember: Fruit canned with too much headroom or too little liquid will tend to darken at the top of the container. So heed the directions.

Apples

Even with root-cellaring and drying (see both), you'll want some apples put by as sauce, dessert slices or pie timber. And of these, probably the handiest thing is to can applesauce and slices done in sirup, and to freeze the slices you'll use for pies. Canning apple cider is described later on under Juices. See Recipes.

CANNING FRUITS

GENERAL HANDLING

Boiling-Water Bath. Use Hot pack only. Use jars or plain cans. Process with Thin Sirup, plain water, or with sweetening as desired.

Because apples oxidize in the air, work quickly and with only small amounts at a time. Wash, peel and core apples (save peels and cores for jelly, as described in Applesauce, below); treat prepared pieces with either of the anti-discoloration solutions on page 38 until you're ready to pack. Drain, and carry on with the specific handling. (See also Freezing for pie timber.)

SLICES

Rinse drained, prepared pieces. Cover with hot Thin Sirup or water, boil gently for 5 minutes. Lift out and drain, saving cooking sirup or water. Pack hot.

In jars. Fill clean, hot jars, leaving ½ inch of headroom. Add boiling-hot Thin Sirup or water, leaving ½ inch of headroom; adjust lids. Process in a Boiling-Water Bath (212 F.)—pints for 15 minutes, quarts for 20 minutes. Remove jars; complete seals if necessary.

In plain cans. Fill, leaving only ¼ inch of headroom. Add boiling-hot Thin Sirup or water to the top of the can. Exhaust to 170 F. (*c.* 10 minutes); seal. Process in a B-W Bath (212 F.)—10 minutes for either No. 2 or No. 2½ cans. Remove cans; cool quickly.

APPLESAUCE

Prepare by your favorite rule and according to how you'll use it—chunky or strained smooth; sweetened or not; with spices (cinnamon, nutmeg, whatever) or plain. Because of complete precooking and being packed so hot, processing time is relatively short and is designed to ensure the seal.

Thrifty idea: Pare crisp, red apples, cut in quarters or eighths and remove core parts; drop pieces in anti-discoloration solution. *Don't throw away the peels and cores: save them to boil up for a beautiful juice for jelly.* Put about 1 inch of water in a large enameled or stainless-steel kettle, fill with well-rinsed apple pieces to within 2 inches of the top. Bring to a boil, stirring now and then to prevent sticking, and cook until apples are tender. Leave as is for chunky sauce, or put it through a sieve or food mill for smoothness. Sweeten it if you like—2/3 cup more or less of honey or sugar is about average—and return it to heat to boil again briefly to dissolve the sweetening. Pack hot.

In jars. Fill clean, hot jars with piping hot sauce, leaving only ¼ inch of headroom; adjust lids. Process in a Boiling-Water Bath (212 F.)—10 minutes for either pints or quarts. Remove jars; complete seals if necessary.

In plain cans. Pack to the top with hot sauce. Exhaust to 170 F. (*c.* 10 minutes); seal. Process in B-W Bath (212 F.)—10 minutes for either No. 2 or No. 2½ cans. Remove cans; cool quickly.

BAKED APPLES

Sometimes people can baked apples. Prepare them in a favorite way and bake until *half done;* pack hot in jars or plain cans as for Apple Slices, adding hot Thin Sirup. Adjust jar lids or exhaust and seal cans. Process in a Boiling-Water Bath (212 F.)—20 minutes for either pint or quart jars, 10 minutes for either No. 2 or No. 2½ cans (reaching 170 F. by exhausting shortens processing time). Complete seals if necessary for jars; cool cans quickly.

Apricots

Can these exactly as you would Peaches (q.v.), but leave the skins on if you like. Some varieties tend to break up when they're heated, so test a couple before you commit a whole batch to Hot pack: if they get ragged, can the rest by Raw pack.

Berries, see grouped handling at the end of Fruits section.

Cherries, Sour (for Pie)

Because these are used primarily as pie timber, they may be canned in water—but they have better flavor in Thin Sirup. Either way, you'll add the extra sweetening at the time you thicken the juice when you're building the pie.

GENERAL HANDLING

Boiling-Water Bath. Use Raw or Hot pack. Use jars or R-enamel cans. Prepare Thin Sirup for Raw pack; heat in their own juice with sugar for Hot pack.

Wash, stem and pit cherries. (Use a small sterilized hairpin or the looped end of a paper clip if you don't have a pitting gadget.) Shake fruit down in the containers for a firm pack.

RAW PACK

In jars. Jog cherries down several times during packing; leave ½ inch of headroom. Add boiling sirup, leaving ½ inch of headroom; adjust lids. Process in a Boiling-Water Bath (212 F.)—pints for 20 minutes, quarts for 25 minutes. Remove jars; complete seals if necessary.

In R-enamel cans. Make a firm pack, leaving only ¼ inch of headroom. Add boiling sirup to top. Exhaust to 170 F. (*c.* 10 minutes); seal. Process in a B-W Bath (212 F.)—No. 2 cans for 20 minutes, No. 2½ cans for 25 minutes. Remove cans; cool quickly.

HOT PACK

Measure pitted cherries and put them in a covered kettle with ½ cup of sugar for every 1 quart of fruit. There should be enough juice to keep the cherries from sticking. Set on lowest burner. Cover the kettle, and bring fruit very slowly to a boil to bring out the juice. Be prepared to add a little boiling water to each jar if you haven't enough juice to go around.

In jars. Fill with hot fruit and juice, leaving ½ inch of headroom; adjust lids. Process in a Boiling-Water Bath (212 F.)—pints for 10 minutes, quarts for 15 minutes. Remove jars; complete seals if necessary.

In R-enamel cans. Fill to the top with hot fruit and juice. Exhaust to 170 F. (*c.* 10 minutes); seal. Process in a B-W Bath (212 F.)—No. 2 cans for 15 minutes, No. 2½ for 20 minutes. Remove cans; cool quickly.

Cherries, Sweet

GENERAL HANDLING

Boiling-Water Bath. Use Raw or Hot pack. Use jars or cans (plain cans for light varieties like Royal Ann; R-enamel for dark red or "black" types like Bing).

If you're going to serve these as is, or combined with other fruits in a compôte, you don't pit them (they'll hold their shape better unpitted); but do prick each cherry with a needle to keep it from bursting while it's processed. Use Medium or Heavy sirup for Raw pack; for Hot pack add more sugar than for Sour Cherries.

Wash cherries, checking for blemishes, and discard any that float (they may be wormy); remove stems. Shake down for a firm pack.

RAW PACK

In jars. Fill firmly, leaving ½ inch of headroom. Add boiling sirup, leaving ½ inch of headroom; adjust lids. Process in a Boiling-Water Bath (212 F.)—pints for 20 minutes, quarts for 25 minutes. Remove jars; complete seals if necessary.

In plain or R-enamel cans. Make a firm pack, leaving only ¼ inch of headroom. Fill to top with boiling sirup. Exhaust to 170 F. (*c.* 10 minutes); seal. Process in a B-W Bath (212 F.)—No. 2 cans for 20 minutes, No. 2½ cans for 25 minutes. Remove cans; cool quickly.

HOT PACK

Measure washed and pricked cherries into a covered kettle, adding ¾ cup of sugar for every 1 quart of fruit. Because there is not much juice in the pan, add a little water to keep fruit from sticking as it heats. Cover and bring very slowly to a boil, shaking the pan gently a few times (instead of stirring, which breaks the fruit). Heat some Medium or Heavy sirup to have on hand in case there's not enough juice to go around when you fill the containers.

In jars. Proceed and process as for Raw pack.

In plain or R-enamel cans. Proceed and process as for Raw pack.

Dried Fruits

FEASIBILITY

Any dried fruit may be freshened and canned. But why do it, when they keep so well as is (see Drying)—unless you foresee a particular need for a few servings of them stewed up ready for the table?

GENERAL HANDLING

Boiling-Water Bath only. Use Raw or Hot pack. Use jars or plain cans.

Freshen by covering with cold water and letting stand overnight. Drain, saving the soaking water (heated to boiling) to use in processing, and proceed with Raw pack.

If you're in a hurry, cover with water, bring to a boil, and simmer until the fruit is plumped. Drain, saving the cooking water for processing, and proceed with Hot pack.

RAW PACK

In jars. Fill, leaving ½ inch of headroom. Add 2 to 4 tablespoons sugar (depending on sweetness of fruit) to pints, 4 to 6 tablespoons to quarts. Add boiling soaking water, leaving ½ inch of headroom; adjust lids. Process in a Boiling-Water Bath (212 F.)–pints for 20 minutes, quarts for 25 minutes. Remove jars; complete seals if necessary.

In plain cans. Fill, leaving only ¼ inch of headroom. Add 2 to 4 table-spoons sugar to No. 2 cans, 4 to 6 tablespoons to No. 2½ cans. Fill to top with boiling soaking water. Exhaust to 170 F. (*c.* 15 minutes; seal. Process in B-W Bath (212 F.)–No. 2 cans for 15 minutes, No. 2½ for 20 minutes. Remove cans; cool quickly.

HOT PACK

In jars. Fill with hot fruit, sweeten, and add hot cooking water as for Raw pack. Process in a B-W Bath (212 F.)–pints for 15 minutes, quarts for 20 minutes. Remove jars; complete seals if necessary.

In plain cans. Fill with hot fruit, sweeten, and add hot cooking water as for Raw pack. Process in a B-W Bath (212 F.)–No. 2 cans for 15 minutes, No. 2½ for 20 minutes. Remove cans; cool quickly.

Figs

The green Kadota variety makes a particularly attractive product.

GENERAL HANDLING

Long B-W Bath. Use Hot pack only. Use jars or plain cans. Prepare Thin Sirup.

Wash ripe, firm figs; do not peel or remove stems. Cover with boil-ing water and let simmer at 180 F. for 5 minutes. Drain and pack.

HOT PACK ONLY

In jars. Fill with hot figs, leaving ½ inch of headroom. Add boiling sirup. For flavor, add 1 teaspoon lemon juice and one thin slice of fresh lemon to pints, 2 teaspoons lemon juice and 1 slice of lemon to quarts. Adjust lids. Process in a Boiling-Water Bath (212 F.)– pints for 85 minutes, quarts for 90 minutes. Remove jars; complete seals if necessary.

In plain cans. Fill, leaving ¼ inch of headroom. Add boiling sirup and 1 teaspoon lemon juice and 1 thin slice of lemon to No. 2 cans, 2 teaspoons lemon juice and 1 thin slice of lemon to No. 2½ cans. Exhaust to 170 F. (*c.* 10 minutes); seal. Process in a B-W Bath (212 F.)–No. 2 cans for 85 minutes, No. 2½ for 90 minutes. Remove cans; cool quickly.

Canning Frozen Fruits and Berries

For delivery in early fall, large farm-supply chain stores (look under Feeds or Grain, in the Yellow Pages) often have good buys in 4-gallon containers of frozen fruits and berries—good buys because you order them ahead, and they usually cost no more than the going price of store-bought fresh fruit; and all the washing and peeling and slicing is already done, to boot. A list from one such outfit offers sweet and sour cherries, strawberries, halved purple plums, sliced peaches, sliced Spy apples and applesauce, all with sugar; and blueberries, blackberries, red raspberries, rhubarb and crushed pineapple, all without sugar.

The hitch: You must take delivery when they come in, and hence be prepared to can your order immediately (unless you have a freezer big enough to hold the bulk packages). And you should be a serious canner: 4 gallons of prepared fruit is a lot to deal with in one swoop, and requires organizing the time and utensils for the job.

HANDLING

Boiling-Water Bath only. Use Hot pack only. Use jars or cans—plain or Re-enamel as recommended for the specific raw food (q.v.).

Defrost fruit slowly in the unopened package. Drain off all juice and measure it: if the fruit was unsugared, add sweetening in proportion to make Thin or Medium sirup, as desired; if it was sugared, add more sweetener to taste if you want to. Bring juice to boiling. Add fruit and boil it gently for 2 or 3 minutes. Proceed with hot-packing and processing in a Boiling-Water Bath as for the specific fresh fruit (you may need to add some boiling water to each container if there's not enough juice to go around).

Grapes

Tight-skinned seedless grapes are the ones to can if you can any—for fruit cocktail, compôtes, gelatine desserts and salads (but grapes for juice may be any sort you have plenty of).

GENERAL HANDLING

Boiling-Water Bath. Use Raw or Hot pack. Use jars or cans (plain, or R-enamel cans if it's a dark grape).

Sort, wash and stem.

RAW PACK

In jars. Fill tightly but without crushing grapes, leaving ½ inch of head-room. Add boiling Medium Sirup, leaving ½ inch of headroom;

adjust lids. Process in a Boiling-Water Bath (212 F.)–pints for 15 minutes, quarts for 20 minutes. Remove jars; complete seals if necessary.

In cans (plain or R-enamel). Fill, leaving ¼ inch of headroom. Add boiling Medium Sirup to top. Exhaust to 170 F. (*c.* 10 minutes); seal. Process in a B-W Bath (212 F.)–No. 2 cans for 20 minutes, No. 2½ for 25 minutes. Remove cans; cool quickly.

HOT PACK

Prepare as for Raw pack. Bring to a boil in Medium Sirup. Drain, reserving sirup, and pack.

In jars. Pack with hot grapes, leaving ½ inch of headroom. Add boiling sirup, leaving ½ inch of headroom; adjust lids. Process in a Boiling-Water Bath (212 F.)–pints for 15 minutes, quarts for 20 minutes. Remove jars; complete seals if necessary.

In cans (plain or R-enamel). Fill with hot grapes, leaving ¼ inch of headroom. Add boiling sirup to the top. Exhaust to 170 F. (*c.* 10 minutes); seal. Process in B-W Bath (212 F.)–No. 2 cans for 20 minutes, No. 2½ for 25 minutes. Remove cans; cool quickly.

Grapefruit (or Orange) Sections

FEASIBILITY

Only if you have a good supply of tree-ripened fruits is canning worthwhile–but canning makes an infinitely handier product than freezing does. Don't overlook Mixed Fruit; and don't forget marmalades and conserves (q.v.).

GENERAL HANDLING

Boiling-Water Bath only. Use Raw pack only. Use jars only (cans could give a metallic taste to home-canned citrus).

Wash fruit and pare, removing the white membrane as you go. Slip a very sharp thin-bladed knife between the dividing skin and pulp of each section, and lift out the section without breaking. Remove any seeds from individual sections. Prepare Thin Sirup.

RAW PACK ONLY

In jars only. Fill hot jars with sections, leaving ½ inch of headroom. Add boiling Thin Sirup, leaving ½ inch of headroom; adjust lids. Process in a Boiling-Water Bath (212 F.)–10 minutes for either pints or quarts. Remove jars; complete seals if necessary.

Juices, see grouped handling at the end of Fruits section.

Peaches

FEASIBILITY

The benefits and pleasures of canning are exemplified in peaches: home-canned peaches are full of flavor, are versatile, and are considered by many cooks to be better than frozen ones. See also Drying, Preserves and cobblers in Recipes.

GENERAL HANDLING

Hot-Water Bath only. Use Raw or Hot pack. Use jars or plain cans.

Wash and scald briefly (by dipping a few peaches at a time in boiling water) and dunk quickly in cold water; slip off loosened skins. Halve, pit; scrape away dark fibers in the pit cavity because they sometimes turn brown in canning. (Save a few pits: old-time canners always tucked one pit in each jar of peaches "for flavor," and you might do the same.) Slice if you like. Treat peeled pieces immediately with either solution described just before Apples, above. Rinse, drain. Pack with Thin or Medium Sirup. If the peaches are especially juicy, make the sirup with their juice instead of water (see "Sirups for Canning Fruits").

RAW PACK

In jars. Pack halves or slices attractively, leaving ½ inch of headroom. Add boiling sirup, leaving ½ inch of headroom; adjust lids. Process in a Boiling-Water Bath (212 F.)—pints for 25 minutes, quarts for 30 minutes. Remove jars; complete seals if necessary.

In plain cans. Fill carefully, leaving only ¼ inch of headroom. Add boiling sirup to the top. Exhaust to 170 F. (*c.* 10 minutes); seal. Process in a B-W Bath (212 F.)—No. 2 cans for 30 minutes, No. 2½ for 35 minutes. Remove cans; cool quickly.

HOT PACK

Heat prepared peaches through in hot sirup. Drain, reserving sirup.

In jars. Fill with hot peaches, leaving ½ inch of headroom. Add boiling sirup, leaving ½ inch of headroom; adjust lids. Process in a Boiling-Water Bath (212 F.)—pints for 20 minutes, quarts for 25 minutes. Remove jars; complete seals if necessary.

In plain cans. Fill with hot peaches, leaving only ¼ inch of headroom. Add boiling sirup to the top. Exhaust to 170 F. (*c.* 10 minutes); seal. Process in a B-W Bath (212 F.)—No. 2 cans for 25 minutes, No. 2½ for 30 minutes. Remove cans; cool quickly.

Skins come easily off scalded peaches, above, and cut fruit is held in an anti-darkening solution; right, boiling-hot sirup will cover the beautifully packed peaches with ½ inch of headroom to spare.

Peaches, Brandied

GENERAL HANDLING

Boiling-Water Bath only. Use Hot pack only. Use jars only (because they look so pretty: which is part of their fun). See also Brandied Peaches Without Brandy, under Preserves.

The peaches should be small to medium in size, firm-ripe, and with attractive color; blemish-free of course. Wash. Using a coarse-textured towel, rub off all their fuzz. Weigh them.

For every 1 pound of peaches, make a Heavy Sirup of 1 cup sugar to 1 cup water. Bring sirup to boiling and, when sugar is dissolved, add the whole peaches and simmer them for 5 minutes. Drain; save the sirup and keep it hot.

HOT PACK ONLY, IN JARS ONLY

Without crushing, fit peaches in hot jars, leaving ½ inch of headroom. Pour 2 tablespoons of brandy over the peaches in each 1-pint jar, using proportionately more brandy for quarts. Fill jars with hot sirup, leaving ½ inch of headroom; adjust lids. Process in a Boiling-Water Bath (212 F.)—pints for 15 minutes, quarts for 20 minutes. Remove jars; complete seals if necessary.

Pears

FEASIBILITY

Bartlett pears are ideal for canning, to serve alone or as a salad or in a compôte. They will be too soft for successful canning, though, if they've ripened on the tree: use ones that were picked green (but full grown) and allowed to ripen in cool storage, between 60 and 65 F.

Very firm-fleshed varieties like Seckel and Kieffer are generally spiced or pickled; they make a satisfactory product if ripened in storage and simmered in water till nearly tender before packing with sirup. The so-called winter pears—such as Anjou and Bosc—are usually eaten fresh; they are cold-stored much the way apples are, but they are not likely to keep as long (see Root-Cellaring).

GENERAL HANDLING

Use a Boiling-Water Bath. Use Raw or Hot pack. Use jars or plain cans.

Wash; cut in halves or quarters. Remove stems, core (a melon-ball scoop is handy for this); pare. Treat pieces against oxidation with either of the solutions described on page 38; proceed with packing.

Make Thin or Medium Sirup.

Small pears may be canned whole: pare them, but leave the stems on. It takes about 9 small whole pears to fill a pint jar or a No. 2 can.

RAW PACK

In jars. Pack halves or quarters attractively, leaving ½ inch of headroom. Add boiling sirup, leaving ½ inch of headroom; adjust lids. Process in a Boiling-Water Bath (212 F.)—pints for 25 minutes, quarts for 30 minutes. Remove jars; complete seals if necessary.

In plain cans. Fill carefully, leaving only ¼ inch of headroom. Add boiling sirup to the top. Exhaust to 170 F. (*c.* 10 minutes); seal. Process in a B-W Bath (212 F.)—No. 2 cans for 30 minutes, No. 2½ for 35 minutes. Remove cans; cool quickly.

HOT PACK

Heat fruit through in hot sirup; drain, reserving sirup.

In jars. Fill with hot pears, leaving ½ inch of headroom. Add boiling sirup, leaving ½ inch of headroom; adjust lids. Process in a Boiling-Water Bath (212 F.)—pints for 20 minutes, quarts for 25 minutes. Remove jars; complete seals if necessary.

In plain cans. Fill with hot pears, leaving only ¼ inch of headroom. Add boiling sirup to the top. Exhaust to 170 F. (*c.* 10 minutes); seal. Process in a B-W Bath (212 F.)—No. 2 cans for 25 minutes, No. 2½ for 30 minutes. Remove cans; cool quickly.

MINT VARIATION

Prepare as above; the pears may be cut up or left whole. To Medium Sirup, add enough natural peppermint extract and green food coloring to give the desired taste and color.

Simmer the pears in this sirup for 5 to 10 minutes, depending on size and firmness of fruit, before packing Hot and processing in a B-W Bath as above.

Pears, Spiced

Seckel, Kieffer and similar hard varieties are best for spicing. Bartletts or other soft pears may be used if they are underripe.

GENERAL HANDLING

Use a Boiling-Water Bath. Use Hot pack only. Use jars only (like Brandied Peaches, these are very attractive to look at; and you could take a ribbon at the fair!).

Wash, peel and core 6 pounds of pears. Gently boil them covered in 3 cups of water until they start to soften.

Make a very heavy sirup of 4 cups sugar and 2 cups white vinegar. Tie in a small cloth bag 10 to 12 3-inch sticks of cinnamon, ¼ cup whole cloves, and 4 teaspoons cracked ginger. Simmer the spice bag in the sirup for 5 minutes.

Add the pears and the water in which they were partially cooked to the spiced sirup, and simmer for 4 minutes. Drain pears, saving the hot sirup and discarding the spice bag.

HOT PACK ONLY, IN JARS ONLY

Pack hot pears attractively in clean hot jars. Add spiced sirup, leaving ½ inch of headroom; adjust lids. Process in a Boiling-Water Bath (212 F.)—pints for 15 minutes, quarts for 20 minutes. Remove jars; complete seals if necessary.

Pineapple

Fresh pineapple is as easy to can as any fruit—and may be packed in any plain or minted and colored sirup (see also "Canning Frozen Fruits").

GENERAL HANDLING

Use a Boiling-Water Bath. Use Hot pack only. Use jars or plain cans.

Scrub firm, ripe pineapples. Cut a thin slice from each end. Cut like a jelly roll in ½-inch slices, or in 8 lengthwise wedges. Remove the skin, the "eyes" and the tough-fiber core from each piece. Leave in slices or wedges, or cut small or chop: let future use guide your hand.

Simmer pineapple gently in Light or Medium Sirup for about 5 minutes. Drain; save the hot sirup for packing.

HOT PACK ONLY

In jars. Fill with fruit, leaving ½ inch of headroom. Add hot sirup, leaving ½ inch of headroom; adjust lids. Process in a Boiling-Water Bath (212 F.)—pints for 15 minutes, quarts for 20 minutes. Remove jars; complete seals if necessary.

In plain cans. Fill with fruit, leaving ¼ inch of headroom. Add hot sirup to the top of the cans. Exhaust to 170 F. (*c.* 10 minutes); seal. Process in a B-W Bath (212 F.)—No. 2 cans for 20 minutes, No. 2½ for 25 minutes. Remove cans; cool quickly.

Plums (and Italian Prunes)

GENERAL HANDLING

Use Boiling-Water Bath. Use Raw or Hot pack. Use jars or cans—R-enamel for red plums, plain for greenish-yellow varieties.

Firm, meaty plums (such as the Greengage) hold their shape better for canning whole than the more juicy types do. Freestone plums and prunes are easily halved and pitted for the tighter pack.

Choose moderately ripe fruit. Wash. If to be canned whole, the skins should be pricked several times with a large needle to prevent the fruit from bursting. Halve and pit the freestone varieties. Prepare Medium or Heavy Sirup, and have it hot.

RAW PACK

In jars. Fill with raw fruit, leaving ½ inch of headroom. Add boiling sirup, leaving ½ inch of headroom; adjust lids. Process in a Boiling-Water Bath (212 F.)—pints for 20 minutes, quarts for 25 minutes. Remove jars; complete seals if necessary.

In cans (R-enamel for red fruit, plain for light-colored). Pack raw fruit, leaving ¼ inch of headroom. Add boiling sirup to the top of the can. Exhaust to 170 F. (*c.* 10 minutes); seal. Process in a B-W Bath (212 F.)—No. 2 cans for 15 minutes, No. 2½ for 20 minutes. Remove cans; cool quickly.

HOT PACK

Heat prepared plums to boiling in sirup. If they're halved and are very juicy, heat them slowly to bring out the juice; measure the juice, and for each 1 cup juice add ¾ cup sugar—give or take a little, according to your taste—to make a Medium Sirup. Reheat to boiling for just long enough to dissolve the sugar. Drain fruit, saving the hot sirup. Have some hot plain Medium Sirup on hand for eking out sweetened juice.

In jars. Pack hot fruit, leaving ½ inch of headroom. Add boiling sirup, leaving ½ inch of headroom; adjust lids. Process in a Boiling-Water Bath (212 F.)—pints for 20 minutes, quarts for 25 minutes. Remove jars; complete seals if necessary.

In cans (R-enamel for red fruit, plain for light-colored). Pack hot fruit, leaving ¼ inch of headroom. Fill to top with boiling sirup. Exhaust to 170 F. (*c.* 10 minutes); seal. Process in a B-W Bath (212 F.)—No. 2 cans for 15 minutes, No. 2½ for 20 minutes. Remove cans; cool quickly.

Rhubarb (or Pie Plant)

Never eat rhubarb LEAVES: they are high in oxalic acid, which is poisonous in large doses.

Safe to eat are the tart, red stalks of this plant, which are excellent pie timber, make a tangy dessert sauce, are a favorite ingredient in old-time preserves; rhubarb juice makes a good hot-weather drink. See Recipes.

Presweetened rhubarb sauce may be canned by Open-Kettle, but do add a seal-ensuring Boiling-Water Bath (see Whole Cranberry Sauce). Rhubarb may also be canned raw and unsweetened by the Cold-Water method (for limited storage, though)—see Cranberries again.

However, your best use would be to can sweetened sauce by the method given below, and to freeze the raw pieces for pies.

GENERAL HANDLING AS SAUCE

Use a Boiling-Water Bath. Use Hot pack. Use jars or R-enamel cans.

For best results, can it the same day you cut it. If the stalks are young enough, they need not be peeled (their red color makes an attractive product). *Discard leaves,* trim away both ends of the stalks, and wash; cut stalks in ½-inch pieces. Measure. Put rhubarb in an enameled kettle (because of the tartness), mixing in ½ cup of sugar for each 1 quart (4 cups) of raw fruit. Let it stand, covered, at room temperature for about 4 hours to draw out the juice. Bring slowly to a boil; let boil no more than 1 minute (or the pieces will break up). Pack.

HOT PACK

In jars. Fill with hot fruit and its juice, leaving ½ inch of headroom; adjust lids. Process in a Boiling-Water Bath (212 F.)—10 minutes for either pints or quarts. Remove jars; complete seals if necessary.

In R-enamel cans. Pack hot fruit and juice to the top of the cans. Exhaust to 170 F. (c. 10 minutes); seal. Process in a B-W Bath (212 F.)—10 minutes for either No. 2 or No. 2½ cans. Remove cans; cool quickly.

Tomatoes

FEASIBILITY

By far and away the most popular canned vegetable (though botanically they're fruit, and their acidity lets them be canned like fruit)—see Recipes; see juice, above, and paste, below; for canning with other vegetables, see Canning Celery and Mixed Vegetables.

CANNING FRUITS

GENERAL HANDLING

Use a Boiling-Water Bath—but the Open-Kettle method for Hot pack is sometimes used (with a finishing B-W Bath recommended to ensure the seal). Use Raw or Hot pack: Raw is better for table-ready whole or cut tomatoes, and Hot is fine for use in combination dishes where attractive shape is not important. Use jars or plain cans.

Choose firm-ripe tomatoes. Peel by dipping, a few at a time, in boiling water for about 30 seconds, dunking immediately in cold water, and then stripping off skins. Gouge out the stem ends; leave whole, or halve or quarter.

RAW PACK

In jars. Pack raw whole or cut tomatoes in clean jars, leaving ½ inch of headroom, pressing gently to fill vacant spaces. *Do not add water:* there will be enough juice for processing. Add ½ teaspoon salt to pints, 1 teaspoon salt to quarts; adjust lids. Process in a Boiling-Water Bath (212 F.)—pints for 35 minutes, quarts for 45 minutes. Remove jars; complete seals if necessary.

In plain cans. Fill to the top with raw whole or cut tomatoes, pressing gently to fill vacancies: you need no headroom, since there's enough slack in the tomatoes. *Do not add water.* Add ½ teaspoon salt to No. 2 cans, 1 teaspoon salt to No. 2½ cans. Exhaust to 170 F. (*c.* 15 minutes; seal. Process in a B-W Bath (212 F.)—No. 2 cans for 45 minutes, No. 2½ for 55 minutes. Remove cans; cool quickly.

HOT PACK

Bring cut tomatoes to a boil in their own juice, stirring gently so they don't stick to the pan. Ladle tomatoes and juice into containers.

In jars. Fill clean hot jars with tomatoes and juice, leaving ½ inch of headroom. Add ½ teaspoon salt to pints, 1 teaspoon salt to quarts. Adjust lids. Process in a Boiling-Water Bath (212 F.)—10 minutes for either pints or quarts. Remove jars; complete seals if necessary.

In plain cans. Pack boiling hot tomatoes and juice, leaving ¼ inch of headroom. Add ½ teaspoon salt to No. 2 cans, 1 teaspoon salt to No. 2½ cans. Exhaust to 170 F. (*c.* 10 minutes); seal. Process in a B-W Bath (212 F.)—10 minutes for either No. 2 or No. 2½ cans. Remove cans; cool quickly.

OPEN-KETTLE PROCESSING

Tomatoes break up readily when precooked for canning by Open-Kettle. Simmer peeled, quartered tomatoes in their own juice until tender, salting to taste during cooking (salting of course is optional here, as elsewhere).

In jars only. Ladle boiling hot, cooked tomatoes and their juice into hot, sterilized jars, leaving 1/8 inch of headroom. Be sure to wipe rims clear of pulp and seeds: they will prevent a perfect seal, thus causing spoilage. Cap and seal immediately.

(Optional Boiling-Water Bath to ensure the seal: Leave more headroom—½ inch. Merely *adjust* lids; process in a B-W Bath (212 F.)—10 minutes for either pints or quarts. Remove jars; complete seals if necessary.)

Tomato Paste

FEASIBILITY

Home-made tomato paste is better and more versatile than most commercial varieties because, since you govern what goes into it, it may be used as a delicate color-booster for otherwise pallid dishes and for sauces, in addition to being a more expectable addition to some Italian-style foods. Forgo seasonings other than salt: you can always add spices and garlic, etc., when you build the particular dish you have in mind.

HANDLING

Boiling-Water Bath. Use Hot pack only. Use ½-pint jars only (you're likely to have them on hand anyway, and an unused dab of paste keeps better in the refrigerator in a jar than it does in a can).

Peel, trim and chop tomatoes (4 to 4½ pounds of tomatoes will make about 4 ½-pint jars). Measure, and add ¾ teaspoon salt for every pint of chopped tomatoes. Simmer in an enameled kettle over very low heat for 1 hour, stirring so it doesn't stick. Remove from heat, put it through a fine sieve, then continue cooking very slowly, stirring occasionally, until the paste holds shape on the spoon—about 2 hours more. Pack hot.

HOT PACK ONLY, IN JARS

Fill ½-pint jars, leaving ½ inch of headroom; adjust lids. Process in a Boiling-Water Bath (212 F.) for 35 minutes. Remove jars; complete seals if necessary.

Canning Berries

Don't get so taken up with making jellies and jams in berry-time that you forget to can some too: they may be done for serving solo and in compôtes and salads; or, with slightly different handling, for use in cobblers, pies and puddings; or they may be put on the shelf until you have more time to make your preserves. (See Recipes, and also look at Freezing, Drying, Root-Cellaring.)

For purposes of general handling, berries—except for strawberries, which are a law unto themselves—are divided in two categories: *soft* (raspberries, blackberries, boysenberries, dewberries, loganberries and youngberries), and *firm* (blueberries, cranberries, currants, elderberries, gooseberries and huckleberries). The texture usually determines which pack to use; but some of the firm ones may be dealt with in more than one way, and such variations are described separately below for the specific berries.

It goes without saying that you'll want to use only perfect berries that are ripe without being at all mushy. Pick them over carefully, wash them gently and drain; stem or hull them as necessary. Work with only a couple of quarts at a time because all berries, particularly the soft ones, break down quickly by being handled.

General Procedure for Most Berries

All berries are acid, so a Boiling-Water Bath for the prescribed length of time is the best process for them. A couple of them, being especially tough-skinned and highly acid, may even be canned by the Cold-Water method (provided that your storage is cold enough and you don't hope to keep them too long). Only rarely would Open-Kettle Canning be adequate—and then for berries precooked as a table-ready sauce with an extra amount of sugar and packed Hot (*but even these are the better for an added short B-W Bath to ensure the seal*).

Use Raw pack generally for *soft* berries, because they break down so much in precooking.

A Hot pack in general makes a better product of most *firm* berries.

Use jars or cans for berries processed by a Boiling-Water Bath— R-enamel cans for all red berries, but plain cans for gooseberries.

All may be canned either with sugar or without—but just a little sweetening helps hold the flavor even of berries you intend to doll up later for desserts. Thin and Medium sirups are used more often than Heavy, with Medium usually considered as giving a better table-ready product than Thin.

RAW PACK (SOFT BERRIES)

In jars. Fill clean, hot jars, shaking to settle the berries for a firm pack; leave ½ inch of headroom. Add boiling Thin or Medium sirup, leaving ½ inch of headroom; adjust lids. Process in a Boiling-Water Bath (212 F.)—pints for 10 minutes, quarts for 15 minutes. Remove jars; complete seals if necessary.

In R-enamel cans. Fill, shaking for a firm pack; leave only ¼ inch of headroom. Add boiling Thin or Medium sirup to the top of the can. Exhaust to 170 F. (*c.* 10 minutes); seal. Process in a B-W Bath (212 F.)—No. 2 cans for 15 minutes, No. 2½ for 20 minutes. Remove cans; cool quickly.

STANDARD HOT PACK (MOST FIRM BERRIES)

Measure berries into a kettle, and add ½ cup of sugar for each 1 quart of berries. On lowest burner, bring very slowly to a boil, shaking the pan to prevent berries from sticking (rather than stirring, which breaks them down). Remove from heat and let them stand, covered, for several hours. *This plumps up the berries and keeps them from floating to the top of the container when they're processed.* For packing, reheat them slowly. As insurance, have some hot Thin or Medium sirup on hand in case you run short of juice when filling the containers.

In jars. Fill with hot berries and juice, leaving ½ inch of headroom. Proceed and process as for Raw pack.

In R-enamel or plain cans. Fill to the top with hot berries and juice, leaving no headroom. Proceed and process as for Raw pack.

UNSWEETENED HOT PACK (MOST FIRM BERRIES)

This is often used for sugar-restricted diets; it is also another way of canning berries intended for pies.

Pour just enough cold water in a kettle to cover the bottom. Add the berries and place over very low heat. Bring to a simmer until they are hot throughout, shaking the pot—not stirring—to keep them from sticking.

Pack hot without adding liquid as for the standard Hot pack—but remove any air bubbles in this very solid pack by running a knife blade around the inner side of the container. Process as above.

Specific Berries—except Strawberries

BLACKBERRIES

Raw pack. Usually considered soft, so for over-all versatility use Raw pack under the General Procedure above. With boiling water or Thin or Medium sirup—but Medium sirup if you want them table-ready. In jars or R-enamel cans.

BLUEBERRIES

Though in the firm category, they actually break down too much in the standard Hot pack (but they make a lovely sauce for ice cream, etc., if you want to can them by Hot pack with a good deal of extra sweetening). Old-timers dried them (q.v.) to use like currants in fruit cake.

Raw pack. With boiling water or sirup (Medium recommended). In jars or R-enamel cans. Proceed and process under General Procedure above.

Raw pack variation. If you want to hold them as much like their original texture and taste as possible when canned (to use like fresh berries in cakes, muffins, pies), you must blanch them. Put no more than 3 quarts of berries in a single layer of cheesecloth about 20 inches square. Gather and hold the cloth by the corners, and dunk the bundle to cover the berries in boiling water until juice spots show on the cloth—*about 30 seconds.* Dip the bundle immediately in cold water to cool the berries. Drain them.

Fill jars, leaving ½ inch of headroom. Add no water or sweetening; adjust lids. Process as for standard Raw pack under General Procedure above.

BOYSENBERRIES

Soft; in Raw pack under General Procedure. Use jars or R-enamel cans.

CRANBERRIES

These hold so well fresh in proper cold storage (see Root-Cellaring) or in the refrigerator, and they also freeze (q.v.), so they probably make the most sense canned if they're done as whole or jellied sauce.

The sauce may be canned successfully by Open-Kettle (with an optional quick Boiling-Water Bath to ensure the seal). Whole raw, unsweetened berries may also be canned by the Cold-Water method.

For both procedures the home-canner is better off using jars only.

Open-Kettle for whole sauce. Boil together 4 cups sugar and 4 cups water for 5 minutes. Add 8 cups (about 2 pounds) of washed, stemmed cranberries, and boil without stirring until the skins burst. Pour boiling hot into *hot sterilized jars,* leaving 1/8 inch of headroom, and run a sterile knife or spatula around the inner side of the jar. Seal immediately with sterilized lids. Makes about 6 pints.

Optional Boiling-Water Bath: After filling with 1/8 inch of headroom, *adjust* lids, and process pints in a B-W Bath (212 F.) for 5 minutes. Remove jars; complete seals if necessary.

Open-Kettle for jellied sauce. Boil 2 pounds of washed, stemmed berries with 1 quart of water until the skins burst. Push berries and juice through a food mill or strainer. Add 4 cups sugar to the resulting purée, return to heat, and boil almost to the jelly stage (not quite to 10 degrees F. above boiling temperature, or just before it begins to sheet from the spoon). Pour hot into sterilized straight-sided jars (so it will slip out easily); seal with sterilized lids as for any jelly. Makes 4 pints.

Cold-Water Canning for raw cranberries. Wash and stem cranberries. Sterilize jars, lids and gaskets. Scrub and scald a deep pail. Fill each jar with cranberries, set it in the pail, and let cold drinking water fill the jar and keep running into the pail until the water comes 6 inches over the top of the jar. Put on the cover and complete the seal under water.

Store the sealed jars in a place that's dry, dark and cold, but where they won't freeze.

CURRANTS

Currants are a novelty in certain sections of the United States where, during the 1920's, the bushes were uprooted because they harbored an insect destructive to the white pine. If you are fortunate enough to have some, by all means make jelly with them. Turn extra ones into dessert sauce; dry some; and they freeze.

Classed as firm berries, they can by Hot pack under General Procedure; in jars or R-enamel cans.

DEWBERRIES

Soft; in Raw pack under General Procedure. Use jars or R-enamel cans.

ELDERBERRIES

Best use is for jelly or wine.

If you do can them, use a Hot pack under General Procedure—and add 1 tablespoon lemon juice for each 1 quart of berries, to improve their flavor. In jars or R-enamel cans.

On the outside chance that you'd want to use them in muffins and cakes, experiment with blanching and the Raw pack variation described under Blueberries.

GOOSEBERRIES

Another scarce fruit in many sections of the country because, like the currant, they harbored the white-pine blister rust insect, and were eradicated as a conservation measure. But they make such heavenly old-fashioned pies, tarts and preserves!

Although they're firm, they do well in Raw pack with very sweet sirup. Or they may be done with Hot pack (where they hold their shape less well). Or the green (slightly underripe) ones may be Cold-Water Canned.

Wash; pick them over, pinch off stem ends and tails. Some cooks prick each berry with a sterile needle to promote a better blending of sweetening and juice (but we can't imagine a quicker way to drive ourselves up the wall; we'll leave it to osmosis).

Raw pack. Heavy Sirup is recommended for these very tart berries. And they'll probably pack better if you put ½ cup of hot sirup in the bottom of the container before you start filling. Use jars or plain cans. Process as in General Procedure above.

Hot pack. Follow the General Procedure for a standard Hot pack—but you may want to increase the sugar to ¾ cup for each 1 quart of berries. Process.

Cold-Water Canning for raw green gooseberries. Follow the method given above for Cranberries. And here you certainly do *not* prick the berries beforehand.

HUCKLEBERRIES

Being cousins of the blueberry, these firm berries are handled like Blueberries (q.v.).

LOGANBERRIES

They're soft, so pack Raw under General Procedure.

RASPBERRIES

Tenderest of the soft berries, these really do better if they're frozen. Put by some as jam or jelly, of course; try canning some sauce or juice. And if you have them in your garden, please don't forget to take a basket of fresh-picked raspberries to some older person who doesn't have a way to get them any more.

If you can them, use Raw pack and Medium Sirup. Use jars or R-enamel cans. Follow the General Procedure above.

YOUNGBERRIES

Another softie. Raw pack, as under General Procedure.

Strawberries

The most popular berry in the United States, these nevertheless are often a disappointment when canned, because they will fade and float if they are handled in the standard way recommended for most other soft berries. Here's how to have a blue-ribbon product—and no short cuts, please.

GENERAL HANDLING

Use a Boiling-Water Bath. Use Hot pack only (even though they're soft). Use jars or R-enamel cans.

Wash and hull perfect berries that are red-ripe, firm, and without white or hollow centers. Measure berries. Using ½ to 1 cup sugar for

each 4 cups of berries, spread the berries and sugar in shallow pans in thin alternating layers. Cover with waxed paper or foil if necessary as a protection against insects, and let stand at room temperature for 2 to 4 hours. Then turn into a kettle and simmer for 5 minutes in their own juice. Have some boiling Thin Sirup on hand if there's not enough juice for packing.

HOT PACK ONLY

In jars. Fill, leaving ½ inch of headroom (adding a bit of hot sirup if needed); adjust lids. Process in a Boiling-Water Bath (212 F.)—pints for 10 minutes, quarts for 15 minutes. Remove jars; complete seals if necessary.

In R-enamel cans. Fill to the top with hot berries and juice. Exhaust to 170 F. (*c.* 10 minutes); seal. Process in a B-W Bath (212 F.)—No. 2 cans for 15 minutes, No. 2½ for 20 minutes. Remove cans; cool quickly.

FOR A NICE SAUCE

Some ½-pint jars of strawberries will be welcome for toppings on ice cream or puddings.

Prepare the berries as above, but use 1 to 1¼ cups sugar to each 4 cups of berries. Process the ½-pints in a B-W Bath (212 F.) for 10 minutes. Remove jars; complete seals if necessary.

Canning Fruit Juices

It might seem a marginal use of time and material to can fruit juices, but they may be used to advantage in several ways: as beverages at breakfast or in place of commercial soft drinks for the family, or as the base for punches served by a country caterer (a Grange group, for instance); or the juices may be put by for future jelly-making.

Beverage juices will have better flavor if they are presweetened at least partially. Use sugar, or the sweetener of your choice. (But for sugar-restricted diets, *use only the non-nutritive sweetener approved by your doctor.)*

Juices intended for jelly are not sweetened until you are making your jelly.

Fruit (and berry) sirups, which are concentrated, are better made from regular canned juice at the time you'll be wanting to use them, because you could run into a problem with pectin in some cases and end up with something too gooey for your purpose.

Nectars—most often made from apricots, peaches and pears—are juices that are thickened with finely sieved pulp; they are usually "let down" (diluted) with ice water when served.

CONTAINERS FOR JUICES

Modern glass canning jars are your best choice for juices because they seal easily and are made to withstand heat and many years of re-use. Their only drawback: *fruit juice in jars must be stored in the dark* so its color won't fade or change.

Cans also are suitable for juices. One manufacturer of cans recommends that the R-enamel type be used for all juices in cans, even though some of the fruits from which they're made do well in plain cans. R-enamel prevents color change inside the can; and of course any can, being light-proof, need not be stored in the dark.

Not suitable are the jars which you bought peanut butter or other food products in. For one thing, the glass in them is not as durable, either for heat-processing or rehandling, as is the glass in modern canning jars; for another, the liners of their tops are not made for re-use (any more than sealers for regular canning jars are), so you cannot count on them for a perfect seal.

Also not suitable are soft-drink bottles, which would not be satisfactory for re-use in home heat-processing.

General Procedure for Most Juices

Because boiling temperature spoils the flavor of almost all fruit juices and may impair their nutritive value, they are usually processed by the *Hot*-Water Bath (180 to 190 F.), which is pasteurization. By the same token, the juices are extracted by simmering rather than being brought to a full boil.

Use Hot pack only (with individual exceptions noted below). Use jars or R-enamel cans.

Choose ripe, blemish-free fruit or berries; wash. Then stem, hull, pit, core, slice—whatever is needed for preparing the particular fruit. Rig up a jelly bag for straining the juice.

APPLE CIDER (BEVERAGE)

Cider, being the raw juice pressed from apples, is packed Raw. Get cider fresh from the mill, strain it through a jelly bag.

Raw pack only, in jars. Pour strained fresh cider into hot sterilized jars, leaving ¼ inch of headroom; adjust lids. Process in a Hot-Water Bath at 185 F.–30 minutes for either pints or quarts. Remove jars; complete seals if necessary.

Raw pack only, in cans (R-enamel suggested). Fill to the top with strained fresh cider leaving no headroom. Exhaust to 170 F. (c. 15 minutes); seal. Process in a H-W Bath at 185 F.–30 minutes for either No. 2 or No. 2½ cans. Remove cans; cool quickly.

APPLE JUICE (FOR JELLY LATER)

Add some underripe apples to the batch for more pectin. Wash and cut up apples, discarding stem and blossom ends. *Do not peel or core* (you may even use the peels left over from making Applesauce). Barely cover with cold water and bring to a boil over moderate heat, and simmer until apples are quite soft—about 30 minutes. Strain hot through a jelly bag.

Pack and process as for Apple Cider, above.

APRICOT NECTAR

Nectars are merely juices that are thickened with finely sieved fruit pulp.

Use a Boiling-Water Bath. Use Hot pack only. Use ½-pint or pint jars or No. 2 cans (R-enamel suggested).

Wash, drain; pit; slice and measure. Add 1 cup boiling water to each 4 cups of prepared fruit, bring to simmering, and cook gently until fruit is soft. Put through a fine sieve or a food mill. To each 2 cups of fruit juice-plus-pulp add about ½ cup sugar, or to taste. (Optional: add 2 teaspoons lemon juice or 1/8 teaspoon crystalline ascorbic acid to each 2 cups of nectar.) Reheat and simmer until sugar is dissolved. Pack.

Hot pack only, in jars. Pour hot nectar into ½-pint or pint jars, leaving ½ inch of headroom; adjust lids. Process in a Boiling-Water Bath (212 F.)–15 minutes for either ½-pints or pints. Remove jars; complete seals if necessary.

Hot pack only, in No. 2 cans (R-enamel suggested). Fill No. 2 cans to the top with simmering nectar, leaving no headroom; seal. Process in a Boiling-Water Bath (212 F.)–for 15 minutes. Remove cans; cool quickly.

BERRY JUICES

Crush and simmer berries in their own juice until soft; strain through a jelly bag—allow several hours for draining. If you twist the bag for a greater yield, the juice should be strained again through clean cloth to make it clear.

If the juice is for a beverage, add 1 to 2 cups sugar to each 4 quarts of juice; if it's for jelly, omit sugar at this time. Reheat juice to simmering—180 to 190 F. Pack.

Hot pack only, in jars. Pour simmering juice into hot sterilized jars, leaving ¼ inch of headroom; adjust lids. Process in a Hot-Water Bath at 190 F.—30 minutes for either pints or quarts. Remove jars; complete seals if necessary.

Hot pack only, in R-enamel cans. Fill cans to the top with hot juice, leaving no headroom; seal (at simmering stage it will already be more than 170 F., so exhausting is not necessary). Process in a H-W Bath at 190 F.—30 minutes for either No. 2 or No. 2½ cans. Remove cans; cool quickly.

CHERRY JUICE

Prepare as for Berry Juice, adjusting sweetening to the tartness of the cherries (or omitting if for jelly). Use Hot pack; process in a Hot-Water Bath at 190 F.—30 minutes for either pint or quart jars or for No. 2 or No. 2½ cans.

CRANBERRY JUICE

Cranberries are so acid that Open-Kettle with a finishing Boiling-Water Bath is satisfactory for processing. Use Hot pack only. Use jars only.

Pick over and wash. Measure, and add an equal amount of water. Bring to boiling, and cook until berries burst. Strain through a jelly bag (squeezing the bag adds to the yield but clouds the juice: re-strain if you want it beautifully clear). Add sugar to taste.

Assuming that you bother to can this juice only for special-diet reasons, either omit sugar or use the *non-nutritive sweetener prescribed by your doctor.*

Bring to boiling to dissolve the sweetener. Pack.

Hot pack only. Pour boiling juice into hot sterilized jars. If you do not plan on a finishing Boiling-Water Bath, leave a mere 1/8 inch of headroom. Cap and seal immediately.

Optional Boiling-Water Bath to ensure the seal: Fill jars, but leave ¼ inch of headroom; adjust lids. Process in a B-W Bath

(212 F.)—10 minutes for either pints or quarts. Remove jars; complete seals if necessary.

CURRANT JUICE

Prepare and process as for Berry Juices, above.

GRAPE JUICE

Hot-Water Bath only. Use Hot pack only. Use jars or R-enamel cans.

The extra intermediate step of refrigerating the juice will prevent crystals of tartaric acid (harmless, but not beautiful) in the finished product. It's easier to work with not more than 1 gallon of grapes at a time.

Select firm-ripe grapes; wash, stem. Crush and measure into an enameled or stainless-steel kettle; add 1 cup water for each 4 quarts of crushed grapes. Cook gently *without boiling* until fruit is very soft—about 10 minutes. Strain through a jelly bag, squeezing it for a greater yield.

Refrigerate the juice for 24 hours. Then strain again for perfect clearness, being mighty careful to hold back the sediment of tartaric acid crystals in the bottom of the container.

Add ½ cup sugar for each 1 quart of juice (or omit sweetening), and heat to 190 F.

Hot pack only, in jars. Pour simmering juice into hot sterilized jars, leaving ¼ inch of headroom; adjust lids. Process in a Hot-Water Bath at 190 F.—30 minutes for either pints or quarts. Remove jars; complete seals if necessary.

Hot pack only, in R-enamel cans. Fill cans to the top with simmering juice, leaving no headroom; seal. Process in a H-W Bath at 190 F.—30 minutes for either No. 2 or No. 2½ cans. Remove cans; cool quickly.

PEACH NECTAR

Prepare and process as for Apricot Nectar, above.

PEAR NECTAR

Prepare and process as for Apricot Nectar, above.

PLUM JUICE (AND FRESH PRUNE)

Hot-Water Bath only. Use Hot pack only. Use jars or R-enamel cans.

Choose firm-ripe plums with attractive red skins. Wash; stem; cut in small pieces. Measure. Put in an enameled or stainless-steel kettle, add 1 cup water for each 1 cup prepared fruit. Bring slowly to simmering, and cook gently until fruit is soft—about 15 minutes. Strain through a jelly bag. Add ¼ cup sugar to each 2 cups juice, or to taste. Reheat just to simmering.

Pack and process as for Berry Juices, above.

RHUBARB JUICE

This makes good sense if you have extra rhubarb, because it can be used for a delicious quencher, and was the main ingredient of a hill-country wedding punch in olden days (see Recipe). And rhubarb is said to be good for our teeth.

May be Open-Kettle Canned because it's so acid. Use Hot pack only. Use jars or R-enamel cans.

Wash and trim fresh young red rhubarb, but *do not peel.* Cover the bottom of the kettle with ½ inch of water, add rhubarb cut in ½-inch pieces. Bring to simmering, and cook gently until soft—about 10 minutes. Strain through a jelly bag. Reheat juice, adding ¼ cup sugar to each 4 cups of juice to hold the flavor, and simmer only until sugar is dissolved.

Hot pack, in jars. Pour simmering juice into hot sterilized jars, leaving only 1/8 inch of headroom. Cap and seal immediately.

Hot pack, in R-enamel cans. Pour simmering juice to the top of the cans, leaving no headroom; seal immediately. Cool cans quickly.

(Optional: Jars or cans may be given a short Boiling-Water Bath to ensure the seal. After filling the containers, proceed as for the Optional B-W Bath for Cranberry Juice, above.)

TOMATO JUICE

Boiling-Water Bath only. Use Hot pack only. Use jars or plain cans.

Wash firm-ripe juicy tomatoes; remove stem ends and cores; cut in pieces. Simmer in their own juice until soft, stirring often. Put through a food mill or fine sieve: the finer the pulp the less the juice will separate in the container. Measure juice and put it in a kettle with 1 teaspoon salt to each 4 cups of juice. Reheat to boiling.

Hot pack only, in jars. Fill hot sterilized jars with boiling juice, leaving ½ inch of headroom; adjust lids. Process in a Boiling-Water Bath (212 F.)—10 minutes for either pints or quarts. Remove jars, adjust seals if necessary.

Hot pack only, in plain cans. Fill to the top with boiling juice, leaving no headroom; seal. Process in a B-W Bath (212 F.)—15 minutes for either No. 2 or No. 2½ cans. Remove cans; cool quickly.

TOMATO JUICE COCKTAIL

Boiling-Water Bath only. Use Hot pack only. Use jars or plain cans.

To make 3 quarts of tomato juice cocktail, prepare 10 pounds of firm-ripe juicy tomatoes as for plain Tomato Juice. Simmer them over low heat for 1 hour with: 16 whole cloves, 2 bay leaves, 4 diced medium onions, 4 teaspoons sugar, ½ teaspoon ground pepper and 2 teaspoons salt.

Strain tomatoes with their juice through a fine sieve, and add ½ cup vinegar and about 1 teaspoon more salt (or to taste) to each 4 cups of juice. Bring again to a full boil. Pack.

Hot pack only, in jars. Fill with hot juice, leaving ½ inch of headroom; adjust lids. Process in a Boiling-Water Bath (212 F.)—10 minutes for either pints or quarts. Remove jars; complete seals if necessary.

Hot pack only, in plain cans. Fill with boiling juice to the tops, leaving no headroom; seal immediately. Process in a B-W Bath (212 F.)—10 minutes for either No. 2 or No. 2½ cans. Remove cans; cool quickly.

Canning Vegetables

Absolutely all natural vegetables are low-acid, and therefore must be processed in a Pressure Canner to avoid possible food poisoning by heat-resistant spores of spoilage organisms.

The only exception among the many specific canning instructions which follow is for Pickled Beets, whose added vinegar makes them acid enough to be processed safely in a Boiling-Water Bath. (Tomatoes, naturally high in acid, are classed as a fruit, and are canned under Fruits.)

Almost all natural vegetables may be canned successfully either by Raw pack or Hot pack, and in jars or cans (plain, C-enamel or R-enamel). Garden greens are packed Hot; certain wild greens must be thoroughly cooked before canning to rid them of toxins or unpalatable qualities, so they too are always packed Hot.

It goes without saying that you will choose for canning only prime vegetables that are at the peak of their garden goodness; and that you will put them through the canning process without delay, refrigerating them if they must be held overnight.

SALT IN CANNING VEGETABLES

Salt is merely a seasoning in canned vegetables: therefore—because it is not a preservative when used in such relatively small amounts as suggested hereafter—it may be omitted.

If you use salt, your regular table salt will do. In the amounts in the specific instructions, iodine or the pure additives that keep it free-running in damp weather will not make the processing liquid cloudy.

Before tasting canned low-acid food, boil it hard for 15 minutes to destroy any hidden toxins (corn and greens require 20 minutes). If it looks spoiled or foams or has an off-odor during boiling, destroy it completely so it can't be eaten by people or animals.

Asparagus

Asparagus keeps more spring flavor if you freeze it; but it cans easily— whole or cut up. See Recipes.

GENERAL HANDLING

Only Pressure Canning for asparagus: it has even less acid than string beans. Use Raw or Hot pack. Use jars or plain cans.

Wash; remove large scales that may have sand behind them; break off tough ends; wash again. If you're canning it whole, sort spears for length and thickness, because you'll pack them upright; otherwise cut spears in 1-inch pieces.

RAW PACK

In jars. Whether asparagus is whole (spears packed upright) or cut up, leave ½ inch of headroom. Add ½ teaspoon salt to a pint, 1 teaspoon to a quart. Add boiling water, leaving ½ inch of headroom; adjust lids. Pressure-process at 10 pounds (240 F.)—pints for 25 minutes, quarts for 30 minutes. Remove jars; complete seals if necessary.

In plain cans. Pack as for jars, leaving only ¼ inch of headroom. Add ½ teaspoon salt to No. 2 cans, 1 teaspoon to No. 2½. Fill to top with boiling water. Exhaust to 170 F. (*c.* 10 minutes); seal. Pressure-process at 10 pounds (240 F.)—20 minutes for either No. 2 or No. 2½. Remove cans; cool quickly.

HOT PACK

Whole spears—stand upright in a wire blanching basket and dunk it for 3 minutes in boiling water up to *but not covering* the tips; drain and pack upright (tight but not squushed). Cut-up—cover clean 1-inch pieces with boiling water for 2 to 3 minutes; drain and pack.

The added processing liquid can be the boiling-hot blanching water—if it's free of grit—instead of fresh boiling water.

In jars. Complete the pack and Pressure-process as for Raw pack, above.

In plain cans. Complete the pack and Pressure-process as for Raw pack, above.

Beans, "Butter," see Beans, Lima (fresh)

Beans (dried), Baked

FEASIBILITY

Freezing makes more sense for several pints or so left over from a meal. But if you can't freeze leftovers, or for your own reasons (the stove goes all day in the winter anyway; you have to make them far ahead of time, climate or facilities being a problem) you want to can whole batches, here's what you do.

See also Recipes; and, below, Beans (dried), in Sauce.

GENERAL HANDLING

Only Pressure Canning (because they're low-acid and dense). Only Hot pack—either hot from the oven or reheated; in either jars or plain cans. If the cooked beans have got cold or too dry, add a bit of hot water as you reheat them, so they'll be juicy enough again.

HOT PACK ONLY

In jars. Pack beans hot, leaving 1 inch of headroom. Pressure-process at 10 pounds (240 F.)—pints for 80 minutes, quarts for 100 minutes. Remove jars; complete seals if necessary.

In plain cans. Pack beans hot, leaving only ¼ inch of headroom. Exhaust to 170 F. (c. 15 minutes); seal. Pressure-process at 10 pounds (240 F.)—No. 2 cans for 95 minutes, No. 2½ for 115 minutes. Remove cans; cool quickly.

Beans (dried), in Sauce

FEASIBILITY

Not prebaked, these are cooked as they process, thereby cutting the total time from raw bean to canned product by about 80 percent—if you are impelled to can these dried "baked" beans in the first place.

GENERAL HANDLING

Only Pressure Canning. Only Hot pack. Use either jars or plain cans.

Use clean beans—kidney, navy, pea or yellow-eye as you prefer—that are free of any musty odor. Cover with boiling water, boil 2 minutes. Remove from heat and let soak 1 hour in their cooking water. Yield: 1 cup dry beans will make about 2 or 2½ cups after soaking.

To pack, reheat to boiling, drain (saving water to use in the sauce), and put hot beans in containers.

To make about 4 cups of sauce, enough to do 4 to 5 pints of beans:

Tomato—4 cups tomato juice, 3 tablespoons sugar, 2 teaspoons salt, 1 tablespoon onion pulp, a pinch of whatever spices you like, a few grains of cayenne. Heat to boiling. (Blah but O.K. in a bind: 1 cup tomato catsup, 3 cups of the drained-off soaking water, and 1 teaspoon salt, or to taste; boil.)

Molasses—4 cups of drained-off soaking water, 3 tablespoons dark molasses, 1 tablespoon vinegar, 2 teaspoons salt, ½ teaspoon dry mustard, ¼ teaspoon ginger; boil. Maple sirup is great in beans; so is some onion pulp. Experiment!

HOT PACK ONLY

In jars. Fill only ¾ full with drained hot beans. Lay on top of the beans a 1-inch-square slice of salt pork or bacon end (more for quarts). Add boiling sauce, leaving 1 inch of headroom. Adjust lids. Pressure-process at 10 pounds (240 F.)—pints for 65 minutes, quarts for 75 minutes. Remove jars; complete seals if necessary.

In plain cans. Fill only ¾ full with drained hot beans. Lay on top of the beans a 1-inch-square slice of salt pork or bacon end (more for No. 2½). Add boiling sauce, leaving only ¼ inch of headroom. Exhaust to 170 F. (*c.* 20 minutes); seal. Pressure-process at 10 pounds (240 F.)—No. 2 cans for 65 minutes, No. 2½ for 75 minutes. Remove cans; cool quickly.

Beans—Green/Italian/Snap/String/Wax

FEASIBILITY

These beans—call them "green" or "snap" or "string," and their close relatives—are one of the most popular vegetables to put by. Don't shy away from canning them because they're the foremost Horrible Example of Bad Processing. Just be sensibly careful, and do them in a Pressure Canner.

They freeze well; maybe you'd like to freeze the very young, just-from-the garden ones, and can the rest. And old-timers used to dry them (see "Leather Britches").

GENERAL HANDLING

Pressure Canning only. Use Raw or Hot pack (Hot makes them supple and permits a more solid pack). Use jars or plain cans.

The name "snap" comes from the crisp way the young ones break when they're fresh-picked; if you must hold them overnight before canning, refrigerate them in bags. Wash, trim ends. Sort roughly for size: you may want some whole in a fancy pack (upright like asparagus spears), or others frenched or cut on a slant in 1-inch pieces. If you're stuck with doing some bigger, older ones, though, break off tips and tails, unzip their strings along their length, cut them in small pieces, and pack them by themselves. There's plenty of use for all types—see Recipes.

RAW PACK

In jars. Fill as tightly as you can, leaving ½ inch of headroom. Add ½ teaspoon salt to pints, 1 teaspoon to quarts. Add boiling water, leaving ½ inch headroom. Adjust lids. Pressure-process at 10 pounds (240 F.)—pints for 20 minutes, quarts for 25 minutes. Remove jars; complete seal if necessary.

In plain cans. Pack as tightly as you can, leaving only ¼ inch of head-room. Add ½ teaspoon salt to No. 2 cans, 1 teaspoon to No. 2½. Fill to top with boiling water. Exhaust to 170 F. (*c.* 10 minutes); seal. Pressure-process at 10 pounds (240 F.)—No. 2 cans for 25 minutes, No. 2½ for 30 minutes. Remove cans; cool quickly.

HOT PACK

Cover clean, trimmed beans with boiling water and boil 5 minutes. Drain, keeping the hot cooking water. Pack whole beans upright; use a wide-mouth funnel to pack the cut ones.

In jars. Fill with hot beans, leaving ½ inch of headroom. Add ½ teaspoon salt to pints, 1 teaspoon to quarts. Add boiling-hot cooking water, leaving ½ inch of headroom. Adjust lids. Pressure-process at 10 pounds (240 F.)—pints for 20 minutes, quarts for 25 minutes. Remove jars; complete seals if necessary.

In plain cans. Fill loosely with hot beans, leaving only ¼ inch of head-room. Add ½ teaspoon salt to No. 2 cans, 1 teaspoon to No. 2½. Fill to top with boiling-hot cooking water. Exhaust to 170 F.

(*c.* 10 minutes); seal. Pressure-process at 10 pounds (240 F.)–No. 2 cans for 25 minutes, No. 2½ for 30 minutes. Remove cans; cool quickly.

Beans, fresh Lima (Shell beans)

FEASIBILITY

If young fresh limas (they're also called "butter beans") are available at a moderate price, can them. They freeze satisfactorily, too.

GENERAL HANDLING

A dense and very low-acid vegetable, limas should be Pressure-Canned only. Use Raw or Hot pack. Use jars or C-enamel cans.

It's good but not vital to deal with one variety at a time–if only because sometimes different-sized types require different amounts of headroom.

Shell the beans and wash them before packing. They must be packed loosely.

RAW PACK

In jars. If it's a small variety, leave 1 inch of headroom for pints, 1½ inches of headroom for quarts; if it's a large variety, leave ¾ inch of headroom for pints, 1¼ inches of headroom for quarts. *Do not press or shake the beans down.* Add ½ teaspoon salt to pints, 1 teaspoon salt to quarts. Add boiling water, leaving ½ inch of headroom (the water will be well over the top of the beans); adjust lids. Pressure-process at 10 pounds (240 F.)–pints for 40 minutes, quarts for 50 minutes. Remove jars; complete seals if necessary.

In C-enamel cans. Fill with beans, leaving ¾ inch of headroom for either No. 2 or No. 2½ cans; *don't press or shake down.* Add ½ teaspoon salt to No. 2 cans, 1 teaspoon salt to No. 2½. Fill cans to top with boiling water. Exhaust to 170 F. (*c.* 10 minutes); seal. Pressure-process at 10 pounds (240 F.)–40 minutes for either No. 2 or No. 2½. Remove cans; cool quickly.

HOT PACK

Cover shelled, washed beans with boiling water and cook 1 minute after water returns to boiling. Drain, saving the hot cooking water.

In jars. Fill loosely with drained hot beans, leaving 1 inch of headroom for either pints or quarts. Add ½ teaspoon salt to pints, 1 teaspoon salt to quarts. Add boiling-hot cooking water, leaving 1 inch of headroom; adjust lids. Pressure-process at 10 pounds (240 F.)–

pints for 40 minutes, quarts for 50 minutes. Remove jars; complete seals if necessary.

In C-enamel cans. Fill loosely with drained hot beans, leaving only ½ inch of headroom. Add ½ teaspoon salt to No. 2 cans, 1 teaspoon salt to No. 2½. Fill to the top with boiling-hot cooking water. Exhaust to 170 F. (*c.* 10 minutes); seal. Pressure-process at 10 pounds (240 F.)—40 minutes for either No. 2 or 2½. Remove cans; cool quickly.

Beets

FEASIBILITY

Beets keep well in a root cellar (and some gardeners even leave them in the ground, well mulched, to harvest piecemeal for the table during the winter). Between canning and freezing, can them: they can beautifully, and, the alternatives considered, are a marginal use of freezer space. Use canned beets plain, titivated as a relish, in hash (see Recipes).

GENERAL HANDLING

Only Pressure Canning for beets: they rank with string beans on the low-acid scale. Because they're firm-fleshed, use Hot pack only. Use jars or R-enamel cans.

Sort for size; leave on tap root and 2 inches of stem (otherwise they bleed out their juice before they get in the containers). Wash carefully. Cover with boiling water and boil until skins slip off easily (15 to 25 minutes, depending on size/age). Drop them in cold water for just long enough to be able to slip off skins; skin, trim away roots, stems, any blemishes. Leave tiny beets whole; cut larger ones in slices or dice. Now they are ready to pickle or can.

HOT PACK ONLY

In jars. Fill with hot beets, leaving ½ inch of headroom. Add ½ teaspoon salt to pints, 1 teaspoon salt to quarts. Add fresh boiling water, leaving ½ inch of headroom; adjust lids. Pressure-process at 10 pounds (240 F.)—pints for 30 minutes, quarts for 35 minutes. Remove jars; complete seals if necessary.

In R-enamel cans. Fill with hot beets, leaving only ¼ inch of headroom. Add ½ teaspoon salt to No. 2 cans, 1 teaspoon salt to No. 2½. Cover to top with boiling water. Exhaust to 170 F. (*c.* 10 minutes); seal. Pressure-process at 10 pounds (240 F.)—30 minutes for either No. 2 or No. 2½ cans. Remove cans; cool quickly.

Beets, Pickled

HANDLING

Boiling-Water Bath only (vinegar makes them so acid that B-W Bath is quite O.K.). Use Hot pack only. Use jars only.

Wash; leave tap root and bit of stem. Boil until tender (how long, depends on size). Dunk in cold water to handle; trim, strip off skins, slice. While beets are cooking, make a Pickling Sirup of 2 parts vinegar (¼ of this may be water, if you like it weaker) to 2 parts sugar, and bring it to a boil.

Fill clean, hot jars with hot beet slices, leaving ½ inch of headroom. Add ½ teaspoon salt to pints, 1 teaspoon to quarts. Add boiling Pickling Sirup, leaving ½ inch of headroom; adjust lids. Process in a Boiling-Water Bath (212 F.)–30 minutes for either pint or quart jars. Remove jars; complete seals if necessary.

Broccoli

FEASIBILITY

Broccoli and similarly strong-flavored vegetables—Brussels sprouts, cabbage (unless it's done as sauerkraut, and see also Root-Cellaring) and cauliflower—usually discolor when canned and grow even stronger in flavor. Broccoli, particularly, is certainly worth freezer space if you have a surplus or a cheap supply; cauliflower freezes well, and so do Brussels sprouts. But here's how you can broccoli and the others if you have to.

GENERAL HANDLING

Low-acid, so only Pressure Canning. Use Hot pack only. Use jars or C-enamel cans.

Wash all-green spears, trimming off leaves, any old blossoms, and woody parts of the stems. Soak in cold salt water (1 tablespoon salt to 1 quart water) for 10 minutes to drive out bugs, etc. Drain and wash in fresh water. Cut in 2-inch pieces, splitting thick stalks; or size as you like.

HOT PACK ONLY

Cover trimmed, clean, cut broccoli with boiling water and boil 3 minutes; drain.

In jars. Pack, leaving 1 inch of headroom. Add ½ teaspoon salt to pints, 1 teaspoon to quarts. Add boiling water, leaving 1 inch of headroom;

adjust lids. Pressure-process at 10 pounds (240 F.)–pints for 30 minutes, quarts for 35 minutes. Remove jars; complete seals if necessary.

In C-enamel cans. Pack, leaving only ½ inch of headroom. Add ½ teaspoon salt to No. 2 cans, 1 teaspoon salt to No. 2½. Fill to top with boiling water. Exhaust to 170 F. (*c.* 10 minutes); seal. Pressure-process at 10 pounds (240 F.)–30 minutes for either No. 2 or No. 2½ cans. Remove cans; cool quickly.

Brussels Sprouts

These really should be frozen (they're hateful soggy and watery). But if canning, treat them like Broccoli, making a special point of the salt-water soak because they may have worms.

Cabbage

This really should be root-cellared. Or put by as sauerkraut (q.v.).

If canned as is, see Broccoli, but pressure-process cans at 10 pounds (240 F.) for *40* minutes.

Carrots

FEASIBILITY

Carrots keep so well in a root cellar–and even, well mulched, are held over in the ground by some cold-climate gardeners (who say they're sweeter and juicier dug as needed in midwinter)–and there are so many uses for them raw, that canned ones are handiest if they're put up when young and tiny or are cut small to be put in combination dishes (see Recipes). It doesn't make much sense to take up freezer space with them, unless you have special plans for serving some baby ones.

Like beets, carrots can be harvested late in the season to can when weather is cooler. Don't bother with overlarge, woody ones: medium-size are best (the fancy tiny carrots come earlier anyway).

GENERAL HANDLING

Only Pressure Canning. Raw or Hot pack. In jars or C-enamel cans.

Sort for size. Wash, scrubbing well, and scrape. (An energetic scrub with your stiffest brush often will do for the very small ones; or parboil them just enough to loosen the skins, dunk them in cold water, slip off their skins, then use Hot pack.) Slice, dice, cut in strips–whatever.

RAW PACK

In jars. Fill tightly, leaving 1 inch of headroom. Add ½ teaspoon salt to pints, 1 teaspoon to quarts. Add boiling water, leaving ½ inch of headroom (water comes above the carrots); adjust lids. Pressure-process at 10 pounds (240 F.)–pints for 25 minutes, quarts for 30 minutes. Remove jars; complete seal if necessary.

In C-enamel cans. Fill tightly, leaving ½ inch of headroom. Add ½ teaspoon salt to No. 2 cans, 1 teaspoon to No. 2½. Add boiling water to top. Exhaust to 170 F. (*c.* 10 minutes); seal. Pressure-process at 10 pounds (240 F.)–No. 2 cans for 25 minutes, No. 2½ for 30 minutes. Remove cans; cool quickly.

HOT PACK

Cover clean, scraped, cut or whole carrots with boiling water, bring again to a full boil; drain, but save the water to put in the jars for processing.

In jars. Pack hot carrots, leaving just ½ inch of headroom. Proceed as for Raw pack, using the cooking water for the added processing liquid.

In C-enamel cans. Pack, leaving only ¼ inch of headroom. Proceed as for Raw pack, using cooking water as the processing liquid, and reducing Pressure-process time–No. 2 cans for 20 minutes, No. 2½ for 25 minutes.

Cauliflower

Immeasurably better frozen; but can it like Broccoli.

Celery

FEASIBILITY

Because late celery can be held over the winter in a root cellar (q.v.), celery is marginal to can for its own sake. It is often an ingredient in canned vegetable combinations, though, and you should know how to process it. And of course a few containers of diced celery come in handy for soup or stew.

GENERAL HANDLING

Pressure Canning only. Use Hot pack only. Use jars or plain cans.

Wash thoroughly, trim off leaves (but if it's destined for stew, a few bits of chopped leaf are good flavor), cut stalks in 1-inch pieces. Cover with boiling water, boil 3 minutes. Drain, saving the cooking water.

HOT PACK ONLY

In jars. Fill with hot celery, leaving 1 inch of headroom. Add ½ teaspoon salt to pints, 1 teaspoon to quarts. Add boiling-hot cooking water, leaving 1 inch of headroom; adjust lids. Pressure-process at 10 pounds (240 F.)–pints for 30 minutes, quarts for 35 minutes. Remove jars; complete seals if necessary.

In plain cans. Fill with hot celery, leaving ½ inch of headroom. Add ½ teaspoon salt to No. 2 cans, 1 teaspoon to No. 2½. Fill to top with boiling cooking water. Exhaust to 170 F. (*c.* 10 minutes); seal. Pressure-process at 10 pounds (240 F.)–30 minutes for either No. 2 or No. 2½ cans. Remove cans; cool quickly.

Corn, Cream Style

FEASIBILITY

Canning is the better, and certainly handier, way of putting by cream-style corn. Its density demands that it be home-canned only in pint jars or No. 2 cans: an extremely low-acid vegetable, it would be pressure-cooked to death for the much longer time needed to process the interior of larger containers.

GENERAL HANDLING

Pressure Canning only. Use Raw or Hot pack. Use pint jars or No. 2 C-enamel cans.

Get it ready by husking, de-silking and washing the ears. Slice the corn from the cob *halfway through the kernels,* then scrape the milky juice that's left on the cob in with the cut corn (this is where the "cream" comes in).

RAW PACK

In pint jars only. Fill with corn-cream mixture, leaving 1½ inches of headroom (more space than usual is needed for expansion). Add ½ teaspoon salt. Add boiling water, leaving ½ inch of headroom (water will be well over the top of the corn); adjust lids. Pressure-process at 10 pounds (240 F.) for 95 minutes. Remove jars; complete seals if necessary.

In No. 2 C-enamel cans only. Fill without shaking or pressing down, leaving ½ inch of headroom. Add ½ teaspoon salt. Fill to top with boiling water. Exhaust to 170 F. (*c.* 25 minutes); seal. Pressure-process at 10 pounds (240 F.) for 105 minutes. Remove cans; cool quickly.

HOT PACK

Prepare as for Raw pack. To each 4 cups of corn-cream mixture, add 2 cups boiling water. Heat to boiling, stirring, over medium heat (it scorches easily).

In pint jars only. Fill with boiling corn and liquid, leaving 1 inch of headroom. Add ½ teaspoon salt (but you don't need more water); adjust lids. Pressure-process at 10 pounds (240 F.) for 85 minutes. Remove jars; complete seals if necessary.

In No. 2 C-enamel cans only. Fill to the top with boiling corn and liquid. Add ½ teaspoon salt (but you don't need more water). Exhaust to 170 F. (*c.* 10 minutes); seal. Pressure-process at 10 pounds (240 F.) for 105 minutes. Remove cans; cool quickly.

Corn, Whole Kernel

FEASIBILITY

Even if (like a lot of people) you prefer to freeze it for more of a just-picked flavor, you'll find that some jars of it on your shelves are a godsend when you're making combination dishes (see Recipes).

CANNING VEGETABLES

GENERAL HANDLING

Pressure Canning only. Use Raw or Hot pack. Use jars or C-enamel cans. Less dense than cream-style corn, it may be canned in quarts and No. 2½ cans just as well as in pints and No. 2 cans.

Husk, de-silk and wash fresh-picked ears. Cut from the cob at about 2/3 the depth of the kernels (this is deeper than for cream-style, but still avoids getting bits of cob).

RAW PACK

In jars. Fill, leaving 1 inch of headroom—and don't shake or press down. Add ½ teaspoon salt to pints, 1 teaspoon salt to quarts. Add boiling water, leaving ½ inch of headroom (water will come well over top of corn); adjust lids. Pressure-process at 10 pounds (240 F.)—pints for 55 minutes, quarts for 85 minutes. Remove jars; complete seals if necessary.

In C-enamel cans. Fill, leaving ½ inch of headroom—and don't shake or press down. Add ½ teaspoon salt to No. 2 cans, 1 teaspoon salt to No. 2½. Add boiling water to top. Exhaust to 170 F. (c. 10 minutes); seal. Pressure-process at 10 pounds (240 F.)—60 minutes for either No. 2 or No. 2½ cans. Remove cans; cool quickly.

HOT PACK

Prepare as for Cold pack. To each 4 cups of kernels, add 2 cups boiling water. Bring to boiling over medium heat, stirring so it won't scorch. Drain, saving the hot liquid.

In jars. Fill with kernels, leaving 1 inch of headroom. Add ½ teaspoon salt to pints, 1 teaspoon salt to quarts. Add boiling-hot cooking liquid, leaving 1 inch of headroom; adjust lids. Pressure-process at 10 pounds (240 F.)—pints for 55 minutes, quarts for 85 minutes. Remove jars; complete seals if necessary.

In C-enamel cans. Fill with hot kernels, leaving ½ inch of headroom. Add ½ teaspoon salt to No. 2 cans, 1 teaspoon salt to No. 2½. Add boiling-hot cooking liquid to top (water will come well over top of corn). Exhaust to 170 F. (c. 10 minutes); seal. Pressure-process at 10 pounds (240 F.)—60 minutes for either No. 2 or No. 2½ cans. Remove cans; cool quickly.

Before tasting canned low-acid food, boil it hard for 15 minutes to destroy any hidden toxins (corn and greens require 20 minutes). If it looks spoiled or foams or has an off-odor during boiling, destroy it completely so it can't be eaten by people or animals.

Eggplant

FEASIBILITY

This loses its looks when it's canned, but some cooks feel that it makes an unhandy product if frozen alone (better to precook it as a favorite casserole, etc., they say, and freeze it as a convenience food). However, there are good dishes to build with canned eggplant and herbs, tomatoes, cheese or whatever: look up some good Italian and Greek recipes.

GENERAL HANDLING

Pressure Canning only. Use Hot pack only. Use jars or plain cans.

Wash, pare and slice or cube eggplant. Sprinkle lightly with salt and cover with cold water (to help draw out its juice). Let soak 45 minutes; drain. In fresh water, boil for 5 minutes. Drain, and pack hot without adding salt.

In jars. Fill clean hot jars, leaving 1 inch of headroom. Add boiling water, leaving 1 inch of headroom; adjust lids. Pressure-process at 10 pounds (240 F.)—pints for 30 minutes, quarts for 40 minutes. Remove jars; complete seals if necessary.

In plain cans. Pack, leaving only ¼ inch of headroom. Fill to top with boiling water. Exhaust to 170 F. (*c.* 10 minutes); seal. Pressure-process at 10 pounds (240 F.)—No. 2 cans for 35 minutes, No. 2½ for 40 minutes. Remove cans; cool quickly.

Greens—Spinach, etc., and Wild

FEASIBILITY

All garden greens—spinach, chard, turnip or beet tops—can nicely; so do wild ones like dandelions and milkweed (fiddleheads and cowslips are usually such treats that they're eaten as they come in). Greens freeze well, and with more garden freshness. (See also Drying and Salting.)

GENERAL HANDLING

Pressure Canning only. Use Hot pack only (to make greens solid enough in the container). Use jars or plain cans.

Using spinach as the example *for garden greens:* Remove bits of grass, poor leaves, etc., from just-picked leaves; cut out tough stems and coarse midribs. Wash thoroughly, lifting from the water to let any sediment settle. Put about 2½ pounds of clean, wet leaves in a large cheesecloth, tie the top, and steam the spinach for about 10 minutes— or until well wilted, and pack.

Prepare *wild greens*—American cowslips, dandelions, milkweed and fiddleheads—according to directions given for the individual greens in Recipes.

HOT PACK ONLY

In jars. Fill with greens, leaving ½ inch of headroom. Add only ¼ teaspoon salt to pints, ½ teaspoon salt to quarts. Add boiling water, leaving ½ inch of headroom; adjust lids. Pressure-process at 10 pounds (240 F.)—pints for 70 minutes, quarts for 90 minutes. Remove jars; complete seals if necessary.

In plain cans. Fill with greens, leaving only ¼ inch of headroom. Add only ¼ teaspoon of salt to No. 2 cans, ½ teaspoon salt to No. 2½. Cover to top with boiling water. Exhaust to 170 F. (c. 10 minutes); seal. Pressure-process at 10 pounds (240 F.)—No. 2 cans for 65 minutes, No..2½ for 75 minutes. Remove cans; cool quickly.

Hominy (Lye-hulled Corn)

FEASIBILITY

This traditional Southern vegetable is made from dried whole-kernel field corn, not from precious home-parched sweet corn (see Drying), after the hulls are removed by long cooking in a weak lye solution.

Alkali—lye, and washing or baking sodas, its much milder cousins—is a quick destroyer of Vitamin C and many of the B vitamins.

WARNINGS ABOUT LYE

The stuff called "lye" may be any one of several highly caustic alkaline compounds that, in the presence of only the moisture in the air on a muggy day, can become activated, burning and eating deeply into animal or other organic tissue—including human skin.

ANTIDOTE FOR SEARING CONTACT: slosh immediately with cold water, follow with boric-acid solution (eyes) or vinegar.

If you buy household lye/caustic soda for hulling corn, *make sure it's suitable for use with food,* and is designated as "lye" or "lycons" on the can and contains no aluminum, nitrates or stabilizers. Above all, avoid commercial drain-openers, either crystalline or liquid. (See Soapmaking for more details.)

Use only enameled- or granite-ware pots or kettles—*never use utensils of aluminum,* which reacts violently with lye in water.

GENERAL HANDLING

Pressure Canning only. Use Hot pack only. Use jars or C-enamel cans. Plan on the rough ratio of 1 cup of dried corn making up to 4 cups of canned hominy; this swelling must take place during precooking, before it is packed.

Hulling and precooking. In an enameled kettle, dissolve 4 tablespoons of suitable household lye in 8 quarts of water; add 8 cups of dried field corn. Boil 30 minutes; let stand off heat 20 minutes more. Drain; wash off lye with several hot-water rinses; cool by rinsing in cold water. Work off the hulls and dark tips of the kernels by rubbing the hominy or washing it vigorously in a colander. When hulls and tips are removed, boil it in fresh water to cover for 5 minutes, drain; *repeat four times* (totaling 25 minutes of boiling in five fresh waters). After last repeat, cook in fresh water until kernels are soft—about 45 minutes. Drain and pack hot.

Hulling with homemade lye. When the liquid that has leached through a barrel of ashes (see Soapmaking) is strong enough to float an egg, put it in an enameled kettle with dried corn in the proportion of 4 parts liquid to 1 part corn. Boil until the hulls can be worked and rinsed off. Proceed with rinses, etc., as above.

P.S.—Using soda. There's an old rule for hulling with soda instead of lye—but it doesn't say whether it's *washing* soda (strong, but less so than lye) or *baking* soda (bland enough to be taken internally). It calls for covering 4 cups of dried corn with 2 quarts of water and 2 tablespoons of "soda"; letting stand overnight; and then, in the same soda water, simmering the corn *for 3 hours*—or until hulls are loosened. Proceed with rinses, hulling, etc., as above.

HOT PACK ONLY

In jars. Fill, leaving ½ inch of headroom. Add ½ teaspoon salt to pints, 1 teaspoon salt to quarts. Add boiling water, leaving ½ inch of headroom; adjust lids. Pressure-process at 10 pounds (240 F.)—pints for 60 minutes, quarts for 70 minutes. Remove jars; complete seals if necessary.

In C-enamel cans. Fill, leaving only ¼ inch of headroom. Add ½ teaspoon salt to No. 2 cans, 1 teaspoon salt to No. 2½. Fill to top with boiling water. Exhaust to 170 F. (*c.* 10 minutes); seal. Pressure-process at 10 pounds (240 F.)—No. 2 cans for 60 minutes, No. 2½ for 70 minutes. Remove cans; cool quickly.

Mixed Vegetables (in General)

Old-fashioned cooks call this "end of the garden"—meaning sort of a patchwork-quilt affair when they have too little of any single ingredient to warrant canning it alone, but welcome a combination that will be a fine base for hearty soups or stews, even for salads. Carrots, celery, corn, lima beans, okra, onions, peas, tomatoes, turnips—all are favorites for this treatment. Combine any two or more that won't be mushy after processing.

GENERAL HANDLING

Pressure Canning only. Hot pack only. Use jars or plain or C-enamel cans (for which type of can, see "About Jars and Cans" at the beginning of the Canning section).

Rule of thumb for processing: Choose the time required by the single ingredient requiring the longest processing (viz. Celery and Tomatoes, following).

Wash, trim vegetables, peeling if necessary. Cut to uniform size. Cover with boiling water and boil 10 minutes. Drain; save the cooking water to use for processing if you like.

HOT PACK ONLY

In jars. Fill with hot mixed vegetables, leaving ½ inch of headroom. Add ½ teaspoon salt to pints, 1 teaspoon salt to quarts. Add boiling water (fresh, or the cooking water), leaving ½ inch of headroom; adjust lids. Pressure-process at 10 pounds (240 F.)—pints for 60 minutes, quarts for 70 minutes. Remove jars; complete seals if necessary.

In plain or C-enamel cans. Fill with hot mixed vegetables, leaving ½ inch of headroom. Add ½ teaspoon of salt to No. 2 cans, 1 teaspoon of salt to No. 2½ cans. Fill to the top with boiling water (fresh, or the cooking water). Exhaust to 170 F. (*c.* 10 minutes); seal. Pressure-process at 10 pounds (240 F.)—No. 2 cans for 60 minutes, No. 2½ for 70 minutes. Remove cans; cool quickly.

Mixed Celery and Tomatoes

GENERAL HANDLING

Pressure Canning only (although tomatoes canned alone are done in a Boiling-Water Bath, the celery requires that this combination be Pressure Canned). Use Hot pack only. Use jars or plain cans.

Have equal parts of clean, cut-up celery and peeled, cored and chopped tomatoes. Mix, and boil for 5 minutes *without added water.*

HOT PACK ONLY

In jars. Pack in hot jars, leaving 1 inch of headroom. Add ½ teaspoon salt to pints, 1 teaspoon salt to quarts. Add boiling water, leaving 1 inch of headroom; adjust lids. Pressure-process at 10 pounds (240 F.)–pints for 30 minutes, quarts for 35 minutes. Remove jars; complete seals if necessary.

In plain cans. Pack, leaving ½ inch of headroom. Add ½ teaspoon salt to No. 2 cans, 1 teaspoon salt to No. 2½ cans. Fill to the top with boiling water. Exhaust to 170 F. (*c.* 10 minutes); seal. Pressure-process at 10 pounds (240 F.)–30 minutes for either No. 2 or No. 2½ cans. Remove cans; cool quickly.

Mixed Corn and Beans (Succotash)

GENERAL HANDLING

Pressure Canning only. Use Hot pack only. Use jars or C-enamel cans.

Boil freshly picked ears of corn for 5 minutes; cut kernels from cobs (as for whole-kernel corn, *without* scraping in the milk). Prepare fresh lima beans or green/snap beans, and boil by themselves for 3 minutes. Measure and mix hot corn with ½ to an equal amount of beans.

HOT PACK ONLY

In jars. Fill with hot corn-and-bean mixture, leaving 1 inch of headroom. Add ½ teaspoon salt to pints, 1 teaspoon salt to quarts. Add boiling water, leaving 1 inch of headroom; adjust lids. Pressure-process at 10 pounds (240 F.)–pints for 60 minutes, quarts for 85 minutes. Remove jars; complete seals if necessary.

In C-enamel cans. Fill with hot mixture, leaving ½ inch of headroom. Add ½ teaspoon salt to No. 2 cans, 1 teaspoon salt to No. 2½ cans. Fill to the top with boiling water. Exhaust to 170 F. (*c.* 10 minutes); seal. Pressure-process at 10 pounds (240 F.)–No. 2 cans for 70 minutes, No. 2½ for 95 minutes. Remove cans; cool quickly.

Mushrooms

Canned mushrooms are handy for sauces and casseroles and make a nice marinated appetizer, but they need treating against discoloration and they're usually put up only in small containers. Once they're prepared, freezing is quicker and they do just as well.

GENERAL HANDLING

Pressure Canning only. Use Hot pack only. Use ½-pint or pint jars, plain No. 2 cans.

Soak them in cold water for 10 minutes, then wash well. Trim blemishes from caps and stems. Leave whole, halve or slice, depending on how you plan to use them later. (If you're using an alternate discoloration preventive instead of the ascorbic acid added during packing, you may have to apply it at this stage; see under canning Apples.) In a covered saucepan heat them gently—*don't boil*—for 15 minutes; or steam for 4 minutes.

HOT PACK ONLY

In jars. Fill with hot mushrooms, leaving ½ inch of headroom. Add ¼ teaspoon of salt to ½-pint jars, ½ teaspoon salt to pints. To prevent color change, add 1/16 teaspoon of crystalline ascorbic acid to ½-pint jars, 1/8 teaspoon to pints. Add boiling water, leaving ½ inch of headroom; adjust lids. Pressure-process at 10 pounds (240 F.)— 30 minutes for either ½-pints or pints. Remove jars; complete seals if necessary.

In plain No. 2 cans. Fill with hot mushrooms, leaving ½ inch of headroom. Add ½ teaspoon salt and 1/8 teaspoon crystalline ascorbic acid. Fill to top with boiling water. Exhaust to 170 F. (c. 10 minutes); seal. Pressure-process at 10 pounds (240 F.) for 30 minutes. Remove cans; cool quickly.

Nut Meats

FEASIBILITY

Nuts are an important source of protein for vegetarian main dishes, and are a popular touch in baked goods, candies, salads, etc. All nuts are rather fatty, and it's this fat that turns rancid and spoils the meats (even nuts in the shell can spoil after a while). The two ways to delay or prevent rancidity are to can the nut meats or freeze them.

GENERAL HANDLING

Pressure Canning or Boiling-Water Bath. Use *dry* Hot pack only (nut meats are oven-dried before canning). Use dry, sterilized jars no larger than pints, and with *self-sealing lids* (see "About Jars and Cans").

Spread a shallow layer of nut meats in baking pans, and bake in a very slow oven—not more than 275 F.—watching the nuts carefully and stirring once in a while, until they are dry but not browned: they must not scorch. Keep hot for packing.

HOT PACK ONLY

In self-sealing jars. For pints (or ½-pints), fill dry, sterilized jars, leaving ½ inch of headroom; adjust lids. Pressure-process at 5 pounds (228 F.)—10 minutes for ½-pints or pints. OR process in a Boiling-Water Bath—*but with the water level well below the tops of the jars*—for 20 minutes. Remove jars; remove bands from self-sealing lids after jars have cooled 12 hours.

Okra (Gumbo)

This vegetable popular in Southern, Creole and West Indian cooking cans and freezes equally well: if you plan to use it cut up in soups and stews, it's probably handier canned.

GENERAL HANDLING

Pressure Canning only. Use Hot pack only. Use jars or plain cans.

Wash tender young pods; trim stems but don't cut off caps. Cover with boiling water and boil 1 minute; drain. Leave whole with cap, or cut in 1-inch pieces, discarding cap.

HOT PACK ONLY

In jars. Fill with hot okra, leaving ½ inch of headroom. Add ½ teaspoon salt to pints, 1 teaspoon salt to quarts. Add boiling water, leaving ½ inch of headroom; adjust lids. Pressure-process at 10 pounds (240 F.)—pints for 25 minutes, quarts for 40 minutes. Remove jars; complete seals if necessary.

In plain cans. Fill with hot okra, leaving only ¼ inch of headroom. Add ½ teaspoon salt to No. 2 cans, 1 teaspoon salt to No. 2½ cans. Fill to top with boiling water. Exhaust to 170 F. (*c.* 10 minutes); seal. Pressure-process at 10 pounds (240 F.)—No. 2 cans for 25 minutes, No. 2½ for 35 minutes. Remove cans; cool quickly.

Onions, White

Onions that are properly cured and stored (see Drying) carry over so well that many cooks don't bother to can them—on top of which home-canned onions are apt to be dark in color and soft in texture. They are often canned in combinations (see Mixed Vegetables for rule-of-thumb).

CANNING VEGETABLES

GENERAL HANDLING

Pressure Canning only. Use Hot pack only. Use jars or C-enamel cans.

Sort for uniform size—1 inch in diameter is ideal—and wash. Peel, trimming off roots and stalks. (If you push a hole downward through the middle with a slender finishing nail, their centers will cook with less chance of shucking off outer layers.) Cover with boiling water, parboil gently for 5 minutes. Drain, saving the cooking water for processing.

HOT PACK ONLY

In jars. Fit whole onions in closely, leaving ½ inch of headroom. Add ½ teaspoon salt to pints, 1 teaspoon salt to quarts. Add boiling cooking liquid, leaving ½ inch of headroom; adjust lids. Pressure-process at 10 pounds (240 F.)—pints for 25 minutes, quarts for 30 minutes. Remove jars; complete seals if necessary.

In C-enamel cans. Fit whole onions closely, leaving ¼ inch of headroom. Add ½ teaspoon salt to No. 2 cans, 1 teaspoon to No. 2½ cans. Fill to brim with boiling cooking water. Exhaust to 170 F. (*c.* 10 minutes); seal. Pressure-process at 10 pounds (240 F.)—No. 2 cans for 25 minutes, No. 2½ for 30 minutes. Remove cans; cool quickly.

Parsnips

This is probably the only vegetable that actually improves by wintering over in frozen ground—so why take the shine off it as the "first of spring" treat?

But if you can't keep them in a garden or a root cellar: wash, trim, scrape, and cut them in pieces, then proceed as for Broccoli (q.v.).

Peas, Black-eyed (Cowpeas, Black-eyed Beans)

FEASIBILITY

These are probably dried—for baking or porridge or canning in sauce (see under "Beans" in Recipes)—more generally than they're canned as a side vegetable.

GENERAL HANDLING

Pressure Canning only. Use Raw or Hot pack. Use jars or C-enamel cans.

Shell and wash before packing. Take care *not* to shake or press down the peas when you pack the containers.

RAW PACK

In jars. Fill with raw peas, leaving 1½ inches of headroom in pints, 2 inches of headroom in quarts. Add ½ teaspoon salt to pints, 1 teaspoon salt to quarts. Add boiling water, leaving ½ inch of headroom (water will come well over the top of the peas); adjust lids. Pressure-process at 10 pounds (240 F.)—pints for 35 minutes, quarts for 40 minutes. Remove jars; complete seals if necessary.

In C-enamel cans. Fill with raw peas, leaving ¾ inch of headroom. Add ½ teaspoon salt to No. 2 cans, 1 teaspoon to No. 2½ cans. Add boiling water, leaving ¼ inch of headroom. Exhaust to 170 F. (*c.* 10 minutes); seal. Pressure-process at 10 pounds (240 F.)—No. 2 cans for 35 minutes, No. 2½ for 40 minutes. Remove cans; cool quickly.

HOT PACK

After shelling and washing, cover with boiling water, bring to a full, high boil. Drain, saving the blanching water for processing with if you like.

In jars. Pack hot, leaving 1¼ inches of headroom in pints, 1½ inches of headroom in quarts. Add ½ teaspoon salt to pints, 1 teaspoon to quarts. Add boiling water (or blanching liquid), leaving ½ inch of headroom in either size of jar; adjust lids. Pressure-process at 10 pounds (240 F.)—pints for 35 minutes, quarts for 40 minutes. Remove jars; complete seals if necessary.

In C-enamel cans. Pack hot, leaving ½ inch of headroom for either size of can. Add ½ teaspoon salt to No. 2 cans, 1 teaspoon salt to No. 2½ cans. Add boiling water, leaving ¼ inch of headroom. Exhaust to 170 F. (*c.* 10 minutes); seal. Pressure-process at 10 pounds (240 F.)—No. 2 cans for 30 minutes, No. 2½ for 35 minutes. Remove cans; cool quickly.

Peas, Green

GENERAL HANDLING

Pressure Canning only (green peas are among the lowest-acid vegetables we have). Use Raw or Hot pack. Use jars or plain cans.

Shell and wash peas. In packing, take care not to shake or press the peas down.

RAW PACK

In jars. Fill, leaving 1 inch of headroom. Add ½ teaspoon salt to pints, 1 teaspoon to quarts. Add boiling water to within 1½ inches of the top of the jar (water will come well below the top of the peas); adjust lids. Pressure-process at 10 pounds (240 F.)—40 minutes for both pints and quarts. Remove jars; complete seal if necessary.

In plain cans. Fill, leaving only ¼ inch of headroom. Add ½ teaspoon salt to No. 2 cans, 1 teaspoon to No. 2½ cans. Fill to top with boiling water. Exhaust to 170 F. (*c.* 10 minutes); seal. Pressure-process at 10 pounds (240 F.)—No. 2 cans for 30 minutes, No. 2½ for 35 minutes. Remove cans; cool quickly.

HOT PACK

Cover washed peas with boiling water, bring to a full boil. Drain, saving the blanching water to process with if you like.

In jars. Fill loosely with hot peas, leaving 1 inch of headroom. Add ½ teaspoon salt to pints. 1 teaspoon to quarts. Add boiling water, leaving 1 inch of headroom; adjust lids. Pressure-process at 10 pounds (240 F.)—40 minutes for either pints or quarts. Remove jars; complete seals if necessary.

In plain cans. Fill loosely with hot peas, leaving only ¼ inch of headroom. Add ½ teaspoon salt to No. 2 cans, 1 teaspoon to No. 2½. Fill to the brim with boiling water. Exhaust to 170 F. (*c.* 10 minutes); seal. Pressure-process at 10 pounds (240 F.)—No. 2 cans for 30 minutes, No. 2½ for 35 minutes. Remove cans; cool quickly.

Peppers, Green (Bell, Sweet)

This is the easiest of our vegetables to freeze (no blanching required, q.v.); and it's fine in a canned mixture, to use for soups and stews; and it's grand in relishes. (See Pickles and Relishes.) But a few containers of straight canned peppers are handy for cooked dishes when fresh ones cost an arm and a leg out of season.

GENERAL HANDLING

Pressure Canning only. Hot pack only. Use jars or plain cans.

Wash, remove stems, cores and seeds. Cut in large pieces or leave whole. Put in boiling water and boil 3 minutes. Drain and pack. (If you like them peeled, take them from the boiling water, dunk in cold water to cool just enough for handling, and strip off the skins; pack.)

It is necessary to add a bit of vinegar (or half the amount in lemon juice) to increase the acidity for safe canning of green peppers within a reasonable processing time (see Hot pack directions following for specific amounts).

In jars. Pack hot peppers flat, leaving 1 inch of headroom. Add ½ teaspoon salt and 1 tablespoon vinegar to pints, 1 teaspoon salt and 2 tablespoons vinegar to quarts. Add boiling water, leaving ½ inch of headroom (water comes over the top of the peppers); adjust lids. Pressure-process at 10 pounds (240 F.)—pints for 35 minutes, quarts for 45 minutes. Remove jars; complete seals if necessary.

In plain cans. Pack flat leaving ½ inch of headroom. Add ½ teaspoon salt and 1 tablespoon vinegar to No. 2 cans, 1 teaspoon salt and 1½ tablespoons vinegar to No. 2½ cans. Fill to top with boiling water. Exhaust to 170 F. (*c.* 10 minutes); seal. Pressure-process at 10 pounds (240 F.)—No. 2 cans for 20 minutes, No. 2½ for 25 minutes. Remove cans; cool quickly.

Pimientos

GENERAL HANDLING

Pressure Canning only. Use Hot pack only. Use ½-pint or pint jars, or No. 2 plain cans.

Wash, cover with boiling water, and simmer until skins can be peeled off—4 to 5 minutes. Dunk in cold water so they can be handled, trim stems, blossom ends, and skin them; pack hot. (If you're doing a large quantity, roast them in a hot oven—400 to 500 F.—for about 5 minutes, until skins blister and can be peeled off; cool them enough to handle, trim, etc.; pack.)

HOT PACK ONLY

In jars. Pack flat in clean, hot ½-pint or pint jars, leaving ½ inch of headroom. Add ¼ teaspoon salt and 1½ teaspoons vinegar to ½-pints, ½ teaspoon salt and 1 tablespoon vinegar to pints. Add *no water;* adjust lids. Pressure-process at 10 pounds (240 F.)—20 minutes for either ½-pints or pints. Remove jars; complete seals if necessary.

In No. 2 plain cans. Pack flat, leaving only 1/8 inch of headroom. Add ½ teaspoon salt and 1½ teaspoons vinegar, but *no water.* Exhaust to 170 F. (*c.* 10 minutes); seal. Pressure-process at 10 pounds (240 F.) for 20 minutes. Remove cans; cool quickly.

Potatoes, Sweet (and Yams)

Sweet potatoes don't keep as well in open storage as white potatoes do, and it makes sense to can some of them to serve hot with butter, or mashed, or glazed.

GENERAL HANDLING

Pressure Canning only. Hot pack only—but either *wet* or *dry* (dry-packed glaze well). Use jars or plain cans.

Sort for size, wash; boil or steam until only half cooked and skins come off easily—20 minutes or so. Dunk in cold water so they can be handled, slip off skins and trim away any blemishes. If they're large, cut them in pieces.

HOT PACK—DRY

In jars. Fill tightly, leaving 1 inch of headroom—pack more or less upright, pressing gently to fill spaces (but not cramming them in a shapeless mush). *Add nothing to them,* not even salt; adjust lids. Pressure-process at 10 pounds (240 F.)—pints for 65 minutes, quarts for 95 minutes. Remove jars; complete seals if necessary.

In plain cans. Fill tightly as for jars, but to the top, leaving no headroom. *Add nothing,* not even salt. Exhaust to 170 F. (*c.* 10 minutes); seal. Pressure-process at 10 pounds (240 F.)—No. 2 cans for 80 minutes, No. 2½ for 95 minutes. Remove cans; cool quickly.

HOT PACK—WET

Prepare as in General Handling (parboiling, skinning, etc.).

In jars. Fill more loosely than for dry-packed, leaving 1 inch of headroom. Add ½ teaspoon salt to pints, 1 teaspoon salt to quarts. Add boiling water or Medium Sirup (see "Sirups for Canning Fruits"); adjust lids. Pressure-process at 10 pounds (240 F.)—pints for 55 minutes, quarts for 90 minutes. Remove jars; complete seals if necessary.

In plain cans. Fill more loosely than for dry-packed, leaving only ¼ inch of headroom. Add ½ teaspoon salt to No. 2 cans, 1 teaspoon to No. 2½. Fill to top with boiling water or Medium Sirup. Exhaust to 170 F. (*c.* 10 minutes); seal. Pressure-process at 10 pounds (240 F.)—No. 2 cans for 70 minutes, No. 2½ cans for 90 minutes. Remove cans; cool quickly.

Potatoes, White ("Irish")

These potatoes don't home-freeze at all well (unless they're partially precooked in a combination dish, q.v.)—so cold-store them (see Root-Cellaring). But it's possible for them to be too immature to store without spoiling—so you can them. Delicate tiny, new potatoes can well, and are good served hot with parsley butter or creamed.

GENERAL HANDLING

Pressure Canning only. Use Raw or Hot pack. Use jars or plain cans. If around 1 to 1½ inches in diameter, they may be canned whole; dice the larger ones.

Wash and scrape just-dug new potatoes, removing all blemishes. (If you're dicing them, prevent darkening during preparation by dropping the dice in a solution of 1 teaspoon salt for each 1 quart of cold water.) Drain before packing by either method.

RAW PACK

In this pack, *diced get 5 minutes longer processing time,* because they're more dense in the containers than whole ones are.

In jars. Fill with whole or diced potatoes, leaving ½ inch of headroom; add ½ teaspoon salt to pints, 1 teaspoon salt to quarts. Add boiling water, leaving ½ inch of headroom; adjust lids. Pressure-process at 10 pounds (240 F.)—*whole,* pints or quarts for 40 minutes; *diced,* pints or quarts for 45 minutes. Remove jars; complete seals if necessary.

In plain cans. Fill, leaving only ½ inch of headroom. Add ½ teaspoon salt to No. 2 cans, 1 teaspoon salt to No. 2½. Fill to the top with boiling water. Exhaust to 170 F. (*c.* 10 minutes); seal. Pressure-process at 10 pounds (240 F.)—*whole,* No. 2 cans for 40 minutes, No. 2½ for 45 minutes; *diced,* No. 2 for 45 minutes, No. 2½ for 50 minutes. Remove cans; cool quickly.

HOT PACK

Cover clean, scraped *whole* potatoes with boiling water, boil 10 minutes; drain. Drain anti-discoloration solution off *diced* potatoes; cover them with boiling fresh water, boil 2 minutes; drain.

In jars. With whole or diced potatoes, leave ½ inch of headroom. Add ½ teaspoon salt to pints, 1 teaspoon to quarts. Add boiling water, leaving ½ inch of headroom; adjust lids. Pressure-process at 10 pounds (240 F.)—*whole,* pints for 30 minutes, quarts for 40 minutes; *diced,* pints for 35 minutes, quarts for 40 minutes. Remove jars; complete seals if necessary.

In plain cans. Fill with whole or diced potatoes, leaving only ¼ inch of headroom. Add ½ teaspoon salt to No. 2 cans, 1 teaspoon to No. 2½ cans. Fill to top with boiling water. Exhaust to 170 F. (*c.* 10 minutes); seal. Pressure-process at 10 pounds (240 F.)—*whole* or *diced*—No. 2 cans for 35 minutes, No. 2½ for 40 minutes. Remove cans; cool quickly.

Pumpkin (and Winter Squash)

The starch in these vegetables changes gradually to sugar as they age; and even in the best cold storage (see Root-Cellaring) their water content increases. So put by some pumpkin or squash by freezing or canning to use in deep winter.

GENERAL HANDLING

Pressure Canning only. Hot pack only. Use jars or R-enamel cans. Cube it or strain it (strained takes longer to process).

Dry-fleshed pumpkin (or winter squash) is best for canning: test it with your thumbnail—it's dry enough if your nail won't cut the surface skin easily.

HOT PACK—CUBED

Wash, cut in manageable hunks, pare and remove seeds; cut in 1-inch cubes. Cover with water and bring to boiling. Drain, reserving hot liquid, and pack hot.

In jars. Fill with hot cubes, leaving ½ inch of headroom. Add ½ teaspoon salt to pints, 1 teaspoon to quarts. Add boiling cooking water, leaving ½ inch of headroom; adjust lids. Pressure-process at 10 pounds (240 F.)—pints for 55 minutes, quarts for 90 minutes. Remove jars; complete seals if necessary.

In R-enamel cans. Fill, leaving only ¼ inch of headroom. Add ½ teaspoon salt to No. 2 cans, 1 teaspoon to No. 2½. Fill to brim with boiling cooking water. Exhaust to 170 F. (*c.* 10 minutes); seal. Pressure-process at 10 pounds (240 F.)—No. 2 cans for 50 minutes, No. 2½ for 75 minutes. Remove cans; cool quickly.

HOT PACK—STRAINED

Prepare as for cubes, but leave in larger pieces if more convenient. Steam or bake until tender; put through a strainer or food mill. Over low heat, simmer until it's heated through, stirring steadily so it won't scorch. Pack hot *with no added liquid or salt.*

In jars. Fill, leaving ½ inch of headroom; adjust lids. Pressure-process at 10 pounds (240 F.)—pints for 65 minutes, quarts for 80 minutes. Remove jars; complete seals if necessary.

In R-enamel cans. Fill, leaving only 1/8 inch of headroom. Exhaust to 170 F. (*c.* 10 minutes); seal. Pressure-process at 10 pounds (240 F.) —No. 2 cans for 75 minutes, No. 2½ for 90 minutes. Remove cans; cool quickly.

Rutabagas (and White Turnips)

FEASIBILITY

Root-cellaring is best (q.v.). But if you don't have adequate cold storage, can some to use as a side vegetable or in quick stews; or freeze some, if you have plenty of freezer space.

Rutabagas are good shredded and soured as for Sauerkraut (see under Salting and Brining); they're better done this way than white turnip is, because they're firmer and sweeter. Rutabaga/turnip "kraut" may be canned like sauerkraut, below.

HANDLING AND PROCESSING

Wash, peel, cube, pack in jars/C-enamel cans, and pressure-process as for Broccoli (q.v.).

Salsify (Oyster Plant)

Like parsnips and horseradish, this delicately flavored, old-fashioned vegetable is able to winter in the ground: so long as it doesn't alternately freeze and thaw, it won't spoil (but getting at it may be a problem). It may be root-cellared. And with a little extra attention so it won't discolor, it cans well. See Recipes.

GENERAL HANDLING

Pressure Canning only. Use Hot pack only. Use jars or C-enamel cans.

Its milky juice turns rather rusty when it hits the air, and you may prevent discoloration of the vegetable by either one of two ways: (1) Scrub roots well, scrape as for carrots, and slice, dropping each slice immediately in a solution of 2 tablespoons vinegar and 2 tablespoons salt for each 1 gallon of cold water; rinse well, cover quickly with boiling water, boil for 2 minutes; pack hot. Or (2) scrub roots; in a solution of 1 tablespoon vinegar to each 1 quart of water, boil whole until skins come off easily—10 to 15 minutes; rinse well in cold water, skin, leave whole or slice; pack hot.

HOT PACK ONLY

In jars. Fill, leaving 1 inch of headroom. Add fresh boiling water, leaving 1 inch of headroom; adjust lids. Pressure-process at 10 pounds (240 F.)—pints for 30 minutes, quarts for 35 minutes. Remove jars; complete seals if necessary.

In C-enamel cans. Fill, leaving ½ inch of headroom; add fresh boiling water to brim. Exhaust to 170 F. (*c.* 10 minutes); seal. Pressure-process at 10 pounds (240 F.)—30 minutes for both No. 2 and No. 2½ cans. Remove cans; cool quickly.

Sauerkraut (Fermented Cabbage)

By all means can your sauerkraut—unless you are able to guarantee storage at from 40 F. to 55 F. (maximum) for as long as you want to hold it in the crock you made it in.

GENERAL HANDLING

Boiling-Water Bath only (pressure-processing is not needed for a food so acid as this has become). Hot pack only. Use jars or R-enamel cans.

HOT PACK ONLY

Heat to simmering—180 to 210 F.—*do not boil,* and pack as directed below. If you don't have enough sauerkraut juice, eke it out with a brine made of 1½ tablespoons salt for each 1 quart of water.

In jars. Fill clean, hot jars, leaving ½ inch of headroom. Add hot juice (or hot brine, above), leaving ½ inch of headroom; adjust lids. Process in a Boiling-Water Bath—pints for 15 minutes, quarts for 20 minutes. Remove jars; complete seals if necessary.

In R-enamel cans. Pack hot, leaving only ½ inch of headroom. Fill to the brim with hot juice or brine (again, as above). Exhaust to 170 F. (*c.* 10 minutes); seal. Process in a Boiling-Water Bath—25 minutes for either No. 2 or No. 2½ can. Remove cans; cool quickly.

Spinach, see Greens

Squash—Chayote, Summer, Zucchini

FEASIBILITY

Since these don't cold-store well, and get mushy from home-freezing (unless they're precooked in a combination dish), canning makes good sense. Zucchini is particularly handy canned with chopped tomatoes and seasoned with grated onion and herbs in the Italian manner; see Mixed Vegetables for the rule-of-thumb for combining.

GENERAL HANDLING

Pressure Canning only. Use Raw or Hot pack. Use jars or plain cans.
Wash, trim ends but do not peel. Cut in ½-inch slices; halve or quarter the slices to make the pieces uniform.

RAW PACK

In jars. Pack tightly in clean, hot jars, leaving 1 inch of headroom. Add ½ teaspoon salt to pints, 1 teaspoon to quarts. Add boiling water, leaving ½ inch of headroom (water will come over the top of the squash); adjust lids. Pressure-process at 10 pounds (240 F.)—pints for 25 minutes, quarts for 30 minutes. Remove jars; complete seals if necessary.

In plain cans. Pack tightly, leaving ½ inch of headroom. Add ½ teaspoon salt to No. 2 cans, 1 teaspoon to No. 2½. Fill to the brim with boiling water. Exhaust to 170 F. (*c.* 10 minutes); seal. Pressure-process at 10 pounds (240 F.)—20 minutes for either No. 2 or No. 2½ cans. Remove cans; cool quickly.

HOT PACK

Prepare as for Raw pack. Cover with boiling water, bring to a boil. Drain, saving the hot cooking liquid for processing.

In jars. Pack hot squash loosely, leaving ½ inch of headroom. Proceed as for Raw pack, but Pressure-process pints for 30 minutes, quarts for 40 minutes. (Hot squash is more dense than raw, so requires longer processing.) Remove jars; complete seals if necessary.

In plain cans. Pack hot squash loosely, leaving ¼ inch of headroom. Proceed as for Raw pack, Pressure-processing both No. 2 and No. 2½ cans for 20 minutes (exhausting to 170 F. gives several minutes' advantage here). Remove cans; cool quickly.

Squash, Winter, see Pumpkin

Tomatoes

Although they're eaten mostly as a vegetable, tomatoes are canned under Fruits (q.v.). This isn't just botanical purism: technically they're fruits, but in addition they're canned the way fruits are—and they are the only natural vegetable that is.

Turnips, White, see Rutabagas

> Before tasting canned low-acid food, boil it hard for 15 minutes to destroy any hidden toxins (corn and greens require 20 minutes). If it looks spoiled or foams or has an off-odor during boiling, destroy it completely so it can't be eaten by people or animals.

Canning Meat and Poultry

Unless you raise food animals yourself (thus taking care that they are housed, fed and slaughtered in the best possible way); or unless you get whole or part carcasses from a local small-scale raiser (whose methods you've investigated carefully beforehand)—your safest buy is from a meat-seller whose goods are purchased under interstate trade regulations. Through improved animal-raising and meat-handling regulations and inspections, most parasites and diseases have been eliminated in meat that passes federal inspection and is allowed to travel in interstate trade. Most notable is the reduction of the feared *Trichina spiralis* in pork, the cause of trichinosis in people.

WARNING ABOUT GAME

Any wild game may be diseased or carry parasites (bear, for example, often have trichinosis). So, if you are a successful hunter or if you've been given a present of venison or other wild meat, *do not eat it cooked Rare.*

Pressure Canning at 10 pounds (240 F.)—for the length of time required for large pieces, small pieces or ground meat, respectively—is the only safe way to put game by in jars or cans.

The Biologist for your state Fish and Game Department in the state capital will be glad to tell you of any disease problems with game in your area.

Although freezing is easier, any fresh, wholesome meats or poultry —beef, pork, lamb and chicken are the most popular—may be canned safely.

Domestic rabbits and small-game animals are canned like Poultry.

Choose only good meat for canning, and handle it with expediency and total cleanliness, because bacteria grow at a frightening rate in meats and poultry if given half a chance.

Note: You must work quickly. Any meat picks up bacteria so don't keep it waiting at room temperature until you can handle it. If you have a large amount to do, temporarily store the part you're not working on in the refrigerator or a meat cooler (32 to 38 F.). Can first thing *tomorrow* what you could not can today: keep right at it until the job is done.

And it is vital to process all canned animals and birds in a Pressure Canner at 10 pounds (240 F.) to destroy possible bacteria—including the potent Botulinus.

HANDLING OF MEAT FROM LARGE ANIMALS

Know what a whole, half or quarter of an animal will yield in the way of cuts before you buy one. There is 20 to 25 percent waste to start with, and usually there will be more pounds of stewing and/or ground meat than pounds of steaks and roasts and chops.

Cutting the meat

Have the carcass cut in serving pieces by a professional meat-cutter to get the most out of your investment.

If you wish to tackle the job yourself, write to the U.S. Department of Agriculture, Washington, D.C. 20250, or ask your County Extension Service office, for a copy of *Farmers Bulletin No. 2209, Slaughtering, Cutting and Processing Beef on the Farm,* and for a copy of *Farmers Bulletin No. 2152, Slaughtering, Cutting and Processing Pork on the Farm.* Both explain and illustrate the full meat-cutting process.

Use the Beef bulletin as a guide to cutting up veal and lamb.

Audrey Alley Gorton's *The Venison Book, How To Dress, Cut up and Cook Your Deer,* a small paperback in most bookstores and libraries, is a helpful guide to field-dressing and butchering large game.

SALT IN CANNING MEAT AND POULTRY

Salt is merely a seasoning in canned meat and poultry: therefore—because it is not a preservative when used in such relatively small amounts as mentioned below—it may be omitted.

If you use salt, your regular table salt will do.

Equipment and its care

A Pressure Canner is essential.

Containers may be jars—we recommend the modern straight-sided ones, because they're easier to get the meat out of—or plain cans (meat sometimes makes the coating flake off the interiors of enameled cans: harmless, but unattractive).

Use good-sized sharp knives, including a 3- to 4-inch boning knife.

Wooden cutting-boards and surfaces are best for working on: they are less likely than harder surfaces to dull the knives, and yet will withstand the necessary scrubbing and disinfecting.

If you plan to do large quantities of meat, you should have a high-sided roasting pan and a very big kettle (at least as large as your Boiling-Water Bath kettle).

All tools and utensils must be scrubbed in hot soapy water and rinsed well with fresh boiling water before each use.

To control bacteria, cutting-boards and wooden working surfaces must be scrubbed hard in hot soapy water *both before and after* you handle meat on them, and must be disinfected with a chlorine-bleach solution that is left on for 15 minutes, then rinsed off with fresh boiling water.

Because meat and poultry—and their broths—are very low-acid, boiling is the best way to determine if such home-canned food is safe to eat. So if there's the slightest possibility of spoilage, boil the food hard for 20 minutes in a covered pan to destroy possible hidden toxins. If it foams unduly or has an off-odor during boiling, destroy it completely so it can't be eaten by people or animals.

Canning Meats

CANNING LARGE PIECES OF MEAT

Pressure Canning only. Use Raw or Hot pack (we prefer Hot pack). Use straight-sided jars or plain cans.

Unlike the canning procedures for Vegetables, in certain instances the air in food in *jars*—as well as cans—is exhausted before processing.

Prime cuts of beef, pork, lamb, veal and large game are best canned in large pieces. The less choice parts are good for stews and ground meats.

Prepare and Pack Raw

Wipe raw meat with a clean damp cloth. Remove bones *and all surface fat* (fat in canned meat is likely to shorten its storage life, and fat is a Number One seal-spoiler).

Cut in jar/can lengths, with the grain running the long way of the container.

A jar-sized chunk of meat needs no liquid packed Raw, but it must be exhausted (right) even though it is processed in glass, not a can.

IN STRAIGHT-SIDED JARS

Push the long pieces into the jars, leaving 1 inch of headroom. *Add no liquid:* there will be enough juice. Exhaust jars in a slow-boil bath to 170 F. (*c.* 70 minutes). Remove jars from exhaust bath. Add ½ teaspoon salt to pints, 1 teaspoon salt to quarts. Adjust lids.

Pressure-process at 10 pounds (240 F.)—pints for 75 minutes, quarts for 90 minutes. Remove jars; complete seals if necessary.

IN PLAIN CANS

Push long pieces into the cans, leaving *no* headroom. *Add no liquid:* there will be enough juice. Exhaust cans in a slow-boil bath to 170 F. (*c.* 70 minutes). Remove from exhaust bath. Add ½ teaspoon salt to No. 2 cans, ¾ teaspoon salt to No. 2½ cans; seal.

Pressure-process at 10 pounds (240 F.)—No. 2 cans for 65 minutes, No. 2½ cans for 90 minutes. Remove cans; cool quickly.

Prepare and Pack Hot (Precooked)

Put large cut-to-measure pieces of boned, de-fatted meat (see Raw pack preparation, above) in a large, shallow pan. Add just enough water to keep meat from sticking; cover, and cook slowly on top of the stove or in a 350 F. oven until the meat is Medium done, turning it now and then so it precooks evenly.

IN STRAIGHT-SIDED JARS

Pack hot meat loosely, leaving 1 inch of headroom. Add ½ teaspoon salt to pints, 1 teaspoon salt to quarts. Add boiling meat juice (extended with boiling water if necessary), leaving 1 inch of headroom. Wipe jar rims carefully to remove any fat. Adjust lids.

Pressure-process at 10 pounds (240 F.)—pints for 75 minutes, quarts for 90 minutes. Remove jars; complete seals if necessary.

IN PLAIN CANS

Pack hot meat loosely, leaving ½ inch of headroom. Add ½ teaspoon salt to No. 2 cans, ¾ teaspoon salt to No. 2½ cans. Fill cans to the top with boiling meat juice (extended with boiling water if necessary), leaving *no* headroom. Wipe can rims carefully to remove any fat; seal (no exhausting is necessary, because long precooking has driven air from the meat).

Pressure-process at 10 pounds (240 F.)—No. 2 cans for 65 minutes, No. 2½ cans for 90 minutes. Remove cans; cool quickly.

Note: You may also roast large pieces of meat as for the table until it is Medium done; pack as above (extending pan juices with boiling broth or water if necessary), and pressure-process at 10 pounds (240 F.) for the full time required above.

CANNING SMALL PIECES OF MEAT

Use the less choice parts of the animal for future use in stews, main-dish pies, etc.

Pressure Canning only. Use Raw or Hot (precooked) pack. Use straight-sided jars or plain cans.

Prepare and Pack Raw

Remove all surface fat from clean meat. Cut the meat off any bones. As you cut in stewing-size pieces, remove any interior bits of fat; cut away any tough muscle-sheath.

IN STRAIGHT-SIDED JARS

Pack, leaving 1 inch of headroom. *Add no liquid:* there will be enough juice. Exhaust jars in a slow-boil bath to 170 F. (*c.* 70 minutes). Remove from exhaust bath. Add ½ teaspoon salt to pints, 1 teaspoon salt to quarts. Wipe jar rims carefully to remove any fat. Adjust lids.

Pressure-process at 10 pounds (240 F.)—pints for 75 minutes, quarts for for 90 minutes. Remove jars; complete seals if necessary.

IN PLAIN CANS

Pack cut-up meat, leaving *no* headroom. *Add no liquid.* Exhaust cans in a slow-boil bath to 170 F. (*c.* 70 minutes). Remove from exhaust bath. Add ½ teaspoon salt to No. 2 cans, ¾ teaspoon to No. 2½ cans. Wipe can rims carefully to remove any fat. Seal.

Pressure-process at 10 pounds (240 F.)—No. 2 cans for 65 minutes, No. 2½ cans for 90 minutes. Remove cans; cool quickly.

Prepare and Pack Hot (Precooked)

Follow Raw pack preparation. Put meat in a large, shallow pan, with just enough water to keep it from sticking; cover. Precook until Medium done. Stewing-size pieces take less tending if you do them in a 350 F. oven; but you can also precook them to Medium on top of the stove, turning or stirring them from time to time.

If you want to brown the meat before canning it, you don't need to dredge it in flour first: just put it under a hot broiler long enough to brown it on all sides; or brown it in a hot skillet, using an absolute minimum of oil to keep it from sticking. Slosh a little water around the pan to pick up any juice, and save the water to use in precooking the meat, as above.

IN STRAIGHT-SIDED JARS

Pack hot meat loosely, leaving 1 inch of headroom. Add ½ teaspoon salt to pints, 1 teaspoon salt to quarts. Add boiling meat juice (extended with boiling water if necessary), leaving 1 inch of headroom. Wipe jar rims carefully to remove any fat. Adjust lids.

Pressure-process at 10 pounds (240 F.)—pints for 75 minutes, quarts for 90 minutes. Remove jars; complete seals if necessary.

Pack hot meat loosely, leaving ½ inch of headroom. Add ½ teaspoon salt to No. 2 cans, ¾ teaspoon salt to No. 2½ cans. Fill cans to the top with boiling meat juice (extended if necessary), leaving *no* headroom. Wipe can rims carefully to remove any fat. Seal.

Pressure-process at 10 pounds (240 F.)–No. 2 cans for 65 minutes, No. 2½ cans for 90 minutes. Remove cans; cool quickly.

CANNING GROUND MEAT

Freezing ground meat gives you a much better product than canning does. But if you must can it, don't can it bulk in a solid mass: make it up in meatballs by your favorite recipe (draining all browning fat off them before packing); or shape it in thin patties–which you may always break up to use later in casseroles, spaghetti sauce or whatever.

Pressure Canning only. Use Raw or Hot pack. Use straight-sided jars or plain cans.

Prepare and Pack Raw

Grind less tender cuts of *lean* meat. Work with fresh, clean cold meat: cold meat is easier to grind than meat at room temperature is. *Don't add any fat.* Make meatballs and brown them quickly on their surface, draining them well; or shape meat in thin patties slightly smaller in diameter than the containers.

IN STRAIGHT-SIDED JARS

Fill with raw patties packed in layers, or with browned raw meatballs, leaving 1 inch of headroom. Add ½ teaspoon salt to pints, 1 teaspoon salt to quarts. Exhaust jars in a slow-boil bath to 170 F. (*c.* 75 minutes). Remove from exhaust bath. Wipe jar rims carefully to remove any fat. Adjust lids.

Pressure-process at 10 pounds (240 F.)–pints for 75 minutes, quarts for 90 minutes. Remove jars; complete seals if necessary.

IN PLAIN CANS

Pack raw patties or browned raw meatballs firmly to the top of the cans. Add ½ teaspoon salt to No. 2 cans, ¾ teaspoon salt to No. 2½ cans. Exhaust in a slow-boil bath to 170 F. (*c.* 75 minutes). Remove from exhaust bath and press meat down in the cans so as to leave ½ inch of headroom. Wipe can rims carefully to remove any fat. Seal.

Pressure-process at 10 pounds (240 F.)—No. 2 cans for 100 minutes, No. 2½ cans for 135 minutes. Remove cans; cool quickly.

Prepare and Pack Hot (Precooked)

Trim and grind *lean* meat as in Raw pack, above. Make meatballs, browning their surface and draining well; or shape thin patties, slightly smaller in diameter than the containers. In a slow oven (325 F.) pre-cook meatballs or patties until Medium done. Skim off all fat from the drippings in the pan, saving the pan juices.

IN STRAIGHT-SIDED JARS

Pack hot patties (in layers) or hot precooked meatballs, leaving 1 inch of headroom. Cover with boiling *fat-free* pan juices (extended with boiling meat broth if necessary), leaving 1 inch of headroom. Wipe jar rims carefully to remove any fat. Adjust lids.

Pressure-process at 10 pounds (240 F.)—pints for 75 minutes, quarts for 90 minutes. Remove jars; complete seals if necessary.

IN PLAIN CANS

Pack hot patties (in layers) or hot precooked meatballs, leaving ½ inch of headroom. Cover with boiling *fat-free* pan juices (extended with boiling meat broth if necessary), leaving *no* headroom. Wipe can rims carefully to remove any fat. Seal.

Pressure-process at 10 pounds (240 F.)—No. 2 cans for 65 minutes, No. 2½ cans for 90 minutes. Remove cans; cool quickly.

CANNING PORK SAUSAGE

Freezing is better for pork sausage, especially in view of the large amount of fat.

Make your sausage by any tested recipe (see how in the Roundup section), *but use your seasonings lightly* because such flavorings change during canning and storage; and *omit sage*—it makes canned pork sausage bitter.

Pressure Canning only. Use Hot pack only. Use straight-sided jars or plain cans.

Prepare and Pack Hot (Precooked)

Shape raw sausage in thin patties, slightly smaller in diameter than the containers. In a slow oven (325 F.) precook patties until Medium done.

Skim off all fat from the drippings in the pan, saving pan juices.

IN STRAIGHT-SIDED JARS

Pack hot sausage patties in layers, leaving 1 inch of headroom. Cover with boiling *fat-free* pan juices (extended with boiling meat broth if necessary), leaving 1 inch of headroom. Wipe jar rims carefully to remove any fat. Adjust lids.

Pressure-process at 10 pounds (240 F.)—pints for 75 minutes, quarts for 90 minutes. Remove jars; complete seals if necessary.

IN PLAIN CANS

Pack hot patties in layers, leaving ½ inch of headroom. Cover with boiling *fat-free* pan juices (extending with boiling meat broth if necessary), leaving *no* headroom. Wipe can rims carefully to remove any fat. Seal.

Pressure-process at 10 pounds (240 F.)—No. 2 cans for 65 minutes, No. 2½ cans for 90 minutes. Remove cans; cool quickly.

CANNING BOLOGNA-STYLE SAUSAGE

If you don't have adequate cold, dry storage for Bologna-style sausage (see under Roundup for recipe and storing), you may can it.

Pressure Canning only—*and at 15 pounds.* Use Hot pack only. Use straight-sided jars or plain cans.

Prepare and Pack Hot (Cooked Completely)

When the sausage has been simmered until it is completely cooked and floats (see recipe under Smoking), remove it from the kettle, saving the cooking water. Cut the hot sausage in lengths the height of your containers for packing.

If the sausage is not fresh from cooking and therefore is cold, heat it through by simmering for 10 to 20 minutes, depending on thickness, in a bland broth (bland, so as not to change the flavor of the sausage). Save the broth, cut the hot sausage to length, and pack.

IN STRAIGHT-SIDED JARS

Fit pieces of hot sausage lengthwise in the jars, leaving 1 inch of headroom. Add boiling broth, leaving 1 inch of headroom. Wipe the jar rims carefully to remove any fat. Adjust lids.

Pressure-process at 15 pounds (250 F.)—pints for 50 minutes, quarts for 60 minutes. Remove jars; complete seals if necessary.

Fit hot sausage lengthwise in cans, leaving ½ inch of headroom. Add boiling broth, leaving ½ inch of headroom. Wipe the can rims carefully to remove any fat. Seal.

Pressure-process at 15 pounds (250 F.)—No. 2 cans for 45 minutes, No. 2½ cans for 60 minutes. Remove cans; cool quickly.

CANNING CORNED BEEF

Corn the beef (see under Brining in the section on Curing).
　　Pressure Canning only. Use Hot pack only (but in this case the meat is not precooked as for fresh meat). Use straight-sided jars or plain cans.

Prepare and Pack Hot (Freshened)

Wash the corned beef and cut it in chunks or thick strips to fit your containers, removing all fat. Put the pieces of meat in cold water and bring to boiling. Taste the broth in the kettle: if it's unpleasantly salty, drain the meat, cover it with fresh cold water, and bring again to boiling. This boiling merely freshens (removes salt), *it does not cook the corned beef.*

IN STRAIGHT-SIDED JARS

Fit hot freshened meat in jars, leaving 1 inch of headroom. Add boiling broth in which the meat was freshened, leaving 1 inch of headroom. Wipe jar rims carefully to remove any fat. Adjust lids.

Pressure-process at 10 pounds (240 F.)—pints for 75 minutes, quarts for 90 minutes. Remove jars; complete seals if necessary.

IN PLAIN CANS

Fit hot freshened meat in cans, leaving ½ inch of headroom. Fill cans to the top with boiling broth in which the meat was freshened, leaving *no* headroom. Wipe can rims carefully to remove any fat. Seal.

Pressure-process at 10 pounds (240 F.)—No. 2 cans for 65 minutes, No. 2½ cans for 90 minutes. Remove cans; cool quickly.

CANNING VARIETY MEATS

Most of the variety meats—liver, heart, tongue (see Recipes) and sweetbreads and brains—are best cooked and eaten right away. Certainly sweetbreads and brains, the most delicate foods of the lot, should be served when they are fresh. For liver and kidneys, freezing is recommended. Tongue may be canned satisfactorily, as well as frozen.

Canning Beef Tongue

The following procedure of course may be used for smaller tongues.

Soak the tongue in cold water for several hours, scrubbing it thoroughly and changing the water twice. Put it in a deep kettle, cover with fresh water, and bring to boiling. Skim off the foam well, then salt the water lightly; cover, and cook slowly until Medium done—*not tender* in the thickest part. Remove from kettle and plunge into cold water for a moment; peel off skin and trim off remaining gristle, etc., from the root.

Cut in container-size pieces, and pack Hot as for Large Pieces of Meat, or slice evenly and pack Hot as for Small Pieces of Meat. Pressure-process at 10 pounds (240 F.) for the times required (q.v.).

CANNING FROZEN MEAT

If you're ever faced with a freezing emergency, you may salvage frozen meat by canning it—provided it is good quality to start with, was correctly frozen and stored (see Freezing, and the table "Freezer Storage Life of Various Foods").

First, thaw it slowly in the refrigerator below 40 F. Then handle it as if it were fresh, using Pressure Canning only, Hot pack only, and the processing times that apply for Canning Large Pieces of Meat/Canning Small Pieces of Meat, above.

CANNING SOUP STOCK (MEAT BROTH)

Bony pieces of meat make good soup stock, and it may be worth your while to can the broth even if you're not canning other meat: some cans/jars of it are often a godsend. Freezing also is satisfactory for putting by soup stock, but it does take up valuable freezer space.

Pressure Canning only. Use Hot pack only. Use jars or plain cans.

Because meat and poultry—and their broths—are very low-acid, boiling is the best way to determine if such home-canned food is safe to eat. So if there's the slightest possibility of spoilage, boil the food hard for 20 minutes in a covered pan to destroy possible hidden toxins. If it foams unduly or has an off-odor during boiling, destroy it completely so it can't be eaten by people or animals.

Prepare and Pack Hot

Cover meat with lightly salted water (or omit salt; at any rate you may always season it to taste when you come to use it). Simmer until the meat falls away from the bones. Skim off all fat—lay absorbent paper toweling on the surface to pick up fat; or cool and refrigerate until the congealed fat may be lifted off in a hard sheet. Remove bones, but leave bits of meat and sediment. Reheat to boiling; continue boiling to concentrate the broth if it isn't strong enough.

IN JARS

Pour boiling hot stock into jars, leaving 1 inch of headroom. Wipe jar rims carefully. Adjust lids.

Pressure-process at 10 pounds (240 F.)—pints for 20 minutes, quarts for 25 minutes. Remove jars; complete seals if necessary.

IN PLAIN CANS

Fill cans with boiling hot broth, leaving *no* headroom. Wipe can rims carefully. Seal.

Pressure-process at 10 pounds (240 F.)—No. 2 cans for 20 minutes, No. 2½ cans for 25 minutes. Remove cans; cool quickly.

Canning Poultry and Small Game

The following instructions—which use chicken as the example for simplicity's sake—may be applied to canning domestic rabbits, wild birds and other small game, as well as canning other domestic poultry such as ducks, guinea hens, geese and turkeys, etc. *All these animals may be canned the same way:* general preparation (with specific exceptions as they come along), packing and processing are the same for all.

> *Note:* Read the introduction under Canning Meat and Poultry for "Warning about Game," necessary equipment, and the special care required in handling all meat for processing.

If you refrigerate adequately, prevent contamination during handling, work quickly, and don't try short cuts in packing and processing, poultry and small game may be canned satisfactorily.

Freezing of course is easier.

Use Pressure Canning only. Use Raw or Hot pack. Use straight-sided jars or plain cans.

WHERE CANNING OF POULTRY, ETC., IS DIFFERENT

Unlike the procedures given in the preceding section for packing meat, the methods that follow include canning with the bone left in.

Also, the skin on large pieces of birds—breast, thighs, drumsticks—is left on: processing at 240 F. compacts the surface of meat next to the sides of the container (making a pressure mark), so the skin you leave on acts as a cushion. Breast meat is skinned if packed in the center of jars/cans (surrounded by skin-on pieces that touch the containers' sides); so skin as you pack.

TO DRESS POULTRY, ETC.

Dressing involves two steps: (1) removing feathers by plucking or removing the fur pelt by skinning, and (2) drawing, which is removing the internal organs in one intact mass. Domestic birds are plucked before being drawn because they are handled for food immediately after they're killed.

However, a hunter *field-dresses* his kill by removing the innards on the spot, since they spoil a great deal more quickly than muscle tissue does; and he waits to skin it after he's home. Immediate drawing therefore reduces the chance of spoiling the rest of the meat en route home, and is especially necessary with mammals. Game birds may be held for several hours before being drawn; but if they cannot be got home for handling within half a day, they too should be drawn in the field, and plucked later.

Plucking a Chicken

Pluck feathers from the still warm, fresh-killed and bled chicken, being careful to get all the pinfeathers. Hold the bird by its feet and pull the feathers toward the head, in the opposite direction to the way they lie naturally. Scalding the whole bird is not necessary, but if the feathers are resisting enough so you're afraid of tearing the skin, you can spot-scald: lift the chicken by the feet with its head dangling, and pour nearly boiling water into the base of the feathers, where it will be trapped momentarily against the skin.

Dry the bird and singe off the hairs. Wipe it clean.

Drawing a Chicken

Cut off the head of the fresh-killed and plucked bird if it is still on; remove feet at the "ankle" joint just below the drumstick. Cut out the oil sac at the top of the tail (it would flavor the meat unpleasantly, so don't break it).

Lay the chicken on its back, feet toward you. Using a sharp knife, cut a circle around the vent (anus), so it can be removed intact with the internal organs still attached. Cut deeply enough to free it, and be careful not to cut into the intestine that leads to it.

Insert the tip of the knife, with cutting edge upward, at the top of the circle around the vent, and cut through the thin ventral wall toward the bottom of the breast bone, making the slit long enough so you can draw the innards out through it with vent attached.

Reach clear to the front of the body cavity and gently pull out the mass of organs. Separate and save the heart, liver and gizzard.

Next, turn the chicken over and slit the skin lengthwise at the back of the neck—if you slit down the *front* of the neck you may cut into the crop; push away the skin and remove the crop and windpipe.

Cut the neck bone off close to the body. Wash the whole bird. Look inside it, and remove any bits of lung, etc., that may remain in the cavity.

Return to the giblets. From the liver, cut away the green gall sac, roots and all; and be mighty careful not to break it, because gall ruins the flavor of any meat it touches. Split one side of the gizzard, cutting until you see the tough inner lining. Press the gizzard open and peel the lining away and discard it and its contents. Trim the heart.

Refrigerate each dressed chicken, either whole or cut up, until you are ready to can it.

Drawing and Skinning a Rabbit, etc.

Lay the fresh-killed rabbit on its back, and proceed to draw it as if it were a chicken: cut around the vent carefully; make a slit in the abdominal wall, reach in and pull out the innards with vent attached; save the liver and heart.

Cut off the feet. Working from the hind legs upward, work the rabbit out of its skin, easing the job with your knife where you need to. The head may be skinned, but chances are you'll prefer to remove it with the skin when you reach it. Cut away the gall sac from the liver; trim the heart. Wash the dressed rabbit and pat it dry. *Refrigerate each dressed rabbit until you are ready to can it.*

If you raise rabbits for the table you'll find it simpler to skin them as soon as they are killed and before drawing them.

Cutting up Poultry

Lay the dressed, clean bird on its back and, using a sharp boning knife, disjoint the legs and wings from the body. Separate thighs from drumsticks at the "knee" joint. If the bird is very large—like a turkey or goose—separate the wing at its two joints, saving the two upper meaty sections for canning with bone in. (Very small birds, such as grouse, etc., may do best merely quartered with poultry shears.)

Turn the chicken crossways to you, hold the bottom of the breast section, and cut under it, through the ribs, until you reach the backbone; separate it from the backbone by cutting through the ribs. Poultry shears or heavy kitchen shears will be handy for use on the stronger bones at the shoulder joint.

Bone the breast meat by cutting down one side of the breast bone and easing the white meat off in a large piece; repeat on the other side.

Remove lumps of fat and any bits of broken bone from each piece of chicken and wipe it with a clean damp cloth.

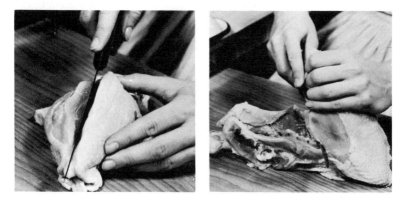

CUTTING UP RABBITS

Because of its anatomy, think of a rabbit as making two forequarters, two hind quarters, and a saddle. Split the saddle down the backbone as you would split the breast of a chicken, boning it if you like. The size of the rabbit has a lot to do with whether you cut up the quarters.

CANNING POULTRY, ETC., BONE IN

Prepare and Pack Raw

Pack meaty pieces loosely and more or less upright in the containers, putting breasts in the center (therefore skinned), surrounded by thighs and drumsticks (skin on) next to the sides of the jars/cans.

IN STRAIGHT-SIDED JARS

Pack, leaving 1 inch of headroom. Exhaust to 170 F. in a slow-boil bath (*c.* 75 minutes). Add ½ teaspoon salt to pints, 1 teaspoon salt to quarts. *Add no liquid:* there will be enough juice. Wipe jar rims carefully to remove any fat. Adjust lids.

Pressure-process at 10 pounds (240 F.)—pints for 65 minutes, quarts for 75 minutes. Remove jars; complete seals if necessary.

(In *this instance alone*—Raw pack in jars with bone in—some cooks omit the exhaust-bath-to-170 F.-step, and pressure-process at 10 pounds/240 F. for longer time: pints for 70 minutes, quarts for 80 minutes.)

IN PLAIN CANS

Pack, leaving *no* headroom. Exhaust to 170 F. in a slow-boil bath (*c.* 50 minutes). Add ½ teaspoon salt to No. 2 cans, ¾ teaspoon salt to No. 2½ cans. *Add no liquid.* Wipe can rims carefully to remove any fat. Seal.

Pressure-process at 10 pounds (240 F.)—No. 2 cans for 55 minutes, No. 2½ cans for 75 minutes. Remove cans; cool quickly.

Prepare and Pack Hot (Precooked), Bone In

Put raw meaty pieces in a large pan, cover with boiling water or boiling unseasoned (chicken) broth. Cover the pan and cook the meat slowly over moderate heat on top of the stove or in a 350 F. oven until Medium done. Pack hot meat with breasts preferably in the center (so skin them), surrounded by legs and thighs (unskinned, because they touch the sides of the containers).

POULTRY WITH BONES IN

IN STRAIGHT-SIDED JARS

Pack hot meat in loosely, leaving 1 inch of headroom. Add ½ teaspoon salt to pints, 1 teaspoon salt to quarts. Cover with boiling unseasoned cooking liquid, leaving 1 inch of headroom. Wipe jar rims carefully. Adjust lids.

Pressure-process at 10 pounds (240 F.)—pints for 65 minutes, quarts for 75 minutes. Remove jars; complete seals if necessary.

IN PLAIN CANS

Pack hot meat in loosely, unskinned if they touch the side of the can; leave ½ inch of headroom. Add ½ teaspoon salt to No. 2 cans, ¾ teaspoon salt to No. 2½ cans. Add boiling unseasoned cooking water to the top of the cans, leaving *no* headroom. Wipe can rims carefully to remove any fat. Seal.

Pressure-process at 10 pounds (240 F.)—No. 2 cans for 55 minutes, No. 2½ cans for 75 minutes. Remove cans; cool quickly.

CANNING POULTRY, ETC., WITHOUT BONES

Whether you pack Raw or Hot, remove bones from good meaty pieces before you start. But leave skin on pieces of birds until you're actually filling the containers; then skin the pieces in the center of the pack (usually breast meat), and leave skin on the pieces that touch the side of the jar/can (usually legs).

Prepare and Pack Raw

IN STRAIGHT-SIDED JARS

Fill with boned raw pieces, skin taken off the ones in the center, skin left on the ones touching the side of the jar. Leave 1 inch of headroom. Exhaust to 170 F. in a slow-boil bath (*c.* 75 minutes). Add ½ teaspoon salt to pints, 1 teaspoon to quarts. *Add no liquid.* Wipe jar rims carefully. Adjust lids.

Pressure-process at 10 pounds (240 F.)—pints for 75 minutes, quarts for 90 minutes. Remove jars; complete seals if necessary.

IN PLAIN CANS

Pack, with skin on pieces that touch the side of the can, leaving *no* headroom. Exhaust to 170 F. in a slow-boil bath (*c.* 50 minutes). Add

½ teaspoon salt to No. 2 cans, ¾ teaspoon to No. 2½ cans. *Add no liquid.* Wipe can rims carefully. Seal.

Pressure-process at 10 pounds (240 F.)—No. 2 cans for 65 minutes, No. 2½ cans for 90 minutes. Remove cans; cool quickly.

Prepare and Pack Hot (Precooked), Without Bones

Remove bones from good meaty pieces, but leave skin on all pieces of poultry until you're filling the containers: then skin the ones in the center of the pack (usually breasts), leaving skin on the ones that touch the sides of jars/cans (usually legs).

Cover boned meat with boiling water or unseasoned broth and cook slowly on stove or in oven until Medium done as for Hot pack, Bone In, above.

IN STRAIGHT-SIDED JARS

Pack hot boned meat loosely (with outside pieces unskinned). Leave 1 inch of headroom. Add ½ teaspoon salt to pints, 1 teaspoon to quarts. Add boiling unseasoned broth, leaving 1 inch of headroom. Wipe jar rims carefully. Adjust lids.

Pressure-process at 10 pounds (240 F.)—pints for 75 minutes, quarts for 90 minutes. Remove jars; complete seals if necessary.

IN PLAIN CANS

Pack hot boned meat loosely, with outside pieces unskinned. Leave ½ inch of headroom. Add ½ teaspoon salt to No. 2 cans, ¾ teaspoon salt to No. 2½ cans. Add boiling unseasoned broth to the top of the cans, leaving *no* headroom. Wipe can rims carefully. Seal.

Pressure-process at 10 pounds (240 F.)—No. 2 cans for 65 minutes, No. 2½ cans for 90 minutes. Remove cans; cool quickly.

CANNING POULTRY GIBLETS

Giblets are more useful if they are canned together, rather than spread out among the cans of meat (use them chopped in gravies, meat sauces or spreads, as fillings for main-dish pies, on rice as a supper dish, etc.). Furthermore, the livers are better and handier if they are canned separately; and being so tender, they need much shorter precooking before Hot packing and processing.

Pressure Canning only. Use Hot pack only. Use straight-sided pint jars or No. 2 plain cans.

Prepare and Pack Hot (Precooked)

Cut clean gizzards in half, trimming off the gristle; cut smaller if necessary. Remove tops of hearts where the blood vessels come in; halve hearts if they're very large. Cover gizzards and hearts with hot water or hot unseasoned broth and cook until Medium done.

Remove all fat from the livers; cut away connecting tissue between the lobes. Cover livers with hot water or hot unseasoned broth and cook gently until firm and Medium done; stir occasionally to prevent sticking.

Pack gizzards and hearts together, pack livers separately.

IN STRAIGHT-SIDED PINT JARS

Fill with hot gizzards and hearts, or hot livers, leaving 1 inch of headroom. Add ½ teaspoon salt. Add boiling cooking liquid, leaving 1 inch of headroom. Wipe jar rims carefully. Adjust lids.

Pressure-process at 10 pounds (240 F.)—pint jars of either livers, or gizzards and hearts for 75 minutes. Remove jars; complete seals if necessary.

IN NO. 2 PLAIN CANS

Fill with hot gizzards and hearts, or hot livers, leaving ½ inch of headroom. Add ½ teaspoon salt. Add boiling cooking liquid to the top of the cans, leaving *no* headroom. Wipe can rims carefully. Seal.

Pressure-process at 10 pounds (240 F.)—No. 2 cans of either gizzards and hearts, or livers for 65 minutes. Remove cans; cool quickly.

CANNING FROZEN POULTRY, ETC.

In case your freezer conks out, or you have a windfall of frozen poultry, domestic rabbits or small game, you may can it—*if:*

(1) it is good quality and was properly frozen (see Freezing, and the table "Freezer Storage Life of Various Foods"), and

(2) it is thawed slowly in the refrigerator below 40 F.

Then treat it as if it were fresh, using Pressure Canning only, Hot pack only, straight-sided jars or plain cans. Follow preparation and processing under Canning with Bone In/Boned, above.

CANNING CHICKEN STOCK (BROTH)

Make broth from bony pieces of chicken (or other poultry, rabbits, wild birds, etc.) as you made it from meat, and pack and pressure-process it the same way (see Soup Stock under Canning Meat).

Because meat and poultry—and their broths—are very low-acid, boiling is the best way to determine if such home-canned food is safe to eat. So if there's the slightest possibility of spoilage, boil the food hard for 20 minutes in a covered pan to destroy possible hidden toxins. If it foams unduly or has an off-odor during boiling, destroy it completely so it can't be eaten by people or animals.

Canning Fish and Shellfish

Even though some people do it, we are not convinced that canning is the safest way to put by fish and shellfish at home.

And even if we did can it successfully, the long pressure-processing required—longer than is needed for the same sized containers of meat packed the same way—would give us a product far inferior in texture and flavor and nutrients to the fresh seafood we started with.

Freezing safely keeps much more of the fresh-caught qualities of fish and shellfish—and it's so much easier! And fish may also be cured by Salting and Smoking (q.v.). See Recipes too.

BUT IF YOU THINK YOU *MUST* CAN IT . . .

However, if you foresee having a large catch to deal with, and canning is the only method you have for preserving it, then write for the latest and best information on the safe way to can fish and shellfish at home—write to:

> Bureau of Fisheries
>
> U.S. Department of the Interior
>
> Washington, D. C. 20242

Allow several weeks for their reply.

Freezing

Any food which is able to be canned is able to be frozen. In addition, some things which are chancy to can, such as seafood, freeze well. Further, a freezer holds safely for later use many table-ready dishes, meal leftovers and home-prepared convenience foods which may not be canned at all.

And usually—provided that preparation for freezing was adequate and that the freezer is working right—frozen food retains more of its original fresh flavor and texture, and generally keeps more of its nutrients.

On the other hand, freezing does not kill the organisms that cause spoilage, as canning does: it merely stops their growth temporarily.

Freezing as a way of preserving food means subjecting each sealed-from-the-air parcel/container of food to the sharpest cold we can—ideally even colder than 20 degrees below Zero Fahrenheit—for 24 hours, and then storing it at a sustained Zero F. Even so, frozen food has a limited storage life; and the warmer the freezer, the shorter the time you can hold it (see "Temperature *vs.* Spoilage" at the start of the Canning section, and "How Long in the Freezer?" coming in a minute).

Other points to bear in mind about freezing are that preparing food for a freezer is quicker than any other method of putting it by except for root-cellaring certain vegetables—and that home freezers represent a hefty capital investment.

CONSIDERATIONS IN GETTING A FREEZER

A proper sharp-freeze at −20 F. followed by Zero F. storage require a mechanical freezer, either one of your own, at home, or as space rented in a freezer-locker plant (see under Warehouses—Cold Storage, in the Yellow Pages). It would be a good idea for young families on a tight budget to rent a drawer in a nearby locker for a while: with such a trial run, they'll (1) decide on a feasible food-storage pattern, (2) learn what size freezer to buy come the time they can afford one, and (3) get the benefit of such special services as professional meat-cutting and commercial wrapping, if they want them. And it takes only a little extra bother to trot down to their locker drawer with a carton of home-packaged specialties or a case of good frozen produce bought at an authentic saving during the frequent supermarket sales.

THOSE FROZEN-FOOD/FREEZER PLANS

There are a number of companies that sell, on time payments, a package deal of freezer and food supply replenished over a period of several years. Some of these plans involve a membership fee of several hundred dollars to join, payable either as a lump sum or by installments; in addition, the buyer contracts in advance to purchase food at stated intervals. Still other plans offer only a food-purchase contract without the freezer.

All such plans undoubtedly are convenient: the householder orders ahead of time, and therefore has always on hand a certain quantity and type of food.

We recommend that everyone who is considering joining any such food/freezer plan check the company's offer with the local Better Business Bureau or other consumer protection group. Any contract which the householder is tempted to sign deserves careful investigation as to quality of product, be it freezer or food; terms of purchase, including carrying charges; and reliability of the firm, including what recourse either the company or the buyer may have if the contract appears to have been violated.

This recommendation is not to be construed as a blanket condemnation, even implied, of group-purchasing agreements. Prior investigation simply makes sense if the family is to get a suitable plan sponsored by a reliable organization.

For tips on selecting freezers and on some ins and outs of frozen-food plans, see the USDA's *Home and Garden Bulletin No. 48, Home Freezers, Their Selection and Use,* and *Consumer and Marketing Service Home and Garden Bulletin No. 166, How to Buy Meat for Your Freezer;* also, ask your County Agent for the latest information available from your state Consumer Education Specialist.

How big a freezer?

Some advisers recommend 6 cubic feet of freezer space for each person in the family, but farm families who raise most of their food and store it in their freezer might need 10 cubic feet per person. A cubic foot holds about 35 pounds of food.

> *Note:* Manufacturers' sales brochures describing cubic-foot sizes in freezers are sometimes approximate, so check the specifications and measurements to determine the actual usable interior space. See the USDA bulletin on selecting a home freezer, referred to above. There is also a discussion of freezers' cubic-foot measurements in the *Consumer Reports Buying Guide for 1972,* which repeats material in the November 1969 issue of *Consumer Reports.*

Of all the ways to put food by, freezing limits storage room most severely, so what you freeze should be given careful thinking-through beforehand. If your freezer is to be more than a place to stash random things you're not going to use right away, figure out a system of priorities. A good rule-of-thumb is to assign freezer space first to the more expensive and heavier foods, and to ones that can't be preserved so well any other way. Therefore, plan to freeze meats and seafood; and plan to freeze certain vegetables (prime example, broccoli) and certain fruits (prime example, strawberries—assuming you don't want all of them in jam), and mentally allot room for some favorite main-dish combinations or desserts.

You needn't be rigid about it, because if you make the best use of your freezer you'll be continually rotating its contents.

What type of freezer?

To do its job, the freezer must have adequate controls, no warm spots ("warm" being a constant temperature higher than the rest of the storage area), and the ability to provide the initial sharp-freeze for 24 hours at −20 F.

The small enclosed space for ice cubes or below 32 F. storage in some refrigerators is not adequate unless it has its own controls for sharp-freeze and storage, and has its own outside door.

CHEST

The chest type with one or more top openings offers best use of the space within it, and it holds its cold better than the others (cold air sinks to the bottom, hence the open frozen-food bins at the supermarket).

To think about: More care is needed when filling it, so that all foods may be arranged in easy-to-reach fashion. Especially if the little woman is a little woman.

UPRIGHT

The upright ones with a refrigerator-type door of course take up less space in the room, they are easier to load and unload than the chests, and the little shelves on the door are handy for temporary storage of dabs and snippets.

To think about: More cold spills out when the door is opened than is lost with opening a chest; and irregular-shaped packages may tumble out at the same time.

TWO-DOOR COMBINATIONS

Side-by-side or stacked (one above the other) freezer-refrigerator combinations save floor space, and the freezer section is an adequate, though usually smaller, variation of the upright type with its own controls.

To think about: The freezer space is usually too limited to accommodate more than a quite modest freezing program and storage for bargains from markets' sales. With care, though, it could hold a balanced supply of food types and varieties for a very small family.

And don't ignore the possible advantages in renting a freezer-locker drawer.

Where to put it?

If possible, locate the freezer in or near the kitchen: you'll use it more (which means using it better) than if it's in the cellar or other remote spot.

If you have a choice of convenient locations, choose the cooler one—so long as the place isn't actually freezing.

Put it in a relatively dry room, because moisture rusts the mechanism and can build up frost inside non-defrosting models, particularly up-right ones.

And *please* place it away from a back wall, so there's adequate air circulation and you can get under and around it to get out the fluff. Lack of air and a build-up of dust can overheat the motor and even cause fire. Mounting it on small rollers is a help in cleaning.

USING A FREEZER

Operating costs per pound of food are less if the freezer is kept at least 3/4 full at all times.

Operating temperatures

For the inital sharp-freeze, set the control at the lowest possible point: at or below −20 F., the temperature that makes smaller ice crystals in the food and gives a better finished product.

Place packages in single layers in contact with the parts of the box which cover the freezing coils—these would be certain shelves or walls or parts of the floor—and leave the food spread there for 24 hours before stacking the packages compactly for storage. For best results, don't try to sharp-freeze, at one time, more than 2 to 3 pounds of food for each 1 cubic foot of available freezer space. Later, when you're not sharp-freezing but simply storing, turn the controls back to no higher than Zero F.

For storing food after it's sharp-frozen, stack packages close together, and keep the storage section temperature at Zero F. or lower.

HOW LONG IN THE FREEZER?

Frozen foods lose quality when subjected to freezer temperatures above Zero F. While the storage life of different products varies, it can be stated generally that each rise of 10 degrees Fahrenheit cuts the storage life in half. (Thus if a food has a storage life of 8 months maintained at Zero F., its safe storage life will be only 4 months maintained at 10 F., and only 2 months if maintained at 20 F.) Foods maintained at −10 F. (10 degrees below Zero Fahrenheit) *in general* will keep their quality longer than shown in the following table—although keeping an item more than 12 months is uneconomical use of freezer space.

Freezer Storage Life of Various Foods
Maintained at Zero Fahrenheit (−18 Centigrade)

FOOD	MONTHS at 0°F.	FOOD	MONTHS at 0°F,
Fruits		*Fish and Shellfish*	
Apricots	12	Fatty Fish (Mackerel,	3
Peaches	12	Salmon, Swordfish, etc.)	
Raspberries	12	Lean fish (Haddock,	6
Strawberries	12	Cod, Flounder, Trout, etc.)	
Vegetables		Lobster, Crabs	2
		Shrimp	6
Asparagus	8 to 12	Oysters	3 to 4
Beans, green	8 to 12	Scallops	3 to 4
Beans, Lima	12	Clams	3 to 4
Broccoli	12		
Cauliflower	12	*Bakery Goods (Precooked)*	
Corn on the cob	8 to 10	Bread:	
Corn, cut	12	Quick	2 to 4
Carrots	12	Yeast	6 to 12
Mushrooms	8 to 10	Rolls	2 to 4
Peas	12	Cakes:	
Spinach	12	Angel	4 to 6
Squash	12	Gingerbread	4 to 6
		Sponge	4 to 6
Meats		Chiffon	4 to 6
Beef:		Cheese	4 to 6
Roasts, Steaks	12	Fruit	12
Ground	8	Cookies	4 to 6
Cubed, Pieces	10 to 12	Pies:	
Veal:		Fruit	12
Roasts, Chops	10 to 12	Mince	4 to 8
Cutlets, Cubes	8 to 10	Chiffon	1
Lamb:		Pumpkin	1
Roasts, Chops	12		
Pork:		*Other Precooked Foods*	
Roasts, Chops	6 to 8	Combination dishes	4 to 8
Ground, Sausage	4	(Stews, Casseroles, etc.)	
Pork or Ham, smoked	5 to 7	Potatoes:	
Bacon	3	French-fried	4 to 8
Variety meats	Up to 4	Scalloped	1
(Liver, Kidneys, Brains, etc.)		Soups	4 to 6
Poultry	6 to 12	Sandwiches	2

Times shown in the table are approximate, and are for foods of good quality that are properly processed/packaged when put in freezer storage.

Keeping an inventory

Running a freezer is like running a small store—you have to know what you have on hand and how long you've had it.

First, label and date each package of frozen food so you know how much of what is in each parcel; and when it was put by, so you'll use it while it's still top quality.

Store similar foods together, and you won't end up with a hodge-podge you have to paw through to find what you're looking for.

Devise some sort of inventory sheet or board that lets you keep track of food going in and coming out of your freezer. Some cooks make a sort of pegboard arrangement by driving part way into a board one nail for each type of food, labeling the nail, and slipping on it some sort of marker (a plastic ring, a washer, even a paper clip) for each package of that food when it is put in the freezer. As a package is taken out, a marker from the corresponding nail is removed.

Check the contents of your freezer every so often, and put maverick or to-be-used-soon items in places where you can't overlook them.

CARING FOR A FREEZER

Freezers need little care—just respect.

Treat the outside the same way that you do your refrigerator. Keep the surface and the door gaskets wiped clean. Clean behind and under it, and keep the protective grid over the motor free of dust.

Many are self-defrosting, but it is easy to do the defrosting yourself. Do it once or twice a year at times when the food supply is low. Disconnect the freezer, remove the food and wrap it in newspapers and blankets to keep it frozen. Use a wooden paddle—or similar tool that won't scratch the finish—to scrape the condensation (frost) from the walls of the cabinet onto papers or towels. Wipe the box with a clean cloth wrung out in water and baking soda. Dry the box before restarting the motor. About once a year, really wash the inside of the freezer.

By the way, have you read the manufacturer's instruction book lately?

WHEN THE FREEZER STOPS FREEZING

Now and again everybody's electricity fails for a time. Or, Heaven forbid, someone accidentally disconnects the freezer. Or the motor isn't working properly. Resist the impulse to open the door to check everything: make a plan of action first.

Find out, if you can, how long your freezer has been, or is likely to be, stopped. If it can be running in a few hours, don't worry: food in a fully loaded, closed freezer will keep for two days; if it's less than half loaded, the food won't keep longer than one day.

A freezer full of meat does not warm up as fast as a freezer full of baked foods.

The colder the food, the longer it will keep.

The larger the freezer, the longer the food will stay frozen.

But you must not open the door.

Emergency measures for a long stoppage

Call your local freezer-locker plant (still under Warehouses—Cold Storage, in the Yellow Pages), to see if they can take care of your food while the emergency lasts. Then take out all the food, wrap it in newspapers and blankets, or pack it closely in insulated cartons, and hurry it down to the locker.

If your good friends have extra space, ask their help, and divvy your food among their freezers—writing your name on each package beforehand, and insulating it well for the trip to your neighbors'.

If you can't parcel it out for temporary storage, and your freezer will be stopped more than one day, try to buy 25 pounds of dry ice. (In the Yellow Pages, look under Dry Ice, or call an ice and fuel company). This amount will hold the inside of a partly full 10-cubic-foot freezer below freezing for 2 or 3 days, and hold longer a 10-foot one that's full.

Consolidate the food packages into a compact pile. Put heavy cardboard directly on the food packages and lay the dry ice on the cardboard. Careful! Handle dry ice with gloves: it burns—or, more accurately, it freezes.

Then cover the entire freezer with blankets, but leave the air-vent openings free so the motor won't overheat in case the current comes on unexpectedly.

But if all that food thaws . . .

If, despite your emergency measures, the food in your freezer thawed, there are several things you can do. You can refreeze some of it, you can cook up some of it and freeze the cooked dishes from scratch; some of it you may can. And some you may have to destroy.

WHEN TO REFREEZE

This calls for good judgment, and a definition of terms.

When food has *thawed,* it still contains many ice crystals; individual pieces may be able to be separated, but they still contain ice in their tissues; and dense foods, or ones that pack solidly, might have a firm-to-hard core of ice in the middle of the package, in addition to the crystals in the tissues. Many thawed foods may be refrozen. Be sure to re-label them for limited storage.

When food has *defrosted,* all the ice crystals in its tissues have warmed to liquid. *No defrosted foods except very strong-acid fruits should be refrozen:* defrosted low-acid foods, if refrozen, are possible sources of food poisoning. Certain defrosted foods, if they have defrosted only within an hour or so, and hence are still quite cold, may be canned; but the resulting quality might not warrant the effort. Remember, however, that defrosted low-acid foods, vegetables, shellfish and precooked dishes may be spoiled although they have no telltale odor; if spoiled, they'd be nasty if pressure-canned, and could be downright dangerous to boot if merely cooked up and served.

WHAT CAN BE SAFELY REFROZEN

The first check of thawed food in a package or a non-rigid container is to squeeze it. *Don't open it.* Squeeze it: if you can feel good, firm crystals inside, the package is O.K. to refreeze—*provided the food is not highly perishable in the first place.*

Of course food in rigid containers must be opened to be inspected for adequate ice crystals.

Even though they're defrosted, strong-acid fruits may be refrozen if they're still cold; there will be definite loss in quality, however.

Refreeze thawed vegetables only if they contain plenty of ice crystals.

Give wrapped meat packages the squeeze test. Beef, veal and lamb that are firm with ice crystals may be refrozen, but you can always cook them up in convenience dishes and freeze them from scratch. The salt in merely thawed short-storage cured pork helps the ice crystals, and it can be refrozen, with a noticeable loss in quality. Unless fresh pork has quite a lot of crystals, it's better to cook it and serve it, or cook it fully in a combination dish, and freeze the dish for later reheating.

If packages of meat seem at all soft in the squeeze test, open them and examine the contents for unnatural color or an off-odor: on the slightest suspicion that they're not perfectly fresh, *destroy them.*

Thawed poultry, being more perishable than beef, veal or lamb to start with, would do better if fully cooked and then refrozen, either as is or in a made dish. Thawed variety meats—liver, kidneys, heart, sweetbreads, brains—are highly perishable and should be cooked and served, rather than cooked and frozen again as a convenience dish; you could make a fully cooked liver loaf (see Recipes), though, and freeze that. Seafood, being extremely perishable, should be cooked and served (cooked clams and oysters get tough in refreezing anyway).

Never refreeze melted ice cream. Never refreeze cream pies, eclairs, or similar foods.

But you can refreeze unfrosted cakes, uncooked fruit pies, bread, rolls, etc.

So what do you do with all the good thawed food that you don't want to refreeze, and that wouldn't can well, and that your family can't manage to eat right away?

Give it to friends who will enjoy it—of course explaining that it's thawed.

Or how about throwing the biggest impromptu dinner party you can imagine?

FREEZER PACKAGING MATERIALS

Freezer packaging materials usually are found at freezer-locker plants, hardware stores, feed and grain stores, and, often, in supermarkets and discount stores.

First, read the fine print

There is no simple definition we can give the homemaker that will enable her to recognize whether the wrappings and bags and rigid containers she should use in freezing food for her family are truly moisture-vapor-proof or moisture-vapor-resistant. But manufacturers are constantly researching improvements in their products, so we say: Read the makers' labels to learn if the materials are designed for freezer use.

The prime purpose of freezer packaging is to keep frozen food from drying out ("freezer-burning"), and to preserve nutritive value, flavor, texture and color. To do this, packaging should be moisture-vapor-*proof*—or at least *resistant*—and be easy to seal. And the seal should do its own job too.

And don't be sad if . . .

Don't expect perfect results from all your work if you package the food for your freezer in household waxed paper or regular aluminum foil or wrappings that are intended for short-term storage in the refrigerator.

And don't expect perfect results if you make-do with those coated-paper cartons that cottage cheese or milk or ice cream came from the store in.

And don't expect perfect results if you seal your good food with the sticky tape you use on Christmas parcels. The adhesive used on made-for-the-freezer tape remains effective at temperatures way below Zero Fahrenheit—and the stuff on regular household tapes does not.

Rigid containers

As the name implies, these hold their shape and may be stood upright, and are suitable for all foods except those with irregular shape (a whole chicken, say); and they are the best packaging for liquids.

Made of aluminum, glass, plastic, or plastic-coated cardboard, these boxes, tubs, jars and pans come fitted with tight-sealing covers. If the rims and lids remain smooth they often may be re-used; however, the aluminum ones have a tendency to bend as the packages are opened.

The cans described in the Canning section may also be used in freezing.

Three rigid containers and the inner bag for a fourth. The strawberries and broccoli are in plastic boxes, above; the peaches, below, are in a can/freeze jar (be sure that it's made for the freezer too). The special funnel and rack aren't required, but they do help make best use of the cardboard freezer box that will protect the bag.

The modern glass jars (also described in "About Jars and Cans" in Canning) may be used for freezing most fruits and vegetables. The wide-top jars with tapered sides are advised for liquid packs: the contents will slide out easily without having to be completely thawed.

Non-rigid containers

Non-rigid containers are the moisture-vapor-resistant bags and sheet materials used for Dry pack fruits and vegetables, meats and poultry, fish, and sometimes liquids. They are made of cellophane, heavy aluminum foil, pliofilm, polyethylene or laminates of paper, metal foil, glassine, cellophane and rubber latex.

The best ways of using sheet wrapping are the *butcher wrap* and the *drugstore fold*—both shown in Freezing Roasts.

Usually food in bags, and sometimes sheet-wrapped foods, are stored in a cardboard carton (re-usable) for protection and easier stacking in the freezer.

> *Note:* The special boil-in bags are available for home freezing, but require a heat-sealing device to close them securely. They are fine for small amounts of really moist cooked dishes, but at home we are unable to withdraw successfully all the drying air from the food package—so we'll say no more about this type of packaging. Yet for raw green peas or similar foods, such bags are good if you can seal them completely.

Sealing and labeling

The packaging is no better than the sealing that closes it.

SEALING RIGID CONTAINERS

Some rigid freezing containers are automatically sealed by their lids, or by screw-type bands, or by flanged snap-on plastic covers.

Then there's the waxed-cardboard freezer box with a tuck-in top that is sealed tight shut with freezer tape. If the contents are already sealed in an inner bag, though, you don't have to seal the box top.

There is also the re-usable container like a coffee can with an extra plastic lid: for your seal, tape the lid to the can all around.

The lids for glass jars must have an attached rubber-composition ring or a separate rubber ring to make a seal.

The lids for cans are put on with their own special sealing machine, as effectively for the freezer as for the Pressure Canner.

SEALING NON-RIGID CONTAINERS

Freezing bags are best sealed by twisting and folding the top, and fastening them with string, a rubber band, or a strip of coated wire.

Heat-sealing is possible—but it's tricky unless you have the special equipment for doing it.

Non-rigid sheet wrappings sometimes can be heat-sealed, but people more often seal all the edges with freezer tape.

LABELING

Use a wide, indelible marking pen to label each package with the name of the contents, the amount, and the date it is packaged.

SOME FREEZING TERMS

Anti-oxidant—Chemical agent, such as ascorbic acid (Vitamin C), added to sugar or sirup to control discoloration of fruits.

Blanch (scald)—To heat vegetables in boiling water or steam in order to slow or stop the action of enzymes.

Dry pack—To package fruits without added liquid or sugar.

Enzymes—Naturally occurring substances that help promote organic change (ripening, decomposition, etc.) in vegetable or animal tissues. Their action must be stopped before certain food is frozen in order to prevent loss of quality, flavor and color.

Freezer burn—Dehydration of improperly wrapped food, leading to loss of color, flavor and texture.

Freezer tape—A pressure-sensitive adhesive tape designed to stick tightly at freezer temperatures (when ordinary tape comes off).

Glaze—To dip frozen food quickly in water iced to just above freezing, so that a thin coat of ice forms over the food.

Headroom—Space left at top of container to allow for expansion of food as it freezes.

Heat seal—To seal closure with pressure from a warm flatiron or special heating device.

Moisture-vapor-proof—Term applied to freezer packaging materials specially treated to prevent evaporation from food or transfer of moisture from the freezer to the food.

Overwrap—The second covering, usually sheet material (and water-vapor-resistant), wrapped around the first sealed container or sealed package, and then completely sealed with freezer tape.

Wet pack—To package fruits in sugar sirup, or with plain sugar (which draws juice to form liquid).

Freezing Fruits

The quality that comes out of the freezer is not one whit better than what goes in it. Use only prime fruit and treat it with respect.

Before freezing specific fruits: look at the chart "Headroom for Fruits and Vegetables," and "Sugar Sirups for Freezing Fruits."

HEADROOM FOR FRUITS AND VEGETABLES

It is necessary to allow ample headroom for foods packed in containers because the contents expand during freezing, and if extra space hasn't been provided, the expansion forces the closures off.

Loosely packed vegetables (like asparagus and broccoli) require no extra headroom, since space between the pieces is adequate for expansion.

The wide-top containers referred to are tall, with sides either straight or slightly flared.

The narrow-top containers referred to include canning jars, which may be used for freezing most fruits and vegetables that are *not packed in water.*

Type of Pack	Wide-top Container		Narrow-top Container	
	Pint	*Quart*	*Pint*	*Quart*
Liquid pack:	½ inch	1 inch	3/4 inch	1½ inches
(Fruit in juice, sugar, sirup or water; or crushed or puréed)				
Fruit juice	½ inch	1 inch	1½ inches	1½ inches
Dry pack:	½ inch	½ inch	½ inch	½ inch
(Fruit/vegetable packed without added sugar or liquid)				

Press air out of bags, then twist and tie the tops. Below, crumpled wrap keeps peaches from floating up to the headroom and darkening.

GENERAL PREPARATION

Handle only a small quantity at a time—2 or 3 quarts. A good way: put them in a wire basket and dunk it up and down several times in deep, cold water. After peeling, trimming, pitting and such, fix fruits much as you would for serving. Cut large fruits to convenient size, or crush. Small ones, such as berries, usually are left whole, or just crushed.

Crush soft fruits with a wire potato masher or pastry blender, firm ones in a food chopper. To make purée, press fruits through a colander, food mill or strainer (blenders can liquify too much).

TO PREVENT DARKENING

Unlike the choice of anti-discoloration procedures used most often in canning apples, apricots, peaches, nectarines and pears (see page 38), these and other oxidizing foods are kept from darkening by the addition of ascorbic acid (Vitamin C) either crystalline or tablets; commercial mixtures with an ascorbic acid base; crystalline citric acid, or plain lemon juice. Or steam-blanching for 3 to 5 minutes, depending on size of the pieces, may be used (see how, under Freezing Vegetables).

Fruit has a tendency to float to the top, where it changes color when exposed to the trapped air; so crumple some moisture-resistant sheet wrapping and put it on the top of the packaged fruit to hold it below the sirup. Seal and freeze.

ASCORBIC ACID, CRYSTALLINE

Usually available from drugstores, or from some freezer-locker plants. If bought in ounces, figure that 1 ounce will give roughly 40 ¼-teaspoons or 20 ½-teaspoons (these being the most common amounts called for in freezing).

There is no record of known undesirable side effects from using ascorbic acid to hold the color of processed foods. It is Vitamin C. (There's more about it in Drying, and in Curing Meats.)

And not only is it the *safest* anti-oxidant to use, it is also the most effective of the agents employed in freezing to prevent darkening, because it will not change the flavor of the food, as the larger amounts needed of citric acid or lemon juice will do.

It dissolves easily in cold water or juices. Figure how much you'll need for one session at a time (see individual instructions), and prepare enough.

For wet pack with sirup. Add dissolved ascorbic acid to cold sirup and stir gently.

For wet pack with sugar. Just before packing, sprinkle the needed amount of ascorbic acid—dissolved in 2 to 3 tablespoons of cold water—over the fruit before you add the sugar.

For wet pack in crushed fruits and purées. Add dissolved ascorbic acid to the prepared fruit; stir well.

In fruit juices. Add dry ascorbic acid to the juice and stir to dissolve.

In dry pack (no sugar). Just before packing, sprinkle dissolved ascorbic acid over the fruit; mix gently but thoroughly to coat each piece.

ASCORBIC ACID TABLETS

It takes 3,000 milligrams (mg) to equal 1 teaspoon of crystalline ascorbic acid. Crush the tablets and dissolve them in the small amount of water. Use as Crystalline, above.

COMMERCIAL ASCORBIC ACID MIXTURES

These mixtures of crystalline ascorbic acid and sugar—or ascorbic acid, sugar and citric acid—are sold under trade names. They are not quite as effective, volume for volume, as plain ascorbic acid, but are readily available and easy to use.

Follow the manufacturer's instructions.

CITRIC ACID

Drugstores carry this in crystalline or powdered form. You need more of this than ascorbic acid to do the job, and sometimes it adds its own flavor to the fruit.

Dissolve the required amount in 2 to 3 tablespoons of cold water. Following directions for the individual fruits, add it as for ascorbic acid, above.

LEMON JUICE

A long-time favorite, it contains both citric and ascorbic acids. Again this is not as effective as crystalline ascorbic acid and it does add its own lemony flavor to the food.

Use it in the same manner as dissolved ascorbic acid.

STEAMING

Steaming in a single layer over boiling water is enough to retard darkening in some fruits (for example, apples). The treatments described above are easier, though.

THE VARIOUS PACKS

A few fruits freeze well without sweetening, but most have a better texture and flavor when packed in sugar or a sugar sirup.

Unlike canning fruits, the size and texture influence the form in which you pack them for freezing. The intended future use is your final deciding factor.

Fruit to freeze whole, in pieces, juiced, crushed or puréed, is packed Dry or Wet.

DRY PACK (ALWAYS SUGARLESS)

The simplest way is just to put whole or cut-up firm fruits in containers (do not add a thing), seal and freeze. This is especially good for blueberries, cranberries, currants, figs, gooseberries and rhubarb.

If you have the space, spread raspberries, blueberries, currants or other similar berries one layer deep on a tray or cookie sheet and set in the freezer. When berries are frozen hard, pour them into polyethylene bags and seal. They won't stick together. Later the bag may be opened; the needed amount taken out, the bag reclosed and returned to the freezer.

Versatile Dry pack lets you use the fruits as if they were fresh.

WET PACKS

This means adding some liquid—such as its own natural juice, sugar sirup, crushed fruit, or water.

Wet pack with sugar. Plain sugar is sprinkled over and gently mixed with the prepared fruit until juice is drawn out and sugar is dissolved. Then you pack and freeze. Fruit fixed this way is especially good for cooked dishes and fruit cocktails. This has less liquid than the Wet pack with Sirup.

Wet pack with sirup. Fruit, whole or in pieces, is packed in containers and covered with a cold sugar sirup to improve their flavor and make a delightful sauce around the fruit. Generally best for dessert dishes.

Plan on using 1/3 to 1/2 cup of sirup for each pint package of fruit.

A 40 Percent Sirup (see "Sugar Sirups for Freezing Fruit") is used for most fruits, but to keep the delicate flavor of the milder ones, use a thinner sirup. A 50 to 60 Percent Sirup is best for sour fruits such as pie cherries.

Wet pack with fruit juice. The fruit—whole, crushed, or in pieces—is packed in the container and covered with juice extracted from good parts of less perfect fruit, and treated with ascorbic acid to prevent darkening. Pack with a piece of crumpled moisture-resistant sheet wrapping on top to hold fruit below the liquid. Seal and freeze. People on sugar-restricted diets can enjoy this unsweetened fruit; or artificial sweeteners *approved by their doctor* may be dissolved

---

SUGAR SIRUPS FOR FREEZING FRUITS

Designation	*Sugar*	*Water*	*Yield*
30 percent (thin)	2 cups	4 cups	5 cups
35 percent	2½ cups	4 cups	5 1/3 cups
40 percent (medium)	3 cups	4 cups	5½ cups
50 percent	4 3/4 cups	4 cups	6½ cups
60 percent (very heavy)	7 cups	4 cups	7 3/4 cups
65 percent	8 3/4 cups	4 cups	8 2/3 cups

Dissolve the sugar thoroughly in cold or hot water (if hot, chill it thoroughly before packing). Sirup can be made the day before and stored in the refrigerator: it must be kept quite cold.

Roughly, estimate ½ to 2/3 cup of sirup for each pint container of fruit.

Substitutions: Generally, ¼ of the sugar may be replaced by light corn sirup without affecting the flavor of the fruit; indeed, the additional blandness is often desirable for delicately flavored fruits, and some cooks prefer substituting even more corn sirup.

Honey or maple sirup may also replace ¼ of the sugar—if the family likes the different flavor either imparts. Raw sugar of course affects the color and, to some degree, the flavor.

---

in the juice to enhance the flavor.

For general use, sugar may be dissolved in the juice in the same proportion used in making a sugar sirup suitable for the particular fruit.

A greater degree of natural flavor is kept in the Juice pack, either sweetened or unsweetened, than in the Sirup pack.

Wet pack, purée. Fruit is puréed by forcing it through a food mill, strainer or colander. Dissolved ascorbic acid or lemon juice is mixed with the purée before packing to prevent darkening. Sweetening may or may not be added.

Wet pack with water. This is similar to the Juice and Sirup packs, except that the added liquid is cold water in which ascorbic acid has been dissolved. The flavor is not as satisfactory as it is in Juice or Sirup packs.

Apples

Apples, more so than most produce, store well by several methods: fresh in a root cellar, or dried, or as canned applesauce or dessert slices (all q.v.). But you may want to freeze a few for late-season cooked dishes—especially in a package shaped for a pie.

SLICES

Prepare. Peel, core and slice. As you go, treat against darkening by coating the slices with ½ teaspoon pure ascorbic acid dissolved in each 3 tablespoons of cold water. Or steam-blanch (page 133). Less satisfactory but easier: drop slices in a solution of 2 tablespoons salt to each 1 gallon of water (no vinegar) for no longer than 20 minutes; rinse well and drain before packing.

Dry pack, no sugar (for pies). Arrange in a pie plate as for a pie, slip the filled plate into a plastic bag and freeze. Remove the solid chunk of slices from the plate as soon as frozen and overwrap it tightly in moisture-vapor-proof material—as if it were a piece of meat (q.v.)— and return to the freezer. (Handy at pie-making time because you lay the pie-shaped chunk of slices right in your pastry, put on the sugar and seasonings, top with a crust and bake.)

Wet pack, sugar. Sprinkle ¼ cup sugar over each 1 quart of slices for pie-making. Leave appropriate headroom.

Seal; freeze.

Wet pack, sirup. Cover with 40 Percent Sirup for use in fruit cocktail or serving uncooked. Leave appropriate headroom.

Seal; freeze.

SAUCE

Prepare. Make applesauce as you like it—strained, chunky, sweetened or unsweetened.

Wet pack, puréed. Fill containers. Leave ½ inch of headroom.

Seal; freeze.

Apricots

HALVES AND SLICES

Prepare. If apricots do not need peeling, heat them for 30 seconds in boiling water to keep their skins from toughening. Cool immediately in cold water. Cut up as you like.

Wet pack, sirup. Pack in container, cover with 40 Percent Sirup to which has been added ¾ teaspoon ascorbic acid to each 1 quart of sirup. Leave appropriate headroom.

Seal; freeze.

Wet pack, sugar. Sprinkle ¼ teaspoon ascorbic acid dissolved in ¼ cup water over each 1 quart of apricots. Mix ½ cup of sugar with each 1 quart of fruit, stir until sugar dissolves. Pack in containers with appropriate headroom.

Seal; freeze.

CRUSHED OR PURÉED

Prepare. Wash and treat skins as for whole fruit. Crush or put through a sieve or food mill.

Wet pack, sugar. Mix 1 cup sugar with each 1 quart of crushed or sieved fruit. Add anti-darkening agent. Pack, leaving ½ inch of headroom.

Seal; freeze.

Avocados

Most versatile if frozen plain. Sweetening for milk shakes or ice cream, etc., may be added when you make them up. And for Guacamole, the further seasonings—minced onion, tomatoes, green peppers, etc.—are also best added shortly before serving this delicious dip/spread.

Prepare. Peel and mash. If intended for future sweet dishes, add 1/8 teaspoon crystalline ascorbic acid to each 1 quart of purée to prevent darkening. If for Guacamole, add 1 tablespoon lemon juice (anti-darkening plus flavoring) and a dash of salt for each 2 avocados as you mash them.

Wet pack, puréed. Leave ½ inch of headroom.

Seal; freeze.

Most Soft Berries

WHOLE

Prepare. Sort, wash gently and drain: blackberries, boysenberries, dewberries, loganberries, youngberries.

Dry pack, no sugar. Pack in containers, leaving ½ inch of headroom. Or see the alternate Dry method in "The Various Packs."

Seal; freeze.

Wet pack, sirup. (For berries to be served uncooked.) Pack and cover with 40 to 50 Percent Sirup. Leave ½ inch of headroom.

Seal; freeze.

Wet pack, sugar. (For berries to be used in cooked dishes.) In a bowl mix ¾ cup sugar with each 1 quart of berries. Mix until sugar dissolves. Pack; leave ½ inch of headroom.

Seal; freeze.

CRUSHED OR PURÉED

Wet pack, puréed. Add 1 cup sugar to each 1 quart crushed or puréed berries. Mix well. Pack; leave ½ inch of headroom.

Seal; freeze.

Most Firm Berries

Prepare. Sort and wash blueberries, elderberries, huckleberries. Optional: steam berries for 1 minute to tenderize skins.

WHOLE

Dry pack, no sugar. (For berries to be used in cooked dishes.) Pack; leave ½ inch of headroom.

Seal; freeze.

Wet pack, sirup. (For berries to be served uncooked.) Pack; cover with 40 Percent Sirup, leaving ½ inch of headroom.

Seal; freeze.

CRUSHED OR PURÉED

Wet pack, puréed. Add 1 to 1½ cups sugar to each 1 quart of crushed or puréed berries; stir to dissolve. Leave appropriate headroom.

Seal; freeze.

Cranberries

WHOLE

Prepare. Wash and drain.

Dry pack, no sugar. Fill containers with clean berries. Leave ½ inch of headroom.

Seal; freeze.

Wet pack, sirup. Cover with 50 Percent Sirup. Leave appropriate headroom.

Seal; freeze.

PURÉED

Prepare. Wash and drain berries. Add 2 cups water to each 1 quart (1 pound) berries and boil until skins burst. Press through a sieve and add 2 cups sugar to each 1 quart purée. Mix.

Wet pack, puréed. Pack; leave appropriate headroom.

Seal; freeze.

Currants

Prepare. Wash; remove stems.

WHOLE

Dry pack, no sugar. Treat like Cranberries.

Seal; freeze.

Wet pack, sugar. Add ¾ cup sugar to each 1 quart of fruit; stir gently to dissolve. Pack; leave appropriate headroom.

Seal; freeze.

Wet pack, sirup. Treat like Cranberries.

Seal; freeze.

CRUSHED

Wet pack, crushed. Add 1 1/8 cups sugar to each 1 quart crushed currants; stir to dissolve sugar. Pack; leave appropriate headroom.

Seal; freeze.

JUICE

For beverages, use ripe currants. For future jellies, mix in some slightly underripe currants for added pectin.

Prepare. Crush currants and warm to 165 F. over low heat. Drain through a jelly bag. Cool.

Wet pack, juice. Sweeten with ¾ to 1 cup sugar to each 1 quart of juice, or pack unsweetened. Leave appropriate headroom.

Seal; freeze.

Gooseberries

Prepare. Wash; remove stems and tails.

Dry pack, no sugar. (Best for future pies and preserves.) Pack whole berries; leave ½ inch of headroom.

Seal; freeze.

Wet pack, sirup. Cover whole berries with 50 Percent Sirup. Leave appropriate headroom.

Seal; freeze.

Raspberries

The versatile and very tender raspberries freeze even better than strawberries do. The wild ones, though small, have fine flavor. Real seedy berries are best used in purée or as juice.

WHOLE

Prepare. Sort; wash very carefully in cold water and drain thoroughly.

Dry pack, no sugar. Fill containers gently, leaving ½ inch of headroom.

Seal; freeze.

Wet pack, sugar. In a shallow pan, carefully mix ¾ cup sugar with each 1 quart of berries so as to avoid crushing. Pack; leave ½ inch of headroom.

Seal; freeze.

Wet pack, sirup. Cover with 40 Percent Sirup. Leave appropriate headroom.

Seal; freeze.

CRUSHED OR PUREED

Prepare. Crush or sieve washed berries.

Wet pack, juice. Add ¾ to 1 cup sugar to each 1 quart of berry pulp; mix to dissolve sugar. Pack; leave appropriate headroom.

Seal; freeze.

JUICE

Prepare. Select fully ripe raspberries. Crush and slightly heat berries to start juice flowing. Strain through a jelly bag.

Wet pack, juice. For beverage, sweeten with ½ to 1 cup sugar to each 1 quart of juice. (For future jelly, do not sweeten.) Pour into containers; leave appropriate headroom.

Seal; freeze.

Strawberries

Choose slightly tart firm berries with solid red centers. Plan to slice or crush the very large ones. Sweetened strawberries hold better than unsweetened.

WHOLE

Prepare. Sort; wash in cold water; drain. Remove hulls.

Wet pack, sugar. In a shallow pan, add ¾ cup sugar to each 1 quart of berries and mix thoroughly. Pack; leave ½ inch of headroom.

Seal; freeze.

Wet pack, sirup. Cover berries with cold 50 Percent Sirup. Leave appropriate headroom.

Seal; freeze.

Wet pack, water (unsweetened). To protect the color of the berries, cover them with water in which 1 teaspoon crystalline ascorbic acid to each 1 quart of water has been dissolved. Leave appropriate headroom.

Seal; freeze.

SLICED OR CRUSHED

Prepare. Wash and hull as for whole berries, then slice or crush partially or completely.

Wet pack, sugar. Add ¾ cup sugar to each 1 quart of berries in a shallow pan. Mix thoroughly. Pack; leave appropriate headroom.

Seal; freeze.

JUICE

Prepare. Crush berries; drain juice through a jelly bag.

Wet pack, juice. Add 2/3 to 1 cup sugar to each 1 quart of juice—or omit sugar if you wish. Pour into containers; leave appropriate headroom.

Seal; freeze.

Cherries, Sour (for Pie)

As pie timber these are better canned; but if you want to freeze them, here's how.

WHOLE

Prepare. Use only tree-ripened cherries. Stem, wash, drain and pit. (The rounded end of a clean paper clip makes a good cherry-pitter.)

Wet pack, sugar. Add ¾ cup sugar to 1 quart of pitted cherries; stir until dissolved. Pack, leaving appropriate headroom.

Seal; freeze.

Wet pack, sirup. Cover pitted cherries with cold 60 to 65 Percent Sirup. Leave appropriate headroom.

Seal; freeze.

CRUSHED

Wet pack, juice. Add 1 to 1½ cups sugar to each 1 quart of crushed cherries. Mix well. Pack; leave appropriate headroom.

Seal; freeze.

PURÉED

Wet pack, juice. Crush cherries; heat just to boiling and press through a sieve or food mill. Add ¾ cup sugar to each 1 quart of purée. Pack; leave appropriate headroom.

Seal; freeze.

JUICE

Home-made cherry juice in a party punch makes it exceptional!

Wet pack, juice. Crush cherries, heat slightly (*do not boil*) to start juice flowing. Strain through a jelly bag. Add 1½ to 2 cups sugar to each 1 quart of juice; or pack unsweetened. Pour into containers; leave appropriate headroom.

Seal; freeze.

Cherries, Sweet

The dark red and "black" varieties are best for freezing—but do handle them quickly to prevent color and flavor changes. Use only tree-ripened fruit and remove the pits: they give an almond flavor to cherries when frozen.

WHOLE

Wet pack, sirup. Cover pitted cherries with 40 Percent Sirup in which you've dissolved ½ teaspoon crystalline ascorbic acid to each 1 quart of sirup. Leave appropriate headroom.

Seal; freeze.

CRUSHED

Wet pack, juice. To each 1 quart of crushed cherries add 1½ cups sugar and ¼ teaspoon crystalline ascorbic acid; mix well. Pack; leave appropriate headroom.

Seal; freeze.

JUICE

Sweet red cherries and sweet white cherries are handled differently for juice.

Prepare. Heat sweet *red* cherries slightly (to 165 F.) to start the juice. Strain through a jelly bag.

Crush sweet *white* cherries *without heating*. Strain through a jelly bag. Then warm this juice in a double boiler or over low heat to 165 F. Cool the red or the white juice and let it stand covered overnight.

Wet pack, juice. Pour off the clear juice into containers, being careful not to include any sediment from the bottom of the kettle. Add 1 cup sugar to each 1 quart of juice; or leave unsweetened if you prefer. Leave appropriate headroom.

144

Seal; freeze. (Sweet cherry juice by itself is pretty blah. So mix some *sour* cherry juice with the sweet to make a better beverage.)

Coconut

If you have a windfall, freeze some simply for fun—you may want to have a Mainland luau!

Prepare. Puncture the "eye" of the coconut; drain out and save the milk. Remove the meat from the broken-open shell. Shred it, or put it through a food chopper.

Wet pack, juice. Cover shredded meat with coconut milk. Leave appropriate headroom.

Seal; freeze.

Dates

Prepare. Wash, if necessary, and dry on paper toweling; remove pits.

Dry pack, no sugar. Pack in containers with no headroom.

Seal; freeze.

Figs

WHOLE OR SLICED

Prepare. Only tree-ripened, soft-ripe fruit, please; and check a sample for good flavor clear through the flesh. Sort, wash and cut off stems. Peeling is optional.

Dry pack, no sugar. Fill containers with the prepared figs; leave appropriate headroom.

Seal; freeze.

Wet pack, sirup. Cover with 35 Percent Sirup to which you have added ¾ teaspoon crystalline ascorbic acid—or ½ cup lemon juice—to each 1 quart of sirup.

Seal; freeze.

Wet pack, water. Pack figs; cover with water to which you have added ¾ teaspoon crystalline ascorbic acid to each 1 quart of water. Leave appropriate headroom.

Seal; freeze.

CRUSHED

Wet pack, juice. Crush prepared figs. Mix 2/3 cup sugar and 1/4 teaspoon crystalline ascorbic acid with each 1 quart of crushed fruit. Leave appropriate headroom.

Seal; freeze.

Fruit Cocktail (or Compôte)

Freezing is excellent for your favorite combinations of fruit to serve either as an appetizer or dessert. A few added blueberries or dark sweet cherries make a nice color contrast.

Prepare. Use any combination of fruits peeled, cored, etc., and cut to suitable size.

Wet pack, sirup. Pack. Cover with cold 30 to 40 Percent Sirup in which ¾ teaspoon crystalline ascorbic acid to each 1 quart of sirup has been dissolved. If cut-up oranges are in the mixture, the ascorbic acid may be omitted. Leave appropriate headroom.

Seal; freeze.

Grapefruit (and Oranges)

Commercial processors do a fine job with citrus fruits. It's hardly worth-while to compete unless you've a surplus of grapefruit and/or oranges. Use heavy, blemish-free, tree-ripened fruits.

SECTIONS OR SLICES

Prepare. Wash; peel, cutting off the outside membranes. Cut a thin slice from each end. With a sharp, thin-bladed knife, cut down each side of the membranes and lift out the whole sections. Work over a large bowl to catch the juice. Remove seeds. Oranges may be sliced.

Wet pack, sirup. Cover fruit with 40 Percent Sirup made with excess fruit juice, and water if needed. (For better quality, add ½ tea-spoon crystalline ascorbic acid to each 1 quart of sirup before packing.) Leave appropriate headroom.

Seal; freeze.

JUICE

Prepare. Use good tree-ripened fruits. Squeeze, using a squeezer that does not press oil from the rind.

Wet pack, juice. Either sweeten with 2 tablespoons sugar to each 1 quart of juice, or pack unsweetened. (For best quality, add ¾ teaspoon crystalline ascorbic acid to each 1 gallon of juice before packing.) Pour into glass freezing jars. Leave appropriate headroom.

Seal; freeze.

Grapes

Canning is probably smarter for these—but you may want to freeze some for gelatine salads and desserts. Juice is likely to be the best frozen use of grapes.

WHOLE OR HALVES

Prepare. Use firm-ripe grapes with tender skins and nice color and flavor. Wash and stem. Leave seedless grapes whole; cut other varieties in half and remove their seeds.

Dry pack, no sugar. Leave appropriate headroom.

Seal; freeze.

Wet pack, sirup. Cover grapes with cold 40 Percent Sirup. Leave appropriate headroom.

Seal; freeze.

JUICE

For a beverage or future jelly-making, use firm-ripe grapes.

Prepare. Wash, stem, crush. Do *not* heat. Strain through a jelly bag. Allow juice to stand overnight in the refrigerator while sediment settles to the bottom. Carefully pour off the clear juice.

Wet pack, juice. Pour into containers; leave appropriate headroom.

Seal; freeze.

(If tartrate crystals—the basis for cream of tartar—form in frozen juice, strain them out after the juice thaws.)

Melons

SLICES, CUBES OR BALLS

Prepare. Cut firm-ripe melons in half; remove seeds and soft tissues holding them. If for slices or cubes, cut off all rind; cut to shape. If for balls, do not cut off rind, but scoop out with a baller, taking care not to include any rind.

Wet pack, sirup. Cover with 30 Percent Sirup. Leave appropriate headroom.

Seal; freeze.

CRUSHED (NOT FOR WATERMELON)

Prepare. Halve, cut off rind; remove seeds and their soft tissue. Crush or put through the food chopper, using a coarse knife.

Wet pack, juice. Add 1 tablespoon sugar to each 1 quart of crushed melon, if you wish (and an added 1 teaspoon lemon juice points up the flavor). Stir to dissolve. Pack; leave appropriate headroom.

Seal; freeze.

Nectarines

These are not as satisfactory frozen as most other fruits are.

HALVES, QUARTERS OR SLICES

Choose only firm, fully ripe nectarines—avoiding overripe ones, which often develop a disagreeable flavor in the freezer.

Prepare. Wash and pit. Peeling is optional.

Wet pack, sirup. Put ½ cup of 40 Percent Sirup in each container and cut fruit directly into it. (For a better product add ½ teaspoon crystalline ascorbic acid to each 1 quart of sirup before packing.) Gently press fruit down and add extra sirup to cover. Top with crumpled moisture-resistant wrap to hold fruit in place. Leave appropriate headroom.

Seal; freeze.

PURÉED

Treat like Peach Purée.

Peaches

Peaches are excellent either canned or frozen.

HALVES AND SLICES

Prepare. Use firm, ripe peaches without any green color on their skins. Wash, pit, and peel. (They are less ragged if peeled without the boiling-water dip.)

Wet pack, sugar. Coat cut peaches with a solution of ¼ teaspoon crystalline ascorbic acid dissolved in each ¼ cup of water to prevent darkening. Add 2/3 cup of sugar to each 1 quart of fruit, and mix gently. Pack, leaving appropriate headroom.

Wet pack, sirup. Put ½ cup 40 Percent Sirup in the bottom of each container. Cut peaches directly into it. (For a better product add ½ teaspoon crystalline ascorbic acid to each 1 quart of the sirup before packing.) Gently press fruit down and add extra sirup to cover. Top with crumpled moisture-resistant wrap to hold fruit in place. Leave appropriate headroom.

Seal; freeze.

Wet pack, water. Cover cut peaches with water in which 1 teaspoon crystalline ascorbic acid has been dissolved in each 1 quart of water. Leave appropriate headroom.

Seal; freeze.

CRUSHED OR PURÉED

Prepare. Loosen skins by dipping peaches in boiling water for 30 to 60 seconds. Cool immediately in cold water; peel and pit.

Crush coarsely. For purée, press through a sieve or food mill; it's easier to make the purée if you heat the peaches in a very little water for 4 minutes before you sieve them.

Wet pack, juice. Mix 1 cup sugar and 1/8 teaspoon crystalline ascorbic acid with each 1 quart of peaches. Pack; leave appropriate headroom.

Seal; freeze.

Pears

Use Bartlett or a similar variety—not any of the so-called winter pears, which keep in cold storage (see Root-Cellaring).

HALVES OR QUARTERS

Prepare. Choose well-ripened pears, firm but not hard. Wash, cut in halves and quarters; core. Cover them with cold water to prevent their oxidizing during preparation (leaching is negligible because immersion time is so short).

Wet pack, sirup. Handling no more than 3 pints at a time in a deep-fry basket, lower cut-up pears into boiling 40 Percent Sirup for 1 to 2 minutes. Drain; cool. (Save the hot sirup for another load of fruit.) To pack, cover cooled pears with cold 40 Percent Sirup to which has been added ¾ teaspoon crystalline ascorbic acid to each 1 quart of sirup. Leave appropriate headroom.

Seal; freeze.

PURÉED

Prepare. Wash well-ripened pears that are not hard or gritty. Peeling is optional. Proceed as for Peach Purée.

Persimmons

PURÉED

Purée made from late-ripening native ones needs no sweetening, but nursery varieties may be packed with or without sugar.

Prepare. Choose orange-colored, soft-ripe persimmons. Sort, wash, peel and cut in sections. Press through a sieve or food mill. Mix 1/8 teaspoon crystalline ascorbic acid—or 1½ teaspoons crystalline citric acid—with each 1 quart of purée.

Wet pack, juice (unsweetened). Pack unsweetened purée. Leave appropriate headroom.

Seal; freeze.

Wet pack, juice (sweetened). Mix 1 cup sugar with each 1 quart of purée. Pack; leave appropriate headroom.

Seal; freeze.

Pineapple

Prepare. Use firm, ripe pineapple with full flavor and aroma. Pare, removing eyes, and core. Slice, dice, crush or cut in wedges or sticks.

Wet pack, sirup. Pack fruit tightly. Cover with 30 Percent Sirup made with pineapple juice, if available, or water. Leave appropriate headroom.

Seal; freeze.

Wet pack, juice (unsweetened). Pack fruit tightly without sugar: enough juice will squeeze out to fill the crevices. Leave appropriate headroom.

Seal; freeze.

Plums (and Prunes)

Frozen plums and prunes are good in pies and jams, salads and desserts. Use the unsweetened pack for future jams. To serve unsweetened whole plums raw, see below.

WHOLE, HALVES OR QUARTERS

Prepare. Choose tree-ripened fruit with deep color. Wash. Cut as desired. Leave pits in fruits you freeze whole.

Wet pack, sirup. Cover with cold 40 to 50 Percent Sirup in which is dissolved ½ teaspoon crystalline ascorbic acid to each 1 quart of sirup. Leave appropriate headroom.

Seal; freeze.

Wet pack, juice (unsweetened). Pack plums tightly. Leave appropriate headroom.

Seal; freeze. (To serve whole plums uncooked, dip them in cold water for 5 to 10 seconds; remove skins, and cover with 40 Percent Sirup to thaw. Serve in the sirup.)

PURÉED

Purée may be made from heated or unheated fruit, depending on its softness.

Prepare. Wash plums, cut in half and pit. *Unheated fruit:* press raw through a sieve or food mill. Add ¼ teaspoon crystalline ascorbic acid—or ½ teaspoon crystalline citric acid—to each 1 quart of purée. *Heated fruit* (the firm ones): add 1 cup water to each 4 quarts of plums; boil for 2 minutes; cool, and press through a sieve or food mill.

Wet pack, juice. Mix ½ to 1 cup sugar with each 1 quart of purée. Pack; leave appropriate headroom.

Seal; freeze.

JUICE

Prepare. Wash plums, simmer until soft in enough water barely to cover. Strain through a jelly bag and cool the juice.

Wet pack, juice. Add 1 to 2 cups sugar to each 1 quart of juice. Pour into containers; leave appropriate headroom.

Seal; freeze.

Rhubarb

Freeze only firm, young, well-colored stalks with good flavor and few fibers. (See also Canning.)

PIECES

Prepare. Wash, trim and cut in 1- to 2-inch pieces, or longer to fit the package. Heating rhubarb in boiling water for 1 minute and cooling immediately in cold water helps to set the color and flavor.

Dry pack, no sugar. Pack either raw or preheated (and now cold) rhubarb tightly in containers. Leave appropriate headroom.

Seal; freeze.

Wet pack, sirup. Pack either raw or preheated (and now cold) rhubarb tightly. Cover with cold 40 Percent Sirup. Leave appropriate headroom.

Seal; freeze.

PURÉED

Prepare. Prepare as pieces. Add 1 cup water to each 6 cups of rhubarb and boil 2 minutes. Cool immediately; press through a sieve or food mill.

Wet pack, juice. Add 2/3 cup sugar to each 1 quart of purée. Pack; leave appropriate headroom.

Seal; freeze.

JUICE

Prepare. Select as for pieces. Wash, trim, and cut in 4- or 5-inch lengths. Add 4 cups water to each 4 quarts of rhubarb, and bring just to a boil. Strain through a jelly bag.

Wet pack, juice. Pour into containers. Leave appropriate headroom.

Seal; freeze.

Freezing Vegetables

With a very few exceptions, any vegetable that cans well freezes equally well at home, if not better. The exceptions at this writing (all raw) are whole tomatoes, greens for salads, white (Irish) potatoes and cabbage. Because they have a high water content, formation of ice crystals ruptures their flesh, and the result is loss of texture or shape when defrosted. The extremely low temperature now being used by some frozen-food companies bypasses the crystal stage in freezing, so commercially frozen white potatoes or whole tomatoes are infinitely superior than those done at home.

Certain vegetable varieties are better for freezing than others, so read your seed catalogs carefully to see which ones you'll have the most luck with. Or ask your County Agent for a listing in your area. Or a truck gardener can tell you (but sometimes the person tending his roadside stand can't).

Because of the investment in nutrition and money that freezing entails, you'll want to freeze only prime vegetables that are garden-fresh. If you can't freeze them the same day they're picked, refrigerate them overnight.

Note: Procedures for cooking frozen vegetables come at the end of this section.

GENERAL PREPARATION

The first step, after you've gathered your packaging, etc., is to wash the vegetables (only peas, lima beans and others that are protected by pods may not need to be washed). Use cold water and lift the vegetables out of it to leave any grit in the bottom of the pan.

You may need to take a further step to draw out possible insects in broccoli, Brussels sprouts and cauliflower: simply soak them for ½ hour in a solution of 4 tablespoons salt to 1 gallon of cold water.

Sort the vegetables according to size, or cut them to uniform pieces. Peel, trim and cut as needed.

Blanching

Even after vegetables are picked, the enzymes in them make them lose flavor and color and sometimes make them tough—*even at freezer temperatures*. Therefore the enzymes must be stopped in their tracks by being heated for a few minutes (how many minutes depends on the size and texture of the vegetable) before the vegetables are cooled quickly and packed. This preheating is necessary for virtually all vegetables: green (sweet) peppers are the notable exception.

IN BOILING WATER

Practically all vegetables are safely blanched in boiling water. Use a large kettle which has a wire basket that fits down in it. Put in at least 4 quarts of water and bring it to a boil. Put prepared vegetables in the basket—not more than a pound or two at a time—and lower it into the boiling water. Start counting the time at once. Shake the basket to let heat reach all parts of its load. When the specified time is up, lift out the basket and immediately dunk the vegetables in ice-cold water to cool them fast.

If you live 5,000 feet or more above sea level, preheat vegetables 1 minute longer than the time called for.

BLANCHING IN STEAM

A few vegetables are better if heated in steam, and some may be done in either steam or boiling water.

For steaming, use a large kettle with a tight lid and a rack that holds a steaming basket at least 3 inches above the bottom of the kettle. Put in 1 or 2 inches of water and bring it to a boil.

Cool food as fast as possible after it's blanched.

Put your prepared vegetables in the basket in only a single layer, so the steam can reach all parts quickly. Cover the kettle and keep heat high. Start counting the time as soon as the cover is on.

For altitudes of 5,000 feet or more above sea level, add 1 minute to steaming time.

OTHER WAYS TO PREHEAT

Pumpkins, squash and sweet potatoes may be heated in a pressure cooker or in the oven before freezing. Mushrooms may be heated in fat in the skillet. And tomatoes for juice may be simmered.

Cool after Blanching

Cool all vegetables as quickly as possible after they've been preheated. Use plenty of cold water—ice-water is ideal—and change it often to keep it cold. It takes about the same time to cool vegetables as it did to blanch them.

When they are completely cooled, drain them well: you don't want to make a wet pack inadvertently to go into the freezer.

THE PACKS

Vegetables for freezing may be packed either dry or in brine. The Dry pack is easier and lets you use the vegetables as you would if they were fresh, so Dry pack is the method we'll use the most.

Incidentally, a trick borrowed from commercial processors will make your packaging of dry-packed vegetables (and some fruits) easier. Just place a single layer of any freezer-ready small vegetable on a tray and sharp-freeze it fast (below −20 F.). Then pour the frozen vegetable into a freezer-type container and seal. Because the pieces are not stuck to each other, you can pour out the amount needed, reclose and seal the container, and return it and its partial contents to the freezer.

COOKING FROZEN VEGETABLES

The secret of cooking frozen vegetables well (if it is a secret), is to cook them in a small amount of liquid, and only until they are tender. When you blanched them for the freezer, you already did a small part of the cooking.

So treat your frozen vegetables like fresh ones—except for a shorter cooking time. This way you'll keep more of the nutrients, as well as more of the natural color, flavor and texture.

TO THAW OR NOT TO THAW

Most are best cooked *without* thawing.

Defrost the leafy ones just enough to separate the leaves.

Partially defrost corn-on-the-cob, else the cob will not be heated through and the cooked kernels will cool too soon at the table. Open only the amount needed of any style corn and cook and serve it at once: holding it either before or after cooking makes it soggy.

BOILING

Generally you bring to the boil ½ cup water for each 1 pint of frozen vegetables. Add the vegetables, cover, and begin to count cooking time when water returns to the boil.

Exceptions: 1 cup water to each 1 pint of lima beans; water to cover for corn-on-the-cob.

Cooking times. Spinach—3 minutes; turnip greens—15 to 20 minutes; all other greens—8 to 12 minutes.

Depending on size of pieces: large lima beans, cut green/snap/ wax beans, broccoli, carrots, cauliflower, corn in all forms, green peas—all from 3 to 10 minutes.

Kohlrabi (and similar-textured vegetables)—8 to 10 minutes.

Summer squash—up to 12 minutes.

At high altitudes, boil a bit longer—water boils at 2 degrees *lower* than 212 F. for each 1,000 feet above sea level.

PRESSURE-COOKING

The best guide is the manufacturer's instructions which come with the pressure saucepan.

BAKING

Most frozen vegetables can be cooked well by baking in a covered casserole. (It takes longer than boiling, but if your oven is running anyway, why not try it?)

Partially defrost the vegetable to separate the pieces; put it in a buttered casserole. Add the seasonings you like. Cover and bake at about 350 F. Most thawed vegetables cook in about 45 minutes.

For corn-on-the-cob, brush the partially thawed ears with butter or margarine and salt, then roast at 400 F. about 20 minutes.

PAN-FRYING

Use a heavy skillet with a cover. Put in about 1 tablespoon of table fat for each 1 pint of the frozen vegetable (which has thawed enough to separate in pieces). Cook tightly covered over moderate heat, stirring occasionally, until tender. Season to taste, and serve right away.

Asparagus, broccoli and peas will cook tender in about 10 minutes. Mushrooms will be done in 15 minutes. Green/snap/wax beans pan-fry to tenderness in 15 to 20 minutes.

REHEATING

Those vegetables fully cooked before freezing—usually leftovers—just need gentle reheating to serving temperature.

Frozen vegetables used in made dishes are treated like fresh ones. They're good creamed or scalloped, served au gratin or added to soufflés, cream soups and salads. See Recipes.

Asparagus

Prepare. Sort for size, wash well. Peel slightly tough ends *c.* 2 inches back from the bottom, cut off the really tough ends. Leave spears in lengths to fit the package, or cut in 2-inch pieces.

Blanch. In boiling water—small-diameter stalks for 2 minutes, medium stalks for 3 minutes, thick ones for 4 minutes. Cool immediately; drain.

Pack. Leave no headroom. With spears, alternate tips and stem ends; if it's a wide-top container, pack tips down.

Seal; freeze.

Beans, Lima

These are handier canned: but freeze the tenderest ones, if you can afford the space.

Prepare. Shell and sort for size.

Blanch. In boiling water—small beans for 2 minutes, medium for 3 minutes, large for 4 minutes. Cool immediately and drain.

Pack. Leave ½ inch of headroom.

Seal; freeze.

Beans, fresh Shell

Prepare. Shell and wash.

Blanch. In boiling water—1 minute. Cool immediately and drain.

Pack. Leave ½ inch of headroom.

Seal; freeze.

Beans—Snap/String/Green/Italian

These also can well. Fancy young tender ones are better frozen.

Prepare. Cut in 1- or 2-inch pieces, or in lengthwise strips (frenching), or leave whole if they're very young and tender.

Blanch. In boiling water—for 3 minutes. Cool immediately, drain well.

Pack. Leave ½ inch of headroom.

Seal; freeze.

Beets

Baby ones are worth freezer space. (Why not can larger ones plain or pickled?)

Prepare. Wash and sort for size—maximum 3 inches, small are best. Leave on tails and ½ inch of stem so their juice won't bleed out while boiling.

Boil. Until tender—25 to 30 minutes for small beets, 45 to 50 for medium. Cool quickly. Slip off skins; trim and cut in slices or cubes.

Pack. Leave ½ inch of headroom for cubes; no headroom for whole or sliced.

Seal; freeze.

Broccoli

Prepare. Peel coarse stalks, trimming off leaves and blemishes; split if necessary. Salt-soak for ½ hour (1 tablespoon salt for each 1 quart cold water) to drive out bugs; wash well. Sort for uniform spears, or cut up.

Blanch. In steam—5 minutes for stalks; in boiling water—3 minutes for stalks. (Reduce blanching time for cut-up or chopped.) Cool immediately; drain.

Pack. Leave no headroom for spears or large chunks; arrange stalks so blossom ends are divided between either end of the container. Leave ½ inch of headroom for cut-up or chopped (they have less air space).

Seal; freeze.

Brussels Sprouts

Give freezer space only to the best heads.

Prepare. Salt-soak as for Broccoli if necessary. Wash well. Trim off outer leaves. Sort for size.

Blanch. In boiling water—small heads for 3 minutes, medium heads for 4 minutes, large heads for 5 minutes. Cool immediately, drain well.

Pack. Leave no headroom.

Seal; freeze.

Cabbage (and Chinese Cabbage)

Plan to use these only in cooked dishes: after being frozen they aren't crisp enough for salads.

Prepare. Trim off coarse outer leaves; cut heads in medium or coarse shreds or thin wedges, or separate into leaves.

Blanch. In boiling water—1½ minutes. Cool immediately and drain.

Pack. Leave ½ inch of headroom.

Seal; freeze.

Carrots

These cold-store and can well, so freeze only the fancy young ones (preferably whole).

Prepare. Remove tops, wash and peel. Leave baby ones whole; cut others into ¼-inch cubes, thin slices or lengthwise strips.

Blanch. In boiling water—tiny whole ones for 5 minutes; dice, slices, or lengthwise strips for 2 minutes. Cool immediately; drain.

Pack. Leave ½ inch of headroom.

Seal; freeze.

Cauliflower

Infinitely better frozen than canned.

Prepare. Break or cut flowerets apart in pieces *c.* 1 inch across. Salt-soak as for Broccoli for ½ hour to get rid of bugs, etc. Wash thoroughly; drain.

Blanch. In boiling salted water (1 teaspoon salt to each 1 quart of water)—3 minutes. Cool immediately; drain.

Pack. Leave no headroom.

Seal; freeze.

Celery

Usable only in cooked dishes, so assign it freezer space accordingly. See also "Dabs and Snippets" at the end of Combination Dishes, in the Freezing section.

Prepare. Strip any coarse strings from any young stalks; wash well, trim, and cut in 1-inch pieces.

Blanch. In boiling water—3 minutes. Cool immediately; drain.

Pack. Leave ½ inch of headroom.

Seal; freeze.

Corn

Feasibility for freezing sweet corn: whole-kernel, Yes (it's better than canning); cream-style, Maybe (it's certainly handier canned, and there's not much difference in the product); on-the-cob, No—unless you've got loads of freezer space and don't mind thawing it before cooking it for the table (it shouldn't be popped frozen into the pot because the kernels will be cooked to death by the time the core of the cob is hot through). See Recipes.

WHOLE-KERNEL

Prepare. Choose ears with thin, sweet milk; husk, de-silk and wash. (Cut from cob *after* blanching.)

Blanch. In boiling water—4 minutes. Cool ears immediately; drain.

Pack. Cut from cob about 2/3 the depth of the kernels, and don't scrape in any milk. Leave ½ inch of headroom.

Seal; freeze.

CREAM-STYLE

Prepare. Choose ears with thick and starchy milk. Husk, de-silk and wash. (Cut from cob *after* blanching.)

Blanch. In boiling water—4 minutes. Cool immediately; drain.

Pack. Cut from the cob at about the center of the kernels, then scrape the cobs with the back of the knife to force out the hearts of the kernels and the juice (milk); mix with cut corn. Pack, leaving ½ inch of headroom.

Seal; freeze.

ON-THE-COB

Prepare. Choose ears with thin, sweet milk (as for whole-kernel). Husk, de-silk, wash; sort for size.

Blanch. In boiling water—small ears (1¼ inches or less in diameter) for 7 minutes, medium ears (to 1½ inches) for 9 minutes, large ears (over 1½ inches) for 11 minutes. Cool immediately; drain.

Pack. In containers, or wrap in moisture-vapor-resistant material.

Seal; freeze.

MAVERICK FREEZING IN THE HUSK

People who know the *Why's* and the *How's* of freezing say: "Never freeze corn without blanching it first to stop enzymatic action." But one hears of corn frozen successfully in its husk (though de-silked), without blanching.

> *Note:* "Successfully" doesn't mean much unless you make the comparison by using identical ears from the same crop, picked and treated and frozen at the same time and for the same period, and cooked the same way for the same meal. Compare it right yourself—prepare it as described below (but eat it before Thanksgiving, because its storage life is bound to be short).

Prepare and pack. Without husking, pull out the silk; and, to save freezer space, remove a little of the outer husk. Do not blanch. Put ears in plastic bags simply to keep the freezer clean.

Freeze.

Greens, Garden

Prepare. Remove imperfect leaves, trim away tough midribs and tough stems; cut large leaves (like chard) in pieces. Wash carefully, lifting from the water to let silt settle.

Blanch. In boiling water—spinach, New Zealand spinach, kale, chard, mustard and beet and turnip greens: all for 2 minutes; collards for 3 minutes.
Cool immediately; drain.

Pack. Leave ½ inch of headroom.

Seal; freeze.

Greens, Wild

Prepare. Collect and clean fiddleheads (ostrich fern) according to directions given in Recipes, blanch for 2 minutes. Drain and cool.

Collect and clean dandelions according to directions given in Recipes. If you like the slightly bitter taste, merely blanch the very tenderest leaves for 1½ minutes; otherwise boil in two or more waters. Drain and cool.

Collect milkweed and boil in several waters according to directions given in Recipes. Drain and cool.

Collect American cowslips (the marsh-marigold) and bring to boiling in several waters, cooking thoroughly to get rid of toxin. Drain and cool.

Pack. Leave ½ inch of headroom.

Seal; freeze.

Jerusalem Artichokes

Treat like Kohlrabi or small Turnips (q.v.).

Kohlrabi

Prepare. Cut off the tops and roots of small to medium kohlrabi. Wash, peel; leave whole or dice in ½-inch cubes.

Blanch. In boiling water—whole for 3 minutes, cubes 1 minute. Cool immediately and drain.

Pack. Whole in containers or wrap in moisture-vapor-resistant material. Cubes in containers, leaving ½ inch of headroom.

Seal; freeze.

Mushrooms

Prepare. Wash carefully in cold water. Cut off ends of stems. Leave stems on fancy small buttons if you like; if mushrooms are larger than 1 inch across the caps, slice or quarter them. If serving cold (in salads, etc.), blanch in steam; if serving hot (as garnish for meats, or in combination dishes), precook.

Blanch. In one layer, over steam—whole for 5 minutes, quarters or small caps for 3½ minutes, slices for 3 minutes. (This also prevents darkening; see "How To Prevent Darkening" at the start of Freezing Fruits.) Cool immediately; drain.

Precooking. In table fat—sauté in a skillet until nearly done. Air-cool, or set the skillet in cold water (you'll freeze them in the good buttery juice from the pan).

Pack. Leave ½ inch of headroom.

Seal; freeze.

Okra (Gumbo)

Use in soups and stews.

Prepare. Wash. Cut off stems, being careful not to open the seed cells.

Blanch. In boiling water—small pods 3 minutes, large pods 4 minutes. Cool immediately; drain. Leave whole, or cut in crosswise slices.

Pack. Leave ½ inch of headroom.

Seal; freeze.

Parsnips

Really best left in the ground over winter for the first fresh treat of spring—freezing is only a second choice.
Treat like Carrots.

Peas, Black-eyed (Cowpeas, Black-eyed Beans)

Prepare. Shell; save only the tender peas.

Blanch. In boiling water—for 2 minutes. Cool immediately, drain well.

Pack. Leave ½ inch of headroom.

Seal; freeze.

Peas, Green

Prepare. Shell; use only sweet, tender peas.

Blanch. In boiling water—for 1½ minutes. Cool immediately; drain.

Pack. Leave ½ inch of headroom.

Seal; freeze.

Peppers, Green (Bell, Sweet)

Here is a vegetable that *does not require* blanching: the brief pre-cooking described below is designed to make them more limp, so you can pack more peppers in the container—and it's for large-ish pieces you plan to use in cooked dishes, at that.

If you plan to serve them raw (for instance in thin rings as a garnish, or diced in a salad), don't bother to blanch.

Prepare. Wash; cut out stems, cut in half, remove seeds. Leave in halves, or cut in slices, strips, rings or dice (depending on future use).

If blanched. In boiling water—halves for 3 minutes, slices for 2 minutes. Cool immediately; drain.

Pack. Blanched, leave ½ inch of headroom. Raw, leave no headroom.

Seal; freeze.

Peppers, Hot

Prepare. Wash and stem.

Blanch. No.

Pack. Leave no headroom.

Seal; freeze.

Pimientos

Prepare. Wash and dry crisp, thick-walled pimientos.

Roast. In a 400 F. oven—for 3 to 4 minutes. Rinse and rub off charred skins in cold water. Drain.

Pack. Leave ½ inch of headroom.

Seal; freeze.

Pumpkin

Pumpkin makes fine pies and breads (see Recipes), but is seldom used as a table vegetable. Why not can it instead?

Prepare. Wash whole pumpkin; cut or break in pieces. Remove seeds. Do not peel.

Precook. Until soft—in boiling water, steam, a pressure cooker or in the oven. Scrape pulp from rind; mash through a sieve. Cool immediately.

Pack. Leave ½ inch of headroom.

Seal; freeze.

Rutabagas

Prepare. Cut off tops of young, medium-sized rutabagas; wash and peel. Cut in cubes to freeze merely blanched, or in large chunks to cook and mash before freezing.

Blanch (for cubes). In boiling water—for 2 minutes. Cool immediately; drain.

Cook (chunks to mash). In boiling water until tender. Drain; mash or sieve. Cool immediately.

Pack. Leave ½ inch of headroom for either cubed or mashed.

Seal; freeze.

Squash, Summer (and Zucchini)

Only young squash with small seeds and tender rinds are suitable for freezing.

Prepare. Cut off blossom and stem ends; wash and cut in slices.

Blanch. In boiling water—for 3 minutes. Cool immediately in ice water; drain well.

Pack. Leave ½ inch of headroom.

Seal; freeze.

Squash, Winter

Root-cellar mature squash with hard rinds. Treat it like Pumpkin if you do freeze it, though.

Soybeans

Prepare. To serve as a vegetable, wash firm, well-filled, bright-green pods (shell *after* blanching).

Blanch. In boiling water—5 minutes. Cool quickly. Squeeze beans out of pods.

Pack. Leave ½ inch of headroom.

Seal; freeze.

Sweet Potatoes (and Yams)

Use medium to large sweet potatoes that have air-dried (to cure) after being dug. Pack whole, sliced or mashed.

Prepare. Sort for size; wash. Leave skins on.

Precook. Cook, until almost tender, in water, steam, a pressure cooker or an oven. Cool at room temperature. Peel; cut in halves, slices or mash.

Prevent darkening. Dip whole peeled sweet potatoes or slices for 5 seconds in a solution of 1 tablespoon citric acid or ½ cup lemon juice and 1 quart of water. For mashed sweet potatoes mix 2 tablespoons orange or lemon juice with each quart.

Pack. Leave ½ inch of headroom.

Pack variations. Roll slices in sugar. Or cover whole or sliced with a cold 50 Percent Sirup. In either case, leave appropriate headroom.

Seal; freeze.

Tomatoes

Tomatoes are so easy to can—and are so handy in several table-ready forms—that we question the feasibility of freezing them. And aside from taking up a good deal of freezer space, a frozen whole tomato has limited appeal: its tender flesh is ruptured by ice crystals, and you have a deflated mush when you defrost it.

STEWED TOMATOES

Prepare. Remove stem ends and cores of ripe tomatoes; peel and quarter.

Cook. In a covered enameled or stainless-steel kettle, cook gently in their own juice until tender—10 to 20 minutes. Set the kettle bodily in cold water to cool the contents.

Pack. Leave appropriate headroom.

Seal; freeze.

TOMATO JUICE

Prepare. Cut vine-ripened tomatoes in quarters or smaller. In an enameled or stainless-steel kettle simmer them in their own juice for 5 to 10 minutes—or until tender with a good deal of liquid. Put through a sieve or food mill. Season with ½ teaspoon salt to each pint of juice, or 1 teaspoon to each quart.

Pack. Leave appropriate headroom.

Seal; freeze.

Turnips, White

Turnips are similar to rutabagas, but they mature more quickly. Freeze them in cubes or fully cooked and mashed. They also keep well in the root cellar.

Cubes: treat like Rutabagas.

Mashed: treat like Winter Squash or Pumpkin.

Freezing Meat

For handling meat from large animals, see the introduction to Canning Meat and Poultry: the same safeguards and methods for cutting meat apply to meat that is to be frozen.

To avoid disappointment, before you buy a whole, half or quarter of an animal, find out what cuts it will yield—and how many. There is 20 to 25 percent waste, regardless; and usually there will be more pounds of stewing and/or ground meat than pounds of steaks and roasts and chops.

COOKING FROZEN MEAT

Generally, any cut of meat may be cooked either frozen or thawed—which leaves the decision up to you. How do you plan to serve it?

THAW THESE:

—Meat to be coated with crumbs before cooking.

—Meat to be browned as the first step in cooking.

—Ground meat that must be shaped for cooking.

—Large roasts: they can overcook on the outside before the inner part is done, if they're not defrosted first.

APPROXIMATE THAWING TIMES FOR MEAT

In the refrigerator: large roasts—4 to 5 hours per pound; small roasts—3 hours per pound.

At room temperature: 1 hour per pound for roasts and packages of stewing-size pieces or ground meat.

THESE MAY BE COOKED FROZEN:

—Preshaped ground meat patties.

—Meat loaves.

—Thin steaks or chops.

—Meatballs in their own gravy or broth.

APPROXIMATE TIMES FOR COOKING FROZEN MEAT

Roasting. If you're caught short of time and must roast a big piece of frozen meat, do it in a preheated oven *about 25 degrees lower* than generally used for roasting unfrozen meat (that is, do it in an oven not more than 300 F.), and *increase the roasting time by one-half.* Neither adjustment need be made for day-long or overnight roasting of frozen meat at below 200 F. temperatures.

Broiling. Broil frozen meat of any thickness *at least 5 to 6 inches below* the heat source, and *increase broiling time by one-half.*

Pan-broiling. Cook frozen *thin* hamburgers, chops and steaks in a *very hot skillet* with a small amount of fat swished around to keep meat from sticking.

Start to cook frozen *thicker* patties, chops and steaks in a *warm skillet* with 1 tablespoon of fat. Heat the meat slowly and turn it until thawed. Then *increase the heat* and pan-broil the meat as for unfrozen thin cuts.

Freezing Roasts

Prepare. Trim away excess fat. Wipe with a clean damp cloth. Pad protruding sharp bones with fat or with extra wrapping, so they can't pierce the package.

Pack and seal. Package individual roasts tightly in sheet wrapping, using either the butcher wrap or drugstore fold.

Label; freeze.

THE DRUGSTORE FOLD	**THE BUTCHER WRAP**

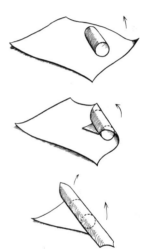

Roll folded edge down, turn over

Fold ends of roll down

Ends up and over, tuck tight

Sides over end

Tuck sides in

Fold tip of point over

Fold up and tape

Roll to end of paper—
seal open edges with tape

Freezing Chops and Steaks

Prepare. Trim away excess fat. Wipe with a clean damp cloth.

Pack and seal. Package, in sheet wrapping, the number needed for one meal. Put a double layer of wrapping between individual chops/ steaks or layers of chops/steaks. Press outer sheet wrapping closely to the bundle of meat to exclude air. Use either the butcher wrap or drugstore fold.

Label; freeze.

Freezing Ground Meat

Use only freshly ground meat to freeze as patties, loaves or in bulk. Freshly made pork sausage (see recipe in the Roundup section) also may be frozen; but its freezer life is short because of its high fat content.

PATTIES

Prepare. Make up ready to cook—but omit onion, which loses its flavor in frozen foods.

Pack and seal. Put double layers of lightweight freezer wrap between patties for easy separation when you are ready to cook them. In each bundle, tightly wrap enough patties for one meal, using either the butcher wrap or drugstore fold.

Label; freeze.

LOAVES, COOKED

Prepare. Cool cooked loaves, remove from baking pan.

Pack and seal. Wrap tightly, using either the butcher wrap or drugstore fold.

Label; freeze.

LOAVES, UNCOOKED

Prepare. Mix loaves as for baking. Line loaf pans with foil; fill with meat-loaf mixture and fold ends of foil over meat. *Freeze.*

Pack and seal. Remove loaves from pans when frozen, and overwrap tightly, using either the butcher wrap or drugstore fold.

Label; store in freezer.

BULK

Pack and seal. Put meal-size quantities in freezer boxes or bags, excluding air. Seal tightly.

Label; freeze.

Freezing Stew Meat

Prepare. Cut in cubes. For easier use later, pan-brown them; but they may be packed without browning.

Pack and seal. Fill rigid containers with meal-size portions of browned cubes. Cover with pan liquid or broth, leaving ½ inch of headroom. Seal.

Pack unbrowned cubes in rigid containers, freezer bags or sheet wrapping, excluding air. Seal tightly.

Label; freeze.

Freezing Cooked Meat

Prepare. It's better to freeze cooked meat or poultry in large pieces (so less surface may be exposed to air). Slices of meat or poultry keep best if covered with broth or gravy.

Pack and seal. Large pieces are wrapped tightly, using either the butcher wrap or drugstore fold. Slices are stored in rigid containers of suitable size and covered with broth or gravy, then closely covered and sealed.

Label; freeze.

Freezing Store-bought Cuts

(Meaning those prepackaged fresh meats from the market's display case.)

Pack and seal. Remove the store wrapping—even though it is well sealed; discard the tray, and rewrap and seal the meat closely in your own freezing materials. This will close out air and give the meat a more durable cover. (There's too much air held in store packages—and this causes freezer burn; also, the clear film that's O.K. to sell it in is not strong enough for freezer storage.)

Label; freeze.

Freezing Poultry and Small Game

For handling domestic poultry, wild birds, domestic rabbits and small game, see the introduction to Canning Meat: the same safeguards apply to freezing these foods. For specifics on dressing–plucking/skinning and drawing–and cutting up the meat, see Canning Poultry.

All freshly killed and dressed birds are better if stored in the refrigerator for 12 hours to develop their greatest tenderness before freezing.

COOKING FROZEN POULTRY

Here again, "poultry" applies to domestic and wild birds, domestic rabbits and small game.

For best results, thaw before cooking (unless you're boiling it to use in a fricassee or such): roasting and broiling is more uniform if the poultry is thawed first, and the meat is less likely to be dry or rubbery. Pieces to be coated before frying, or browned before stewing, should always be thawed beforehand. It's easier to stuff a thawed bird than one that's still frozen.

Cook all poultry immediately after thawing.

APPROXIMATE THAWING TIMES FOR FROZEN POULTRY

Thaw it in its freezer wrappings.

In the refrigerator: 2 hours per pound.

At room temperature: 1 hour per pound.

Before a cold-air fan: 20 minutes per pound. Don't try to hasten thawing by using a hot-air fan.

Freezing Birds Whole

Any bird may be frozen whole for future stuffing and roasting.

Prepare. Tie legs of dressed, washed birds together with thighs close to body; press wings snugly against breast.

Pack and seal. Put bird in a freeze bag, press out air and tightly close the bag top. Or wrap the bird in moisture-vapor-resistant material (see wrapping illustrations); seal tightly. Pack and freeze giblets separately.

Label; freeze.

STUFF IT LATER

Even if the cook is careful at every step, dangerous bacteria causing food spoilage can develop in poultry stuffed at home and then frozen: *normal roasting will not kill heat-resistant bacteria in the center of the densely stuffed cavity.* Prestuffed frozen birds sold by big commercial processors are prepared under controlled conditions of temperature and humidity, etc., that cannot be duplicated in the home.

Freezing Birds in Halves

Prepare. Split dressed, washed birds lengthwise and cut off the backbone (use it in soup stock).

Pack and seal. Put a double layer of freezer paper between the halves. Pack and seal in a freezer bag or wrap as for Whole.

Label; freeze.

Freezing Birds in Smaller Pieces

Prepare. Cut in pieces suitable for intended use (see Canning Poultry).

Pack and seal. Put meaty pieces close together in freezer bag or carton; wrap tightly in sheet material. Seal.

Label; freeze.

Freezing Birds in Cooked Dishes, see Convenience Dishes.

173

Freezing Fish and Shellfish

Freezing is the best method for preserving the fresh qualities of fish and shellfish (see also Salting and Smoking).

For ideal results, freeze all seafood immediately after it's caught. At least do it within 24 hours, and keep the fish packed in ice in the refrigerator while it waits.

Any fish or shellfish are safely and easily frozen, although certain species' characteristics dictate slight differences in the way you prepare them for the freezer.

All fish and shellfish must be stored at ZERO FAHRENHEIT (−18 Centigrade) *after initial sharp freezing at* c. −20 F.

PRELIMINARIES TO FREEZING FISH

For handling, fish may be divided into two categories: Lean and Fat.

The Fat—mackerel, pink and chum salmon, ocean perch, smelt (herring), lake trout, flounder, shad and tuna—are more perishable than the leaner varieties; plan to freezer-store these not more than 3 months.

The Lean fish—cod, haddock, halibut, yellow pike, yellow perch, fresh-water herring, Coho and King and red salmon—all keep well in frozen storage up to 6 months.

DRESSING (CLEANING)

Scale the fish (or skin it, depending on the variety); remove fins and tail. Slit the belly with a thin-bladed sharp knife and remove the entrails, saving any roe. Cut off the head if you wish. Wash the fish in cold water.

FLAVOR-PROTECTING DIPS

The Fat fish (and roe) are given a 20-second dip in an *ascorbic-acid* solution—2 teaspoons crystalline ascorbic acid dissolved in 1 quart of cold water—to lessen the chance of rancidity and flavor change during storage.

The Lean fish are dipped for 20 seconds in a *brine* of 1 cup salt to 1 gallon of cold water; this firms the flesh and reduces leakage when the fish thaws.

GLAZING WITH ICE

Sometimes whole fish or pieces of fish are ice-glazed before wrapping. This helps keep the air away, thus saving the flavor. The fish is frozen until solid, then dipped quickly in and out of ice-cold water, whereupon a thin coat of ice will form on the fish. Repeat several times to thicken the ice, then wrap the fish for storage.

CUTTING TO SIZE

Fish are frozen whole if they are small enough (under 2 pounds); or are cut in steaks—crosswise slices about 1 inch thick, or are filleted. Exception: large-ish fish you expect to bake whole, you freeze whole.

Fillets are made usually from fish weighing 2 to 4 pounds. Lay the cleaned fish on its side on a clean cutting-board. Run a thin-bladed sharp knife the length of the backbone and slightly above it, and continue cutting to separate the side of the fish from the backbone and ribs; repeat on the opposite side. (This works on most fish; but not on shad— whose build is so complicated that it takes special skill to fillet them.)

COOKING FROZEN FISH AND SHELLFISH

With two exceptions, frozen seafood may be cooked when still frozen— the exceptions being a large whole fish you're baking and pieces that are to be crumbed or coated with batter before cooking.

Small whole fish—under ½ pound—may be defrosted just enough to separate them before they're fried (without crumbs or batter coating) or broiled on a greased broiler.

Fish fillets and steaks are baked or poached from the frozen state; they're partially defrosted before broiling or frying (without crumbs or batter coating).

Shellfish and fish for stews, chowders and Newburgs are cooked still frozen.

Freezing Large Whole Fish

Prepare. Dress (clean) as above, removing the head if you wish.

Pack and seal. Glaze with ice (q.v. above). Wrap snugly with moisture-vapor-proof covering, using the butcher wrap or drugstore fold—then overwrap for security. Seal.

Label; freeze.

Freezing Small Whole Fish

Prepare. Dress as for large whole fish, leaving on heads if you like.

Pack and seal. Small whole fish are most often packed in rigid containers with added cold water to fill crevices between the fish. Hold the lid tightly on the container with freezer tape wrapped around the rim, and overwrap with moisture-vapor-proof freezer paper, using the butcher wrap or drugstore fold. Seal.

For easy separation in thawing, individual small fish may be enclosed in a household plastic bag or other clear wrapping before going into the rigid freezer containers. Proceed with overwrap, and seal.

Sport fishermen often freeze their catch covered with water in large bread pans or the like, the whole thing sealed in a freezer bag, and frozen. When solid, the block of fish-in-ice is removed from the pan and tightly wrapped in moisture-vapor-proof material, closed with the butcher wrap or drugstore fold, then sealed.

Label; freeze.

Freezing Fish Fillets and Steaks

Prepare. Dress and cut up strictly fresh fish. Treat Fat fish pieces with the ascorbic-acid dip, or Lean fish pieces with the brine dip (q.v.). Fillets may also be glazed with ice before wrapping.

Pack and seal. Fill rigid containers with layers of fillets or steaks, dividing layers with double sheets of freezer wrap for easy separation when frozen. Cover and seal.

For even greater odor prevention, overwrap the container with sheet freezer material, using the butcher wrap or drugstore fold.

Layers of fillets and steaks may also be wrapped in bundles and sealed instead of going into rigid containers; the bundles are then overwrapped and sealed.

Label; freeze.

Freezing Fish Roe

Roe is more perishable than the rest of the fish, so it should be frozen and stored separately from the fish.

Prepare. Carefully wash each set of roe from strictly fresh fish and prick the covering membrane in several places with a sterilized fine needle. Treat the roe with an ascorbic-acid dip (q.v.), even though it may come from a Lean fish.

Pack and seal. Wrap each set of roe closely in lightweight plastic for easy separation when frozen, smoothing out all air. Pack in flat layers in rigid containers and seal; then overwrap the containers in moisture-vapor-proof material, using the butcher wrap or drugstore fold. Seal.

Label; freeze. (Sharp-freeze at −20 F.; store at Zero F. or below for not more than 3 months before using.)

Freezing Eels

Prepare. Skin the eel. Tie a stout cord tightly around the fish below the head and secure the end of the cord to a strong, fixed support (a post or whatever). About 3 inches behind the head, cut completely through the skin around the body of the eel, necklace fashion. Grip the cut edge of the skin and pull it downward, removing the entire skin inside out.

Remove the entrails; wash the eel.

Cut in fillets or in the more usual steak-type rounds.

Because eel is a Fat fish, treat the pieces with an ascorbic-acid dip. Pack as for fillets or steaks of other fish, above. Seal.

Label; freeze.

Freezing Crab and Lobster Meat

Prepare. Boil absolutely fresh live crabs or lobsters in their shells for 10 to 20 minutes (depending on size), or until the shells become red; cool quickly in cold water. Pick out the meat.

Pack and seal. Fill rigid containers solidly with meal-size amounts; add no liquid, but leave ½ inch of headroom. Seal.

Label; freeze.

Freezing Shrimp

As with other shellfish, shrimp you freeze must be absolutely fresh. They are best frozen raw, though they may be precooked as for the table before you freeze them.

RAW SHRIMP

Prepare. Wash, cut off the heads and take out the sand vein. Shelling is optional. Wash again in a mild salt solution of 1 teaspoon salt to each 1 quart of water. Drain well.

Pack and seal. Pack snugly in rigid freezer containers without any headroom. Seal tightly.

Label; freeze.

COOKED SHRIMP

Prepare. Wash in a mild salt solution of 1 teaspoon salt to each 1 quart of water; remove heads. Boil gently in lightly salted water for 10 minutes. Cool. Slit the shell and remove the sand vein (for table-ready use remove shells and vein). Rinse quickly. Drain.

Pack and seal. Pack snugly in rigid freezer containers, without any headroom. Seal tightly.

Label; freeze.

Freezing Oysters, Clams, Mussels and Scallops

Probably the most perishable of the shellfish, these should be frozen within hours of the time they leave the sea and *held at refrigerator temperature* (c. *36 F.*) during any waiting period.

Cooked oysters, clams and mussels toughen in the freezer: freeze them raw.

Prepare. Wash in cold water while still in their shells to rid them of sand. Shuck them over a bowl to catch the natural liquid. Wash them quickly again in a brine of 4 tablespoons salt to 1 gallon of water.

Shucking is removing the shells. Since shucking bivalves (oysters, clams, etc.) involves severing the two strong muscles that close the two halves of the shell, you can cut yourself badly if you go about it wrong. *DO NOT USE a sharp or pointed knife.* Instead, use a dull blade with a rounded tip; insert it between the lips of the shell just beyond one end of the hinge, twist to cut the muscle at that point, and repeat at the other end of the hinge. A good shucker does it in one continuous *safe* motion: get someone who knows how, to show you.

Pack and seal. Put in rigid containers and cover with their own juice, extended with a weak brine of 1 teaspoon salt to 1 cup of water. Scallops are packed tightly, then covered with the brine (they have little juice). Leave ½ inch of headroom—unless the container is larger than 3-cup size (more than 3-cup is not advised: it takes too long to defrost; see the table "Headroom for Freezing Fruits and Vegetables"). Seal tightly.

Label; freeze.

Freezing Dairy Products and Eggs

Freezing Milk

Homogenized milk freezes smoothly and may be stored for up to 3 months. But the fat in milk that is not homogenized separates out as flakes, and these won't blend again when the milk thaws.

Prepare and seal. Homogenized milk in its tightly sealed carton—just as it comes from the dairy—is ready for the freezer. Or it may be transferred to rigid freezer containers and sealed with appropriate headroom.

Label; freeze.

Freezing Cream

Frozen heavy cream whips nicely, but it separates and sends an oily film to the top of hot coffee. Probably it is frozen best as dollops of whipped cream to be used on individual cold desserts.

Prepare and seal. Whip; sweeten if you like. Drop in small mounds on a cookie sheet. Freeze uncovered. Remove; pack with a double layer of plastic wrap between the dollops in rigid freezer containers. Seal.

Label; freeze.

Freezing Butter

Salted butter. Freeze in its store carton for a month or two. For longer storage, overwrap and seal.

Unsalted (fresh) butter loses flavor more quickly than salted does. Over-wrap, seal, and freeze it immediately after you make it or get it.

Freezing Ice Cream

Either purchased or home-made ice cream keeps its quality up to 2 months in the freezer.

Prepare and seal. Purchase or make the ice cream. Pack in rigid, tight-sealing containers. Seal.

Label; freeze. (When using up only part of a container, cover the remainder with a sheet of plastic to keep air away, so crystals won't form.)

Freezing Cheese

Cheeses which freeze well are Camembert, Port du Salut, Mozarella, Liederkrantz and their cousins, and Parmesan.

Cheeses with a high fat content (such as Cheddar, Swiss, and American brick, etc.), are best kept at refrigerator temperatures (32 to 40 F.). If you have more than you can use soon, though, cut it in ½-pound (or less) pieces, wrap each piece tightly, label and freeze.

Plain cream cheese (fatty) mixed with cream for dips, etc., will freeze satisfactorily.

If the curds of cottage cheese are *not washed,* it keeps quite well. This means you can freeze home-made cottage cheese, but not the commercial kind.

Freezing Eggs

Freezing is a fine way to save seasonably abundant eggs (see also Water-glassing), because, properly frozen, they do their cooking thing just as well as fresh ones do.

Use only strictly fresh eggs—those kept refrigerated from nest to freezer.

Open the eggs (freezing expansion would break the shells) and pack them in meal- or recipe-size quantities.

You'll need about 10 whole eggs *or* 16 large egg whites *or* 24 egg yolks to fill a 1-pint container.

Note: Examine each egg for quality before adding it to others, whether you're freezing them whole or separated. For whole eggs, break each into a saucer, and look for desirable firm whites and plump, high-standing yolks; for separated eggs, put each white and each yolk in a saucer before adding either to the batch you are freezing.

WHOLE EGGS

Prepare. Examine each egg as above. Break all yolks with a fork, then slowly and carefully mix them with the whites so as to get *no foam*: beaten-in air bubbles will dry out the eggs.

To keep the yolks from thickening add 1 teaspoon salt to each 1 pint for scrambled eggs, etc., or 1 tablespoon sugar to each 1 pint of eggs for future desserts.

Pack and seal. Fill rigid containers, leaving ½ inch of headroom. Seal

Label; freeze. (Labeling is extra important here, unless you don't mind sweet scrambled eggs.)

EGG YOLKS ALONE

Prepare. Mix yolks well but without foaming; add ½ teaspoon salt to each ½-pint of yolks for main dishes or 1½ teaspoons sugar to each ½-pint for future dessert uses.

Pack and seal. Fill rigid containers, leaving ½ inch of headroom. Seal.

Label; freeze.

EGG WHITES ONLY

Prepare. Separate whites from yolks of good-quality eggs.

Pack and seal. Just fill containers *without* added salt or sugar, leaving ½ inch of headroom. Seal.

Label; freeze.

Thawing Frozen Eggs

It's best to thaw eggs in the refrigerator, where it takes 8 to 10 hours to thaw a pint. They may be thawed in their containers under cold *running* water in 2 to 3 hours.

After defrosting, use them as you do fresh eggs.

Never refreeze thawed eggs!

Freezing Convenience Dishes

Keep your freezer busy—at least ¾ full. Restock it with cooked or ready-to-cook dishes as the traditional meats and vegetables, etc., are used up. You'll be ready for unexpected guests, parties, emergencies or a "goof-off" day.

MAKE YOUR OWN BONUS

Fix a larger amount than normal of a food your family likes; eat some and freeze the surplus in meal-size packages. Certain slow-cooked foods, or ones calling for special equipment that's a nuisance to use, are freezer-fodder. Best feature: you can work at your convenience.

PACKAGING

Cool food quickly. Pack in family-size amounts, using appropriately sealed freezer wraps and/or containers; and, for surest results, overwrap and seal most convenience foods with a second layer of freezer wrapping. Store at Zero F. or lower.

A good trick for casseroles: Line the dish you'll later reheat and serve it in with heavy-duty foil, fill with food, and freeze until solid; remove the shaped block of food and its foil liner and overwrap it and seal. Label; store in the freezer.

Freezing Main Dishes, in General

EASY TO FREEZE

Creamed foods, stews, most casseroles, meat pies, croquettes and spaghetti sauce freeze well, as do cooked meats if covered with broth or gravy.

Undercook any vegetables you're including in such a main dish: they finish cooking when the whole thing is reheated.

BEST THICKENERS

If you're making a sauce to be frozen, use to thicken it (if you can find them) as much waxy corn or waxy rice flour as you would wheat flour, or twice as much as you would cornstarch.

PITFALLS TO SUCCESS:

—Fried foods almost always tend to become rancid, tough and dry; store them for only a short time.

—Sauces heavy in fat are likely to separate when reheated; stirring well usually recombines them.

—Sauces with much milk or cheese often curdle from freezing (but they're still good to eat).

—Uncooked potatoes change texture unpleasantly when frozen.

—Hard-cooked egg *whites* become tough when frozen.

—Flavors of garlic and clove grow stronger during freezing; onion, salt and herb flavors vanish.

—Crumb-and-cheese toppings on casseroles (see "Packaging" above) get soggy in the freezer, so add them when food is to be reheated.

TO REHEAT

Stews and creamed dishes are reheated in a double-boiler, or in a heat-proof dish set in a pan of hot water in a 350 F. oven. Stir as little as possible.

Thaw croquettes or other breaded foods uncovered in the refrigerator before heating or frying.

Freezing Baked Goods

BREADS

Fresh-cooked muffins, biscuits, yeast bread and rolls, thoroughly cooled and snugly wrapped, freeze nicely.

Loaves of garlic-buttered bread can be prepared, foil-wrapped, and frozen for later heating.

Uncooked *thin-rolled* biscuits can be frozen.

Uncooked loaves of bread dough—made with double the usual quantity of yeast—may be frozen. Let them rise after defrosting at room temperature before you bake them.

PIE PASTRY

Pie pastry you plan to freeze should have the maximum amount of shortening your recipe calls for, so the crust will have the desired tenderness (freezing could make the texture cardboardy if you scamped on the fat).

Both baked and unbaked pie crusts freeze well.

Baked crusts. These break less if wrapped and frozen in their pie pans.

Unbaked crusts. Roll these out to size and stack on heavy cardboard cut to the same size and covered with waxed paper. Lay on it a flat rolled crust, cover the crust with *two* sheets of waxed paper, then add another rolled crust. Up to 6 crusts may be stacked, ending with a waxed-paper cover. Wrap and seal the entire pile; label and freeze.

To use uncooked pastry, remove one or more crusts; let thaw

for 15 minutes with the waxed paper still above and below each crust to keep moisture from condensing on crust as it thaws.

Label; freeze.

FILLED PIES, UNCOOKED

Fresh fruit or mincemeat are the best fillings for freezing.

Prepare and seal. Prepare pies as usual—except brush the bottom crust with shortening to prevent the filling from soaking into it; and brush the top crust of the finished pie with shortening (*not* milk, water or egg), to keep it from drying out.

Wrap tightly in freezer wrap, using the butcher wrap or drugstore fold. Seal. An outer cardboard box safeguards against breakage in storage.

Label; freeze.

FILLED PIES, COOKED

Cooled fresh fruit, mincemeat and chiffon pies freeze well.

Prepare and seal. Make and bake the pies as for immediate use. *Thoroughly cool them,* and then wrap securely with freezer wrap, using the butcher wrap or drugstore fold. Seal.

Label; freeze.

TO COOK FROZEN PIES

Bake *uncooked* pies in the frozen state in a 450 F. oven for 15 to 20 minutes, then reduce heat to 375 F. until done.

Precooked pies to be served cold are thawed at room temperature for 8 hours. To serve hot, heat the frozen pie in a 400 F. oven for 30 to 35 minutes.

FREEZING CAKES AND COOKIES

Butter, sponge, angel, pound, chiffon and fruit cakes and almost all cookies, are successfully frozen after baking.

Icing is better put on when you are ready to serve the cakes—except for the butter-confectioner's-sugar type (which does freeze well).

Prepare and seal. Make by your favorite recipe. Remove from pan; cool thoroughly. Use the butcher wrap or drugstore fold; use an outer rigid container for cookies. Seal.

Label; freeze. (To defrost: leave, wrapped, at room temperature.)

COOKIE DOUGH

Prepare and seal. Shape the dough in rolls for easy slicing (or in bulk—

which must be thawed before cookies can be shaped).

Also, cookies may be cut, frozen on a tray, then packaged with freezer paper between layers for easy handling later.

Package rolls of dough or cut cookies tightly with freezer wrap and seal.

Label; freeze.

Freezing Your Own TV Dinners

Meal leftovers can make better-than-store-bought TV dinners if they are carefully frozen. Freeze the portions either assembled on divided aluminum-foil plates, or freeze them separately and assemble them later when you're reheating them to serve. If you're using divided foil plates or trays, be most careful to press your covering of freezer foil tightly to the food to expel as much air as possible, and to seal the edges completely. Overwrap and seal. Label carefully; freeze.

IDEAS FOR COMBINATION PLATE DINNERS:

 —Swiss steak, french-fried potatoes, peas.
 —Beef stew, hot bread, asparagus.
 —Meat loaf, candied sweet potatoes, spinach.
 —Corned-beef-hash patties, pan-fried potatoes, string beans.
 —Ham steak, candied sweet potatoes, peas.
 —Breaded veal cutlet, mashed potatoes, carrots.
 —Turkey and dressing, giblet gravy, mashed sweet potatoes, peas.
 —Pot roast, gravy, brown potatoes, corn, peas.
 —Fried chicken, mixed vegetables, mashed potatoes, gravy.
 —Ham croquettes, stuffed baked potatoes, broccoli.

FREEZING DABS AND SNIPPETS

When you're chopping onions or celery or green peppers anyway, cut up extra amounts and package them individually or combined in packets the right size for future dishes.

Other foods good to have ready to use in a minute are snipped chives, chopped nuts and breadcrumbs. And freeze a bunch of tied-together parsley. Just snip off what you need while the bunch is still frozen, then rewrap the remainder and return it quickly to the freezer before it has a chance to defrost.

 —But let your own originality take over! Try what tempts you.

The Preserving Kettle

Jellies, pickles and relishes are the items that prompt the most questions to Extension Service home economists. This seems to indicate that beginning homemakers get their early canning experience via the preserving kettle; then, with confidence gained, they graduate to canning meal basics. And meanwhile the preserves add so much to any table —plus an extra thrill if they've won a prize at the fair!

There are many good sources for recipes. Most women's magazines offer them in season; many cookbooks have chapters on all types of preserves and pickles. Four standbys are the USDA's *H&G Bulletin No. 56, How To Make Jellies, Jams; and Preserves at Home,* and *H&G Bulletin No. 92, Making Pickles and Relishes at Home;* the *Ball Blue Book,* sold by the Ball Corporation, Muncie, Indiana 47302; and the *Kerr Home Canning Book,* sold by Kerr Glass Manufacturing Corporation, Sand Springs, Oklahoma 74063. Also, the containers of store-bought pectin—liquid or crystalline—include folders of recipes for jellies, jams and the like.

The following "receipts," to use the pleasant old term, are from Beatrice Vaughan's heirloom collection, and she has translated many nineteenth-century instructions into today's measurements and methods. Most notably, she has tailored the ingredients to small, easy-to-work-with batches; especially with jellies, she says, you get best results if you handle no more than 3 to 6 cups of juice at a time.

EXTRA PROCESSING TO OFFSET POOR STORAGE

Preserves and pickles can suffer from mold and other spoilage micro-organisms when storage is not the ideal 30—50 F. and dark and dry—conditions not always possible in warm, humid climates or in modern centrally heated homes. So, for needed insurance: treat all jars of food from the preserving kettle *except jelly* to a short Hot-Water/Boiling-Water Bath before storing. See section introductions or recipes.

Jellies, Jams and Such

Jellies, jams, preserves, conserves, marmalades and butters are the six cousins of the fruit world. All have fruit and sugar in common, but differences in texture and fruit-form distinguish one from another.

Jelly. Made from fruit juice, it is clear and tenderly firm. Quiveringly, it holds its shape when turned out of the jar.

Jam. Made from crushed or ground fruit, it almost holds its shape, but is not jelly-firm.

Preserves. These are whole fruits or large pieces of fruit in a thick sirup that sometimes is slightly jellied.

Conserves. These glorified jams are made from a mixture of fruits, usually including citrus. Raisins and nuts also are frequent additions.

Marmalade. This is a tender jelly with small pieces of citrus fruit distributed evenly throughout.

Butters. These are fruit pulps cooked with sugar until thick.

THE FOUR ESSENTIAL INGREDIENTS

FRUIT

This gives each product its special flavor and provides at least a part of the pectin needed for successful gels.

Full-flavored fruits are preferred, because the large proportion of sugar added for good consistency and keeping quality dilutes the flavor.

PECTIN

This substance, which is what makes jelly gel, is found naturally to a greater or lesser extent in most fruits (apples and quinces have a lot). Pectin content diminishes as the fruit becomes fully ripe.

In the old days apple juice was combined with less pectin-rich juices to make them gel.

Today the readily available powdered or liquid commercial pectins take the guesswork out of jellies and such.

ACID

None of the fruits will gel or thicken without acid. The acid content of fruits varies, and is *higher in underripe* than in the fully ripe fruit.

Lemon juice is a common addition to low-acid fruits. Or 1/8 teaspoon crystalline ascorbic acid may be substituted for each 1 tablespoon of lemon juice called for in specific recipes.

SUGAR

This helps the gel to form, is a preserving aid and adds to the flavor of the final product.

Corn sirup or honey may replace part of the sugar, up to ¼ in jelly and up to ½ in the other products. (See "Sugar Sirups for Canning Fruits" for other substitutions.)

STEPS IN MAKING COOKED JELLY

The recipes that follow are for cooked jellies—that is, ones boiled with sugar and pectin as indicated. For uncooked jellies, see the references noted above.

Always work with the recommended batch. The quantities given are tailored for success: the longer boiling needed for larger amounts can prevent desired flavor and texture in the finished product.

Preparing the fruit

Choose the amount of fruit called for, making sure that it is not overripe. When the rule does not call for commercial pectin, choose ¾ the amount in just-ripe fruit, ¼ the amount slightly underripe.

Wash quickly and gently, never letting the fruit soak. Cut up solid fruits (such as apples), retaining the cores and peels—which contain the greatest amount of natural pectin—and add the water required for heating. Crush juicy soft berries to start their juice without heating; strain. Crush firm berries, add enough water to prevent scorching, and heat to start the juice flow.

Extracting juice

Drain the prepared fruit in a damp jelly bag suspended above a large bowl; do not squeeze the bag, lest the juice become cloudy. If you do squeeze the bag or use a food mill to get maximum yield, strain the juice again through a fresh jelly bag or through four layers of damp cheesecloth laid in a colander. Measure the juice and proceed with the recipe.

Sugar and pectin

When you add the sugar depends on the type of commercial pectin you use. Each recipe stipulates the type—*and they are not interchangeable.* Always follow the recipe exactly, because time and quantity variations almost always bring failure.

Powdered pectin is added to the strained juice *before* heating. Heat rapidly, bringing to a full rolling boil—i.e., a boil which cannot be stirred down; *then add the sugar,* bring again to a full rolling boil, and boil for 1 minute.

Liquid pectin is added to the strained juice and sugar *after* the mixture is brought to a full boil. Stir constantly during heating. Add pectin, bring again to a full rolling boil, boil for 1 minute.

WITHOUT ADDED PECTIN

Jellies made without pectin (like apple jelly) require less sugar per cup of juice than pectin-added jellies do. The longer cooking needed to reach the jelly stage also concentrates the juice to the right relationship to the sugar content.

DIET JELLIES

Sugarless jellies, etc., are made with added pectin but with sugar substitutes (use only those approved by your doctor). These jellies are good, but need to be stored in refrigerator or freezer, since, lacking the sugar that acts as a preservative, they spoil readily in temperatures above 40 F. Several manufacturers of sugar substitutes provide recipes for diet jellies and preserves.

Testing for doneness

Because barometric pressure as well as altitude affects the boiling point, make necessary adjustments for heights above 1,000 feet above sea level, and for whether the day is close and damp, or clear and dry.

Jelly with added pectin will be done if boiled as the individual instructions for time and quantity specify.

Jelly without added pectin is done when it reaches 8 degrees F. above boiling; usually, under good conditions at 1,000 feet or less, this is 220 F.

220 F. and a full rolling boil in all its glory: the jelly is done.

If you have no jelly thermometer, use the Sheet Test. Dip a cold metal spoon in the boiling jelly and, holding it 12 to 18 inches above the kettle and out of the steam, turn it so the liquid runs off the side. If a couple of drops form and run together and then tear off the edge of the spoon in a sheet, the jelly is done.

Or use the Refrigerator Test. Remove the kettle from the heat (so it won't raise Cain while your back's turned) and pour a tablespoon of jelly into a saucer. Put the saucer in the ice-cube compartment of your refrigerator for a minute or two: if it has become tender-firm, your jelly is ready to pour and seal.

Pouring, sealing, storing

The moment your jelly tests done, remove the kettle from the heat and skim the foam so carefully that you do not stir any of it down into the jelly. Ladle boiling-hot jelly immediately into clean sterilized glasses (see how to sterilize glasses and caps in "About Jars and Cans" in the Canning section). Take care not to slop any around the rim of the glass; if you seal with paraffin, be sure no jelly has dribbled on the top ½ inch inside the glass.

Allow 1/8 inch of headroom with modern jelly glasses having screw-band tops. Put on sterilized tops and caps, and screw tight. Invert the capped glass for a moment and right it immediately. As the jelly cools, the vacuum will form a perfect seal.

If you seal with paraffin, leave ½ inch of headroom and cover jelly immediately with an 1/8-inch layer of paraffin which has been melted slowly in a double boiler (you can have a scary fire on top of your stove if you melt paraffin in a saucepan over high heat). You can also melt wax in an old metal teapot set in a larger pan of hot water; and it makes a fine container for pouring the melted paraffin.

Prick any air bubbles that appear on the wax surface, because they're likely to cause holes in your wax as it cools—and there goes your seal. One thin layer, properly applied, seals best.

When the paraffin is cool, cover the glass with a metal lid if you have one. Or use a double layer of foil, held tight all around with tape, string or a twist of wire.

Label all jelly and store the glasses in a cool, dark dry place.

MAKING COOKED JAM, MARMALADE, ETC.

Jams, conserves and marmalades call for the same general preparation that jellies do. Select fruit, wash gently; stem, core, peel as required; crush or cut fine.

Some are made with added pectin; others rely on just the pectin that nature put in them, and are boiled for an extended time.

Sugar and pectin

With added pectin, the crystalline type is mixed with the unheated prepared fruit. Liquid pectin is added to the cooked fruit-and-sugar mixture after the kettle is removed from heat. With either form of pectin the cooking time is the same: 1 minute at a full boil.

Without added pectin, the cooking time is increased to a range of from 15 to 40 minutes, depending on the character of the fruit. Jam is more likely to scorch than jelly is, so stir it often during cooking.

For *diet jam,* etc., see jelly, above.

Testing for doneness

Jams, etc., with added pectin will be done when they are boiled according to the individual instructions for time and quantity.

Without added pectin, jam is done when it reaches 9 degrees F. above boiling, usually 221 F. at 1,000 feet of altitude or below.

No thermometer? Jam is ready when it begins to hold shape in the spoon (the Sheet Test does not apply to jam, etc.). Or use the Refrigerator Test for jelly, above.

Pouring, sealing, processing, storing

Remove the kettle from heat, skim carefully, and then stir the jam gently for 5 minutes to cool it slightly and thus prevent floating fruit.

Ladle the still-hot jam carefully into glasses, allowing adequate headroom; proceed as for jelly. Where storage is not suitably cool and dry (see page 186), pack in hot jars, leave ¼-inch headroom, adjust lids and process 10 minutes in a B-W Bath to kill possible yeasts and molds.

MAKING FRUIT BUTTERS

Butters may be made from most fruits or fruit mixtures. Probably apple is the best-known ingredient, but apricots, crabapples, grapes, peaches, pears, plums and quinces also make good butters.

Prepare the fruits as for preserves, above, but mash the soft ones and dice or chop the hard fruits. Add a little water and cook the fruit until soft enough to be pressed through a food mill or sieve to make the smooth butter-texture.

For cooking, usually ¾ cup of sugar to 1 cup of fruit pulp makes a fine butter. Use at one time not more than 4 cups of pulp, plus the added sugar. This stuff sticks easily while on the heat, so *stir constantly during cooking.* Let the sugar dissolve in the pulp on low heat, then bring the mixture to a rapid boil and cook until thick.

Finish by skimming off any foam, then pour while hot into hot sterile jars and seal. In warm, humid climates, pack and process as for jam (see "Pouring, sealing" etc., on page 192).

MAKING PRESERVES

Wash the fruit and remove stem and blossom parts. Peel peaches, pears, pineapples, quinces and tomatoes. Shred pineapple, less the core. Cut slits in tomatoes and gently squeeze out the seeds, cut large tomatoes in quarters, leave small ones whole. Pears and quinces are thinly sliced after halving and coring. Take the pits from sour cherries. Of course strawberries and raspberries are left whole.

To cook, carefully follow the specific recipe. Generally, dry sugar is added to the soft fruits to start the juice flowing. There should be enough juice to cook the fruit. Hard fruits are cooked in a sugar-and-water sirup. The recipe will tell you how long to cook each of the preserves.

Ladle hot preserves into sterile canning jars and seal at once (again, see page 192). Label and store in a cool, dark, dry place.

Basic Apple Jelly

    4 cups prepared apple juice
    3 cups sugar

To prepare apple juice, cut up apples, discarding stem and blossom ends. Just barely cover with cold water and set over moderate heat. Cover pan and cook slowly for about 30 minutes, or until apples are quite soft. Turn into a jelly bag and drain well. Don't squeeze the bag, or your jelly will be cloudy. Measure out 4 cups of the juice and bring to boiling. Boil about 5 minutes, then add the sugar. Boil rapidly until the jelly sheets from the spoon (220 F.). Remove from heat and skim off foam. Fill hot sterilized glasses and seal at once with melted paraffin. Makes 5 to 6 medium glasses.

Old-fashioned Dried Apple Jelly

> 1 pound dried apples
> about 5 cups sugar
> ¾ cup fresh lemon juice

Soak dried apples overnight in water just covering. Cook until very tender in the same water, mashing fruit with a spoon. Strain well through a jelly bag. Measure juice and combine with an equal amount of sugar. Add lemon juice. Place over high heat and stir until sugar has melted. Bring to a full, rolling boil and boil hard until the mixture sheets (220 F.). Remove from heat and skim. Seal in hot sterilized glasses. Makes about 8 medium glasses.

Blackberry-Apple Jelly

> 2 quarts cup-up apples, unpeeled and uncored
> 1 quart fresh blackberries
> sugar

Combine cup-up apples and the blackberries. Just barely cover with water and set over moderate heat. Bring to boiling and cook about 25 minutes, or until apples are very tender. Turn into a cloth jelly bag and let drain several hours. Measure juice and add an equal amount of sugar. Set over high heat and bring to a full, rolling boil, stirring until sugar melts. Boil hard until mixture sheets (220 F.). Seal in hot sterilized glasses. Makes about 6 glasses.

Apple-Herb Jelly

> 2½ cups prepared apple juice
> ¼ cup dried herb (such as tarragon, sage, thyme or savory)
> ¼ cup white vinegar
> 4 cups sugar
> few drops red or green coloring (optional)
> ½ bottle liquid fruit pectin (3 ounces)

Heat apple juice just to boiling. Pour over the herb and let stand about 20 minutes. Strain through 2 thicknesses of cheesecloth. Add vinegar and sugar. Bring to a full, rolling boil, stirring frequently. Add coloring to suit taste. Stir in the pectin and bring again to a full, rolling boil. Boil hard 1 minute, stirring constantly. Remove from heat and skim. Seal in hot sterilized glasses. Makes about 6 medium glasses.

Cinnamon-Cider Jelly

    4 cups sweet cider
    2 tablespoons red cinnamon candies
    1 (1¾-oz.) package powdered fruit pectin
    4½ cups sugar

Combine cider, cinnamon candies and the pectin. Stir over high heat until mixture comes to a full, rolling boil. Stir in sugar and bring again to a full boil. Boil hard 1 minute, stirring constantly. Remove from heat and skim. Seal in hot sterilized glasses. Makes about 8 medium glasses.

This tangy jelly is excellent with roast pork.

Rhubarb-Orange Jelly

    4 cups chopped uncooked rhubarb, not peeled
    2 1/3 cups water
    1 (6-oz.) can frozen concentrated orange juice, thawed
    1 (1¾-oz.) package powdered fruit pectin
    4 cups sugar

Combine rhubarb and 2 cups of the water and cook over moderate heat for about 15 minutes. Strain in a sieve, rubbing pulp through. Measure out 2 cups and add the orange concentrate. Add remaining 1/3 cup water. Set over high heat and bring to a full, rolling boil, stirring frequently. Stir in pectin and bring again to full boil, stirring constantly. Boil 1 minute. Remove from heat and skim. Seal in hot sterilized glasses. About 2½ pints.

Rhubarb-Strawberry Jelly

    1½ pounds unpeeled raw rhubarb
    1 quart ripe strawberries, hulled
    1 (1¾-oz.) package powdered fruit pectin
    5 cups sugar

Put rhubarb through food grinder, saving all juice. Mash strawberries and add to rhubarb. Place in a jelly bag to drain, pressing out juice. Measure: there should be 3½ cups. Add pectin and set over high heat. Bring to a full, rolling boil, stirring constantly. Add sugar and bring again to full boil, stirring constantly. Boil hard 1 minute. Remove from heat and skim. Seal in hot sterilized glasses. About 8 medium glasses.

Wild Plum Jelly

 6 cups prepared juice
 4½ cups sugar

Prepare juice by covering cut-up plums with cold water and slowly bringing to a boil. Cook until very tender, stirring frequently. Press through a coarse sieve, then turn pulp into a jelly bag. Drain well, but do *not* squeeze the bag or jelly will be cloudy. Measure 6 cups of the juice and combine with 4½ cups sugar. Set over high heat and bring to a full, rolling boil, stirring constantly. Boil hard until jelly sheets (220 F.), stirring frequently. Remove from heat and skim. Seal in hot sterilized glasses. Makes about 8 medium glasses.

Raspberry-Plum Jelly

 4 cups raspberries, fresh or frozen
 6 red plums, pitted and cut up
 1 medium lemon
 sugar

Combine raspberries and cut-up plums. Quarter the lemon, then slice very thin, discarding seeds. Add to the raspberries and plums. Place all in a heavy kettle and crush fruit with the base of a heavy glass tumbler. Add ½ cup water and cover kettle. Simmer until fruit is very tender, then drain in a jelly bag. Measure juice and add 3/4 as much sugar. Place over high heat and bring to a full, rolling boil, stirring frequently. Cook rapidly until jelly sheets (220 F.). Remove from heat and skim. Seal in hot sterilized glasses. About 6 small glasses.

Lemon-Honey Jelly

 2½ cups honey
 ¾ cup fresh lemon juice, strained of all pulp
 1 tablespoon grated lemon rind
 ½ bottle liquid fruit pectin (3 ounces)

Combine honey, lemon juice and grated rind. Stir over moderate heat until mixture reaches a full boil. Add pectin and bring again to a full, rolling boil, stirring constantly. Boil hard 1 minute. Remove from heat and stir 3 minutes. Seal in hot sterilized glasses. Makes about 2 pints.

Fresh Mint Jelly

1 cup fresh mint leaves and stems, firmly packed
½ cup apple cider vinegar
1 cup water
3½ cups sugar
4 drops green food coloring
½ bottle liquid fruit pectin (3 ounces)

Do *not* remove leaves from the stems. Wash the mint, drain and place in a saucepan. Bruise well with the bottom of a heavy glass tumbler. Add vinegar, water and sugar. Bring to a full, rolling boil over high heat, stirring until sugar melts. Add coloring and pectin and bring again to a full, rolling boil, stirring constantly. Boil hard for 30 seconds. Remove from heat and skim. Pour through a fine sieve into hot sterilized glasses; seal. Makes about 2 pints.

This is a traditional accompaniment to any lamb dish.

Orange-Wine Jelly

4 cups sugar
1½ teaspoons grated orange rind
½ cup fresh orange juice
2 tablespoons fresh lemon juice
1½ cups white wine
½ bottle liquid fruit pectin (3 ounces)

Combine all ingredients except the pectin. Stir over moderate heat until the sugar melts and the mixture comes to a full, rolling boil. Boil hard 2 minutes, stirring constantly. Remove from heat and stir in the pectin. Stir for 2 minutes, skimming off the foam. Seal in hot sterilized glasses. Makes about 7 half-pint glasses.

Tomato Jelly

1¾ cups canned tomato juice
½ cup strained fresh lemon juice
2 teaspoons Tabasco sauce
4 cups sugar
½ bottle liquid fruit pectin (3 ounces)

Combine all ingredients except pectin. Stir over high heat until mixture reaches a full, rolling boil. Stir in pectin and bring again to a full, rolling
(Continued on the next page)

boil. Boil 1 minute, stirring constantly. Remove from heat. Stir and skim for about 3 minutes. Seal in hot sterilized glasses. Makes about 6 medium glasses.

This "lively" flavored jelly is equally good served with meats or spread on hot bread.

"Make Do" Corn Cob Jelly

> 12 cobs of red field-corn
> water
> 1 (1¾-oz.) package powdered fruit pectin
> 4 cups sugar

Remove kernels, boil cobs in water to cover for 20 minutes. Drain liquid through a jelly bag. Measure 3 cups strained liquid into a large saucepan; stir in pectin. Bring to a full, rolling boil, then add the sugar. Bring again to boiling, stirring until the sugar is melted; boil hard 1 minute. Remove from heat, skim, and seal in hot sterilized glasses. Makes about 5 medium glasses.

This is a clear jelly, tasting a little like mild honey. It can be tinted, if desired, with food coloring.

Pear Pancake Syrup

> 4 cups sweetened syrup from canned pears
> juice of 1 medium lemon
> 1½ packages powdered fruit pectin

Combine pear syrup with lemon juice. Bring to a boil. Stir in pectin and bring to full, rolling boil. Remove from heat and seal in hot sterilized jars. Makes about 2 pints.

A delicious and unusual addition to pancakes or waffles.

Corn Cob Syrup

> 12 cobs of red field-corn
> 4 quarts water
> 1½ cups light brown sugar
> 2½ cups white sugar

Break up cobs after kernels have been removed. Boil in the water for about 30 minutes. Drain, reserving liquid. Add the sugars to the liquid

(Continued on the next page)

and bring to boiling. Simmer until of syrup consistency.

Transplanted New Englanders, homesick for their native maple syrup, came up with this substitute in their new homes in the West.

Basic Rule for Berry Jam

Weigh hulled and washed berries. Measure out an equal amount of sugar and set it aside. Crush berries well and set over low heat; bring to boiling slowly, stirring frequently. Add sugar and bring again to boiling. Simmer until thick, stirring frequently to prevent scorching as the mixture thickens. Seal in hot sterilized jars.

Aunt Mabel Berry's Rose-Hip Jam

1 pound rose hips*
1 cup water
sugar

Simmer rose hips and water until fruit is very tender. Rub it through a sieve and weigh the pulp. To each pound or fraction, add an equal weight of sugar. Return to heat and simmer until thick, stirring frequently. Seal in hot sterilized jars.

This jam makes an attractive present, being noncommercial (as well as having a high Vitamin C content).

* Rose hips should be gathered after the first frost of autumn. Take care not to gather them from bushes that have been treated with insecticides or fungicides.

Sun-cooked Strawberry* Jam

You need a blistering hot, still day to do this. Have a table set up in the full sun, its legs set in cans or small pans of water to keep crawling insects from the jam. To protect it from flying insects, have handy a large sheet of clean window glass, the means to prop it at a slant over the platters, and cheesecloth or mosquito netting to tape like a curtain around the three sides left open to the air. And work in *small* batches.

Wash and hull berries, and measure them to determine how much sugar you need. Put a layer of berries in the bottom of a big kettle, cover with an equal number of cups of sugar; repeat a layer of berries

(Continued on the next page)

and cover it with sugar. Set aside for about 30 minutes to let the berries "weep" and the juice start drawing. Place over very low heat and bring slowly to simmering, stirring occasionally to prevent scorching, until the sugar is dissolved.

Pour sirupy berries ½ inch deep into large plates or platters. Set platters on the table in strong sun. Prop the glass over them with one edge on the table, the opposite edge raised 4 to 6 inches high (this allows any condensation to run harmlessly down the glass onto the table, instead of dripping back on the jam to slow the jelling process). Arrange netting around the open sides.

As the fruit cooks in the sun, turn it over with a spatula—2 or 3 times during the day. When it has obviously jelled enough, pour it into sterilized jars and seal. [Newer knowledge suggests a 10-minute finishing B-W Bath to prevent mold, etc.—Editor]

If the sun is not strong or if there's wind, jelling can take 2 or 3 days. In that case, bring the platters indoors each night.

* Or cherries. Or raspberries—but *not washed* before layering.

Ginger-Pear "Honey"

> 5 pounds firm pears, peeled, cored and cut up
> 3¾ pounds sugar
> 1 tablespoon powdered ginger
> grated rind of 2 small lemons
> juice of 2 small lemons

Put pears through the food grinder, using a coarse knife. Combine with remaining ingredients. Stir over moderate heat until sugar melts. Bring to boiling, and simmer until thick. Stir frequently to prevent scorching. Seal in hot sterilized jars. About 3 pints.

This is absolutely delicious as a topping for vanilla ice cream.

Old-time Chokecherry Jam

Remove stems from chokecherries and wash. Drain. Add 1 cup water to every 4 cups fruit. Place over low heat and simmer until fruit is very tender, stirring occasionally. Rub pulp through a medium sieve; measure, and add an equal amount of sugar. Place over moderate heat and stir until sugar has melted. Bring to a full, rolling boil and cook until mixture sheets (220 F.). Stir frequently. Seal in hot sterilized jars. Three cups pulp will make about 3 half-pints.

Sweet Cherry (or other) Preserves

    4 cups pitted sweet cherries, tightly packed
    3 cups sugar

In a 4-quart saucepan crush the cherries lightly to start the juice flow. Boil cherries and their juice about 10 minutes—or until fruit is tender. Add sugar to the cherries, stir well, and boil for 5 minutes more. Now cover the kettle and let the cherries stand for 2 minutes while they absorb more of the sugar. Stir the hot preserves to prevent floating fruit, then pour into hot sterilized jars and seal. Makes about 2 pints.

This is a basic rule for similar fruit preserves, and offers scope for variations of your own devising. Be individual!

Southern Peach "Honey"

    ripe peaches
    sugar

Peel and halve peaches, discarding pits. Mash fruit thoroughly. Measure, and add 2 cups sugar to each cup of peach pulp. Set over low heat and bring to boiling, stirring constantly. Simmer until thick and clear— about 30 minutes. Stir frequently to prevent scorching. Seal in hot sterilized glasses.

Some Southerners prefer this to all other spreads as a complement to hot biscuits.

Applesauce Marmalade

    4½ cups applesauce
    2 medium oranges, unpeeled
    2 small lemons, unpeeled
    ½ cup water
    4 cups sugar

Turn applesauce into a heavy saucepan. Put oranges and lemons through food grinder, using medium knife; discard seeds but reserve all juice. Add to the applesauce, then add water and sugar. Stir over low heat until boiling, stirring constantly. Reduce heat and simmer until thick— about 1 hour. Stir frequently: this marmalade will scorch easily during latter part of cooking time (an asbestos pad under the pan will help too). Seal in hot sterilized jars. About 3 pints.

Honeyed Marmalade

2 cups diced, peeled apples
2 cups diced, peeled carrots
1 cup diced, peeled peaches
2 tablespoons grated lime rind
juice of 2 large limes
2 cups sugar
1 cup honey

Combine all ingredients in order, mixing well. Set over low heat and bring slowly to boiling, stirring frequently. Simmer until thick. Stir frequently to prevent scorching as the mixture thickens. Seal in hot sterilized jars. Makes about 3 pints.

Ripe Tomato Marmalade

3¼ cups chopped, peeled, ripe tomatoes
¼ cup fresh lemon juice
grated rind of 1 large lemon
6 cups sugar
1 bottle liquid fruit pectin (6 ounces)

Place chopped tomatoes in small pan and set over low heat and cover. *Do not add any water.* Bring to boiling, reduce heat and simmer about 10 minutes, stirring frequently. Remove from heat and measure out 3 cups of the tomatoes and liquid. In a large kettle, combine the 3 cups tomatoes with the lemon juice, grated rind and sugar. Stir over moderate heat until boiling. Boil hard 1 minute. Turn off heat and add pectin. Stir for 5 minutes. Seal in hot sterilized glasses. About 1½ pints.

Rhubarb-Carrot Marmalade

6 cups diced, peeled, raw rhubarb
3 cups ground, peeled, raw carrots
2 medium oranges, unpeeled
4½ cups sugar

Combine rhubarb and carrots. Put oranges through the food grinder, using a medium knife. Discard seeds but reserve all juice. Add to rhubarb mixture, then add the sugar. Let stand overnight. Stir over low heat until boiling; reduce heat and simmer until thickened—about 2 hours. Stir frequently. Seal in hot sterilized jars. Makes about 5 pints.

This is a very old rule indeed, and as good and honest as it is "out of the way."

Green Tomato Marmalade

2 quarts sliced, small, green tomatoes
½ teaspoon salt
4 lemons, peeled (save the rind)
4 cups sugar

Combine tomatoes and salt. Chop lemon rind fine and add. Cover with water and boil 10 minutes. Drain well. Slice the peeled lemons very thin, discarding seeds but reserving all juice. Add lemon slices and juice and the sugar to the tomato mixture. Stir over moderate heat until sugar melts. Bring to boiling, reduce heat and simmer until thick—about 45 minutes. Stir frequently. Seal in hot sterilized jars. Makes about 2 pints.

This classic from long ago is especially good served with meat to add a "company dinner" touch.

Old-fashioned Pumpkin Marmalade

1 small pumpkin (*c.* 5 pounds, to give 4 pounds, cubed)
4 pounds sugar
3 lemons
1 orange

Peel pumpkin and cut in small cubes, discarding seeds and inner pulp. Add sugar and let stand overnight. Put lemons and orange through food grinder, discarding seeds but reserving all juice. Add to pumpkin. Stir over low heat until boiling. Simmer until thick and clear—about 3 hours. Stir frequently to prevent scorching. Seal in hot sterilized jars. About 4 pints.

The flavor of this prettily colored jam is predominantly citrus.

Carrot Marmalade

4 cups cooked, sliced carrots
2 lemons
2 oranges
6½ cups sugar

Put carrots and seeded lemons and oranges through the coarse knife of a food grinder: be sure to save all juice. Add sugar, and cook very slowly until thick. Pour hot into hot sterilized jars and seal at once. Makes about 3 pints.

This marmalade is beautifully colored and of excellent flavor, and is as much a favorite today as it was many years ago.

Old-style Apple Butter

½ peck unpeeled apples — 4 qts - (Solid)
2 cups sweet cider
about 5 cups sugar
1 teaspoon ground cloves
1 tablespoon ground cinnamon
½ teaspoon ground allspice

Cut up apples and put them in a heavy kettle. Add the cider and cover. Cook over low heat until very tender, stirring occasionally. Cool slightly, then rub all through a sieve (or use a food mill). Measure and combine with ½ as much sugar. Stir in the spices. Simmer over low heat until dark and thick—about 2 hours. Stir frequently, for *this scorches easily:* an asbestos pad under the kettle will help. Remove from heat and pour into hot sterilized jars, leaving ¼ inch headroom. Adjust lids, process pints or quarts in a Boiling-Water Bath for 10 minutes to ensure the seals. The butter will thicken as it stands. About 5 pints.

Georgia Peach Conserve

4 cups coarsely chopped peaches*
½ cup coarsely chopped pitted prunes, uncooked
1/3 cup seeded raisins
1 medium orange, seeded and ground
½ cup water
1 cup light corn sirup
¼ cup chopped pecans (or other nuts)

Turn peaches into a big heavy saucepan and, with the edge of a serving spoon, chop the fruit coarsely. Add the prunes, raisins, ground orange, water and the corn sirup. Bring to a boil; reduce heat and simmer until dark and thick—about 1 hour. Add nuts and cook 5 minutes longer. Seal in hot sterilized jars. Makes about 2 pints.

   *One quart of undrained canned peaches may be used, omitting the ½ cup of water and using only ¾ cup corn sirup.

Midwinter Plum Conserve

1 quart canned purple plums, undrained
½ cup seeded raisins
1 cup sugar
1 medium orange, peeled and thinly sliced

(Continued on the next page)

1 tablespoon fresh lemon juice
¾ cup chopped nuts

Turn plums into a heavy saucepan, breaking them up with a spoon and discarding the pits. Add raisins, sugar and orange slices. Bring to a boil, reduce heat and simmer until thick—about 45 minutes. Add lemon juice and nuts. Cook 2 minutes longer, then pour boiling hot into hot sterilized jars and seal. About 2 pints.

Pickles and Relishes

Pickles and relishes are first cousins. Their major difference is that vegetables and/or fruits for relishes are chopped before being put with the vinegar mixture, and those for pickles are left whole or cut to size for the recipe.

Any firm-fleshed vegetable or fruit may be used. There are some that hold their shape and texture particularly well in pickles, such as the black-spine type of cucumber and the Seckel pear.

Pickle products are sealed and stored as you do other canned foods. However, pickle flavors reach their peak only after 6 or more weeks in the jars.

HEAT PROCESSING FOR PICKLES

Pickle products require heat treatment to destroy organisms that cause spoilage, and to render inactive the enzymes that may affect flavor, color and texture. Adequate heating is generally achieved best by processing in a Boiling-Water Bath.

ESSENTIAL INGREDIENTS

THE PRODUCE ITSELF

Fresh, prime ingredients are basic. Move them quickly from garden or orchard to pickling solution. They lose moisture so quickly that even one day at room temperature may lead to hollow-centered or shriveled pickles.

Perfect pickles need perfect fruits or vegetables to start with. A tiny bit of overlooked mold makes a musty taste. The *blossom ends* of cucumbers must be removed (since any enzymes located there can cause pickles to soften while brining); but do leave ¼ inch or so of *stem.*

SALT

Use only pickling, dairy or kosher salt. These are plain, pure salt, either coarsely or finely ground.

Do not use table salt. Although pure, the additives in it to keep it free-running in damp weather make the pickling liquids cloudy; the iodine in iodized salt darkens the pickles.

Do not use the so-called rock salt or other salts that are used to clear ice from roads and sidewalks: they are not food-pure.

Salt, as used in brining pickles, is a preservative. A 10-percent brine, about the strongest used in food preservations, is 1½ cups salt dissolved in each 1 gallon of liquid. Old-time recipes often call for a brine "that will float an egg"; translate this to "10-percent brine."

Brine draws the moisture and natural sugars from foods and forms lactic acid to keep them from spoiling.

Brine weakens as the juices come out of the food.

VINEGAR

Use a high-grade cider or white distilled vinegar of 4 to 6 percent acidity (40 to 60 grain). Avoid vinegars of unknown acidity or your own home-made wine vinegar. The latter develops "mother" that clouds the pickling liquid. Use white vinegar if you want really light pickles.

And *never reduce the vinegar* if the solution is too tart: instead, add more sugar. There is a finely balanced relationship of acidity to keeping quality.

SUGAR

Use white sugar unless the recipe calls for brown. Brown, or raw, makes a darker pickle. Sometimes a cook in the northern United States or in Canada may use maple sugar or sirup in her pickles for its flavor—but this is feasible only if she has lots of it to spare.

SPICES

Buy fresh spices for each pickling season. Spices deteriorate and lose their pungency in heat and humidity, so they should be kept in air-tight containers in a cool place.

ALUM (OPTIONAL)

Alum, sometimes used to keep pickles crisp, isn't really necessary if ingredients are perfect and directions are well followed. Grape leaves serve the same purpose.

EQUIPMENT

We've talked earlier about equipment for canning and preserve-making. The main point to remember here is that pickles are acid or prepared with a heavy salt solution, so check to make sure what you have is suitable.

FOR HEATING PICKLING LIQUIDS

Use utensils of unchipped enameled ware, stainless steel, aluminum or glass. Never use anything that's galvanized, or copper, brass or iron. These metals react with the acids or salts to cause undesirable color changes and form undesirable compounds.

FOR FERMENTING OR BRINING

Use a crock or stone jar, unchipped enamel-lined pan, or large glass jar, bowl or casserole. Use a heavy plate or large glass lid topped with a weight to keep vegetables below the surface of the brine. A glass jar filled with water makes a good weight.

METHODS

LONG-BRINE

Vegetables such as cucumbers are washed and dropped into a heavy salt solution (plus sometimes vinegar and spice) and left in a cool place to cure for 2 to 4 weeks. Scum is removed from the brine each day. Following this the pickles are packed loosely in clean jars and covered with the same or freshly made brine and processed in a Boiling-Water Bath.

SHORT-BRINE

Vegetables are left overnight in a brine to crisp up. The next day they are packed in jars, covered with a pickling solution and processed in a Boiling-Water Bath for a suitable time

OPEN-KETTLE

Followed by processing in a Boiling-Water Bath, Open-Kettle is used for relishes and other cut-up pickle mixtures that cook in a sweet-sour sirup or brine.

Sweet Mixed Pickles

    1 quart unpeeled cucumber cubes (¾-inch)
    1 quart tiny pickling onions, peeled
    1 medium head cauliflower, broken into flowerets
    1 large sweet red pepper, seeded and chopped
    ½ cup salt
    4 cups vinegar
    2 cups firmly packed light brown sugar (or raw)
    ¼ teaspoon turmeric
    1 tablespoon mixed pickling spices
    2-inch stick whole cinnamon
    6 whole cloves
    1 teaspoon mustard seed

Combine the four vegetables and sprinkle with the salt. Cover with cold water and let stand overnight. Drain; rinse in fresh water and drain again thoroughly. Combine vinegar, sugar and turmeric in a large enamelware kettle. Tie spices in a small cloth bag and add. Place over moderate heat and bring to boiling. Cook 10 minutes, then add vegetables. Bring again to boiling and cook 5 minutes. Put hot in hot sterilized pint jars, process in a Boiling-Water Bath 10 minutes. Makes about 3 pints.

Dill Cucumber Pickles (Short-brine)

17 to 18 pounds of pickling cucumbers (3 to 5 inches)
2 gallons of 5 percent brine (¾ cup pickling salt to each
    1 gallon of water)
6 cups vinegar
¾ cup salt
¼ cup sugar
9 cups water
2 tablespoons whole mixed pickling spices
14 teaspoons whole mustard seed (2 teaspoons go in each quart jar)
7 to 14 cloves garlic (1 to 2 cloves go in each quart jar)
21 dill heads (3 heads go in each quart jar)
    OR
7 tablespoons dill seed (1 tablespoon to each quart jar)

Put washed and brush-scrubbed cucumbers in a noncorroding crock or kettle and cover with the 5 percent brine. Let stand overnight, then drain and pack cucumbers in clean, hot quart jars. Add the mustard seed, dill and garlic to each jar.

Combine vinegar, salt, sugar and water; tie pickling spices loosely in a clean, thin, white cloth and drop it into the mixture. Bring to a boil. Take out the spice bag and pour boiling liquid over cucumbers in jars, leaving ½ inch of headroom. Adjust the lids and process in a Boiling-Water Bath (212 F.) for 20 minutes. Makes about 7 quarts.

Pickled Carrot Sticks

1 pound carrots, peeled
¾ cup vinegar
¾ cup water
½ cup sugar
1 teaspoon mixed whole pickling spices

Slice carrots in thin sticks. Cover with boiling salted water and cook 10 minutes. Drain. Combine remaining ingredients and bring to boiling. Reduce heat and simmer 3 minutes. Pack carrot sticks in hot sterilized jars and cover with the hot spiced liquid, allowing headroom, then process in a Boiling-Water Bath for 5 minutes to ensure the seal. Makes 2 pints.

Dilled Green Beans

    3 pounds whole green beans
    1½ teaspoons cayenne pepper
    6 garlic cloves
    6 dill heads, or 2 tablespoons dill seed
    3¼ cups vinegar
    3¼ cups water
    6 tablespoons salt

Wash beans; cut off ends. Pack lengthwise in clean, hot, pint jars, leaving ¼ inch of headroom. Add 1 clove of garlic, 1 head of dill (or 1 teaspoon dill seed) and ¼ teaspoon cayenne pepper to *each* pint jar. Mix together in an enameled kettle the water, vinegar and salt; bring to a boil and pour, boiling hot, over the beans in the jars. Leave ¼ inch of headroom. Adjust the lids and process in a Boiling-Water Bath (212 F.) for 10 minutes. Makes about 6 pints.

    It takes about 2 weeks for the full flavor to develop.

    The added vinegar raises the naturally low-acid beans to the strong-acid category, so a B-W Bath is adequate for safe processing.

Sweet Pumpkin Pickle

    6 cups prepared pumpkin
    2 cups vinegar
    2 cups sugar
    2 large sticks whole cinnamon

Prepare pumpkin by peeling and cubing flesh, discarding seeds and inner pulp. Place pumpkin cubes in a colander and set over boiling water: make sure water does *not* touch the pumpkin. Cover and steam until just tender. Drain. Simmer vinegar, sugar and cinnamon for 15 minutes. Add pumpkin cubes and simmer 3 minutes. Set aside for 24 hours. Heat and simmer 5 minutes more. Remove cinnamon. Pack boiling hot in sterilized jars, adjust lids and process in a Boiling-Water Bath for 5 minutes to ensure the seal. Makes 3 pints.

    This pickle compares favorably with that made of cantaloupe.

Sweet Mustard Pickle

    1 quart small green tomatoes, quartered
    1 quart *small* unpeeled cucumbers (about 2 inches)

 (Continued on the next page)

1 quart unpeeled *medium* cucumbers
1 quart tiny pickling onions
1 small head cauliflower, broken into flowerets
3 green peppers, seeded and diced
2 cups green beans, cut in 1-inch slices
1 cup salt
1 cup flour
1/3 cup dry mustard
2 teaspoons turmeric
2 cups sugar
2 quarts vinegar

Combine vegetables and sprinkle with the salt. Cover with cold water and let stand overnight. Place over moderate heat and bring just to boiling point, then drain thoroughly. Combine remaining ingredients smoothly. Stir over moderate heat until smooth and thick. Add well-drained vegetables and bring *just to boiling point*: they should never be overcooked and mushy. Ladle hot into hot sterilized jars, allow ½ inch headroom, and process in a Boiling-Water Bath for 10 minutes for quarts. Makes about 4 quarts.

Ripe Cucumber Pickle

9 large ripe cucumbers
1/3 cup salt
4 cups vinegar
4 cups sugar
2 tablespoons mixed whole pickling spices
2 tablespoons mustard seed

Pare cucumbers and cut in half lengthwise. With a silver spoon, scrape out seeds and pulp, then cut in pieces about 1 x 2 inches. Sprinkle with the salt and cover with cold water. Let stand overnight. Drain; rinse with fresh water, and drain again. Combine vinegar and sugar in a large enamelware kettle. Tie spices in a small cloth bag and add. Bring to boiling and cook 5 minutes. Add drained cucumber slices and bring again to boiling. Reduce heat and simmer until cucumber is tender and appears translucent. Discard the spice bag; ladle into hot sterilized pint jars and process for 5 minutes in a Boiling-Water Bath for the seal. Makes about 6 pints.

Sometimes this old recipe included 1 teaspoon of alum to the overnight soak in order to retain crispness, but it's really not necessary if you're careful not to overcook.

Watermelon Pickles

8 cups prepared watermelon rind
½ cup pickling salt
4 cups cold water
4 teaspoons whole cloves
4 cups sugar
2 cups white vinegar
2 cups water

Choose thick rind. Trim from it all dark skin and remains of pink flesh; cut in 1-inch cubes. Dissolve salt in cold water, pour it over rind cubes to cover (add more water if needed); let stand 5 to 6 hours. Drain, rinse well. Cover with fresh water and cook until barely tender—no more than 10 minutes (err on the side of crispness); drain. Combine sugar, vinegar and water, add cloves tied in a cloth bag, and bring to boiling; reduce heat and simmer for 5 minutes. Pour over rind cubes, let stand overnight. Bring all to boiling and cook until rind is translucent *but not at all mushy*—about 10 minutes. Remove spice bag, pack cubes in hot sterilized pint jars; add boiling sirup, leaving ½ inch of headroom; adjust lids. Process in a Boiling-Water Bath for 5 minutes to ensure seal. Remove jars and complete seals if necessary. Makes about 4 pints.

Golden Glow Pickle

3 quarts prepared ripe cucumbers
6 medium onions, peeled and diced
2 green peppers, seeded and diced
2 sweet red peppers, seeded and diced
¼ cup salt
3 cups vinegar
3½ cups sugar
15 whole cloves
2 tablespoons mustard seed
1 teaspoon celery seed
1 teaspoon turmeric

To prepare cucumbers: peel and cut lengthwise; discard seeds and pulp, and cut in ¾-inch cubes. Combine with diced onions and peppers. Sprinkle with the salt and let stand overnight. Drain; rinse in fresh water, and drain again thoroughly. Combine vinegar, sugar and spices in a large enamelware saucepan. Bring to boiling, then add the drained vegetables. Bring again to boiling, reduce heat and simmer 20 minutes:

(Continued on the next page)

the cucumber cubes *should be just tender,* not mushy. Ladle hot into hot sterilized jars, process in a Boiling-Water Bath for 10 minutes for pint jars. Makes about 6 pints.

Zucchini Pickle

2 quarts thin slices of unpeeled, *small* zucchini squash
2 medium onions, peeled and thinly sliced
¼ cup salt
2 cups vinegar
2 cups sugar
1 teaspoon celery seed
2 teaspoons mustard seed
1 teaspoon turmeric
½ teaspoon dry mustard

Combine zucchini and onions. Sprinkle with the salt, cover with cold water and let stand 2 hours. Drain; rinse with fresh water, and drain again. Combine remaining ingredients in an enamelware kettle and bring to boiling. Cook 2 minutes. Add zucchini and onions, remove from heat, and let stand 2 hours. Bring again to boiling and cook 5 minutes. Ladle hot into hot sterilized pint jars, and process in a Boiling-Water Bath for 5 minutes to ensure a seal. Makes about 4 pints.

This astounding recipe makes a delicious bread-and-butter pickle— almost like one made from cucumbers. It is feasible only if you have a large amount of zucchini available at low cost.

Corn Relish

4 cups corn kernels (about 9 ears' worth)*
1 cup diced sweet green peppers
1 cup diced sweet red peppers
1 cup finely chopped celery
½ cup minced onion
1½ cups vinegar
¾ cup sugar
2 teaspoons salt
1½ teaspoons dry mustard
1 teaspoon celery seed
¼ teaspoon Tabasco sauce
½ teaspoon turmeric, for color (optional)
2 tablespoons flour, for thickening (optional)

(Continued on the next page)

Prepare corn by boiling husked ears for 5 minutes, cooling, and cutting from cob (do not scrape). In an enameled kettle combine peppers, celery, onion, vinegar, sugar, salt, celery seed and Tabasco sauce; boil 5 minutes, stirring occasionally. Dip out ½ cup hot liquid, mix it with dry mustard and turmeric, and return it to the kettle. Add the corn. (If you want the relish slightly thickened, blend the 2 tablespoons flour with ¼ cup cold water and add to the kettle when you put in the corn.) Boil for 5 minutes, stirring extra well if the relish has been thickened, so it won't stick or scorch. Immediately fill clean hot pint jars within ½ inch of the top, adjust lids, and process in a Boiling-Water Bath for 15 minutes. Complete seal if necessary; cool and store. Makes 3 pints.

   * You can use frozen whole-kernel corn that's been thawed slowly: 3 10-ounce packages will equal 4 cups of fresh kernels.

Piccalilli

   6 medium-size green tomatoes
   6 sweet red peppers, seeded
   6 medium onions, peeled
   1 small cabbage
   ¼ cup salt
   2 cups vinegar
   2½ cups light brown sugar (or raw)
   2 tablespoons mixed pickling spices

Put vegetables through the food grinder, using a coarse knife. Sprinkle with the salt, cover and let stand overnight. Drain; then cover with fresh water, and drain again. When thoroughly drained, put into a large kettle and add vinegar and sugar. Tie spices in a small cloth bag and add. Bring to boiling, then reduce heat and simmer about 20 minutes, stirring frequently. Remove the spice bag and turn the hot piccalilli into hot sterilized jars; adjust lids and process in a Boiling-Water Bath for 5 minutes to ensure a seal. Makes about 4 pints.

Rhubarb and Onion Relish

   8 cups sliced raw rhubarb
   4 cups sliced onion
   4 cups firmly packed light brown sugar (or raw)
   2 teaspoons salt
   1 teaspoon ground ginger

(Continued on the next page)

1 teaspoon ground cinnamon
1 cup vinegar
1 garlic bud, peeled and minced
1 tablespoon whole mixed pickling spices

In a large heavy kettle, combine all except the last two ingredients. Tie the garlic and pickling spices in a small cloth bag and add. Bring to boiling, reduce heat and simmer until rhubarb is *just* tender—about 10 minutes. Don't overcook: the rhubarb should not be mushy. Remove the spice bag, ladle the hot relish into hot sterilized jars, adjust lids, and process in a Boiling-Water Bath for 5 minutes to ensure the seal. About 3 pints.

This wonderful garnish is from a very old rule indeed. You won't see its like on supermarket shelves.

Beet Relish

12 cooked medium beets (fresh or canned)
1 medium onion, peeled and chopped
2 cups finely chopped cabbage
1 sweet red pepper, seeded and finely chopped
1½ teaspoons salt
¾ cup sugar
1½ cups vinegar
2 tablespoons prepared horseradish

The vegetables may all be put through the food grinder, using a coarse knife. Combine all ingredients in a large saucepan. Bring to a boil, then reduce heat and simmer about 15 minutes, stirring frequently. Ladle hot relish into hot sterilized jars, adjust lids, and process in a Boiling-Water Bath for 10 minutes for pint jars. Makes about 3½ pints.

Quick Pickled Beets, a side dish that's not canned, is given in the Vegetables Recipes.

Red Pepper Jam

12 sweet red peppers, seeded
1 tablespoon salt
2 cups vinegar
2 cups sugar

(Continued on the next page)

Grind peppers, using a medium knife. Add salt and let stand overnight. Drain well, then combine with the vinegar and sugar. Stir over moderate heat until mixture boils. Reduce heat and simmer until thick as any jam, stirring frequently. Seal in hot sterilized jars. About 2 pints.

This sweet relish is unequaled as a spread for sandwiches when used with cream cheese.

Tomato-Fruit Relish

8 pounds ripe tomatoes (about 20 large)
8 pears, peeled and cored
8 peaches, peeled and pitted
6 large onions, peeled
2 large sweet red peppers, seeded
3 cups vinegar
4 cups sugar
2 tablespoons salt
3 tablespoons mixed whole pickling spices

Peel tomatoes and chop coarsely. Put pears, peaches, onions and red peppers through the food grinder, using a coarse knife. Combine fruits and vegetables in a large enamelware kettle. Add vinegar, sugar and salt. Tie spices in a small cloth bag and add. Bring to boiling; reduce heat and simmer until thick—about 2 hours—stirring frequently. Remove the spice bag and pour hot into hot sterilized jars. Adjust lids and process in a Boiling-Water Bath for 5 minutes. About 8 pints.

"Short-term" Garden Relish

Before you embark on this very good relish, prized by our grandmothers for the lively, fresh accent it imparted to midwinter meals, note that *it is uncooked,* and therefore may present a storage problem in today's heated pantries and cellars. Recommendations for lengthening its life are added at the end of the rule.

1 small cabbage
4 medium onions, peeled
4 large carrots, peeled
2 medium sweet red peppers, seeded
2 medium green peppers, seeded
¼ cup salt

(Continued on the next page)

2 cups vinegar
2 cups sugar
2 tablespoons mustard seed
2 tablespoons celery seed

Put vegetables through the food grinder, using a medium knife. Place vegetables in a large bowl, stir in the salt, and let stand about 3 hours. Drain; then rinse with fresh water, and drain again, pressing vegetables with your hand to squeeze out excess water. Combine vinegar, sugar and spices. Mix with the vegetables, stirring gently but thoroughly. Fill sterilized pint jars, cover tightly, and keep in the refrigerator if you lack cold storage.

Although some of the crispness is lost with heat processing, ensure a seal that gives leeway for storing by filling jars to within ½ inch of the top, adjusting lids, and start in *warm* water for a 15-minute Boiling-Water Bath (cold jars can break if plunked in water already boiling; start timing when bath comes to the boil).

Another idea: put relish in sterile freezer jars, allowing enough headroom, seal; and store in the freezer up to 3 or 4 months.

Pear and Tomato Chutney

3 cups sliced peeled pears
3 cups peeled, quartered tomatoes
1 medium green pepper, seeded and chopped
1 medium onion, peeled and chopped
1¼ cups sugar
1 cup water
½ cup vinegar
1 teaspoon salt
½ teaspoon ground ginger
½ teaspoon dry mustard
1/8 teaspoon cayenne pepper
1 canned pimiento, chopped

Combine ingredients in order in a heavy kettle, except the pimiento. Bring to boiling, stirring occasionally. Reduce heat and simmer slowly about 1 hour, stirring frequently. Break up pears and tomatoes with the edge of a spoon. Add the pimiento and cook 5 minutes longer. Pour hot into hot sterilized jars, adjust lids, and process in a Boiling-Water Bath for 5 minutes to ensure the seal. Makes about 2 pints.

Spiced Pears, see under Canning.

Green Tomato Mincemeat

    3 quarts prepared green tomatoes
    3 quarts prepared apples
    1 cup ground suet
    1 pound seedless raisins
    2 tablespoons grated orange rind
    2 tablespoons grated lemon rind
    5 cups well-packed light brown sugar (or raw)
    ¾ cup vinegar
    ½ cup fresh lemon juice
    ½ cup water
    1 tablespoon ground cinnamon
    ¼ teaspoon ground cloves
    ¼ teaspoon ground allspice
    2 teaspoons salt

To prepare tomatoes: put through the food grinder, using a coarse knife. Peel and core apples and put through grinder. Repeat with the suet. Combine all ingredients in order in a large kettle, and bring to boiling, stirring frequently. Reduce heat and simmer until dark and thick—about 2½ hours. Stir occasionally. An asbestos pad under the kettle will help prevent scorching. Pour boiling hot into pint jars, allowing ½ inch headroom, and process in a Boiling-Water Bath for 25 minutes. Complete seal if necessary. Makes 8 pints, enough for 8 nine-inch pies.

    Directions for this very old recipe originally did not mention the Boiling-Water Bath step included here, but today's generally too-warm storage requires it in order to avoid spoilage. *Pressure-processing* is not needed with this rule, because of the very long cooking time.

Mincemeat

    1 pound boiled lean beef
    ½ pound beef suet
    2½ cups seeded raisins
    ¼ pound chopped citron
    3 cups coarsely chopped apples
    2 cups dried currants
    2¼ cups light brown sugar

(Continued on the next page)

3 tablespoons light molasses
2 cups sweet cider
¾ teaspoon ground cinnamon
¾ teaspoon ground mace
¾ teaspoon ground cloves
¼ teaspoon ground nutmeg
¼ teaspoon ground allspice
¼ teaspoon salt
1 cup brandy

Put beef, suet and raisins through the food grinder, using a coarse knife. Put citron and apples through the grinder. Combine all in a heavy kettle and add remaining ingredients in order, *except the brandy.* Bring to boiling, stirring constantly. Reduce heat and simmer about 1 hour, stirring frequently. *The mixture will scorch easily, so use an asbestos pad under the kettle.* Remove from heat and stir in brandy. Ladle hot into pint jars, allowing ½ inch headroom, and process at 10 pounds pressure for 20 minutes, or in a Boiling-Water Bath for 1 hour and 30 minutes. Makes 5 pints, enough for 5 nine-inch pies.

Lack of adequate cold storage in modern homes dictates the final processing to prevent spoilage.

Brandied Peaches, see under Canning.

Brandied Peaches without Brandy

Use peaches that are not overripe. Wash and drain. Spread a ¼-inch layer of white sugar in the bottom of a small earthenware crock. Add a layer of peaches; fill in around the peaches with sugar. Repeat layers until the jar is full, making sure the top layer is well covered with sugar. Cover crock tightly, set it in a large brown paper bag, and tie the top of the bag shut. Set in a dark place. Brandy will form in about 2 weeks, but more satisfactory results are obtained if left for 3 or 4 months. When the crock is opened, the peaches will be shriveled and the liquid will be quite a heady drink.

Strain the brandy through a muslin jelly bag and store in sterilized jars: do not heat-seal, or you'll lose alcohol.

Serve as a liqueur; add it to berry sirups to make cordials; use it in compotes or on fresh or canned fruits for a Continental dessert; put it in your mincemeat.

Drying

Drying as a way of putting food by goes back to pre-Biblical times, and it is still a prime method of preserving staples at home in areas of the world where other means are not feasible. Early settlers from Europe, taught much of the art by the American Indian, practiced it extensively. Even after canning became popular, country householders continued to dry some fruits, a few vegetables, certain meats and fish, and always, of course, herbs.

THE FEASIBILITY OF DRYING

Aside from their much greater keeping quality than when they were fresh and raw, properly home-dried foods, uncooked, have roughly 1/6 to 1/3 the bulk and only around 10 to 20 percent of the water of their original fresh state. Therefore when dried foods are eaten without having their water restored by cooking, ounce for ounce they are nutritionally superior in a number of aspects to the same foods when fresh and raw—although their content of vitamins sensitive to heat, light or air of course is reduced in the drying process.

Unlike canning and freezing, which have acquired uniform methods as the result of intensive research and widespread use, home-drying does not yet possess a body of firmly established procedures. For one thing, drying is done either outdoors in the sun or indoors by artificial means, depending on the climate. For another, there is considerable variety in the recommendations for treatment before drying, for temperatures and lengths of drying time, and for conditioning prior to storage.

So if you have a choice of preserving methods, continue to can and freeze and root-cellar and cure those foods that are less good when dried—even though they're dried carefully: therefore it's likely that drying is *not* your answer for almost all meats and fish, a majority of our vegetables, and many of our fruits. If you are new to drying, start out with herbs and a few of the easier fruits, and you'll soon discover by trial and error which of the drying techniques described below is best suited to your interest, your facilities and your tastes.

WHAT DRYING DOES

The main purpose of drying is to take out enough water from the material so that spoilage organisms are not able to grow and mutiply during storage. The amount of remaining moisture that is tolerable for safety varies with the type of food—whether it is strong-acid or low-acid natural material, or whether it has been treated with a high concentration of salt—and, to some degree, with the type of storage. (See pages 1—6 for what the spoilers are, and how temperature, acidity and moisture affect them.)

In general, more water can be left in strong-acid food like fruits, less water is left in low-acid things like vegetables. If meats and fish, both of which are nonacid, are heavily salted before being dried, in some cases they can contain safely more residual water than dried fruits do—though they should be cold-stored, and their storage life is comparatively shorter.

> *Note:* Although "drying," "dehydrating" and "evaporating" are often used casually as meaning the same thing, the USDA Research Service's fine *Agriculture Handbook No. 8, Composition of Foods: Raw, Processed, Prepared* lists as dehydrated those foods containing only 2.5 to 4 percent water—the other 96+ percent having been removed by highly sophisticated processes that we can't hope to equal at home. It lists as dried those foods still containing roughly 10 to 20 percent water (the amount depending on whether they're vegetables or fruits). We can take out all but this much moisture with the equipment and methods described in this section—and we'll call it *drying.*

GENERAL PROCEDURES IN DRYING

Choose perfectly fresh food in prime condition—just as you do for every food you put by—and handle it quickly and with absolute cleanliness at every step. Peel it, pit it, cut it up: whatever is required. Small or fairly thin pieces usually make the best product.

Many foods require some sort of treatment before drying to preserve color and nutrients, prevent decomposition, ensure even drying and prolong storage life. Depending on the type of food, these treatments are usually coating with an anti-oxidant, blanching, sulfuring, and, in the case of fish and some meat, salting (see also Smoking).

Good drying is done as rapidly as possible, so long as it doesn't actually cook the material and thereby spoil its looks and texture: the idea is to have the drying process outstrip decomposition. For most foods the heat is increased as the drying proceeds.

The specific appearance of proper dryness is described in the instructions for drying each food. See also "Tests for Dryness in Produce" on page 235.

Some foods are better for being subjected to pasteurizing temperatures for a short time after they test dry.

Many foods require a conditioning period after they test dry: they are stored temporarily in bulk to distribute remaining moisture more evenly; periodic stirring and examination disclose which pieces are not dry enough for storage, and these are removed.

Properly dried foods are stored in a dry place, and in containers safe from insects and animals. Meat and fish, which are high in protein, should be kept under 40 degrees Fahrenheit to increase their storage life.

EQUIPMENT FOR DRYING

Keep everything simple, even rudimentary, in the beginning: aside from saving money it's a lot more fun in this hypertechnical age to return to elementals. You can always branch out with more sophisticated gear when you get your technique down pat for one type of food and start with a new one that requires a different treatment. Try for as much uniformity in size as possible, though, so you can swap equipment from one system to another.

Trays first

Shallow wooden—*never metal*—trays are necessary whether you dry outdoors in sun or shade, or indoors in a dryer or an oven. They should have slatted, perforated or woven bottoms to let the air get at the underside of the food. Don't make them of green wood—which weeps and warps; and don't use pine, which imparts a resinous taste to the food; and don't use oak or redwood, which can stain the food. Ingenuity will turn up many suitable materials: the following ideas are just a sampling.

The simplest frames to make would be those cut from wooden crates that produce comes in: saw the crates in several sections horizontally, rather as you'd split a biscuit.

If you're making frames from scratch, you can use 1-inch x 1-inch material of the kind you're likely to be using anyway for vertical cleats at the corners of a dryer or for bracing. It will give your trays only 1 inch of depth for holding food; this could be a disadvantage for sun-drying—which requires that food be protected by netting of some sort stretched over the top of the tray—but this extreme shallowness doesn't matter much in a dryer.

Tempered hardboard (this is not underlayment) would be good. It is strong despite its thinness and comes in 4-foot x 8-foot sheets that is fine material for making dryers and sulfuring boxes. One sheet will give you a dryer 14 inches wide, 24 inches deep and 36 inches high, plus frames for 6 trays to fit inside, and some usable trimmings left over. For each tray with sides 2 inches high, cut two sides and two ends and fasten them together in a rectangle by nailing them, not to each other, but to 1-inch x 1-inch cleats; fourpenny box nails will do the job well. Diagonal cross-bracing of the cleat material to form an X, with the end of each arm nailed to the corner cleat, will strengthen the frame, and will also provide valuable extra air space when trays are stacked; put it on after the bottom of the tray is attached.

HOW BIG?

Each 1 square foot of tray space will dry around 1½ to 2½ pounds of prepared food.

Loaded trays shouldn't be too large to handle easily, and they should be uniform in size so they stack evenly. The flimsier the construction, the smaller they should be; but even well-built ones for sun-drying are better if they're not more than 2 feet by 2 feet.

However, since you can have an emergency that means you will need to finish off in an oven or dryer a batch you've started outdoors, it makes sense to have the trays smaller, and rectangular. Make the trays narrow enough for clearance when you slide them inside, and 3 to 4 inches shorter than the oven or dryer is from front to back: you'll want to stagger the trays to allow air to zigzag its drying way up and over each tray as it rises from the intake at the bottom to the venting at the top.

Consider having the trays 1 to 2 inches deep, 12 to 16 inches wide, 16 to 20 inches long—but first having found the inner dimensions of the oven or dryer (less the fore-and-aft leeway for staggering the trays).

NO METAL FOR THE BOTTOMS EITHER

Don't use metal screening for the bottom. Aluminum discolors and, more important, it corrodes easily (but the amount of aluminum oxide absorbed by food processed in contact with aluminum is apparently no worry, or such a fighter against contaminants as Adelle Davis wouldn't recommend cooking in aluminum pots). Copper destroys Vitamin C. And galvanized screen has been treated with zinc and cadmium—and cadmium is dangerous stuff indeed to mix with food (when old-time instructions ask for "hardware cloth" they mean galvanized screen, by the way).

Vinyl-coated screen in beguiling ¼-inch and ½-inch mesh looks like the answer at first glance, but what will it do at 140 F., the average heat in a dryer—melt? peel? And how will it react with the food after awhile? Certainly you could test a bit of it in sun-drying.

Any cloth netting will do if its mesh isn't larger than ½-inch. Two layers of cheesecloth work, as does mosquito net, etc.—but they're hard to clean without getting frazzled. Old clean sheets let less air up through, but they're stouter. (In a pinch you can dry food on sheets laid flat in the direct, hot sun.) When cutting cloth for tray bottoms, allow 2 inches more all around so you can fold it over itself on the outside of the frame; then staple it in place.

We've seen good trays with bottoms of hay-bailing twine strung back and forth and then cross-hatched the other way. Draw the twine tight and flat, staple each loop to the outside of the frame-strip before you turn around and go back, keeping the strands ½ inch apart.

Strong, serviceable bottoms are made by nailing ½-inch wood strips to the bottom of the frame ½ inch apart; the strips run in only one direction. More finished—but worth it, because they're smooth and easy to clean—are ¼- or ½-inch hardwood dowels; these are nailed inside the frame with small box nails driven through from the outside, and they also go in only in one direction.

One thickness of cheesecloth laid over bottoms will keep sugar-rich food from sticking to them while it dries; so will a thin coating of oil. Even a few recent publications suggest mineral oil for lubricating the trays—it doesn't impart flavor and doesn't get rancid—but if you're leary of its effect on your body's vitamin absorption, use any fresh, low-flavored vegetable oil. You'll be scrubbing your trays anyway, regardless of what oil you use.

Simple dryers and drying aids

As with trays, there's somehow more satisfaction in using unfancy dryers, especially if you're just starting out. But the USDA *Farmers' Bulletin No. 984, Farm and Home Drying of Fruits and Vegetables* has explicit directions for making several types and sizes of dryers, ranging from a portable one that sits spang on the top of the cookstove (not recommended nowadays, particularly in view of the alternatives) to an elaborate affair suitable for a co-operative project. Unfortunately this very good pamphlet is out-of-print, but probably it can be seen at your County Agent's. The Extension Services in states where much drying is done also have material containing plans.

AN INDOOR BOX DRYER

The 14-inch x 24-inch x 36-inch dryer mentioned in the directions for making trays, above, will hold from 17 to 28 pounds of prepared food on its 6 trays if they're spaced a generous 4 inches apart, and 4 inches are allowed at the bottom and 6 inches at the top for circulation of air. This should be large enough for a small family who are going in for drying seriously. The sketch indicates the general construction of a drying box supported on legs tall enough to accommodate underneath it an upright space heater or a stand for raising an electric hot plate, etc., functionally close to the bottom of the dryer. Consider what you'll be heating with before you start to build: it makes sense to enclose the heat source, so, in order to have the 6 to 8 inches of clearance necessary all around an uninsulated radiant heater (such as an old metal laundry stove), you may have to increase the dimensions of the box or of the area inside the supports. See "Miscellaneous Furnishings" below for suggestions on heaters.

A simple box like this one is portable, a virtue for a modest operation. With a heat source that's not hard to move or that merely depends on a safe extension cord to a safe electrical outlet, the dryer can be set up in any handy dry area with good cross-ventilation—pantry, unused room or large passageway, shed, protected porch, even in the kitchen itself out of the traffic pattern. It should stand free and well away from walls at back and sides, with easy access to the front so you can regulate the heater, take frequent looks at the food and shift the trays during drying.

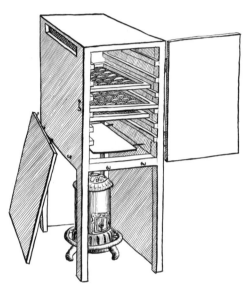

Make the dryer of the same tempered hardboard mentioned earlier, or of 3/8-inch *exterior* type plywood. Use 2-inch x 2-inch stock for the frame, to which the panels and top are nailed, and for the supporting posts, and 1-inch x 2-inch material for bracing and the door frame. Runways for the trays are of 1-inch x 1-inch material, and are placed 6 inches from the top and 6 inches from the bottom of the box, and spaced at 3-inch intervals (which gives 4 inches from the top of one runway to the top of the one below).

Cut the side and back panels 3 inches less than the box is tall, and nail them to the framing so they leave a 3-inch space on three sides for the warm moisture-laden air to escape at the top. Cover these ventilators with fine screen (non-galvanized metal screening is O.K. here, being away from the food).

Leave the bottom of the box open; but, 3 inches below the lowest tray runway, screw in partially—but substantially—several long screws on the interior of each side to support a heat-spreader that will be several inches smaller all around than the interior of the dryer. (The spreader, used whenever the type of heat is likely to be too intensely localized, should be metal; maybe we're hyper-finicky, but we'd steer clear of galvanized material here too—sheet aluminum would work all right; a beaten-up tin cookie sheet, cut down to size if need be, would be fine.

To prevent heat loss below the dryer and control the intake of air at the bottom, enclose the sides and back of the underpinning. The simplest thing is to staple a double thickness of pure aluminum building paper—which is fire-retardant—to the supporting legs. More durable is skirting of hardboard or plywood protected on the heat side by two thicknesses of the aluminum paper; either nail the panels to the legs or hang them with hooks and screw-eyes snugly from the base of the dryer (or from the top horizontal cross-braces between the legs if, in order to contain an uninsulated metal stove, the table-like supporting arrangement is wider and deeper than the dimensions of the drying box proper). The fourth, and front, panel is shorter, leaving about 12 inches of clearance from the floor; and removable, so it's easy to tend the heater.

DRYING OVER A FLOOR REGISTER—NO

Drying food over a floor register leading from the furnace is not recommended: too much dust—even with scrupulously clean air filters; and there are usually fumes from the combustion—even though they're so mild as to be unnoticeable in the room.

A SOLAR DRYER

For small-scale drying outdoors with plenty of sunshine but higher humidity than is desirable for drying in direct sun, you can put together a dryer that looks, and acts, much as a coldframe does (see sketch).

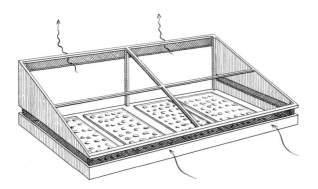

The tilted glass panel—one or more pieces of storm sash are fine—intensifies the heat from the sun, and this rise in temperature inside lowers the relative humidity correspondingly, so that drying occurs faster than is possible outside the dryer. The ample screened venting allows circulation of air.

This dryer is not effective on overcast days.

PROTECTIVE COVERINGS

Food dried in the open, whether outdoors or in a warm room, needs protection from insects and airborne gurry. If the trays have high enough sides (*c.* 2 inches) so the metal can't touch the food, fine-mesh non-galvanized screen does the job. If the trays are so shallow that the covering is likely to sag on to the food, a layer of cloth netting, stretched tight, is better. The problem is not so much what to use, as how to fasten it adequately and still have it easy to remove and replace at the times when the food is stirred or turned over to hasten drying.

Many people cut the covering 2 inches larger all around than the tray it's intended for, bend it over, and thumbtack the overlap to the sides of the tray. Or sometimes it's easier to stretch cheesecloth, etc., over several trays laid side by side, and fasten the cloth to the surface the trays rest on. Or you can use the framed screen from a window: it's weight is usually adequate to keep it lying on top of a drying tray. And there's always simply laying a cloth net over the trays and weighting it down all around outside the trays.

Food that's drying outdoors must be protected from dew at night —unless it is brought inside outright. So stack the trays under a shelter and cover the stack with a big carton found at a supermarket or a store that sells large household appliances. Or drape the stack with a clean old sheet. If there's chance of rain, use a light tarpaulin if you have one (putting a clean sheet between the food and the tarp); a plastic shower curtain or tablecloth; or a painter's dropcloth, plastic or not, but certainly without paint or turpentine on it.

MISCELLANEOUS FURNISHINGS

Trestles, racks, benches. No set sizes or types for these, so just know where you can get bricks or wood blocks for raising the first course of trays off the ground; scrap lumber for building rough benches or racks to hang drying food from; smaller stuff to use as spacers. And not all at once and none of it fancy.

Sulfuring box. We're going to suggest sulfuring in certain instances, and we'll tell how to make and use a sulfuring box in a minute.

Auxiliary heaters. A wood-burning "globe" laundry or chunk stove small enough to go inside the skirts under the dryer throws fine radiant heat and is easy to regulate and pleasant to live with; *don't* use coal- or oil-burners, though: the fumes from freshly added coal "gassing off" or from burning oil are to be avoided in this enclosed little space (directly under food to boot). A cooking-gas ring is O.K.

An upright electric heater, thermostatically controlled and with a built-in fan, does well too (but any front-blowing heater laid on its back to direct the heat upward is a fire hazard).

An electric hot plate with low-medium-high settings can do an adequate job.

A cluster of 150- or 200-watt light bulbs (totaling around 750 watts for the smallish dryer we've been talking about) gives good, even heat—sometimes *too* even: unless there's an automatic control, you must unplug the whole thing or unscrew some of the bulbs to reduce the heat when you need to. Because the bulbs overheat themselves in a cluster, especially in such a confined space, they should be in porcelain sockets; and get extended-service bulbs with a heavy-duty element for longer bulb life.

The wiring of all electrical heating and blowing units must meet all safety crieteria.

Electric fan. To boost the natural draft in an indoor dryer or to augment a cross-draft when drying in an open room or outdoors. It needn't be large; it should be directable, and *it must have a safety grill covering the blades.*

Thermometers. Even with a dryer or oven having a thermostat, you'll need a food thermometer—a roasting, candy or dairy type will do—to check on the heat of food being processed; plus the most inexpensive kind of oven thermometer to move around between the top and bottom trays to keep track of the varying temperatures.

Scale. Not vital but a great help is a scale weighing in pounds (25 goes high enough, with quarter- and half-pound gradations); use it for judging water-loss by weight, per-pound treatments before drying.

Blanching kettle. Your preserving kettle or Boiling-Water Bath canner will do. Enamelware is best; and with a close-fitting cover. Plus a rack or basket—or even a cheesecloth bag—to hold the food above the steam.

Assorted kitchen utensils. Dishpan, colander, crockery or enameled bowls; stainless sharp knives for cutting and paring; apple-corer and a melon-ball scoop; cutting-board; vegetable slicer or a coarse shredder; spoons—some wooden, at least one slotted; also plenty of clean towels and paper toweling, and an extra packet of cheesecloth.

Materials for storing. Several large covered crocks for conditioning dried food before storing—or strong cartons, moisture-proofed with a lining of plastic sheeting; plastic or paper bags (not big) for packaging dried food in small quantities; mouse-proof, sealable containers for the packages. And cool, dark, dry storage when you're done.

The Drying Methods

Basically, home-drying combines sustained mild heat with moving air to accomplish its purpose—heat adequate to extract moisture but moderate enough so it doesn't cook the material, accompanied by currents of air dry enough to absorb the released moisture and carry it off. These conditions can occur outdoors naturally, or they can be reproduced indoors in dryers.

SUN-DRYING

Successful outdoor drying is possible only in sun-drenched regions with prolonged low humidity, where foods are processed either in direct sun—in open air or in the solar "coldframe" described a moment ago—or in the shade. Because the food is covered or brought inside after dark so nighttime condensation won't undo the sun's work, sun-drying takes a minimum of several days, and generally longer.

Where to sun-dry?

In North America, the interior of California and the Southwestern states possess the ideal climate for sun-drying: predictably long periods of hot sun and low humidity. Next come the wide Plains east of the Rockies in the United States and Canada, where occasional showers are not a great problem if the food hasn't got wet and drying can be resumed in sunshine the next day. Despite their heat, the very humid areas of the South are less good; but sun-drying can be done in a limited way in parts of the Northwest, South and Northeast that are away from the moisture-laden air of the seacoasts.

Locate the drying area near enough to the house so you can tend the food several times during the day and put it under cover easily at night—but keep away from places where dust can be stirred up or where animals are quartered or pastured.

Don't dry food outdoors IF: you're in a smog belt; you're in urban sprawl with superhighways surrounding your community; or even if you're rural but have a well-traveled secondary road within a thousand yards of your home. (Dr. Henry A. Schroeder cites the case of a cow which aborted her calf after eating hay cut from a vacant lot in a small New England town: the hay was heavily polluted with lead from the exhausts of cars using the street, which is a numbered highway.)

What to sun-dry

The happiest-sounding source we've found for step-by-step procedures is the USDA Federal Extension Service's *Sun Dry Your Fruits and Vegetables* (1958), apparently compiled for groups like the Peace Corps to use abroad, and drawing on material from Greece and the Philippines as well as from universities in our Southwestern and South Central states. This pamphlet is the credential for the following list of sun-dryable produce—but please keep in mind that the list is based on (*a*) completely ideal conditions of continued sunshine, high temperatures and low humidity, and (*b*) the seeming lack of facilities for drying in the shade or with artificial aids.

It is also important to mention that most of the fruits were exposed to extensive sulfuring before drying—the length of the sulfur dioxide treatment presumably compensating for the long time required for total drying in the sun.

Fruits easier to sun-dry—Apples, apricots, cherries, coconut, dates, figs, guavas, nectarines, peaches, pears, plums and prunes.

Fruits harder to sun-dry—Avocados, blackberries, bananas, breadfruit, dewberries, Loganberries, mameys (tropical apricots), and grapes.

Vegetables easier to sun-dry—Mature shell beans and peas, lentils and soybeans in the green state, chili (hot) peppers, sweet corn, sweet potatoes, cassava root, onion flakes, and soup mixture (shredded vegetables, and leaves and herbs for seasoning).

Vegetables harder to sun-dry—Asparagus, beets, broccoli, carrots, celery, greens (spinach, collards, beet and turnip tops, etc.), green/string/snap beans ("leather britches" to old-timers), green (immature) peas, okra, green/sweet peppers, pimientos, pumpkin, squash, and tomatoes.

MEAT (JERKY)

Fresh meat—the lean muscles of beef, lamb or deer—sometimes is dried in the sun with moderate success only in extremely dry sections of North America that have good air drainage, such as the high plains of the Rocky Mountain region. This classic jerky is never salted; cut in strips, it is hung on racks in direct sun (rather as some peoples in Africa dry their "biltong" in the fierce tropical sunlight of the veldts, with attendants to wave away the flies). More often, though, jerky is dried high over a bed of coals, so as not to cook or be smoked, in semi-shade; this is more generally the Indian method.

The usual treatment, however, is to salt the meat before drying it in the sun, or in shade with slow fire to aid the process. See the individual instructions.

UNDER MORE TEMPERATE CONDITIONS

Because micro-climates and facilities vary from one sun-drying area to another, it's worth noting that authorities who speak only for conditions in the North Temperate Zone agree that vegetables dried in the sun are often inferior in quality to sun-dried fruits and are more likely to spoil during processing. Furthermore, even with some of the "easier" fruits consensus seems to be that color and flavor are better when they finish drying in stacks in the shade—if humidity is low enough—or are brought indoors to a dryer if it isn't.

In general, then, you might start with sun-drying herbs and flavoring leaves, slices of apples and large-stone fruits, kernel corn and slivers of pumpkin and squash and peppers, before undertaking more.

WHAT TO DRY IN SHADE

If high temperatures are constant, humidity is low even at night, and there is a good breeze, produce capable of being dried in direct sun may be dried well (and sometimes better) in the shade—if it has been given one of the pre-drying treatments and "started" in strong sun or in artificial heat, and provided that the stacks of trays are well ventilated.

Fish are not dried in hot sun, and much of their moisture is removed by thorough salting beforehand. See the individual instructions later.

Drying produce in the sun

Wash, peel, core, etc., and pre-treat according to individual instructions. Because vegetables must have more of their water removed than fruits do for safe drying, cut vegetables smaller than you cut fruits so they won't take too long to dry (being low-acid, vegetables are more likely to spoil during drying).

Spread prepared food on drying trays one layer deep (½ inch, or depending on size of the pieces); put over it a protective covering as described above; place trays in direct sun on a platform, trestles, or merely raised from the ground on stones or wood blocks—on any sort of arrangement that allows air to circulate underneath them. The trays may be laid flat or tilted by means of an extra support under one end; often a slanting low roof is a good place.

If you use clean sheets or the like to hold the food, a table, bench or shed roof is a good place. (Naturally you lose the benefit of air circulating under the food in this case.)

Stir the food gently several times each day to turn it over and let it dry evenly.

Before the dew rises after sundown, bring the trays indoors or stack them in a sheltered spot outdoors. If the night air is likely to remain very dry, the outdoor stack need not be covered; otherwise wait a little until the warmth of the sun has left the food, then drape a protecting sheet over the stack. Return the food to the direct sun the next morning.

At the end of the second day, start testing the food for dryness after it has cooled. If it doesn't test dry (see "Testing for Dryness" below), put it out in the sun again until it does. Then it's ready for conditioning and packaging and storing (see "Treatment After Drying," also below).

Stack-drying produce in shade

This variation of sun-drying relies on extremely dry air having considerable movement, and therefore shouldn't be attempted in muggy areas even though the sun is hot. But where you have hot, dry breezes this method gives a more even drying with less darkening than if the food was done entirely in direct sun; apricots, particularly, retain more of their natural color when shade-dried.

Prepare the food, cutting it in small pieces; put the trays in direct sun for one day or more—until the food is 2/3 dry. Then stack the trays out of the sun but where they'll have the benefit of a full cross-draft, spacing them at least 6 inches apart with chocks of wood or bricks, etc. After several days the dried food is conditioned and packaged for storing.

You can also stack-dry small quantities of food on an open porch by using an electric fan to boost the movement of the air and thus increase its evaporating power. Separate the trays of partly dried food with 6-inch blocks and set the fan at one end of the stack, directing its blast across the trays (which you'll have to shift around a good deal, since the food nearest the fan dries first). Condition and store.

Using a solar dryer

Because of the conditions it is designed to overcome, a solar dryer (sketched earlier) accommodates only a relatively small amount of material at one drying session, and the food "started" in it usually cannot be finished off by stack-drying. On the plus side, however, are the fact that it dries faster than would be possible in the open air, and it costs nothing to operate.

Prepare the food as for sun-drying and spread it one layer deep on the trays. Check the material every hour or so, stirring it gently so it dries evenly; if convenient, turn the dryer several times so it faces direct sunshine. As soon as the interior has cooled when the sun gets

TESTS FOR DRYNESS IN PRODUCE

According to *Composition of Foods,* none of the fruits we'll be telling how to home-dry has less than 80 percent water in its fresh raw state, and the average comparable water content of the vegetables is not less than 85 percent.

The safe maximum percentages of water to leave in home-dried produce are: no more than 10 percent for vegetables, and no more than 20 percent for fruits. Commercially dried fruits often contain more water—especially when they're "tenderized"—but also they may contain additives other than simple sulfur dioxide to protect against spoilage from the higher content of moisture. But we don't have the food industry's highly refined means of testing for and controlling moisture, so we rely on appearance and feel to judge dryness.

Fruits generally can be considered adequately dry when no wetness can be squeezed from a piece of it when cut; and when it has become rather tough and pliable; and when a few pieces squeezed together fall apart when the pressure is released. "Leathery"—"suède-like"—"springy"—these are descriptions you'll see in the individual instructions. Several, such as figs and cherries, also are slightly "sticky."

Vegetables are generally "brittle" or "tough to brittle" when they're dry enough; an occasional one is "crisp." Again, instructions for specific vegetables will tell you what to look for.

When they are very nearly dry, some foods will rattle on the trays; this is another thing to check on when they're in natural heat/draft or in a dryer.

And then there's the *2/3 dry* judgment. Without using refined correlations of drying rate against percentage of natural water and weight of solids before drying, we offer this rough rule-of-thumb: Compare the weight of a fresh sample of produce with its weight at some point during the total drying period—if it has lost ½ of its original weight, consider it 2/3 dry for your purposes.

Finally, foods still warm from the sun or hot from the dryer will seem softer, more pliable, more moist than they actually are. *So cool a test handful a few minutes before deciding it's done.*

low, cover all the ventilators. Remove the covering the next morning and set the dryer to get the full benefit of the sun's heat.

If the sun is hot enough and there is no exposure to humidity from the outside, the food should be dried in about two days. Condition and store.

INDOOR DRYING

Almost every food that sun-dries satisfactorily can make a better product dried indoors with applied heat and a natural or forced draft of air; and for some foods, especially low-acid vegetables, processing in an indoor dryer is recommended even though outdoor drying conditions are reliable during the harvest months.

Herbs dry best in the natural heat and draft of a well-ventilated room.

Depending on the water content and size of the prepared food, and whether the dryer is loaded heavily or skimpily, good drying is possible within 12 hours in an indoor dryer—and some materials, if cut small, may be dried in as little as 3 hours.

On a smaller scale, the oven of a cookstove can be made to perform as a dryer; the processing time is about the same.

Meats, fresh or lightly salted, dry better in an oven (which is an indoor dryer of sorts) than they do on trays in a regular drying box.

Salt fish is best done by shade-drying, since a breeze outdoors on a sunny day is preferable to the limited ventilation afforded by a dryer or an oven. But if the weather turns poor, and you don't mind the aroma indoors, you can finish off a batch in the dryer, or do a small amount in the oven.

Using a dryer

Here you're increasing the speed of drying by use of temperatures higher than those reached outdoors in the sun, so be prepared to regulate heaters and shift trays around if you want the best results.

HEAT—WHY / HOW MUCH / WHEN

There's no single across-the-board temperature ideal for box-drying everything, as you'll see from the individual instructions. Generally speaking, however, a steady 140 degrees Fahrenheit is a good heat to fall back on if your dryer is cranky and you don't mind some extra fiddling with trays. Preheat the dryer.

The *How* of drying by artificial heat is simple if you keep in mind a few *Why's*.

(1) In the usual home dryer—which has the heat source directly under the box, and relies on natural draft sometimes augmented by a small fan—the temperature at the top of the stack is less than the temperature at the bottom, near the heater.

So always keep track of the temperature at the lowest tray, so you can use this heat as the base for judging the temperature higher up.

And rotate the trays up or down every ½ hour to correct this difference and ensure even drying.

(2) Fresh food won't dry well if it is exposed to too much heat too soon: either it will case-harden—its exterior being seared and toughened, so natural moisture can't exude and be evaporated—or it will cook, with the cells rupturing and creating an unattractive product. (As a general thing, the juicier the food, the more likely it is to rupture, and the lower is the temperature at which it should be started in the dryer.)

So if you add fresh food to a batch already drying, always put it in at the top of the dryer.

If the whole load is fresh, have the heat inside the cabinet 20 or so degrees below the maximum temperature you'll hold it at later. After probably not much more than 1 hour, start increasing the heat by 10 degrees each ½ hour till you reach the recommended maximum.

(3) But for the majority of its total drying time the food must have enough heat to kill the growth cells of some spoilers, as well as to remove moisture that lets other ones thrive (see "Temperature *vs.* Spoilage" again, page 1). This means that, no matter how low the temperature at which you start food in order to prevent case-hardening, etc., you have to raise the heat to a killing level and hold it there long enough to make it effective.

For more than half the total drying time, the heat must be sustained at at least 140 F.

(4) The first 2/3 of drying is accomplished at a faster rate than the last 1/3 is, and at this point—having been exposed for some time to maximum drying temperature, and having less protection through evaporation—the food can get too hot for the state it's in, and scorch. And just a hint of scorch will hurt the flavor.

When the food has reached the 2/3-dry stage, tend it with extra care to make sure it won't scorch. Keep rotating trays away from the heat source. If you need to, during the last 1 hour reduce the heat by 10 degrees or so, but stick to the 140-F. rule just above.

HANDLING FOOD IN A DRYER

Line or oil the trays—see the comments on tray bottoms under "Equipment for Drying"; spread prepared food on them one layer deep if it's in large pieces, not more than ½ inch deep if it's small. Place halved, pitted fruit with the cut side up (rich juice will have collected in the hollows if it was sulfured).

At this point newcomers to drying by artificial heat may want to weigh a sample tray of food for comparison with the weight of the same trayful after it's been in the dryer for a while, as a help in judging how much moisture has been lost.

Stagger the trays on the slides: one pushed as far back as possible, the next one as far forward as possible, etc. (as in the sketch earlier).

Check the food every ½ hour, stirring it with your fingers, separating bits that are stuck together. Turn over large pieces halfway through the drying time—but wait until any juice in the hollows has disappeared before turning apricots, peaches, pears, etc. Pieces near the front and back ends of the trays usually start to dry first: move them to the center of the trays.

If you add fresh food to a load already in progress, put the new tray at the top of the stack.

Make needed room for fresh food by combining nearly dry material in deeper layers on trays in the center of the dryer; it can be finished here without worry, but keep stirring it.

Using an oven

As far as you can, use an oven as you would a dryer, following general procedures and the specific instructions for each food.

Disengage the upper element of an electric oven; simply refrain from lighting the upper burner of a gas oven. (There are some tips on using the oven of a wood-burning range in the Roundup section at the end of the book.)

If the oven isn't vented, during drying time leave the door ajar about 1 inch for an electric oven, 6 inches for a gas one.

If your oven isn't thermostatically controlled, hang an oven thermometer where you can see it on the shelf nearest the source of heat, leave the door ajar—and be prepared to hover more than usual over the food that's drying.

Preheat the oven to 140 F. *If the oven cannot be set this low, skip the lowest slide you would otherwise be using: keep the bottom tray at least 8 inches from the heat source.*

From casual experience we found that an oven whose burner goes on and off allows wide variations in temperature—sometimes too wide to be practical for anything but a modest batch.

Don't overload the oven: with limited ventilation (even with a fan aimed toward the partly opened door) it can take as much fuel to dry a batch too big as might be used to dry two fairly modest batches.

Room-drying

Also done indoors is what can be called, for simplicity, room-drying. By this method food is hung in a warm room—the kitchen or the attic— for the days required to dry the material. Old-timers would suspend racks of drying food above the big wood-burning range, finish off a flitch of beef near by, and festoon strings of apple or pumpkin rings near the ceiling. Herbs are still usually dried in attics or the kitchens of country houses, hung either in the open or in paper bags to protect them from dust.

In extremely dry areas it may be feasible to stack-dry certain fruits and vegetables indoors, following enough time in sun or dryer to get them better than halfway along. Stack the trays with 6 inches of space between them, open windows to allow a free circulation of air, and force a draft across the trays with an electric fan. Shift the trays end for end occasionally and turn the food to ensure even drying.

PRE-DRYING TREATMENTS FOR PRODUCE

Before being dried at home by any method, fruits make a better product if they undergo one or more of the treatments given hereafter, while all vegetables are treated to stop the organic action that allows low-acid foods to spoil.

And, still speaking generally, a pre-drying treatment for fruits is optional for safety, but the pre-drying treatment for vegetables is a must.

The optional treatments for fruit involve (1) temporary anti-oxidants, to hold their color while they're peeled/pitted/sliced; (2) blanching in steam or in sirup as a longer-range means of helping to save color and nutrients; (3) very quick blanching—either in boiling water or steam (lye is not recommended)—to remove or crack the skins; (4) sulfuring as longest-range protection for some nutrients and for color. We'll sum up for or against these fruit treatments as best we can after we describe them. Then it's up to you to use them or not.

The treatment for vegetables is steam-blanching. The quick dunk in boiling water that's used in freezing is not adequate to protect them against spoilage in drying; and the much longer boiling time needed here would waterlog the material, in addition to leaching away a number of its nutrients.

The following descriptions are given in the order that the treatments are likely to occur in handling produce for drying: they're not necessarily in order of importance.

Temporary anti-oxidant treatment

Even though you intend to blanch or sulfur certain fruits to protect them during the long haul of drying and storage, chances are that you'll want to do something to prevent their darkening piecemeal while you're actually cutting a batch up.

SOAKING?—NO

The argument against soaks to retard the rusty look of oxidation is double-barreled: primarly, they *add* water to material you'll be working hard to take a great deal of the natural water out of; and then, since all the B vitamins, many minerals, the sugars and Vitamin C are water-soluble, these nutrients are lost to some degree in soaking.

THE GOOD ASCORBIC-ACID COAT

Pure ascorbic acid is our best safe anti-oxidant, and is used a lot in preparing fruits for freezing (q.v.). Use it here too. But with the difference that the solution will be many times stronger, and thus food coated with it can hold its color in transit in the open air for a longer time.

One cup of the solution will treat around 5 quarts of cut fruit, so prepare your amount accordingly. Sprinkle it over the fruit as you proceed with peeling, pitting, coring, slicing, etc., turning the pieces over and over gently to make sure each is coated thoroughly.

For apples: dissolve 2½ teaspoons of pure crystalline ascorbic acid in each 1 cup of cold water.

For peaches, apricots, pears, nectarines: dissolve 1 teaspoon of pure crystalline ascorbic acid in each 1 cup of cold water.

If the variety of fruit you're working with is likely to become especially rusty-looking when the flesh is exposed to air, it's O.K. to increase the concentration of ascorbic acid as needed. The proportions above usually do the job.

The commercial anti-oxidant mixtures containing ascorbic acid don't work as effectively, volume for volume, as the pure Vitamin C does, but they're often easier to come by. Follow the directions for Cut Fruits on the package.

Blanching fruits in heavy sirup

Adelle Davis, discussing candy substitutes, observes that natural sugar accounts for around 75 percent of the weight of most dried fruits. With this in mind, it seems excessive to precook fruit in heavy sirup in order to help prevent discoloration while drying—particularly when we have better ways to do the job. (And why not go ahead and *can* the stuff?—it's the old Open-Kettle process, plus long drying tacked on at the end.)

But if you want to turn fruit into an extra-sweet confection, here is the sirup-blanch most often described for apples, apricots, figs, nectarines, peaches, pears, plums and prunes.

Make a sirup of roughly 1 part sweetener to 1 part water, using refined or raw sugar, or part corn sirup or honey (and see "Sugar Sirups for Canning Fruits" on page 37); heat it to 212 F., and in it simmer the fruits for 10 to 15 minutes, depending on the size of the pieces. Remove the kettle from the heat and let the fruit stand in the hot sirup for about 15 minutes more. Then lift the fruit out and drain it well on paper toweling to remove as much surface moisture as you can. Save the sirup for the next batch.

Dry the fruit by whichever method you like. Take extra care that it doesn't stick to the trays, or scorch during the last stage of drying in artificial heat. Fruit treated this way is more attractive than usual to insects, so cover it well during sun-drying. And package it well for storage in a really cool, dry place.

Treating fruit skins without lye

Not only is lye tricky to work with in its own right (do see especially "Warnings About Lye" in canning Hominy on page 81, and Soap-making), but the alkali in soda compounds hurts many B vitamins and Vitamin C. Nevertheless lye—also known as caustic soda—is sometimes suggested for weakening the skins of some whole fruits and berries before they're dried, and for removing the skins of others. The boiling lye solutions for peeling are about eight times harsher than those for just weakening.

But a very quick dip in boiling water, *quite apart from the steam-blanching that helps keep the color and nutrients of certain cut fruits,* works well instead of the lye treatment. And it's safer for you and for your food.

FOR CHECKING THE SKINS

Nature provides a wax-like coating on the skins of cherries, figs, grapes, prunes and small dark plums, and certain firm berries like blueberries and huckleberries, and they all dry better if this waterproofing substance is removed beforehand.

The chances of case-hardening and rupturing (q.v.) are also reduced if the relatively tough skins of such fruits and berries are cracked minutely in many places; this is called "checking," and it allows internal moisture to be drawn through to the surface and there to be evaporated.

Because the 30 to 60 seconds required for the de-waxing and checking operation is often too short to let live steam be effective for the contents of the blanching basket, the answer is a very quick dip in briskly boiling water, followed by a dunk in very cold water, and thorough draining. Use the method described on page 57 for treating the skins of blueberries in the Raw pack variation, or use the one on page 154 for blanching vegetables before freezing.

Length of the dip depends on the relative toughness of the fruits' skins (cranberries are tougher-skinned than currants, for instance). Lay absorbent toweling on the fruit to remove excess moisture from their surface, and continue with the next step in handling the specific fruits.

FOR PEELING

We don't recommend following the advice of otherwise good old manuals when they say to peel peaches by rolling them around in a hot, strong lye solution until their skins rub away.

Routine peeling of any fruit except apples isn't necessary for making a good dried product anyway (see "When To Peel" in Drying Fruits). But if you feel that you must remove the skins from peaches, and even from apricots and nectarines, simply dip them, a few at a time, in boiling water for 30 to 60 seconds—ample time for firm-ripe fruit—cool them quickly in cold water, and pull their skins off by hand.

Steam-blanching before drying

On the whole, vegetables to be dried are blanched in full steam at 212 degrees F. for longer time than they are blanched, either in steam or boiling water, before being frozen. The length of blanching time is given for each vegetable in the individual instructions.

Steam-blanching also is suggested for certain fruits as an aid to discouraging oxidation, and for softening berries, as well as for checking (cracking) the skins of grapes, prunes and figs instead of treating them with lye. In addition to stopping the decomposing action of the enzymes and helping to fix the color of the food, steam-blanching protects some of the nutrients and loosens the tissues so drying is actually quicker.

Put several inches of water in a large kettle that has a close-fitting lid; heat the water to boiling, and set over it—high enough to keep clear of the water—a rack or wire basket holding a layer of cut food not more than 2 inches deep. Cover, and let the food steam for half the time required; then test it to make sure that each piece is reached by steam. A sample from the center of the layer should be wilted and feel soft and heated through when it has been blanched enough.

In a pinch you can use a cheesecloth bag, skimpily loaded with food, and placed on the rack to steam. Be careful not to bunch the food so much that steam can't get at all of it easily.

Remove the food and spread it on paper toweling or clean cloths to remove the excess moisture while you steam the next load; lay toweling over it while it waits for further treatment or to go on the drying trays.

Sulfuring for certain fruits

With more and more people digging in their heels against having things added to their food merely for looks—sometimes at the expense of nutritive values and in a few notable cases at the expense of safety—we thought it important to try for a cross-bearing on the matter of treating cut fruits with sulfur before drying them at home. So we went through the material we'd collected (though scattered, it can be got by any homemaker interested in nutrition), and came up with the following points.

SULFUR, SPOILAGE AND NUTRIENTS

For many years sulfur has been used to preserve the color of drying fruits whose flesh darkens when exposed to air. The fruits generally treated with sulfur have been apples, apricots, nectarines, peaches and pears; light-fleshed varieties of cherries, figs, plums and prunes have also been treated with sulfur to prevent oxidation, though not so routinely. Meanwhile it was noted that unsulfured fruits appear more likely to sour, get moldy or be attacked by insects during prolonged drying or in storage than is the case with the sulfur-treated dried fruits.

Further, sulfur is a mineral essential for life, and therefore is not harmful *per se* in the quantities used in home-drying (which allow plenty of leeway). The sulfur forms sulfurous acid when it unites with the water in the fruits' tissues, and the sulfurous acid evaporates during prolonged sun-drying, during storage, and from cooking; the residue that is eaten is turned into an innocuous compound that is then excreted. The more strongly acid the food, the greater is the power of sulfurous acid to inhibit the growth of molds and the bacteria that cause souring.

O.K. so far, but what of the nutrients lost in drying, particularly from cut fruits that are sulfured beforehand?

Nutritionists have published the results of research showing that, among others, Vitamins A (carotene), B_1 (thiamine) and C (ascorbic acid) are destroyed by exposure to air, but that sulfur aids in retention of A and C when they're hit by air, but helps to destroy what's left of B_1. (In addition, the sugars, the minerals, all the B vitamins and Vitamin C are water-soluble, and therefore soaking removes them.)

The problem, then, turns out to be more complex than the simple choice between having pretty color from sulfuring or losing thiamine from sulfuring. It means choosing to sulfur to save A and C, thereby losing thiamine, or forgoing sulfur to protect the remaining thiamine, and thus losing out on A and C.

And the choice brings up another consideration: deciding which nutritive ingredients are the reasons for choosing certain foods in the first place. Of course there are many other important nutrients beyond Vitamins A, B_1 and C to bear in mind, but these three vitamins are stressed below because they are notably affected by sulfur.

As an example, we can look up apples, apricots, peaches and pears in the USDA's *Composition of Foods*, because they are the only fruits listed that are dried with sulfur, and none of the four when fresh and raw has more than .03 milligram of thiamine—not quite 1/3 that of oranges, 1/2 that of tomatoes, and very little compared with some greens and minute compared with soybeans or wheat germ; their amount of Vitamin C is modest compared with many fresh raw vegetables, especially tomatoes (which in turn have about 1/2 the C in fresh oranges and 1/6 the C of fresh collards and turnip tops); apples and pears are mighty low in Vitamin A compared with oranges and tomatoes, but apricots have almost 14 times as much A as oranges and 3 times as much as tomatoes, and peaches have about 1/2 the amount of A that apricots do.

All four fruits are high in food energy to start with, and this is roughly 5 times greater, weight for weight, when they are dried—and so is the significant amount of Vitamin A in apricots. The Vitamin C, again weight for weight, is roughly doubled for dried apples, peaches and pears, but increases only 20 percent with apricots. The thiamine of dried apricots, peaches and pears is reduced by at least half, but is shown as nearly double for apples when dried.

This is the merest sampling from *Composition of Foods,* but it might suggest that all these fruits would be eaten primarily for their food energy, with apricots—and maybe peaches—also chosen for their Vitamin A; that the Vitamin C in all four is welcome but perhaps incidental; and that none of them is likely to be selected as an important source of thiamine.

Summarizing. These points seem to be adequate support for the consensus of the country's leading authorities on home-drying—

to sulfur certain cut fruits to ensure better storage, less darkening, and less loss of Vitamins A and C (albeit with a greater proportion of Vitamin B_1 usually lost). Sulfuring is optional: the results of drying without sulfur may be disappointing as to color, flavor and some aspects of nutrition, but food safety relies mainly on how competently these fruits are dried.

A POOR WAY TO SULFUR (SOAKING)

There are two ways generally given for sulfuring at home, and we'll mention the quicker but unsatisfactory method first, to get it out of the way.

As in all soaks, cut fruits held in a sulfite solution lose some of their water-soluble nutrients and tend to get waterlogged; in addition, the sulfur compound may often penetrate the tissues unevenly.

Further, for us the available instructions offered too wide a spread for comfort. The substances were given variously as sodium sulfite, sodium bisulfite and potassium metabilsufite, with the amount to use in each 1 gallon of water ranging from 1½ teaspoons on up to 3½ tablespoons. And soaking times, seemingly not geared closely enough to the strength of the solutions, were from 15 to 30 minutes.

HOW TO SULFUR WELL (FUMES, IN A BOX)

We'll describe this at some length because, having decided that *sulfuring is O.K. in certain cases,* we experimented with the mechanics of the procedure in order to amplify the sketchy instructions found so far.

The main bother in burning pure sulfur for the dioxide treatment is that the raw fumes irritate eyes and breathing passages, and therefore the business must be done outdoors in the open air. (All to the good, though, is the fact that they are so irritating: one whiff and you duck away—as you do from ammonia or activated lye, though perhaps not as fast—so you're not likely to keep on breathing them unknowingly.)

Otherwise, it's very simple and direct. And fun, if you relax and think of sulfur as something the ancients knew well, for it's the brimstone of the Bible. Anyway, sulfur first melts—at around 240 F.—becoming a brown goo before it ignites and burns with a clear blue flame that produces the acrid sulfur dioxide that penetrates evenly and is easy to judge the effect of. The usual amount to use is 1 level teaspoon burned for each 1 pound of prepared fruit.

Local drugstores had several kinds of dry sulfur, but we chose the "sublimed" variety—99½ percent pure, to be taken internally mixed with molasses (the classic folk tonic); it's a soft yellow powder with no taste and the faintest of scents that's nothing like the rotten-egg odor of hydrogen sulfide. The 2-ounce box was enough to do 16—18 pounds of prepared fruit. Also, from the hardware store we got a 4-ounce cake of 100 percent refined sulfur (with a short wick to start it melting and burning, because it's a fumigating candle to use in sealed rooms to get rid of bugs in the woodwork). This cake we found much harder than the powder to gauge the dose of: its weight figured in teaspoons, the amount of sulfur needed for a batch of fruit took longer to burn than the time required for exposure to the fumes.

Loading and stacking the trays. You'll be weighing your prepared fruit to determine how much sulfur to use in the treatment, and thus you can keep the batch within limits of what your sulfuring box will handle effectively. Nor should you sulfur more food in one session than your drying arrangements will accommodate as soon as the sulfuring is done—6 trays' worth, for example, if you use an indoor dryer the size of the one described earlier. Spread the fruit one layer in thickness on the trays (which *don't* have metal bottoms), placing any convex pieces with their hollow side up in order to prevent loss of the rich juice that collects during treatment. Limit each sulfuring batch to food of the same type and size: you won't be able to shuffle the food around to compensate for different exposure times, as you do in a dryer. And don't overload the trays or crowd the sulfuring box, because it's easier in the long run to deal with two short stacks, widely spaced, than with one stack too tall and inadequately spaced.

Put the bottom tray on blocks of some kind to raise it at least 4 inches above ground. Separate the trays above it with wooden spacers to hold them 3 inches or so apart. Allow for 6 inches of clearance between the top of the stack and the sulfuring box that will be inverted over it.

The sulfuring box. This you can make from the same materials used for the indoor dryer (q.v.); or you can cover a slatted crate snugly with building paper; or you can use a stout, large carton of the sort that household appliances are shipped in. The box should be tall enough to cover an adequately spaced stack of up to 6 trays, and be about

12 inches longer than the trays from front to back so there'll be room for the sulfuring dish *beside* the stack.

At the bottom near one corner cut out a slot 6 inches wide by 1 inch high if the box is large, 3 x 1 inch if it's just the average supermarket carton; this will be the only air intake needed to keep the sulfur burning, and you'll cover the slot after the sulfur is consumed. Near the top of the side opposite the intake slot, make a hole the diameter of a pencil; this also will be covered when the sulfur has burned. (The need for this tiny upper hole is Norman Rogers's discovery: it wasn't mentioned in the various directions we started out with, but he found that, without it, the sulfur stopped burning prematurely and required relighting; and the escape of fumes through it was negligible.)

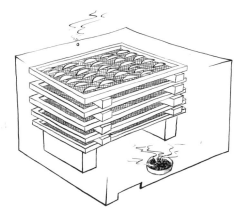

Lighting and burning. Experimenting with sulfur either loose in a small pan/dish or twisted in a bit of paper, Norman found that the powder spread in a shallow container burned better than the same amount in a paper spill: it caught with no trouble, forming under the match a brown puddle that spread and fed the flame until the sulfur was consumed. A spent match left in the sulfur prevented complete melting and burning, as did scraps of charred paper, he said.

Also, the sulfur burned best—i.e., steadily, without relighting, quickly and completely—when the powder was in a smooth layer *not more than ½ inch deep,* settled by tunking the bottom of the burning dish. And the depth, not the total amount, apparently determines the rate of burning, because a little mound of 2 teaspoons' worth burned in 12 minutes, and it took about 15 minutes to burn 12, 18 and 24 teaspoons of sulfur spread a scant ½ inch deep and lit in one, two, and three places, respectively; the melting puddles soon converged into one burning pool.

He said he wasn't bothered by the little sulfur dioxide that escaped when he tilted the box to snake out the sulfuring dish to check on the burning. And the brimstone smell had evanesced from his hands within an hour after he was through with his experiments.

The sulfuring container should be set at the side or in front of the stack: if it were underneath, the food on the bottom tray directly above it would discolor from concentrated exposure to even the small amount of smoke involved in the combustion.

Whatever you have for a burning dish, it should be perfectly clean before each use. The dish can be metal, enameled, or heavy crockery. Metal corrodes from the sulfur after a number of uses (one reason why tray bottoms of metal screening are never put in a sulfuring chamber), and aluminum becomes pitted most quickly; he simply made one-time-use dishes by molding a double thickness of household foil around the bottom of a flat-bottomed container of the appropriate size. He made the sides of his dishes a good 1 inch higher than the layer of sulfur—about 1½ inches all told—because if the sides are too high in proportion to the burning surface of the powder, the flame can smother for lack of air. A flat round dish 3 inches in diameter takes about 12 teaspoons of powdered sublimed sulfur smoothed ½ inch deep; a 4-inch one takes about 18, and a 5-incher about 24 teaspoons.

Be careful about using bright red or yellow ceramic dishes: certain of these pigments on glazed pottery can contain cadmium. Unless you know that the glaze of either color is cadmium-free, don't use such pottery for sulfuring. Or for anything else.

How much sulfur? Weigh the prepared fruit before spreading it in a single layer on the treatment trays, and use 1 teaspoon of powdered pure sulfur for each 1 pound of fruit. This 1-for-1 ratio is conservative but, so far as we can find out, it's adequate for the average small-family operation; much better to adjust sulfuring *time* to your method than to increase the sulfur you burn per pound.

How long to sulfur? Sulfuring time varies according to the texture of the fruit, whether it's peeled, how big the pieces are, and whether it's exposed for a long time in air—as in sun- and shade-drying outdoors —or has a relatively short exposure, as in a drying box or an oven. Specific times are given in the instructions for individual fruits.

Start to count sulfuring time *after* the sulfur has finished burning, which will take about 15 minutes (see above), and you have tightly closed off the air-intake slot at the bottom of the box and the tiny breathing hole at the top. The reason: the necessary amount of sulfur dioxide must first be created by total combustion of the sulfur which has been measured for the weight of the batch being treated; then the fumes must be given time to reach and penetrate the surfaces of the fruit on the stacked trays. With the sulfuring box made airtight, you simply leave it inverted over the stacked trays for the required period.

In general, apples, apricots, peaches and pears are sulfured twice as long for sun-drying as they are for an indoor dryer. And a practical rule-of-thumb is to sulfur small slices of these fruits for the box dryer for a minimum of 20 to 30 minutes, and larger pieces for comparatively longer. Therefore, since we *recommend sulfuring for sun-drying* because of the extended time in vitamin-destructive open air, these fruits would be sulfured for about 60 minutes if they're to be sun-dried as slices, with double that sulfuring when they're quartered, and more than two hours when they're halved.

On the other hand, home-drying done in an indoor box or an oven is often a small-batch affair—and in such cases it's not always feasible to get cranked up to for the sulfuring operation. Though not as effective over-all as sulfuring, there are other measures that can be substituted for all or part of the sulfur treatment for fruit to be dried by artificial heat in small batches; they're correlated in the "Summary of Pre-drying Treatments" in a minute.

Unloading the sulfur box. Stand to windward of the box so the fumes won't come your way, reach across the top, and tilt the whole thing toward you until the box rests on its side or end: it's like lifting the lid of a Pressure canner to let the steam escape away from your direction (as in the picture on page 25).

Remove the trays from the top, being careful not to spill any juice that has collected in the hollows of the fruit. If sulfuring was done on trays that fit a dryer, just slide them as is into the preheated drying box or oven; otherwise lift the fruit on to trays all ready for going immediately out in the sun or in artificial heat.

POST-DRYING TREATMENTS FOR PRODUCE

Even after a sample from each tray of food has shown no moisture when cut and pressed, and feels the way its test says it should, you can't take for granted that the whole batch is uniformly dry. And especially if it's been dried outdoors do you need to get rid of any spoilers—airborne micro-organisms or bugs you can see—that may have got to it somewhere along the line.

Conditioning

This makes sense particularly for food done in a dryer because there's often more chance of spotty results than in sun-drying, and you'll want moisture content equalized between under- and overdried pieces.

Cool the food on the trays, then pour it all into a large, open, non-porous container *that's not aluminum*—a big crock, enamel- or graniteware canner, even a washtub lined first with plastic and then with clean sheeting (washtubs are generally galvanized). Have the containers raised on trestles or tables, and in a warm, dry, airy, well-screened, animal-proof room.

Stir the food once a day—twice if you can manage to—for 10 days or 2 weeks, depending on the size of the pieces. It's O.K. to add freshly dried food to the conditioning batch, but naturally not if the food in a container is almost ready to store.

Fruits, usually being in larger pieces (and therefore more likely to need finishing off) than vegetables, need more conditioning time.

Pasteurizing

Recommended strongly for sun-dried fruits and vegetables and for dryer-processed vegetables that have been cut small enough so their drying time perhaps hasn't been long enough to kill the spoilers.

Don't bother cranking up the dryer for this, and don't do large amounts at a time: use an oven with a thermometer in it, and time the process.

Preheat the oven to 175 F. Spread the food loosely not more than 1 inch deep on the trays; don't do more than two trays' worth at the same time. Heat brittle-dried vegetables, cut small, for 10 minutes at 175 F.; treat fruits—cut larger and therefore needing more time—for 15 minutes at 175 F.

Remove each pasteurized batch and spread it out to cool on clean toweling, etc. Cover lightly with cheesecloth to keep dried food clean. Package one batch while other batches are pasteurizing.

PACKAGING AND STORING

Have dried, treated produce thoroughly cooled before putting it up in small amounts (if packaged warm it will sweat, especially in plastic bags).

Use small paper or plastic bags; twist the tops and secure the closures with string, wire tape, rubber bands, etc.; store packets in large critter-proof containers with heavy lids in a dry, cool place (in humid climates, store in glass jars). Label if necessary.

Drying Fruits

The following instructions are merely individual applications of the principles, methods and treatments described up till now in this section, and newcomers to drying are likely to have better results if they look at the introductory *Why-How* (and sometimes pro/con) before they tackle specific fruits.

In general below, sulfuring is strongly recommended for all cut fruits that are *sun-dried,* in order to help save important vitamins, prevent insect infestations and hold color; steam-blanching is recommended for fruits processed in a *dryer;* a temporary ascorbic-acid coating is suggested for certain fruits that oxidize readily, whether dried in the sun or in artifical heat outdoors; some whole fruits are "checked" with boiling water to crack their skins; pasteurizing is recommended for sun-dried fruits, to kill off any bugs that have got to them. All these treatments are optional: they are included because they result in a more nutritious and attractive product.

It is assumed that all the fruits are firm-ripe, without blemishes, and have been washed carefully in cold water as a preliminary to preparation.

See "Tests for Dryness in Produce" on page 235.

COOKING DRIED FRUITS

Pour boiling water over them in a saucepan *just to cover*—no more now: they shouldn't be drowned, and you can always add more if you need to—and simmer the fruit, covered, for 10–15 minutes, depending on the size of the pieces. Remove from heat and let cool, still covered. Sweeten to taste at the very end of cooking, or when removed from heat (sugar tends to toughen fruit fibers in cooking). For best flavor, chill the fruit overnight before serving.

If the fruit is to be "reconstituted" to use in a cooked dish (a pie or a cream dessert, say), put it in a bowl, add boiling water just to the top of the fruit; cover; and let it soak up the water for several hours, or until tender. Add water sparingly and only if the pieces seem still to be tough, because the liquid is full of good things and should be included in the recipe as if it were natural juice.

APPLES

Best for drying are late-autumn or early-winter varieties, including: Baldwin, Ben Davis, Northern Spy, Spitzenburg; then Winesap, Jonathan, Greening, Rome Beauty, both Delicious, the Russets.

Prepare. Peel, core, slice in 1/8-inch rings. As you go, coat slices with strong ascorbic-acid solution to hold color temporarily.

Dryer. Steam-blanch 5 minutes; remove excess moisture. Begin them at 130 F.; raise gradually to 150 F. after the first hour; when nearly dry, reduce to 140 F. Test dry. Condition. Package; store. Average total drying time: up to 6 hours, depending on size of slices.

Sun-drying. Prepare as above, using ascorbic-acid coating. If not steam-blanched for 5 minutes, sulfur for 60 minutes; if blanched, sulfur for 30 minutes. Proceed with drying. Test dry. Pasteurize. Package; store.

Room-drying. Prepare as above. Steam-blanch 5 minutes *and* sulfur 30 minutes; or sulfur only for 60 minutes. Thread on clean string, and festoon near the ceiling of a warm, dry, well-ventilated room (attic), or above the cookstove (kitchen). Test dry. Pasteurize.

The slices may also be dried on stacked trays with an electric fan blowing across them.

DRY TEST: Leathery, suede-like; no moisture when cut and squeezed.

APRICOTS

Pick before they are so ripe they drop from the tree.

Prepare. Halve and stone. Hold against oxidizing with ascorbic-acid coating.

Dryer. Steam-blanch halves 15 minutes, slices 5 minutes. Remove excess moisture and start in the dryer at 130 F., raise gradually after the first hour to 150 F. Reduce to 140 F. for last hour or when nearly dry. Test dry. Condition; store. Average total drying time: up to 14 hours for halves, up to 6 hours for slices.

Sun-drying. Prepare as above with ascorbic-acid coat. If steam-blanching (above, as for a dryer) sulfur slices 30 minutes, halves 90 minutes. If not blanched, sulfur slices 1 hour, halves 2 hours. Remove halves carefully to drying trays so as not to spill juice in the hollows, and place cut-side up in the drying trays. Turn when all visible juice has disappeared. Test dry. Pasteurize; store.

DRY TEST. Leathery, pieces fall apart after squeezing; no moisture when cut.

BERRIES, FIRM

Prepare. Check (crack) the skins of blueberries, huckleberries, currants and cranberries, etc. by dipping for 15–30 seconds (depending on toughness of skin) in rapidly boiling water. Plunge into cold water. Remove excess moisture.

Dryer. Start at 120 F., increase to 130 F. after one hour, then to 140 F.; they will rattle on the trays when nearly dry. Keep at 140 F. until dry. Test dry. Condition; store. Average total drying time: up to 4 hours.

Sun-drying. Check the skins as above for the dryer. Remove excess moisture and put on trays one layer deep in the sun. Test dry. Pasteurize; store.

DRY TEST. Hard. No moisture when crushed.

BERRIES, SOFT

There are so many better ways to use these—canned, frozen, in preserves —that there's not much use in drying them. Strawberries are especially blah and unrecognizable when dried.

CHERRIES

If not pitting cherries, check their skins with a 15—30-second dunk in boiling water; cool immediately. Some people sirup-blanch (q.v.) before drying cherries.

Dryer. Remove excess moisture from checking treatment. Start at 120 F. for one hour, increase gradually to 145 F. and hold there until nearly dry. Reduce to 135 F. the last hour if danger of scorching. Test dry. Pasteurize. Cool and store. Total drying time: up to 6 hours.

Sun-drying. Pit. Sulfur for 20 minutes. Dry. Test dry. Pasteurize. Cool and store.

TEST DRY. Leathery and sticky.

FIGS

Prepare. Small figs or ones that are partly dry on the tree may be dried whole. Large juicy figs are halved.

Dryer. Check skins by a quick dunk in boiling water for 30—45 seconds. Cool quickly. If cut in half, steam-blanch for 20 minutes. Some people sirup-blanch (q.v.) whole figs before drying. To dry, start at 120 F., increase temperature after the first hour to 145 F. When nearly dry, reduce to 130 F. Test dry. Condition. Cool and store. Total average drying time: up to 5 hours for halves.

Sun-drying. Check the skins as above if drying whole. Sulfur light-colored varieties (like Kadota) for 1 hour before drying. If figs are to be halved, do not check the skins—instead, steam-blanch the halves for 20 minutes and then sulfur for 30 minutes. Test dry. Pasteurize. Cool and store.

DRY TEST. Leathery, with flesh pliable; slightly sticky to the touch, but they don't cling together after squeezing.

GRAPES

Use only Thompson or other seedless varieties for drying.

Prepare. Check the skins by dipping 15–30 seconds in boiling water and cooling immediately. Proceed as for whole Cherries.

Dryer. Proceed as for Cherries. Total average drying time: up to 8 hours.

Sun-drying. Handle like Cherries, but don't sulfur.

NECTARINES

Prepare as for Apricots.

Dryer. Steam-blanch halves 15–18 minutes, slices for 5 minutes. Dry with the same heat sequence as for Apricots. Test dry. Condition; store. Drying time will be roughtly the same as for Apricots.

Sun-drying. Prepare and handle like Apricots. Test dry. Pasteurize. Cool and store.

DRY TEST. Pliable, leathery.

PEACHES

Yellow-fleshed freestone varieties are the best for home-drying.

Prepare. Commercially dried peaches are dried in halves, and next to never peeled. For home-drying in slices, however, peel either by a knife as you are working along, or dip whole fruit in boiling water for 30 seconds, cool quickly and strip off skins.

Halve and stone the fruit; leave in halves or cut in slices. Scoop out any red pigment in the cavity (it darkens greatly during drying). Treat slices or halves with ascorbic-acid coat as you go along to hold color temporarily.

Dryer. Steam-blanch slices 8 minutes, unpeeled halves 15–20 minutes. Start drying at 130 F., increase gradually to 155 F. after the first hour. Turn over halves when all visible juice has disappeared. Reduce to 140 F. when nearly dry to prevent scorching. Average total drying time: up to 15 hours for halves and up to 6 hours for slices.

Sun-drying. Prepare as for the dryer. If steam-blanching slices and halves as above, sulfur slices 30 minutes, halves for 90 minutes. If not blanched, sulfur 60 minutes and 2 hours, respectively. Be careful not to spill the juice in the hollows when transferring the halves to drying trays, where they're placed cut-side up. Proceed as for Apricots. Test dry. Pasteurize. Cool and store.

DRY TEST. Leathery, rather tough.

PEARS

Best for drying is the Bartlett. (Kieffer is better used in preserves.) For drying, pears are picked quite firm and before they are ripe. They are then held at not more than 70 F. in boxes in a dry, airy place for about 1 week—when they are usually ripe enough for drying.

Prepare. Split lengthwise, remove core with a melon-ball scoop, take out the woody vein. Leave in halves or slice (pare off skin if slicing); coat cut fruit with ascorbic acid as you work, to prevent oxidizing.

Dryer. Steam-blanch slices 5 minutes, halves 20 minutes. Start at 130 F., gradually increasing after the first hour to 150 F. Reduce to 140 F. for last hour or when nearly dry. Test dry. Condition; cool and store. Average total drying time: up to 6 hours for slices, 15 hours for halves.

Sun-drying. Sulfur as for Peaches; dry like Peaches. Test dry. Pasteurize; cool and store.

DRY TEST. Suede-like and springy. No moisture when cut and squeezed.

PLUMS AND PRUNES

These may be dried whole, halved or sliced.

Prepare. Check the skins with a 30—45-second dunk in boiling water. Cool immediately.

Dryer. Steam-blanch 15 minutes if halved and stoned, 5 minutes if sliced. Start *slices* and *halves* at 130 F., gradually increase to 150 F. after the first hour; reduce to 140 F. when nearly dry.

Start *whole,* checked fruit at 120 F., increase to 150 F. gradually after the first hour; reduce to 140 F. when nearly dry. Test dry. Condition; cool and store. Average total drying time for slices: up to 6 hours; halves, up to 8 hours; whole, up to 14.

Sun-drying. Check the skins of whole fruit. Sulfur whole fruit for 2 hours. Sulfur slices and halves for 1 hour. Test dry. Pasteurize. Cool and store.

DRY TEST. Pliable, leathery. A handful will spring apart after squeezing.

Drying Vegetables and Herbs

See the over-all introduction to this section for a description of the techniques involved in the directions given below.

Vegetables are precooked by steam-blanching before being dried. *This treatment is NOT optional:* it helps stop the spoilers occurring in low-acid foods.

Except for corn dried on the cob, all vegetables are pasteurized if their processing heat has not been high enough, or prolonged enough, to destroy spoilage organisms. Pasteurizing is particularly important for sun-dried vegetables.

Vegetables are cut smaller than fruits are, in order to shorten the drying process—for the faster the drying, the better the product (so long as the food isn't *cooked*). The approximate total drying times in a dryer are not given below, but they range from around 4 to 12 hours, depending on the texture and size of the pieces.

See "Tests for Dryness in Produce" on page 235.

COOKING DRIED VEGETABLES

Before being cooked, all vegetables except greens are soaked in cold water just to cover until they are nearly restored to their original texture. Never give them any more water than they can take up, and always cook them in the water they've soaked in.

Cover greens with enough boiling water to cover and simmer until tender.

BEANS—GREEN / SNAP / STRING / WAX (LEATHER BRITCHES)

Prepare. String if necessary. Split pods of larger varieties lengthwise, so they dry faster. Steam for 15—20 minutes.

Dryer. Start *whole* at 120 F. and increase to 150 F. after the first hour;

reduce to 130 F. when nearly dry. For *split beans,* start at 130 F., increase to 150 F. after first hour, and decrease to 130 F. when nearly dry. Test. Condition; pasteurize. Cool and store.

Sun-drying. Handle exactly as for the dryer. Test dry. Pasteurize certainly. Cool and store.

Room-drying. Prepare as above but do not split. String through the upper 1/3 with clean string, keeping the beans about ½ inch apart. Hang in warm, dry, well-aired room. Test. Pasteurize certainly. Cool and store. (Old-timers would drape strings near the ceiling over the wood cookstove; they gave the name "leather britches" to these dried beans—probably because they take so long to cook tender.)

DRY TEST. Brittle.

BEANS, LIMA (AND SHELL)

Allow to become full-grown—beyond the stage you would when picking them for the table, or for freezing or canning—but before the pods are dry. Shell. Put in very shallow layers in the steaming basket and steam for 10 minutes. Spread thinly on trays.

Dryer. Start at 140 F., gradually increase to 160 F. after the first hour; reduce to 130 F. when nearly dry. Test dry. Condition; pasteurize. Cool and store.

Sun-drying. Not as satisfactory for such a dense, low-acid vegetable as processing in a dryer is. However, follow preparation as for a dryer. Test dry. Condition if necessary; pasteurize certainly. Cool and store.

DRY TEST. Hard, brittle; break clean when broken.

BEETS

Prepare. Choose beets small enough so they have no woodiness. Leave ½ inch of the tops (they will bleed during precooking if the crown is cut). Steam until cooked through, 30—45 minutes. Cool. Trim roots and crowns. Peel.

Slice crosswise no more than 1/8 inch thick; OR shred them with the coarse blade of a vegetable grater: the smaller, thinner pieces dry more quickly, but of course their use in cooking is more limited.

Dryer. Put slices in at 120 F. and increase to 150 F. after first hour; reduce to 130 F. when nearly dry.

Put finer shreds in at 130 F. Increase gradually to 150 F. after first hour; turn down to 140 F. when nearly dry. Test dry. Condition; pasteurize. Cool and store.

Sun-drying. Prepare as for dryer, but shreds are recommended here instead of slices because they dry more quickly. Condition if necessary; pasteurize certainly. Cool and store.

DRY TEST. Slices very tough, but can be bent; shreds are brittle.

BROCCOLI

Prepare. Trim and cut as for serving. Cut thin stalks lengthwise in quarters; split thicker stalks in eighths. Steam 8 minutes for thin pieces, 12 minutes for thicker pieces.

Dryer. Start at 120 F., gradually increasing to 150 F. after the first hour; reduce to 140 F. when nearly dry. Test dry. Condition; pasteurize. Cool and store.

Sun-drying. Prepare as for dryer. Test dry. Condition if necessary; pasteurize certainly. Cool and store.

DRY TEST. Brittle.

CABBAGE

Most people put it by in a root cellar (q.v.) or as Sauerkraut (see under Salting); but some of it dried can be handy for soup.

Prepare. Remove outer leaves. Quarter; cut out core, and shred with the coarse blade of a vegetable grater, about the size for cole slaw. Steam 8—10 minutes. Cabbage—as do all leaf vegetables—packs on the trays during drying, so spread it evenly and not more than ½ inch deep. At a time, you'll dry only about half as much by weight of leaf vegetables as you do with other types of food, because they need more room to prevent matting.

Dryer. Start at 120 F., increase gradually to 140 F. after the first hour; reduce to 130 F. when nearly dry: the thin part of the leaves dries more quickly than the rib, and therefore is more likely to scorch and turn brown. Keep lifting and stirring the food on the trays to keep it from matting. Test dry. Condition if necessary; pasteurize. Cool and store.

Sun-drying. Follow procedure for dryer. Test dry. Pasteurize certainly. Cool and store.

DRY TEST. Extremely tough ribs; the thin edges crumble.

CARROTS

Like beets, above, they keep so well in a root cellar (q.v.) that it seems a shame to dry them—unless it's a choice between dried carrots or no carrots at all.

Choose crisp, tender carrots with no woodiness. Leave on ½ inch of the tops.

Prepare. There's no need to peel good young carrots: just remove whiskers along with the tails and crowns—which is done *after* they're steamed. Steam until cooked through but not mushy—about 20–30 minutes, depending on the size. Trim off tails, crowns with tops, and any whiskers. Cut in 1/8-inch rings, or shred.

Dryer. Proceed as for Beets, either sliced or shredded. Test dry. Condition; pasteurize. Cool and store.

Sun-drying. Proceed as for Beets, either sliced or shredded. Test dry. Condition if necessary; pasteurize certainly. Cool and store.

DRY TEST. Slices very tough and leathery, but will bend; shreds are brittle.

CELERY

For drying *leaves,* see Herbs.

Prepare stalks. Split outer stalks lengthwise, leave small center ones whole; trim off leaves to dry as herb seasoning. Cut all stalks across in no larger than ¼-inch pieces. Steam for 4 minutes.

Dryer. Start at 130 F., increase to 150 F. after the first hour; reduce to 130 F. when nearly dry. Test dry. Condition; pasteurize, because the maximum heat may not be long enough to stop spoilers. Cool and store.

Sun-drying. Prepare as for the dryer. Test dry. Pasteurize certainly. Cool and store.

DRY TEST. Brittle chips.

CORN-ON-THE-COB

Use popcorn and flint varieties for this. (Flint corn was the food-grain of the Colonists, who were taught by the Indians to use it. It is different from "dent" corn, which shrinks as it dries.) The kernels of both flint and popcorn remain plump when hard and dry.

These varieties are allowed to mature in the field and become partly dry in the husk on the stalks. Both are usually air-dried in the husk. However, in some hot countries the husks are peeled back from the partly dried ears and braided together or tied together. In northern Italy, in the fall, whole sides of brick-lattice buildings are golden with corn being finished in the sun. Both popcorn and flint corn (which is ground into meal) rub easily from the cob when the kernels are dry. Save the cobs for smoking home-cured meats (q.v.).

DRY TEST for popcorn: rub off a little and pop it. If the result's satisfactory, then immediately put it into moisture-vapor-proof containers with tight closures, to prevent it from getting too dry to pop (the remaining moisture in the kernel is what makes it explode in heat).

DRY TEST for flint corn: brittle—it cracks when you whack it. Store in sound air- and moisture-proof barrels; but if you must hold it in large cloth bags, invert the bags every few weeks: this prevents any moisture from collecting on the bag where it touches the floor.

CORN, PARCHED

Correctly dried sweet corn is more than a stop-gap for the many people who consider it superior in flavor to canned corn. Any variety of sweet corn will do.

Prepare. Gather in the milk stage as if it were going straight to the table. Husk. Steam it on the cob for 15 minutes for more mature ears, 20 minutes for quite immature ears (the younger it is, the longer it takes to set the milk). It's a good idea to separate the corn into lots with older/larger and younger/smaller kernels so you can handle them uniformly. When cool enough to handle, cut it from the cob as for canning or freezing whole-kernel corn (q.v.). Don't worry about the glumes and bits of silk: these are easily sifted out after the kernels are dry.

Dryer. Spread shallow on the trays. Start at 140 F.; raise to 165 F. gradually after the first hour; reduce to 140 F. when nearly dry, or for the last hour. Stir frequently to keep it from lumping together as it dries. Test dry. Condition. (Pasteurizing is not necessary following processing in a dryer *if the temperature has been held as high as 165 F. for an hour.*) The silk and glumes will separate to the bottom of the conditioning container; but if you don't condition, shake several cupfuls at a time in a colander whose holes are large enough to let glumes and silk through. Best stored in moisture-vapor-proof containers in small amounts.

Sun-drying. Prepare exactly as for the dryer. Stir frequently to avoid lumping. Pasteurize certainly. Shake free of glumes and silk. Package and store.

Historical note. The Colonists learned from the Indians to loosen the the husks lightly at the top just enough to allow the silk to be pulled out; then they pressed the husk together, and laid the ears on a bed of hot coals, turning them frequently so they wouldn't scorch. When the corn was roasted—in about 25 minutes—ears were air-cooled and husked. Then the kernels were cut from the cobs and spread on a sheet to dry in the sun for about 3 days, being brought in each evening before dew-time.

DRY TEST. Brittle, glassy and semi-transparent; a piece cracks clean when broken.

GARLIC

It keeps so well when it's conditioned after harvesting that it's seldom dried at home. If you do want to dry it, though, treat it like Onions.

HERBS

This category includes celery *leaves* (described after we're done with the others) as well as the greenery from all aromatic herbs—basil, parsley, sage, tarragon: whatever you like to grow and use.

All such seasonings are air-dried, at temperatures never more than 100 F. (higher, and they lose the oils we value for flavor); and as much light as possible should be excluded during the process.

For the best product, dry only the tender and most flavorful leaves from the upper 6 inches of the stalk.

Gather and prepare. Cut them on a sunny morning after the dew has dried, and choose plants that have only just started to bloom; cut them with plenty of stem, then strip off tougher leaves growing lower than 6 inches on the stalk, and remove blossom heads. Hold in small bunches by the stems and swish the leaves through cold water to remove any dust, or soil thrown up from a rain. Shake off the water and lay on absorbent toweling to let all surface moisture evaporate.

Bag-drying. Collect 6 to 12 stems loosely together, and over the bunched leaves put a commodius brown-paper bag—one large enough so the herbs will not touch the sides. Tie the mouth of the bag loosely around the stems 2 inches from their ends, and hang the whole business high up in a warm, dry, airy room. When the leaves have become brittle, knock them from the stems and package them in air-tight containers and store away from light. You can pulverize the leaves by rubbing them between your hands; then store.

Tray-drying. Prepare as for drying in bags. Cut off the handle-stems, spread the leafed stalks one layer deep on drying trays. Put the trays in a warm, dark room that is extra well ventilated (if you use a fan, don't aim it *on* the trays—the herbs could blow around— instead, "bounce" the forced draft off a wall, so it will be gentler). Turn the herbs several times to ensure even drying. Test dry. Remove from stems, and package as above.

Celery leaves. Cut out the coarsest midribs. Tray-dry as for any leaf herb.

DRY TEST. Readily crumbled.

MIXED VEGETABLES

These are never dried in combination: drying times and temperatures vary too much between types of vegetables. Dry vegetables and sea-soning separately, *then* combine them in small packets to suit your taste and future use.

MUSHROOMS

Only young, unbruised, absolutely fresh mushrooms should be dried.

Prepare. Wash quickly in cold water if necessary; otherwise wipe with a damp cloth. Remove stems (they're denser than the caps as a rule, so shouldn't be dried in the same batch with the tops). Slice the caps in 1/8-inch strips—cut stems across in 1/8-inch rings—and treat them with the ascorbic-acid coating if it's important to you to keep them from darkening as you work. Steam for 12—15 minutes.

Dryer. Start at 130 F., increase gradually to 150 F. after the first hour; reduce to 140 F. when nearly dry. Test dry. Condition; pasteurize. Cool and store.

　　Sliced caps and stems process at the same temperature sequences, but stem pieces usually take longer.

Sun-drying. Prepare as for the dryer. Test dry. Condition if necessary; pasteurize certainly. Cool and store.

DRY TEST. Brittle.

ONIONS

Prepare. Peel; slice in rings about 1/8-inch thick. Uniformity is important here, because slices too thin can brown and scorch; it's better to have evenly thicker pieces than some 1/8 inch and other paper-thin. No steaming is necessary.

Dryer. Put them in at 140 F. and keep them there until nearly dry, watching carefully that thinner pieces are not browning. Reduce to 130 F. for the last hour if necessary. Test dry. Condition. Cool and store.

Sun-drying. Prepare as for the dryer. Test dry. Pasteurize. Cool and store.

DRY TEST. Light-colored, but brittle.

PEAS, BLACK-EYED, treat like Beans (Shell), above.

PEAS, GREEN

Choose young, tender peas as you'd serve them fresh from the garden. From there on, treat them like Shell Beans, above.

DRY TEST. Shriveled and hard; shatter when hit with a hammer.

PEPPERS, HOT (CHILI)

Choose mature, dark-red pods. Thread them on a string through the stalks, and hang them in the sun on a south wall. When dry, the pods will be shrunken, dark, and may be bent without snapping.

PEPPERS, SWEET (GREEN OR BELL)

Prepare. Split, core, remove seeds; quarter. Steam 10–12 minutes.

Dryer. Start at 120 F., gradually increase to 150 F. after the first hour; reduce to 140 F. when nearly dry (if any are thin-walled, reduce to 130 F. toward the end, and keep stirring them well). Test dry. Condition. Cool and store.

Sun-drying. Prepare as for the dryer. Test dry. Condition if necessary; pasteurize certainly. Cool and store.

DRY TEST. Crisp and brittle.

POTATOES, SWEET (AND YAMS)

Only firm, smooth sweet potatoes or yams should be used.

Prepare. Steam whole and unpeeled until cooked through but not mushy, about 30—40 minutes. Trim, peel; cut in 1/8-inch slices, or shred.

Dryer. Proceed as for sliced or shredded Beets. Test dry. Condition; pasteurize. Cool and store.

Sun-drying. Prepare as for dryer. Test dry. Condition if necessary; pasteurize certainly. Cool and store.

DRY TEST. Slices extremely leathery, not pliable; shreds, brittle.

POTATOES, WHITE (IRISH)

These root-cellar too well to bother drying. But dry like Turnips, below.

PUMPKIN

Deep-orange varieties with thick, solid flesh make the best product. There's not much use in drying in chunks, because they're to be mashed after cooking.

Prepare. Take them directly from the garden (they shouldn't be conditioned as for root-cellaring). Split in half, then cut in manageable pieces for peeling and removing seeds and all pith. Shred with the coarse blade of a vegetable grater (less than 1/8 inch thick). In shallow layers in the basket, steam for 6 minutes.

Dryer. Proceed as for shredded Beets, above. Test dry. Condition; pasteurize if length of maximum processing heat isn't enough to stop spoilers. Cool and store.

Sun-drying. Prepare as for the dryer. Test dry. Pasteurize certainly. Cool and store.

DRY TEST. Brittle chips.

Historical note. In olden days, pumpkins were often halved at their equators, then cut in rings about 1 inch thick; rind and seeds and pith were removed from each ring. The rings were hung on a long stick and dried slowly in front of a fire until they were like tough leather.

SPINACH (AND OTHER GREENS)

Prepare. Use only young, tender, crisp leaves. Place loosely in the steaming basket and steam for 4—6 minutes, or until well wilted. Remove coarse midribs; cut larger leaves in half. Spread sparsely on drying trays, keeping overlaps to a minimum (leaves tend to mat).

Dryer. Start at 140 F., increase to 150 F. after the first hour; if necessary, reduce to 140 F. when nearly dry, to avoid browning. Test dry. Condition. Cool and store.

Sun-drying. Prepare as for the dryer. Test dry. Pasteurize certainly. Cool and store.

DRY TEST. Easily crumbled.

SQUASH (ALL VARIETIES), treat like Pumpkin.

TURNIPS AND RUTABAGAS

Like white (Irish) potatoes, which root-cellar extremely well if handled right (q.v.), turnips and rutabagas are seldom dried.

If you're compelled to dry them, though, quarter and peel them, then shred—and steam and dry as for shredded Carrots.

DRY TEST. Brittle chips.

Drying Meat and Fish

For 99 percent of North America's householders, drying meat and fish would come under the heading of "Playing with Food," since they lack either the appropriate conditions (see page 231–232) or the need to do it—and climate and necessity are what make the remaining 1 percent masters of the art.

We're not going to try to give blow-by-blow instructions for making jerky as the Mountain Men did, or drying codfish with the expertise of a Newfoundland native. The following are the basic steps, with the *Why.* Adapting them to your own circumstances is up to you.

USING DRIED MEAT AND DRIED FISH

Jerky traditionally was shaved off (or gnawed off) and eaten as is, because it was a staple for overland wanderers who were traveling light and far from assured supplies of fresh meat. (Helpful ins-and-outs of concentrated journey food are to be found in Horace Kephart's

Camping & Woodcraft; see "pemmican" especially.) Today several versions of it appear in stick form as snacks, for either the Long Trail or a cocktail party.

Dried salt fish—the type described below—is always freshened by soaking beforehand, either in cold water or fresh milk; the soaking liquid is discarded here, because of the extremely high salt content.

Such fish were standard fare even in the hinterlands far from salt water. A small roadway in our wooded Green Mountains is still called by old-timers "Codfish Alley"—so named by homesteaders who went down to the flatboats coming up the Connecticut River to buy salt codfish, which they carried home in armloads like billets of stove-wood. See Recipes.

DRYING MEAT (JERKY)

Jerked meat is roughly ¼ the weight of its fresh raw state.

Preferred meats for jerking are mature beef and venison (elk is too fatty), and only the lean muscle is used. Cut lengthwise of the grain in strips as long as possible, 1 inch wide and ½ inch thick.

DRY TEST. Brittle, as a green stick: it won't snap clean, as a dry stick does. Be sure to test it *after* it cools, because it's pliable when still warm, even though enough moisture is out of it.

Unsalted Jerky

This does not mean unseasoned—there's a bit of salt for flavor—but the meat is not salted heavily to draw out moisture or to act mildly as a preservative.

Lay cut strips on a cutting-board, and with a blunt-rimmed saucer or a meat mallet, pound the following seasonings (or your own variations thereof) into both sides of the meat: salt, pepper, garlic powder, your favorite herb. Use not more than 1 teaspoon salt for each 1 pound of fresh meat, and the other seasonings according to your taste.

Arrange seasoned strips ½ inch apart on wire racks—cake-cooling ones, or the racks from the oven; put them in a preheated 150 F. oven, and immediately turn the heat back to 120 F. Prop the oven door open 1 inch to allow the extra amount of moisture to escape. After 5 to 6 hours turn the strips over; continue drying at the same temperature for 4 hours more, when you check for dryness. When dry enough, jerky is shriveled and black, and is brittle when cooled.

Wrap the sticks of jerky in moisture-vapor-proof material, put the packages in a stout container with a close-fitting lid, and store below 40 F. Because it contains too little salt to cause leeching when the meat is frozen, it may also be stored in the freezer.

Salted Jerky

Try this in the sun; or, if you're emulating the frontiersmen, over a very slow, non-smoking fire that's not much more than a bed of coals.

Prepare a brine of 2½ cups of pickling salt for 3 quarts of water, and in it soak the cut strips of meat for 1 or 2 days. Remove and wipe dry.

OVER COALS

Arrange a rectangular fire-bed and drive forked poles into the ground at each corner; the forks should come about 4 feet above the ground. Two hours before you're ready to begin drying the salted meat, start a fire of hardwood and let it burn down to coals.

Cut two fairly heavy poles to go from fork to fork on the long sides, and sticks as thick as a finger—and sharpened at one end—to lay at right angles over the side-poles. The salted strips may be draped over the cross-sticks; or they may be suspended from the sticks (pass the sharpened stick through the meat about 3 inches from one end) and spaced several inches apart.

Feed the fire with small hardwood so carefully that juice does not ooze out from the excess heat, or the meat start to cook.

Depending on conditions, drying could take 24 hours. Test for dryness; package and store.

IN THE SUN

This is nothing to try in a back yard—or indeed in any place near civilization. It needs clear, pure air, uncontaminated by animals or human beings: after all, it is a method used on old-time hunting trips deep into the High Plains.

Choose a time when you'll have good—but not roasting—sun, dry air day and night, and a gentle breeze. Hang the salted strips from a drying frame such as described above (of course with no fire), and leave them there until they become brittle-dry.

A BASIC PROCEDURE FOR DRYING FISH

The amateur possibly could home-dry *salted* fish with reasonable safety, but drying fish *without salt* is best left to commercial processing plants that have controlled atmosphere and sanitation.

Salt-dry any abundant fish, but keep in mind that lean varieties keep better than the fatty types do. Shade-drying is best, except where the sunlight is comparatively weak: fish spoils easily in strong sun.

Cut the throat of a fresh-caught fish; remove the gills but leave the bony structure behind them (this holds the flesh together after the backbone is removed). Drain off the blood, wash the fish and remove the head. Remove the back and rib bones (as for Freezing, see page 175); discard them along with any innards from the cavity. Brush-scrub the fish, then put it in weak brine (1 cup salt to each 1 gallon of water) for 20 minutes to firm the flesh. Drain very well.

Coat all surfaces of each fish liberally with fine pickling salt, using 1 pound of salt for 4 pounds of fish, and stack the opened fish flesh-side up on a slatted wooden rack outdoors. Don't make the stacks more than 12 layers deep, with the top layer skin-side up. Leave them stacked from several days up to 1 week, depending on the height of fish and the dryness of the air. Brine made by the salt and fish juices will drain away. Move the pile inside each night and weight it down to press out more brine.

Scrub the fish again to remove the salt, and put them on wooden frames outdoors to complete the necessary removal of moisture from their tissues. Hang or spread the fish on cross-pieces, preferably in an open shed with good ventilation. However, in far northern latitudes people do dry fish in the sun's weak rays.

To store, wrap dried fish in waxed paper or plastic, pack in wooden boxes, and store in a cool place, 50 F. or less.

DRY TEST. No imprint is left when the fleshy part of a fish is pinched between thumb and forefinger.

Root-Cellaring

Of all the time-tested ways of putting food by, only wintering·over in cold storage is less satisfactory today than it was a century or more ago. And the reason is simple: all the technological advances we're so pleased with in construction and heating have given us cozy, dry basements instead of cool, damp cellars, and the chilly shed off the pantry has given way to a "utilities room" or a warm passageway between carport and kitchen.

So this section is telling how to turn back the clock and create conditions that several generations of North Americans have devoted themselves to improving. It includes some indoor areas that are warmer and drier than the traditional outbuilding or cellar with stone walls and a packed earthen floor, and it also includes some arrangements outdoors that are a good deal more rough-and-ready.

Several of the ones described may require outlays of money or effort or hardihood beyond the expectations of the usual householder.

And most of them need more maintenance than does any other type of storage discussed up till now. This means constantly watching the weather to forestall the effects of sudden extra cold/warmth/wetness, and constantly checking the food for signs of spoil—but it's maintenance just the same.

HOW IT WORKS

Root-cellaring is a homemade verb embracing ordinary winter storage for fresh, raw, whole vegetables and fruits that have not been processed to increase their keeping quality. Used commonly, it means to hold these foods for several months after their normal harvest in a cold, rather moist atmosphere that will not allow them to freeze or to complete their natural cycle to decomposition.

271

The freezing points and warmth tolerances of produce vary. The range to shoot for generally, though, is 32 to 40 degrees Fahrenheit—the effective span for refrigeration—with only a couple of vegetables needing warmer storage to keep their texture over the months. In this range the growth of spoilage micro-organisms and the rate of enzymatic action (which causes overripening and eventual rotting) are slowed down a great deal.

Good home root-cellaring involves some control of the amount of air the produce is exposed to, since winter air is often let in to keep the temperature down. But fresh whole fruits and vegetables respire after they're harvested (some more than others: apples seem almost to *pant* in storage), so the breathing of many types is reduced by layering them with clean dry leaves, sand, moss, earth, etc., or even by wrapping each individually in paper. These measures of course aren't as effective as those of commercial refrigerated storage, which rely in part on drastic reduction of the oxygen in the air supply, but they work well enough for the more limited results expected from home methods.

THE HUMAN LIMITATIONS

We'll be describing a variety of storage arrangements in a minute, including a couple that are drier and sometimes warmer than the traditional ones (since we can't leave in limbo those foods that require something different from the classic old cellar treatment). But first a word about practicality.

The beauty of root-cellaring is that it deals only with whole vegetables and fruits and there are no hidden dangers: if it doesn't work, we know by looking and touching and smelling that the stuff has spoiled, and we don't eat it.

On the other hand it's something that sounds a lot more feasible than it may really turn out to be.

First, the householder must learn something about the idiosyncrasies of the fruits and vegetables he plans to store on a fairly large scale: for example, apples and potatoes—the most popular things to carry over through winter—can't be stored near each other, and the odor of turnips and cabbages in the basement can penetrate up into the living quarters, and squashes want to be warmer than carrots do.

Then he casts around for the right sort of storage. And the solution may cost more than its value to his over-all food program, especially if it's a structure more elaborate or permanent than the family's make-up warrants.

But aren't there the less pretentious outdoor pits, or the more casual barrels sunk in the face of a bank? Yes; and they're fun to use—except in deep-snow country when they can be a worry to get at.

Samuel Ogden of Landgrove, Vermont, organic gardener and noted Green Mountain countryman, warns the newcomer to cold-climate root-cellaring to avoid three things: counting too heavily on cold storage, having too much diversity, and having it inaccessible in bad weather. But for the family with a serious, long-term food program that depends in great degree on its own efforts, though, he recommends the Vermont experience of Helen and Scott Nearing described in *Living the Good Life:* the Nearings' last two root cellars are well-thought-out and substantial affairs—and represent total dedication to a way of life.

EQUIPMENT FOR ROOT-CELLARING

Storage place, indoor or outdoor (see below)
Clean wooden boxes/lugs/crates or barrels; or stout large cardboard
    cartons (for produce that wants to be dry, not damp)
Plenty of clean paper for wrapping individually, or shredding
Plenty of clean dry leaves, sphagnum, peat moss or sand
A tub of sand to keep moistened to provide extra humidity if needed
Simple wall thermometer certainly; humidity gauge (optional)

INDOOR STORAGE

The classic root cellar downstairs

There are fewer of these to be found as the years go by, even in the old houses in our part of the country. Usually in the corner of the original cellar-hole, they have two outside walls of masonry (part of the foundation), the floor is packed earth, and any partitions are designed more to support shelving than to keep out warmth from a nonexistent furnace. They incorporate at least one of the small windows that provide cross-ventilation for the whole cellar to keep overhead floor joists from rotting; propped open occasionally during the winter, it's the answer for regulating temperature and humidity.

Such a place can be ideal today, although the house is "restored" and now contains a furnace (protected from seepage in the springtime by a surrounding pit and an automatic sump pump). Just complete boarding-off the two inside walls, cut and hang a door in one of them, and apply whatever is handiest for insulation against heat from the furnace.

To be perfect, it should have an inner partition to separate storage of fruits and vegetables; and its own electric light. For the rest, build stout shelves or put up trestles to hold boxes, crates and baskets off the floor on the sides away from the window. Reserve one well-drained corner for the vegetables that will be clumped upright with their roots set in soil or sand and moistened by hand to keep them fresh.

Darken the window(s)—potatoes turn green in light when they're stored, and this isn't good. If necessary, keep clearing snow from the areaway that's below ground leading to the window.

And check the whole thing for places where field mice can get in and feast on your crops during the lean winter months, and stop them up.

A modern basement store room

To some extent, in a closed-off corner of a modern basement you can copy the conditions of the old-time downstairs root cellar.

Choose a corner preferably on the north or east (where the temperature is likely to be most even); it should have no heating ducts or oil or water pipes running through it. And if it has a window you'll be saved having to figure out a system for governing temperature, ventilation and humidity.

The store room should be at least 6 x 6 feet if you're going to bother building it at all.

The existing right-angled outside walls of the basement will become the outside walls of the store room. Make two inner right-angled walls of fiberboard or ½-inch lumber nailed to 2 x 4 studding spaced 2 feet apart and secured to a footing. Leave open space on one side to frame and hang a door.

Insulate the new room from the inside—glass batts that include a vapor barrier go easily between the studs. Finish the inside with wall-boarding if you want to, covering the seams with common lath. Insulate the door and give it a simple latch. *Insulate the inside walls only.*

Make an air-duct box to cover at least the lower 2/3 of the window when it's opened, and carry the box part way down the side of the wall (see detail of the sketch). The duct brings cold incoming air to the lower part of the room and lets warm air from the upper part be drawn out-doors through the upper 1/3 of the opened window.

Ideally you should have a fruit-storage room too—or at least a part of the all-purpose store room blocked off for fruit. If you have a window in the fruit room too, build an air-duct box for it. Otherwise you'll regulate temperature/humidity by opening and closing the entrance to the fruit section.

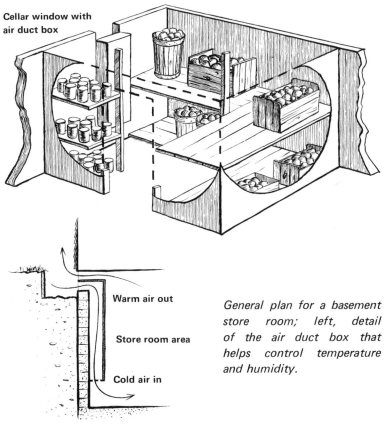

Cellar window with
air duct box

Warm air out

Store room area

Cold air in

General plan for a basement store room; left, detail of the air duct box that helps control temperature and humidity.

Using a bulkhead

Many middle-aged houses have an outside entrance to the cellar: a flight of concrete steps down to the cellar wall, in which a wide door is hung to give access to the cellar. The top entrance to the steps—the hatch—is a door laid at an angle 45 degrees to the ground.

On the stairway, which probably is closed from the outside during the coldest months anyway, you can store barrels/boxes of produce. You could put up rough temporary wooden side walls along the steps; but certainly lay planks on the steps to set your containers on. Insulate the door into the cellar proper with glass batts. If you need to, keep a pail of dampened sand on one of the steps to add humidity. You're likely to be propping the hatchway door open a few inches from time to time to help maintain proper temperature on the steps. This means shoveling snow from the bulkhead, and piling it back on when this outside door is closed again.

A dry shed

This takes the place of the garage advocated by some people—but not by us: too much oil and gasoline odor (some produce soaks stray odors up like a sponge), and far too great a quantity of lead-filled emissions from running motors. And anyway temperature is often uncontrollable.

Instead of using the garage, partition off storage space in the wood-floored shed leading into the kitchen, if you have an old house in the country. Or segregate a storage area in a cold, seldom used passageway.

Storage areas like these are usually not fit for such long-term storage as the basement root cellar or store room is.

Up attic

An old-fashioned attic generally is the last place in the house to cool off naturally as cold weather sets in; and unless the roof is well insulated, the attic temperature rises on sunny winter days. This fluctuation doesn't matter much for some foods, however (see the chart), though it does for onions, say. The answer is to wall off, and ceil, a northeast corner for anything that needs maintained low temperature and dryness. Then you can put pumpkins and such near the stairway leading to the attic—and leave the hall door downstairs open whenever you need to.

SMALL-SCALE OUTDOOR STORAGE

There's a good deal of information around that contains ideas for full-dress outdoor buildings for root-cellaring. Of these we suggest two: the USDA *Home and Garden Bulletin No. 119, Storing Vegetables and Fruits in Basements, Cellars, Outbuildings, and Pits*—available from your County Agent—and the September 1971 issue of *Organic Gardening and Farming* (Rodale Press, Emmaus, Pennsylvania 18049), with more variety.

Use either one to take off from in designing an elaborate building within your climate zone and your means. We limit the discussion below to arrangements for small-scale outdoor storage.

Some mild-climate pits, etc.

The USDA bulletin and the other sources describe several easy-to-make and cheap outdoor storage facilities, all either on well-drained ground or sunk only several inches below the surface. See the chart for which produce likes the conditions they provide.

However, such arrangements can be counted on *only in places with fairly mild winters* that have no great extremes in temperature. At any rate, make a number of small storage places, fill them with only one type of produce to each space, and be prepared to bring the entire contents of a store-place indoors for short storage once the space is opened.

MILD-CLIMATE CONE "PITS"

Most instructions call a storage place like this a pit, but it's really a conical mound above ground. To make it, lay down a bed of straw or

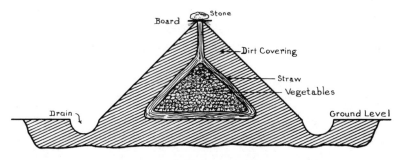

leaves, etc.; pile the vegetables *or* fruits (don't mix them together) on the bedding; cover the pile well with a layer of the bedding material. With a shovel, pat earth on the straw/leaf layer to hold it down, extending a "chimney" of the straw to what will be the top of the cone to help ventilate and control the humidity of the innards of the mound. Use a piece of board weighted by a stone to act as a cap for the ventilator. Surround the "pit" with a small ditch that drains away surface water.

As colder weather comes, add to the protective layer of earth, even finishing with a layer of coarse manure in January.

MILD-CLIMATE CABBAGE "PIT"

This is quite like the cone above, except that it's longer and allows stored food to be removed piecemeal.

Lay the uprooted cabbages head-down on a bedding of straw, etc., pack insulating straw/leaves around them, and cover all with earth. Cut a drainage carry-off on each side of the pit.

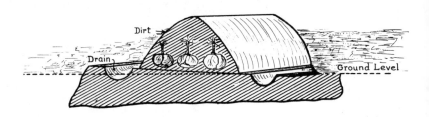

MILD-CLIMATE COVERED BARREL

Still called a "pit" is a barrel laid on its side on an insulating bed of straw, chopped cornstalks, leaves, etc. Put only one type of produce in the barrel on bedding of straw/leaves. Prop a cover over the mouth of the barrel; cover all with a layer of straw, etc., and earth on top to hold it down.

OUTDOOR FRAME FOR CELERY, ETC.

Dig a trench 1 foot deep and 2 feet wide, and long enough to hold all the celery you plan to store. Pull the celery, leaving soil on the roots, and promptly pack the clumps upright in ranks 3 to 5 plants wide.

Covered barrel, above, and celery frame—both for a mild climate.

Water the roots as you range the plants in the trench. Leave the trench open until the tops dry out, then cover it with a slanted roof. This you make by setting on edge a 12-inch board along one side of the trench, to act as an upper support for the cross-piece of board, etc., that you lay athwart the trench. Cover this pitched roof with straw and earth.

Walter Needham's cold-climate pit

As he told in *A Book of Country Things,* he was raised in rural Vermont by a grandfather for whom a candle-mold was a labor-saving device. So whenever we want to learn about totally practical methods of pioneer living in the cold country, we turn to Walter Needham. He was the first to point out that the conical "pit" wouldn't do an adequate job in 20-below Zero weather. This is his alternative:

Choose the place for your pit on a rise of ground to avoid seepage. There, shovel out a pit about 1½–2 feet deep and 4 feet wide at the bottom, throwing dirt up all around to build a rim that will turn water away; dig a V-shaped drainage ditch around it for extra protection (see sketches). Take out any stones near the sides of the pit because frost will carry from one stone to another in rocky ground. The pit needn't go below the deep frost-line if such frost conductors are removed. Pack the bottom of the pit with dry mortar sand 2 to 3 inches deep: the loam, having retained moisture, will freeze; the sand holds the food away from the loam.

On the layer of sand make a layer of vegetables not more than 1 foot deep; cover the vegetables with more fine sand, dribbling it in the crevices, to fill the pit nearly to ground level. Cover the sand with straw or spoiled hay, mounded to shed the weather. Hold down this cover with a thin layer of sod—or, nowadays, plastic sheeting weighted down with 1 to 2 inches of earth. Cover one end of the mound with a door laid on its side and slanted back almost like a bulkhead entrance. In winter you'll move the door away to dig in for the vegetables, and, as they're taken out, move the door back along the mound.

This root-pit is best for beets, carrots, turnips and potatoes.

Walter Needham's sunken barrels

Again, these are for cold-winter areas with uneven temperature.

Into the face of a bank dig space to hold several well-scrubbed metal barrels with their heads removed—one barrel for apples, say;

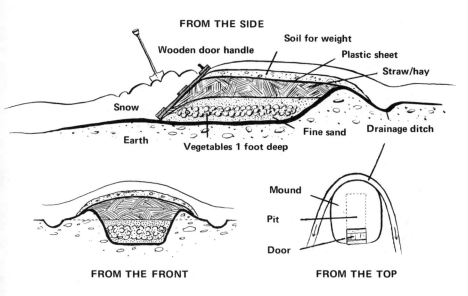

Cold-climate storage in a pit, above, and in sunken barrels.

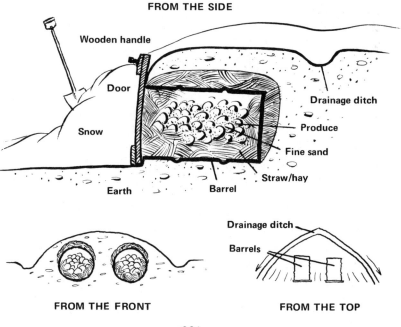

one for potatoes, one for turnips. Take out any large stones that would touch the barrels and conduct frost to them, and provide a bedding of straw/dry leaves, etc., for the barrels to rest on. Slant the open end of the barrels slightly downward, so water will tend to run out.

Put straw or whatever in the barrels for the produce to lie on, and fill the barrels from back to front, using dry leaves or similar material to pack casually around the individual vegetables or fruits if they need it.

Over the opening put a snug cover propped against it—a stout wooden "door" with a wooden handle (did you ever have the skin of your palm freeze on to metal in below-Zero weather?). Dig a shallow V-shaped drainage ditch to carry surface water away from the barrels (as in the top-view sketch above).

The snow will be added protection in the deepest cold of the winter. Shovel it back against the door after removing food from the barrels.

Root-Cellaring Fruits and Vegetables

ROOT-CELLARING FRUITS

Only several of the most popular fruits root-cellar well; and of these, apples retain their texture and flavor longest, with several varieties of pears next in storage life.

Like vegetables, fruits to be stored over the winter should be harvested as late as possible in the season, and be as chilled as you can get them before they're put in their storage containers (it will take even a properly cold root cellar a good deal of time to remove the field heat from a box of warm apples).

Because they absorb odors from potatoes, turnips and other "strong" vegetables, fruits should have their own special section partitioned off in the root cellar if they are stored in quantity; otherwise put them in another area where the conditions simulate those of a root cellar (see the chart), or keep them as far from the offending vegetables as possible.

We recommend clean, stout cartons, wooden boxes or splitwood fruit baskets over the classic apple barrels for storing fruits for a small family. Metal barrels are best used for fruits in underground storage, with the barrel well insulated from frost in the earth.

Some fruits are individually wrapped for best keeping, but all should be bedded on a layer of insulating—and protecting—straw, hay, clean dry leaves, with the straw, etc., between each layer of fruit, and several inches of bedding on top of the container.

All fruits need checking periodically for spoilage. If you're afraid your fruit will deteriorate faster than you can eat it fresh, have a midwinter preserve-making session. They're fun on a cold lowery day.

APPLES

Best keepers: *late* varieties, notably Winesap, Yellow Newton, Northern Spy; then Jonathan, McIntosh in New England, Cortland, Delicious. Pick when mature but still hard, and store only perfect fruit. Apples kept in quantity in home cold storage usually will be "aged" from Christmas on.

Apples breathe during storage, so put them in the fruit room of a root cellar so they don't give off their odor (or moisture) to vegetables. Wrap individually in paper (to cut down their oxygen intake); put them in stout cartons, boxes, barrels that can be covered, and have been insulated with straw, hay or clean dry leaves. If you use large plastic bags or liners for the boxes, etc., cut ¼-inch breathing holes in about 12 places in each bag.

They also may be stored in hay- or straw-lined pits or in buried barrels covered with straw and soil, etc.

Farmers in Vermont often store wrapped apples in milk cans (not used now since bulk-tank regulations went into effect) with tight-fitting lids; as they respire, the apples make their own humidity. Cans then may be held in a dry shed where they won't freeze, rather than in a root cellar.

Check periodically and remove any apples that show signs of spoiling. See the chart for ideal conditions.

GRAPEFRUIT AND ORANGES

Store unwrapped in stout open cartons or boxes in the fruit room of a root cellar (see chart for conditions). Inspect often for spoilage, removing spoiled ones and wiping their mold off sound fruit they've touched.

Recommended Conditions for Over-the-winter Cold Storage

Produce	Food Freezes At (F.)	Type of Storage	Ideal Temperature (F.)	Relative Humidity (%)	Air Circulation	Average Storage Life
Fruits:						
Apples	29.0	RC-F	at 32	MM: 80–90	moderate	4–6 months
Grapefruit	29.8	RC-F	at 32	MM: 80–90	slight	1–1½ months
Grapes	28.1	RC-F	at 32	MM: 80–90	slight	1–2 months
Pears	29.2	RC-F	at 32	MM/M: 85–90	slight	2–7 months
Vegetables:						
Beans, dried	won't	DS; A	32–50	D: 70	moderate	12+ months
Beets	(c. 30)	BSR; P/B; RC	32–40	M: 90–95	slight	4–5 months
Cabbage	30.4	P/B; RC; DS	at 32	MM/M: 85–90	slight	late F–W
Carrots	(c. 30)	BSR; P/B; RC	32–40	M: 90–95	slight	6 months
Cauliflower	30.3	RC	at 32	MM: 80–90	slight	1½–2 months
Celery	31.6	BSR; frame; RC	at 32	MM/M: 85–90	slight	late F–W
Chinese cabbage	(c. 31.9)	BSR; frame; RC	32–34	VM: 95–98	slight	3–4 months
Dried seed, live	won't	A	32–40	D: 70	slight	12+ months
Endive	31.9	frame	at 32	MM/M: 85–90	moderate	2–3 months

284

Horseradish	(c. 30.4)	BSR; P/B; RC	at 32	M: 90–95	slight	4–6 months
Kale	(c. 31.9)	frame	at 32	VM: 95–98	moderate	1 month
Kohlrabi	(c. 30)	BSR; P/B; RC	32–40	M: 90–95	slight	2–3 months
Leeks	(c. 31.9)	BSR; P/B; RC	at 32	MM: 80–90	moderate	1–3 months
Onions	30.6	DS; A	at 32	D: 70	moderate	F–W
Parsnips	30.4	BSR; P/B; RC	at 32	M: 90–95	slight	F–W
Peas, dried	won't	DS; A	32–50	D: 70	moderate	12+ months
Peppers	30.7	BSR; RC; DS	45–50	MM: 80–90	slight	½–1 month
Popcorn	won't	A	to 75	D: 70	slight	12+ months
Potatoes	30.9	BSR; P/B; RC	35–40	MM: 80–90	slight	F–W
Pumpkins	30.5	BSR; A	at 55	MD/D: 70–75	moderate	F–W
Salsify	(c. 30.4)	BSR; P/B; RC	at 32	M: 90–95	slight	4–5 months
Squash	30.5	BSR; A; RC	at 55	VD: 50–70	moderate	F–W
Sweet potatoes	29.7	BSR; DS	55–60	MD/D: 70–75	moderate	F–W
Tomatoes, green	31.0	BSR; DS	55–70	MM: 80–90	moderate	1–1½ months
Turnips	(c. 30)	P/B; RC	at 32	M: 90–95	slight	2–4 months
Winter radishes	(c. 30)	BSR; P/B; RC'	at 32	M: 90–95	slight	2–4 months

A = attic : BSR = basement store room : DS = dry shed : frame = coldframe : P = outdoor pit : B = buried barrel : P/B = pit or barrel : RC = root cellar : RC-F = root cellar for fruit : D = dry : VD = very dry : MD/D = moderately dry to dry : M = moist : MM = moderately moist : MM/M = moderately moist to moist : VM = very moist : F = fall : W = winter.

GRAPES

Catawbas keep best, then Tokays and Concords. Pick mature but before fully ripe.

Grapes absorb odors from other produce, so give them their own corner of the root-cellar fruit room (see chart for conditions). Hold in stout cartons or boxes lined with a cushion of straw, etc., with straw between each layer; don't burden the bottom bunches with more than three layers above them, fitting the bunches in gently. Cover with a layer of straw. Check often for spoilage.

PEARS

Best keeper of the dessert varieties is Anjou, with Bosc and Comice popular among the shorter keepers. (Bartlett and Kieffer ripen more quickly and earlier: the former is especially good for canning, the latter for spicing whole or used in preserves; see Canning and The Preserving Kettle.)

Pick mature but still green and hard. Hold loosely in boxes in a dry, well-aired place at 50–70 F. for a week before storing. Then store them like apples. See chart for conditions.

Warning: Pears that have started ripening above 75 F. during the interim between picking and storage, or are root-cellared at too high a temperature, will spoil, often breaking down or rotting inside near the core while the outside looks sound.

ROOT-CELLARING VEGETABLES

Root-cellared vegetables freeze sooner than fruits do, as a rule; and, if you store a variety beyond the commonest root crops—beets, carrots, potatoes, turnips and rutabagas—you need several different kinds of storage conditions. See the chart again, and the individual instructions below.

Wooden crates and movable bins, splitwood baskets, stout cartons— all make good containers for indoor storage. Insulating and layering materials are straw, hay, clean leaves, sphagnum and peat moss, and dry sand. The moist sand suggested for certain vegetables shouldn't be at all puddly-wet: if it's cold to the touch and falls apart when squeezed, leaving a few particles stuck to your hand, it should be the right degree of dampness.

Don't fill containers so deeply that the produce at the bottom is ignored in the periodic examinations for spoilage. And forgo building permanent bins that can't be moved outside for between-season scrubbing and sunning—stout shelving for the containers at convenient heights off the floor is a much better use of storage space.

BEANS (SHELL), DRIED

Cool the finished beans and package in plastic bags which you then put in large, covered, insect- and mouse-proof containers. See chart for conditions.

BEETS

Harvest in late fall after nights are 30 F. (they withstand frosts in the field) but when the soil is dry. Do not wash. Leave tails and ½ inch of crown when removing the tops. Pack in bins, boxes or crates between layers of moist sand, peat or moss; or line containers with a large plastic bag that has ¼-inch breathing holes cut in about 12 places. See chart for conditions.

CABBAGE, LATE

Cabbage is not harmed by freezing in the field if it's thawed slowly in moist sand in the root cellar and not allowed to refreeze. Late cabbage can be stored effectively in several ways. (1) Roots and any damaged outer leaves are removed and the heads are wrapped closely in newspaper before being put in bins or boxes in an outdoor root cellar (the odor is more noticeable when they are wrapped than when covered with sand or soil). (2) With roots removed, the heads are covered with moist soil or sand in a bin in the root cellar. (3) In pit storage, stem and root are left on and they are placed head-side down. Straw, hay or clean, dry leaves may be packed between the heads for added protection and the whole business covered with soil. (4) The outer leaves are removed and cabbages are hung upside down in a dry place at normal room temperature for several days or until they "paper over." Then they are hung upside down in the root cellar.

Warning: Cabbages have one of the strongest odors of all vegetables, so don't store them where the smell can waft through the house. See chart for conditions.

CARROTS

Carrots may stay in the garden after the first frosts. After digging, handle like Beets. See chart for conditions.

CAULIFLOWER

Another hardy vegetable that can withstand early frosts. Cut off the root and leave plenty of protecting outer leaves; store in boxes or baskets with loose moist sand around and covering the heads. See chart for conditions.

CELERY

Celery should not be stored near turnips and cabbages, which taint its flavor.

Pull the plant, root and all; leave the tops on. Do not wash. Place the roots firmly in moist sand or soil, pressing it well around the roots. Water the covered roots occasionally to keep them moist *but do not water the leaves.*

The procedure for celery may be followed in a trench, a coldframe-bed, or in a corner of the root-cellar-floor that has been partitioned off to a height of six inches. The closer the celery is stood upright, wherever it's stored, the better. See chart for conditions.

CHINESE CABBAGE

Pull and treat like Celery. See chart for conditions.

DRIED SEED (LIVE)

So long as it is kept quite dry, live seed won't germinate. Store in plastic bags that are then put in a large, mouse-proof covered container; or in canning jars that are wrapped in newspaper to keep out the light. It can't be hurt by natural low temperatures: see chart for conditions.

ENDIVE

Pull as for Celery. Do not trim, but tie all the leaves close together to keep out light and air so the inner leaves will bleach. Set upright and close together with moist soil around the roots, again as for Celery. See chart for conditions.

HORSERADISH

One of the three vegetables that winters-over beautifully in the garden *when kept frozen.* Mulch carefully until the weather is cold enough to freeze it, then uncover to permit freezing and, when it has frozen in the ground, mulch heavily to prevent thawing. For root-cellaring, prepare and handle like Beets. See chart for conditions.

KALE

Treat like Celery right on down the line. See chart for conditions.

KOHLRABI, handle like Beets; see chart.

LEEKS, see Celery and chart.

ONIONS

Pull onions after the tops have fallen over, turned yellow and have started to dry—but examine for thrips (which can cause premature wilting, etc.).

Bruised or thick-necked onions don't store well.

Onions grown from sets are stored in a cool, very dry place on trays made of chicken wire with the tops pointing down through the mesh.

Onions must be conditioned—allowed to "paper over"—in rows in the field; turn them several times so their outsides dry evenly. Smaller amounts may be surface-dried on racks in a dry, airy place under cover; or the tops may be braided and the bunches hung in a dry room. After they are conditioned, trim the tops and hang the onions in net bags or baskets in a dry, airy storage place. See chart for conditions.

PARSNIPS

Actually *improved* by wintering frozen in the garden (and not allowed to thaw), but may be root-cellared if necessary. Treat like Beets or Horseradish. See chart for conditions.

PEPPERS

Careful control of temperature and moisture is imperative in storing peppers (see chart): they decay if they get too damp or the temperature goes below 40—45 F.

Pick before the first frost; sort for firmness; wash and dry thoroughly—handling carefully because they bruise easily.

Put them one layer deep in shallow wooden boxes or cartons lined with plastic in which you cut about 12 ¼-inch holes; close the top of the plastic. Even under ideal conditions the storage life is limited.

POPCORN, see Beans (Shell), dried; see chart.

POTATOES, EARLY

Don't harvest after/during heavy rains, or on a hot day. Dig them carefully early in the morning when the temperature is no more than 70 F. Condition them for 2 weeks at 60–70 F. in moist air to allow any injuries to heal: early potatoes will not heal if they are conditioned in windy or sunny places. After conditioning, store at 60 F. for 4 to 6 weeks. These early varieties do not keep long, and spoil readily held at over 80 F.

POTATOES

Late potatoes are much better keepers than early varieties. Dig carefully. Hold them in moist air about 2 weeks between 60–75 F. to condition: do *not* leave them out in the sun and wind. Put them, not too deep, in crates, boxes or bins stored in a dark indoor or outdoor root cellar; cover to keep away all light (to prevent their turning green, which could mean the presence of selenium, not good in large doses).

After several months' storage, potatoes held at 35 F. may become sweet. If they do, remove them to storage at 70 F. for a week or so before using them. Potato sprouts must be removed whenever they appear, especially toward the end of winter. Early sprouting indicates poor storage conditions. See chart for conditions.

Warning: Potatoes make apples musty, so don't store these two near each other unless the apples are well covered.

PUMPKINS

Harvest before frost, leaving on a few inches of stem. Condition at 80 F. for about 2 weeks to harden the rind and heal surface injuries. Store them in fairly dry air at about 55 F. (see chart). Watch the temperature carefully: too warm, and they get stringy; and pumpkins (and squashes) suffer chill damage in storage below 50 F.—they're not for outdoor cellars or pits. Just because they are big and tough doesn't mean they can be handled roughly, so place them in rows on shelves, not dumped in a pile in a corner.

SALSIFY

The third vegetable (with parsnips and horseradish) that winters-over to advantage in the garden—so long as it remains frozen. If they must be stored, dig them when the soil is dry late in the season but before they freeze. Handle and root-cellar like Beets (and see chart).

SQUASHES, condition and store like Pumpkins—but dried (see chart).

SWEET POTATOES

If a killing frost comes before you can dig them, cut the plants off at soil level, so decay in the vines can't penetrate down into the tubers.

Sweet potatoes are really quite tender, so handle them gently: sort and crate them in the field. Condition at 80—85 F. for 10 days to 2 weeks near a furnace or a warm chimney, maintaining high humidity by covering the stacked crates (which have wooden strips between for spacing) with plastic sheeting or a clean tarpaulin, etc. Then store in fairly dry and warm conditions (see chart). Like Pumpkins and Squashes, they damage from chill below 50 F.

TOMATOES, MATURE GREEN

For storing, harvest late but before the first hard frost, and only from vigorous plants. Wash gently, remove stems, dry; sort out all that show any reddening and store these separately.

Pack no more than two layers deep with dry leaves, hay, straw or shredded paper (plastic bags with air-holes are more likely to cause decay). Sort every week to separate faster-ripening tomatoes. See the chart.

TURNIPS

These and rutabagas withstand fall frosts better than most other root crops, but don't let them freeze/thaw/freeze. Storage odor can penetrate up from the basement, so store them by themselves outdoors (see chart for conditions).

Handle like Beets; pack in moist sand, peat, etc.

WINTER RADISHES, handle like Beets; see chart.

Curing

Salting and Smoking

Curing—that is, impregnating with a heavy concentration of salt—is almost as old as drying is, and, because it isn't dependent on climate, it has been used even more widely throughout the world as a means of putting by certain foods.

"Certain foods" again—— Here are the limitations.

Obviously, only those foods whose flavor is compatible with salt may be cured in the first place.

And all such foods are simply not edible unless (1) most of the salt is washed out—along with a good deal of some of the nutrients—before they are cooked, or (2) not enough salt is used to stop spoilage all by itself, so the food must have something further done to it to make it safe to eat, or even make it seem appetizing. This additional handling involves simple refrigeration, or fermenting and refrigeration, or smoking and refrigeration, or canning or freezing, depending on how long you hope to keep it.

Salting

WHAT SALTING DOES

A concentrated brine—which is salt + juice drawn from the food by the salt (called "dry salting"), or salt + water if juice is limited or not easily extracted (called "brining")—cuts down the activity of spoilage micro-organisms in direct proportion to the strength of the solution. These are the general proportions to give the idea:

A 5 percent solution (1 pound, or 2½ cups, of salt to 19 pints of juice/water) *reduces* the growth of most bacteria.

A 10 percent solution (1 pound, or 2½ cups, of salt to 9 pints of juice/water) *prevents* the growth of *most bacteria.*

A solution from 15 percent (1 pound, or 2½ cups, of salt to 5½ pints of juice/water) to 20 percent (1 pound, or 2½ cups, of salt to 4 pints of juice/water) *prevents* the growth of *salt-tolerant bacteria.*

The amounts of salt given in the individual instructions are designed to give the necessary protection to the food being cured, provided that any further safeguards are followed as well. Sometimes a brine is added to make sure that enough liquid is present to carry out the curing process, because you can't add plain water without diluting the strength of the salt required to treat the particular food satisfactorily.

Because salt draws moisture from plant and animal tissues in proportion to its concentration, heavy salting is often a preliminary step in drying or smoking high-protein foods.

USE PURE MEDIUM-COARSE PICKLING SALT FOR ALL CURING

NEVER USE "FREE-FLOWING" OR IODIZED TABLE SALT FOR CURING

EQUIPMENT FOR CURING (SALTING)

Especially for vegetables:

Large stoneware crocks or jars (5-gallon size is good here)
> OR

The biggest wide-mouth canning jars you can get—or ask the high-school cafeteria or your friendly neighborhood snack bar for empty gallon jars (wide-top) that their mayonnaise or pickles came in
> OR

Sound, unchipped enamelware canner (if you can spare it) with lid

Vegetable grater with a coarse blade; large old-style wooden potato-masher

Safe storage area at c. 65–70 F. for fermenting vegetables; plus cooler—c. 38 F.—storage for longer term

(Continued on the next page)

Especially for meats and fish:

Large stoneware crocks (10-gallon or larger)
    OR
Wooden kegs or small barrels—new, or thoroughly scrubbed and
    scalded used ones (before curing in them, though, fill them
    with water to swell the staves tight together, so the con-
    tainers won't leak when they're holding food)
Moisture-vapor-proof wrappings; plus stockinet—tubular cotton-
    knit—for holding the wrap tight to the meat after it's
    packaged
Safe, cold storage area (ideally 36—38 F.) for curing meats and
    fish—and for longer-term storage of meats and vegetables
    in their curing solutions

For both vegetables and meats, etc.:

Cutting-boards and stainless-steel knives (see Canning Meats)
Large enameled or glass/pottery pans or bowls for preparing
    the curing mixtures
Big wooden spoons, etc., for mixing and stirring
China or untreated hardwood covers that fit down inside each
    curing container: an expendable plate, a sawed round, etc.
Weights for these covers, to hold the food under the curing
    brine—a canning jar filled with sand is good; but nothing of
    limestone or iron, which mess up the curing solutions
Plenty of clean muslin (old sheets do beautifully) or double-
    weight cheesecloth
Glass measuring cups in 1-cup and 4-cup sizes
Scale in pounds (up to 25 is plenty, with ¼- and ½-pound
    gradations)
Good-sized working space, particularly for dealing with meats

Salting Vegetables

Unless you're fermenting vegetables—as for sour cabbage (sauerkraut),
etc., below—there's only one reason for salting them: you have no other
way to put them by, so you either salt your vegetables now or do
without vegetables later.

Vegetables are brined whenever they don't release enough natural juice to form adequate liquid during their cure, i.e., when they are not cut small or when they have little natural juice to start with.

Juicy or finely cut vegetables are dry-salted. If a relatively small amount of salt—2½ percent by weight—is added to certain vegetables, they ferment to make a "sour" product (sauerkraut again); but if 25 percent salt by weight is added to these or other prepared vegetables, the high concentration of salt prevents the growth of the yeasts and bacteria that cause fermentation, and thereby preserves them.

DRY SALTING TO PRESERVE

Corn, green/snap/string/wax beans, greens, even cabbage and Chinese cabbage and a number of root vegetables may be dry-salted, but some are more interesting—and certainly more nutritious, since freshening isn't necessary before cooking—if they are fermented instead.

It's not good to add newly prepared vegetables to any already curing, so use a container that will hold the batch you're working with. Just be sure to allow enough headroom to keep the food submerged under the weight: 4 inches should be enough for a 5-gallon crock, less for a smaller one; and the weight can rise above the rim of the container.

Salted Sweet Corn

Select sweet corn in the milk stage as you'd choose it for serving in season as corn-on-the-cob. Husk, remove the silk, and steam it for 10 to 15 minutes over rapidly boiling water or until the milk is set. Cut it from the cob about 2/3 the depth of the kernels (as for whole-kernel processing); weigh it. Mix 4 parts of cut corn with 1 part salt—1 pound of pure pickling salt for each 4 pounds of corn; or 1 cup of salt to 4 cups of cut corn if you don't have a scale.

Pack the corn-salt mixture in a crock to within about 4 inches of the top, cover with muslin sheeting or a double thickness of cheesecloth, and hold the whole business down with a clean plate or board on which you place a weight. If there isn't enough juice in 24 hours to cover the corn, add a salt solution in the proportions of 3 tablespoons salt to each 1 cup of cold water; replace the weighted plate to submerge the corn.

Store the crock in a safe, cool place (about 38 F.). The corn will be cured in from 3 to 5 weeks. Remove meal-sized amounts by dipping out corn and juice with a glass or china cup (don't use metal). Change the cloth as it becomes soiled, and always replace the weighted plate. Keep the crock in cool storage.

To cook the corn, freshen it (soak in cold water a short time, drain, and repeat) until a kernel tastes sweet. Simmer until tender in just enough water to prevent scorching; serve with butter or cream and seasoning to taste.

Salted Green/Snap/String/Wax Beans

Use only young, tender, crisp beans. Wash, remove tips and tails; cut in 2-inch pieces or french. Steam-blanch 10 minutes and cool. Weigh the beans, and measure 1 pound (1½ cups) of pure pickling salt for every 4 pounds of beans. Sprinkle a layer of salt in the bottom of a crock, add a layer of beans; repeat until the crock is filled to within 4 inches of the top or until the beans are used; top with a layer of salt. Cover with clean muslin sheeting or doubled cheesecloth and hold down with a weighted plate. If not enough brine has formed in 24 hours to cover the beans, eke it out with a solution in the proportions of 3 tablespoons of salt to each 1 cup of cold water.

Proceed as for Salted Sweet Corn, above.

Salted Dandelion (or other) Greens

Green salads were a rarity with New England hill folk in the early nineteenth century; nor did they go in for leaf vegetables much, except for dandelions in early spring and beet or turnip tops from their gardens in late summer.

Sometimes they salted their greens according to the 1-to-4 rule. Nowadays we'd go them one better, though, and steam-blanch the washed, tender leaves until they wilt—from 6 to 10 minutes, depending on the size of the leaves. Cool the greens, weigh them, and layer them in a crock with 1 pound (1½ cups) of pure pickling salt for every 4 pounds of greens. Proceed as for Salted Sweet Corn and Salted Green Beans, above.

To cook, rinse well and freshen in cold water for several hours, rinse again, drain, and simmer gently in the water adhering to them. Season with small dice of salt pork cooked with them, or serve with vinegar.

Salted White Turnips (or Rutabagas)

Choose young, crisp turnips without any woodiness. Peel; cut in ½-inch cubes. Steam-blanch from 8 to 12 minutes, depending on size of the pieces; cool. Weigh the prepared turnips and proceed with the 1-to-4 rule—1 pound (1½ cups) of pure pickling salt for each 4 pounds of turnips—and handle thereafter like Salted Sweet Corn, above.

To cook, rinse and freshen for several hours in cold water, rinse again; then simmer until tender in just enough water to keep from scorching. Mash if you like, and serve with butter and seasoning to taste.

Salted Cabbage

Remove bruised outer leaves; quarter, cut out the core. Shred as you would for cole slaw. Steam-blanch for 6 to 10 minutes until wilted. Cool, weigh; follow the 1-to-4 rule for Salted Greens above, and continue with the cure.

To cook, rinse and freshen for several hours, rinse again; then simmer until tender in just enough water to prevent scorching. Season during cooking with 2 teaspoons of vinegar and ¼ teaspoon caraway; or drain and return to low heat for 3 minutes with crumbled precooked sausage or small dice of salt pork; or serve with butter and seasoning to taste.

DRY SALTING FOR "SAUERKRAUT" VEGETABLES

Most often fermented are cabbage (sauerkraut) and Chinese cabbage, white turnips and rutabagas.

Generally speaking, the sweeter vegetables make a more flavorful product, while firmer ones provide better texture. Don't relegate tough, old, woody vegetables to the souring crock—use the best young, juicy ones you can get.

If you feel like experimenting with a small batch (5 pounds, say, in a 1-gallon jar, or less in a smaller container) you could add with the salt the traditional German touches of caraway or dill; or try a bay leaf or two, or some favorite whole pickling spice, or some onion rings, or even a few garlic cloves, peeled (but whole, so you can fish them out before serving).

Some rules advocate starting fermentation with a weak brine, but this procedure offers a loophole for too low a concentration of salt, and the likelihood of mushy food or even of spoilage instead of the desired acidity. Unless you're an old hand with sauerkraut and its relatives, you'll do well to stick to dry salting here.

As with vegetables preserved with salt earlier, you should never mix a fresh batch with one already fermenting.

Produce to be soured is not blanched: you want to encourage the micro-organisms that cause fermentation.

For fermenting you use 1/10 the amount of salt you needed for the preserving just described. This means 2½ percent of pure pickling salt by weight of the prepared food: 10 ounces (15 tablespoons or a scant 1 cup) of salt to 25 pounds of vegetables; 4 ounces (6 level tablespoons) of salt for 10 pounds of vegetables; 2 ounces (3 level tablespoons) of salt for 5 pounds of prepared food. This ratio of salt turns the sugar in the vegetables to lactic acid, and the desired souring occurs.

The vegetables should be kept around 65 F. during the fermenting period, which takes from 10 days to 4 weeks, depending on the vegetable being processed. Temperatures below 60 F. will slow down fermentation; above 70 F., and you court spoilage.

As a rough estimate, allow 5 pounds of prepared vegetables for each 1 gallon of container capacity, with the crock/jar holding a slightly greater weight of dense food that's cut fine. The instructions below use 10-pound batches, but you may want to deal with 25 or 30 pounds of cabbage or turnips at a time, using a 5-gallon crock.

Keep all souring vegetables covered with a clean cloth and weighted below the brine during fermentation. A top-quality vegetable should release enough juice to form a covering brine in around 24 hours; if it hasn't, bring the level above the food by adding a weak brine in the proportions of 1½ teaspoons of pickling salt for each 1 cup of cold water.

By the second day a scum will form on the top of the brine. Remove it by skimming carefully; then replace the scummy cloth with a sterile one, and wash and scald the plate/board before putting it back and weighting it.

Take care of this scum every day, and provide a sterile cloth and plate every day; otherwise the scum will weaken the acid you want, and the food will turn mushy and dark. If the brine gets slimy from too much warmth it's best not to tinker with it: do the simplest thing and decant the batch on the compost pile—and wait until cooler weather to start over again.

Fermentation will be continuing as long as bubbles rise to the top of the brine. When they stop, remove the cloth and weighted plate, wipe around the inside of the headroom; cover the vegetable with a freshly scalded plate/board, and put a close-fitting lid on the container. Then store the whole thing in a cool place at c. 38 F.

Dip out with a glass or china cup what you need for a meal, making sure that enough brine remains to cover the vegetable so it won't discolor or dry when exposed to air. Always keep the container well closed.

Fermented vegetables may be canned. See individual instructions below.

Sauerkraut (Fermented Cabbage)

Quarter each cabbage, cut out the core; shred fine and weigh. Using 2½ percent of pickling salt by weight—6 tablespoons to each 10 pounds of shredded cabbage (or see other amounts in the general method above)—pack the container with alternate layers of salt and cabbage, tamping every two layers of cabbage to get rid of trapped air and to start the juice flow—you don't need to get tough with it: just tap it gently with a clean wooden potato-masher or the bottom of a small jar. Top with a layer of salt. Cover with a sterile cloth and weight it down with a plate, etc.

Follow the daily skimming procedure given above. When fermenting has stopped in about 2 weeks or so, the sauerkraut will be a clear, pale gold in color and pleasantly tart in flavor. It's a good idea to lay a clean plate on it to keep it below the brine's surface; at any rate cover the container with a close-fitting lid. Store in a cool place and use as needed.

If your storage isn't around 38 F., you'd better can the sauerkraut. See the directions on page 95.

Chinese Cabbage Sauerkraut

Follow the method for Sauerkraut. The result usually has more flavor than regular fermented cabbage does, thanks to more, and sweeter, natural juice.

Sour White Turnip (Sauer Rüben)

Peel and quarter young, juicy turnips. Shred fine; or put through the medium knife of a food grinder, catching stray juice in a bowl placed underneath. Pack with layers of salt as for Sauerkraut, but do not tamp down—there should be juice aplenty without tamping, and it's enough to press down on the topmost layer to settle the pack.

Proceed in every way as for Sauerkraut.

Sour Rutabagas, handle like White Turnips

Souring Other Lower-acid Vegetables

Even though properly created fermentation raises the *pH* acidity rating of lower-acid raw vegetables (see page 5), *unless they are heat-processed for storage* they cannot be regarded as safe from spoilage or from growth of certain dangerous heat-sensitive bacteria.

So, because you should can them anyway for safe storage, it doesn't make much sense to go through the business of fermenting them as a preamble to putting them by for serving later as accompaniments to meat or whatever.

Especially when there are recipes for relishes and pickles made from corn, green beans, carrots and beets in The Preserving Kettle section.

Especially when, if you're strapped for canning jars, the chances are that you can rig up some kind of heat to dry them with (see Drying).

BRINING TO PRESERVE VEGETABLES

This is not the same thing as the preparation for making pickles, which is designed either to crisp the ingredients or to season them as a base for adding vinegar, sugar, spices, etc.

What you're doing here is to reproduce the 25 percent, 1-to-4, rule for Dry Salting to Preserve, above—but you're making up for the scarcity of natural juice by using water with a heavy concentration of salt.

It's easier to gauge the amounts of brine and salt needed if you think in terms of 10 pounds of whole vegetables (or large pieces of cut ones) held in a 5-gallon container: there'll be extra room, but that doesn't matter—you'll weight the vegetables to keep them under the surface of the cure. If you'd rather work in 5-pound lots, use a 2-gallon container and halve the given amounts of brine and salt.

Weigh out 10 pounds of fresh, perfect vegetables, and to them add 2 gallons of brine of the strength specified below; this much brine should cover them, but make a bit more if it doesn't. Cover the brined vegetables with clean muslin or doubled cheesecloth, and on it lay a weighted plate to keep them submerged.

The next day you start gradually to increase the salt in the solution, thus compensating for the natural juice that's drawn out to weaken the brine.

First, for each 10 pounds of vegetable, pour 1 pound (1½ cups) of pickling salt on the wet cloth where it will dissolve slowly into the brine; replace the weight on the mound of salt.

One week later, put 4 ounces (6 tablespoons) more salt on the cloth to absorb. Repeat once a week for 3 or 4 weeks more—making a total of 1 to 1¼ pounds of salt added in the weekly doses.

The vegetable is cured in 4 to 5 weeks. Take away the cloth, cover the container with a close-fitting lid, and store at an ideal 38 F.

To cook, freshen the vegetable in several cold waters, and simmer in a very little water until tender, seasoning to taste.

Brined Green Peppers

Halve firm, crisp peppers, remove their seeds; weigh. For 10 pounds of peppers make 2 gallons of strong brine—around a 15 percent solution— by dissolving 4 1/3 cups of pure pickling salt in 8 quarts of water. Pour it over the peppers in a 5-gallon crock (it should cover them, but make a bit more if it doesn't). Cover with cloth and weight down. About 24 hours later, put your first addition of salt on the cloth, carrying on with the general method described above.

Brined Cauliflower

Wash heads of fresh young cauliflower, remove leaves and core, and break apart the flowerets in *c.* 1-inch pieces. Continue as for Brined Green Peppers, above.

Brined Onions

Peel whole, fresh onions, not large ones—and not grown from sets (these can have an inner core wrapped in brown "paper"). Weigh. For every 10 pounds of onions prepare 2 gallons of very strong brine—around a 20 percent solution—by dissolving 4 pounds (6 cups) of pure pickling salt in 8 quarts of water.

From here on, follow the method for Brined Green Peppers, above.

Salting Meat

The salt cure for meat is virtually always followed by exposure to smoke from smoldering hardwood or corncobs in order to dry the surface of the meat, to add flavor to and discourage attacks by insects: indeed, the only two examples below where smoking does not follow salt curing are Corned Beef and Salt Pork.

Checking with a meat thermometer, hold the internal temperature of the largest pieces of meat as constantly at 38 degrees Fahrenheit as possible before and during the process of curing. The countryman takes this need for a thoroughly cooled carcass into account when he butchers hogs and beeves only in winter weather; then he knows that the meat quickly cools and will stay well within the limits for making a wholesome product.

Salt penetrates too slowly at temperatures below 36 F., and the chance of spoilage increases above 38 F. If the temperature of the storage area drops below freezing and stays there for several days, increase the salting time by that number of days.

In general, meats that have been frozen at home do not cure well, even though they're thoroughly defrosted before being treated with salt. Their texture is changed just enough by home-freezing so the penetration of the cure is not likely to be uniform enough to make a satisfactory product.

For information on cutting and handling meat to best advantage for home-curing, see two USDA publications: *Farmers Bulletin No. 2209, Slaughtering, Cutting and Processing Beef on the Farm,* and *Farmers Bulletin No. 2138, Slaughtering, Cutting, and Processing Pork on the Farm.* (They deal in 100-pound batches, by the way; 25-pound lots are used below, as being usually more suited to the needs of the average householder.)

Time out for terms. "Pickle" is used in some manuals to designate a sweetened brine—one containing salts *and* some sugar; it is not the solution with added vinegar that is used for pickling vegetables. "Sugarcure" usually means the addition of ¼ as much cane or beet sugar as there is salt in the mixture; in this amount it has little value as a flavoring agent on its own, but it is important as food for flavor-producing bacteria in meat during long cures.

Smoking procedures are described in detail in the section following this one.

Before we go any further, though, it's necessary to talk about nitrate preservatives.

THE NITRATE/NITRITE WORRY

A number of the procedures below for curing meat include the words " . . . ounces of saltpeter–*optional*."

We include the saltpeter because it's in the recipes in concentrations which, at this writing, have been passed by the Food and Drug Administration as being safe for human beings who eat these foods in normal amounts.

BUT we add *optional* because there's increasing protest over the use of this substance in commercially prepared meats like cold cuts, hot dogs, ham and bacon, etc.: and if you wouldn't dream of buying foods that contain it, then there's no earthly sense in adding it to food you put by at home.

The nitrates are currently under intense scrutiny by the FDA and the USDA, which have set up a government/industry task force to evaluate the problem they raise. Which is: most of the nitrate converts –in the tissues of the food and in our bodies–to a nitrite, which is known to combine with the red blood cells, and, if in sufficient quantity, could limit the oxygen-carrying power of the hemoglobin–thus hindering vital bodily functions.

What saltpeter is and why it's used

"Saltpeter" is either potassium nitrate or sodium nitrate (the latter often called "Chilean nitrate"). If you ask for saltpeter at the drugstore, you're likely to get potassium nitrate (labeled as a diuretic, actually), which is preferred over sodium nitrate because it doesn't absorb moisture during storage the way the sodium compound does. Only once in both the USDA meat-processing bulletins mentioned above is "saltpeter" defined–and then as potassium nitrate.

But if you buy a commerical ready-to-use-at-home mixture for curing your meat, the chances are that it will contain sodium nitrate (along with sodium nitrite and other preservatives, principally salt, NaCl).

For centuries saltpeter has been added to curing mixtures for meat as a means of intensifying and holding the red color considered so appetizing in ham and allied pork products, and in corned beef, etc. It's anti-microbial action is so incidental that we can declare: *the most important substance limiting bacterial growth in cured meat is SALT.*

So when saltpeter is included in a rule for home-cured meat it is being added for cosmetic reasons.

And whether you add it is up to you.

So what do we use instead?

There's no getting around the fact that, for many people, color is psychologically important in food.

Therefore, we suggest that you use pure crystalline ascorbic acid in place of saltpeter. But we honestly don't know how much you should use. We do know, though, that the amount of pure crystalline ascorbic acid (Vitamin C) that you're likely to use can't do you an iota of harm. So be free to experiment: look back at Freezing Fish for ideas to take off from. Add the ascorbic acid to the dry cure or the brine.

Ascorbic acid will improve the red color, and retard the loss of color as time goes by. But, unlike the nitrates, it will not protect the color indefinitely; and this is a backhanded comfort, too: it is highly unlikely that color fading would be delayed by ascorbic acid to such an extent that the meat would be spoiled by bacteria and *still look appetizing.*

Some commercially prepared foods contain lecithin as a means of retarding rancidity. *We certainly do not recommend lecithin*, for the simple reason that we know nothing about using it in home-processed foods, and neither does anyone else that we can discover.

A final parenthesis: It's not fair to lay blame for using a possibly dangerous substance entirely at the door of what has been called "the establishment." We were beguiled by an advertisment in a leading publication in the natural/organic food movement. When we got the material we'd sent (and paid) for, we found that it included a recipe for homemade luncheon meat done in what the author called "the natural way"—

and it included, as a seasoning, eight times the amount of saltpeter as is used in a comparable USDA recipe. P.S. In our version of this Bologna-style Sausage—it's in the Roundup section—we don't have any saltpeter. The sausage may not be a pretty pink, but it's mighty good eating.

STORING CURED MEAT

Their heavy concentration of salt protects Corned Beef and Salt Pork for several months if the brine in which they're held is kept below 38 F.

Freezer storage of sausage and cured meats is relatively limited: after more than 2 to 4 months at Zero F., the salt in the fat causes it to become rancid.

Note of warning. A home-cured ham is not the same as a commercially processed one that has been "tenderized," etc. *Home-cured pork is still RAW.*

SALTING BEEF

Because they lack what producers and butchers call "finish," veal or calf meat shouldn't be used to make corned or dried beef. The product is disappointing.

Corned Beef

Use the tougher cuts and those with considerable fat. Bone, and cut them to uniform thickness and size.

To cure 25 pounds of beef, pack it first in pickling salt, allowing 2 to 3 pounds of salt (3 to 4½ cups) for the 25 pounds of meat. Spread a generous layer of coarse pickling salt in the bottom of a clean, sterilized crock or barrel. Pack in it a layer of meat that you've rubbed well with the salt; sprinkle more salt over the meat. Repeat the layers of meat and salt until all the meat is used or the crock is filled to within a couple of inches below the top.

Let the packed meat stand in the salt for 24 hours, then cover it with a solution of 1 gallon of water in which you've dissolved 1 pound (2 cups) of sugar, ½ ounce (*c.* 1 tablespoon) of baking soda, and 1 ounce (*c.* 2 tablespoons) of saltpeter—*the saltpeter is optional: see "Nitrate Worry" above.*

Put a weighted plate on the meat to hold every speck of it below the surface of the brine; cover the crock/barrel; and in a cool place— not more than 38 degrees F.—let the meat cure in the brine from 4 to 6 weeks.

The brine can become stringy and gummy ("ropy," in some de- scriptions) if the temperature rises above 38 F. and the sugar ferments. The baking soda helps retard the fermentation. But watch it: if the brine starts to get ropy, take out the meat and wash it well in warm water. Clean and sterilize the container. Repack the meat with a fresh sugar-water-etc. solution (above), to which you now add 1½ pounds (2¼ cups) of pickling salt; this salt replaces the original 2 pounds of dry salt used to pack the meat.

To store it, keep it refrigerated in the brine; or remove it from the brine, wash away the salt from the surface, and can or freeze it (q.v.).

Dried (Chipped) Beef

Dried beef—which has about 48 percent water when produced com- mercially—is made from whole muscles or muscles cut lengthwise. Select boneless, heavy, lean-muscled cuts—rounds are best—and cure as for Corned Beef (above) *except* that you add an extra ¼ pound of sugar (½ cup) for each 25 pounds of meat.

The curing is completed in 4 to 6 weeks, depending on size of the pieces and the flavor desired. After it has cured satisfactorily, remove the meat, wash it, and hang it in a cool place to air-dry for 24 hours.

Then it is smoked at 100 to 120 F. for 70 to 80 hours (see Smoking) —or until it is quite dry.

To store, wrap large pieces in paper and stockinette (tubular, small- mesh material, which holds the wrap close to the meat) and hang them in a cool (below 50 F.), dry, dark, insect-free room; certainly refrigerate small pieces. Plan to use all the dried beef before spring.

SALTING PORK

All parts of the pig may be cured by salting. Some—such as the fat salt pork for baked beans, chowders, etc.—are used as they come from the salting process. The choice hams, bacon and, perhaps, loins are carried one step further and are smoked (q.v.) after being cured.

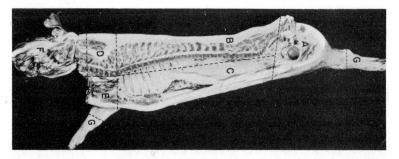

Parts of a pig: A—ham; B—loin and backfat; C—bacon strip with leaf fat; D—shoulder butt and plate; E—picnic shoulder; F—head; G—feet.

Have the meat thoroughly chilled, and hold it as closely as possible to 38 F. during the process of curing: salt penetrates less well in tissues below 36 F., and spoilage occurs with increasing speed in meat at temperatures above 38 F.

"Pumping"—i.e., forcibly injecting a strong curing solution into certain parts of a large piece of meat—is not included in the instructions below because we're leary of it: much safer to allow safe curing time than to try to speed the process by localized "spot" applications of the cure.

Allow 25 days as the minimum curing time for Dry Salted pork, with some of the larger pieces with bone taking longer. Allow at least 28 days for Sweet Pickled (Brined) pork, and more for the larger pieces. The days-per-pound are given for each cut cured by each method.

Before smoking or storing large pieces containing bone, run a skewer up through the meat along the bone, withdraw the skewer and sniff it. If the odor is sweet and wholesome, fine—proceed with the smoking or storing; but if there's any "off" taint, any whiff of spoilage, destroy the entire piece of meat, because it is unsafe to eat.

Dry Salting Large Pieces (Hams and Shoulders)

For each 25 pounds of hams and shoulders mix together thoroughly 2 pounds (*c.* 3 cups) of coarse-fine pickling salt, ½ pound (*c.* 1 cup) brown or white sugar, and ½ ounce (*c.* 1 tablespoon) saltpeter—*optional: see "Nitrate Worry," above.* Use ½ the mixture to rub well on all surfaces of the meat. Poke it generously into the shank ends along the bone (you can even make a fairly long internal slit with a slender boning knife inserted at the shank, and push the mixture up

Heavy salting for heavy cuts, left; then into the barrel/crock to cure.

into it: this is better than relying on "pumping" a strong solution to such areas where the salt must penetrate deeply). Plan to leave an 1/8-inch layer of the mixture on the ham face (the big cut end), with a thinner coating on the rest of the ham and on the shoulders.

Fit the salt-coated meat into a clean sterilized barrel or crock, taking care lest the coating fall off. Cover with a loose-fitting lid or cheesecloth and let cure in a cold place, 36 to 38 F.

One week later, remove the meat, re-coat it with the remaining half of the curing mixture, and pack it again in the barrel/crock.

Curing time: At least 25 days. Allow 2 or 3 days for each 1 pound of ham or shoulder, being sure to leave them in the curing container even after all surface salt is absorbed.

Then smoke them (q.v.).

Dry Salting Thin Cuts (Bacon, "Fat Back," Loin, etc.)

For each 25 pounds of thin cuts of pork, mix together thoroughly 1 pound (*c.* 1½ cups) of pickling salt, ¼ pound (½ cup) of brown or white sugar, and 1½ teaspoons of saltpeter—*optional: see "Nitrate Worry," above.*

Coat the cuts, using all the mixture. Pack the meat carefully in a sterilized crock or barrel, and cover it with a loose-fitting lid or layer of cheesecloth, and let it stand at 36 to 38 F. for the *minimum* total curing time of 25 days; allow 1½ days per pound. Thin cuts do not require an interim salting—that's why you used all the mixture in the first place. And leave them in the crock even after the surface salt has been absorbed.

All but the "fat back" (Salt Pork) is then smoked (q.v.). Wrap the Salt Pork in moisture-vapor-proof material; refrigerate what is intended for immediate use, and freeze the rest.

"Sweet Pickle" Salting Large Pieces (Brining Hams, etc.)

Curing hams and shoulders in brine is slower than the Dry Salting treatment just described, and therefore is well suited to colder regions of the country.

Pack the well-chilled (38 F.) hams and shoulders in a sterilized crock or barrel. For every 25 pounds of meat, prepare a solution of 2 pounds (*c.* 3 cups) of pickling salt, ½ pound (1 cup) of sugar, ½ ounce (*c.* 1 tablespoon) of saltpeter—*optional: see "Nitrate Worry" above*—and 4½ quarts of water. Dissolve all thoroughly, and pour over the meat, covering every bit of it: even a small piece that rises above the solution can carry spoilage down into meat submerged. Put a weighted plate or board over the meat to keep it below the brine, and cover the barrel/crock. Hold the storage temperature to 38 F.

After 1 week, remove the meat, stir the curing mixture, and return the meat to the crock/barrel, making sure that every bit of it is weighted down below the surface of the brine.

Remove, repack, and cover with the stirred brine at the end of the second and fourth weeks.

If at any time during the cure you find that the brine has soured or become ropy or sirupy, remove the meat, scrub it well, and clean and

Cover with cold brine, then weight it all down below the surface.

scald the barrel/crock. Chill the container thoroughly, and return the meat, covering it with a fresh, cold curing solution made like your original brine, except that you *increase the water to 5½ quarts.*

Curing time: A minimum of 28 days; allow 3½ to 4 days for each 1 pound of ham or shoulder.

"Sweet Pickle" Salting Small Pieces (Bacon, Loin, "Fat Back")

Pack the pieces in a sterilized crock or barrel, and cover with a brine like that for large pieces, except in a milder form: use 6 quarts of water, rather than 4½ quarts.

Proceed as for hams and shoulders, keeping the pieces well submerged, and overhauling the contents as above at the end of the first, second, and third weeks.

Curing time: A minimum of 15 days for a 10-pound piece of bacon, allowing 1½ days per pound; but 21 days for heavier pieces of bacon, or for the thicker loins.

Pork that is not to be smoked may be left in the brine until it is to be used—but it will be quite salty.

Smoking

Without intending either to pun or to discuss the pro/con of this traditional finishing process for many cured meats and a few cured fish, we feel duty-bound to note that smoking any food is under fire nowadays from some critics.

However, as we indicated in the individual salting instructions above, meats may be left in brine or dry salt until they're ready to be used. Or remove them from the cure, scrub them well to remove surface salt, and hang them in a cool, dry, well-ventilated place for from several days to a week to let them dry out a bit before storage.

We do not recommend using so-called "liquid smoke" or "smoke salt" in place of bona fide smoking. Either smoke your meat or call it a day at the end of the salt cure.

WHAT "COLD SMOKING" DOES

We're not concerned here with what is known as "hot smoking"—which in effect is cooking in a slow, smoky barbecue for several hours, thus making the food partially or wholly table-ready at the end of the smoking period.

What we'll do is hold the food in a mild smoke at never more than 120 F., and usually from around 70 to 90 F., for several days to color and flavor the tissues, help retard rancidity and, in many cases, increase dryness—the actual length of time depending on the type of food.

The food is then stored in a cool, dry place, or is frozen, to await future preparation for the table.

MAKING THE SMOKE

Use only hardwood chips for the fire—never one of the evergreen conifers, whose resinous smoke can give a creosote-y taste, or other softwoods. Among the most popular woods are maple, apple and hickory.

Or use corncobs. These should be the thoroughly dried cobs from popcorn or flint corn that has dried on the ear: cobs saved from a feast of sweet corn-on-the-cob aren't the same thing at all. If you don't have your own cobs or can't get them from a neighboring farmer, look in the Yellow Pages for a handler of hardwood sawdust or shavings; such a dealer often has chopped cobs to use as a tumbling medium for polishing. Merrill Lawrence of Newfane, Vermont—whose family has been curing and smoking meat for generations—says 2 bushels of cut corncobs can produce 72 hours of smoke, or enough to do a whole ham in a small smoke-box.

Avoid chemical kindlers, either fluids or small bricks impregnated with flammable mixtures, because their fumes can take a long time to dissipate (you don't want your meat to taste of them). Small, dry hardwood laid tepee-fashion over crumpled pieces of milk cartons catch well, and form a good base for the fire. Get your fire well established and burning clean, but do not have it hot; keep it slow, just puttering along evenly so the meat is in no danger of cooking. Hang a thermometer beside the food closest to the fire: fish, which is so highly perishable (even when lightly salted for smoking), should be smoked at 40 to 60 F., and then for a relatively short time compared to the temperature for meats.

The fire can be made and held in any sort of iron or tin brazier suitable for the size of the smokehouse or box.

If you use sawdust or fine chips or chopped corncobs, the smoke might also be maintained well enough by using an electric hot plate to fire a tin pie pan that's filled with the smoke-making material. Set the hot plate on High to start the pan of stuff smoldering, then reduce the heat to Medium or Low. Experiment.

No matter which smoke-making fuel you use, it's important to know how it burns, and how much air intake you need to keep it going or to quiet it down for the type of smoker you have, before you commit a batch of cured meat to the smoking process.

Smoking Meat

Because bacteria in meat grow fastest between 70 and 100 F., you should smoke meat in fairly cold weather, in late fall or early spring, when temperatures are between 30 and 50 F. during the day. However, really cold weather, down to Zero, is not for the beginner who's using the highly simplified smoke-boxes described below.

Smoking should be as sustained as is reasonably possible, simply because you want to get it over with and get the meat cooled and wrapped in moisture-vapor-proof material and stored in a cool, dry place (or frozen). But it won't suffer from the hiatus if you can't smoke at night: the weather will probably keep it cold enough without freezing so you can leave it in the smokehouse and just start your smoke-maker again in the morning.

If you have a sudden sharp drop in temperature, though, you had better bring inside to cool storage any meat that shows danger of freezing without the warmth of the smoke. Resume counting the total smoking time when the smokehouse is operating again.

PREPARING THE MEAT FOR THE SMOKEHOUSE

Remove the meat from the salting crock, scrub off surface salt, using a brush and fresh lukewarm water. Then hang the meat in a cool, airy place for long enough to get the outside of it truly dry—up to 24 hours.

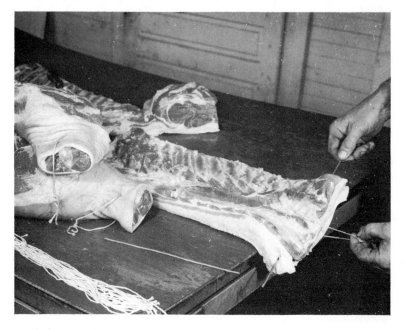

Run several thicknesses of bailing twine or a strong stainless-steel wire through each piece of meat several inches below one end; tie the string or double-twist the wire to form a loop that will hold the weight of the meat. Hams are hung from the shank (small) end. It's a nuisance to have the meat fall to the bottom of the smoke-box because either the loop or the meat has given way.

SMALL HOMEMADE SMOKE-BOXES

The USDA bulletin on processing pork, cited earlier, contains plans for a full-fledged smokehouse, and also a description of a barrel smoke-box. Here are our variations of the barrel, and a description for making use of a discarded refrigerator.

A barrel

You can get the smoking parts of half a 200-pound pig in a 55-gallon steel barrel that you make into a "smokehouse." This means that one ham, one shoulder, and one side of bacon cut in pieces can be smoked at the same time (assuming that you've put a jowl and two feet into Head Cheese, q.v.).

Wooden barrels large enough to do the job are (1) hard to come by these days, and (2) their staves shrink when dried out (as they'd be after several days' worth of warm smoke) and open. So use a metal barrel with one head removed. If it's had oil in it, set the residue of oil on fire and let it burn out; then scour the drum thoroughly inside and out with plenty of detergent and water; rinse; scald the inside, and let it dry in the air.

OUTSIDE ON THE GROUND

In the bottom of the barrel cut a hole large enough to take the end of an elbow for whatever size of stovepipe you want to use (see the sketch). Set the barrel on a mound of earth—with earth banked high enough around it to hold it firm and steady—and dig a trench from it down to a fire-pit at least 10 feet away, and inclining at an angle of

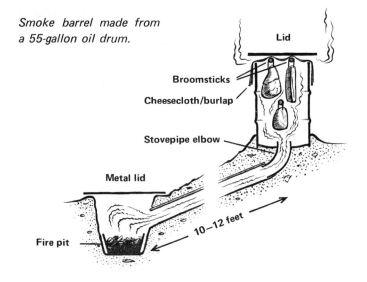

Smoke barrel made from a 55-gallon oil drum.

Lid

Broomsticks

Cheesecloth/burlap

Stovepipe elbow

Metal lid

10–12 feet

Fire pit

something like 30 degrees. Via the trench either connect the barrel to the pit with stovepipe, or build a box-like conduit (stovepiping is easier to remove and clean). You should have the length in order to cool the smoke on its way to the meat, and the pitch to encourage the draft.

Put a cover of close-fitted boards over the fire-pit, arranged so it can be tilted to increase the draft when necessary.

ON THE PORCH, OR IN A GARAGE

The electric-plate/pan-of-sawdust arrangement should be used only in a dry place with fire-retardant material underneath it. This can be sheet metal, or a concrete floor.

Set your barrel on supports—cinder-blocks or trestles of some sort— to hold the elbow well away from the floor. Connect the stovepipe, and lead it from the barrel to the electric smoke-making unit. Make a wooden box, lined with fire-retardant material, to house the hot plate and the pan of sawdust, cut adequate slits for regulating air intake; and merely lift off the box when you want to add more fuel for making smoke.

SMOKING IN THE BARREL

Get the fire or smoke-maker well established and producing evenly before hanging the meat to smoke. There should be good ventilation from the top in order to carry off moisture the first day (to keep the fire from getting too hot, though, reduce the air intake at the bottom of the fire-pit as much as you can without letting the fire go out).

Hang the ham, shoulder and chunks of bacon (or comparable sizes of beef pieces) from broom-handles or stainless-steel rods—not galvanized, not brass, not copper—laid across the top of the barrel. Stagger the meat so that none of it touches other pieces or the side of the barrel; suspend smaller pieces on longer loops of strong steel wire so they drop below the large pieces. Hang your thermometer.

Over the whole business lay a flat, round wooden cover slightly bigger than the barrel's top. It will be held up from the rim by the thickness of the supporting rods. If this isn't enough clearance at the beginning, or if the draft seems to be faltering, prop the lid higher with several cross-pieces of wood laid parallel to the supporting rods.

Close down the ventilation on the second day by draping a piece of clean burlap or several thicknesses of cheesecloth over the supporting rods *under* the lid. The cloth will also protect the meat inside from debris, or from insects attracted to it if the smoke stops. Weight the lid down over the cloth with a good-sized rock to keep it in place.

HOW LONG?

Smokiness—color and flavor of the meat—is a matter for individual taste. If it's oversmoked, the meat is likely to be too pungent, especially on the outside. And you can always put the meat back for more smoking if the flavor isn't enough for you.

So try out your system in a small way. Give a shoulder of cured pork, say, 45 to 55 hours of smoking; take it out and slice into it—you may want to give it a few hours more: 60 hours is about average for a smoked shoulder.

The average ham takes about 72 hours of total smoking time.

Bacon, being a thinner piece of meat, is usually smoked enough in a total of 48 hours.

BUT ALL THESE TIMES ARE APPROXIMATE—they're mentioned merely as guides.

An old refrigerator as a smoke-box

This rig has the disadvantage of being likely to smoke hotter than the ideal 90 F. maximum. Still, the USDA bulletin says the smokehouse can be 100 to 120 F.—just warm enough to melt the surface grease on pork—so if you can keep the inside of the refrigerator box within this maximum you'll probably be all right. You can always extend the distance from the smoker into the box by using a short length of stovepipe to get cooler smoke.

Ask a friendly dealer in household appliances to give you a one-door electric refrigerator of the simplest type, and that's beyond repair. Or ask the people in charge of your community's sanitary landfill to save you one (and make sure the hinges were not damaged irreparably when the door was taken off before the box was dumped).

Remove the compressor unit at the bottom, and the ice-cube compartment; block off any places where ducts may have entered the interior of the box. Take out all galvanized inside parts. While you're at it, get rid of all plastic fittings too: who knows how they'll act if the smoke gets too hot? And you can always use the room.

Cut a hole at least 6 inches in diameter low on one side of the refrigerator, just above the floor of the box (see the sketch). Cover any ventilating grids snugly on front, back and sides of the space that once held the motor.

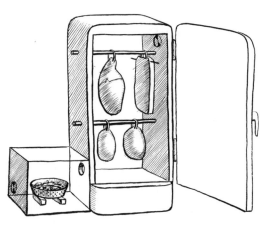

On the top, close to one corner, set in a butterfly vent that you can open in the early stage of smoking. This vent can also be used later to encourage a slight draft, and so keep the smoke from backing up and smothering the fire.

If you can rest cross-rods on the supports that formerly held the shelving, so much to the good. Otherwise you'll have to bore holes in opposite sides of the box to carry the rods from which you'll hang the food.

Set your smoke-maker (either an electric hot plate heating a pan of hardwood sawdust, or a brazier of smoldering chips or corncobs—see above) to one side of the refrigerator. House it in a box that sits over it and fits against the side of the refrigerator and over the hole you have cut without leaking any smoke. In a far corner of this housing box set a butterfly vent that can be used to regulate the air intake of the smoke-maker. Hang an oven thermometer on the side of the refrigerator near the smoke-hole, so you can move the box away for a reading—a rough way of gauging the smoking temperature, but the alternative is to install a thermometer through the refrigerator wall which lets you know the interior heat without opening the door.

Hang the meat inside the refrigerator, close the door and carry on as with the barrel smoke-box above.

Smoking Fish

Remove whole dressed fish or fish fillets from the salt cure (see Drying, page 270). Scrub off all salt with a cloth or soft brush and rinse well. Air-dry for several hours, using an electric fan if necessary, until the fish feel dry when touched lightly.

Run stout string under the bony "collar" under the gills of whole fish and hang them from the cross-rods inside the smoke-box; drape fillets over the rods so they hang evenly. Because fish is so perishable, the smoke should be kept below 70 degrees F. for best results.

Smoke whole small fish for 100 or more hours, or for 4 to 5 days. Since fish is likely to be smoked during warmer weather than meat is, it must be refrigerated thoroughly between sessions if the smoking is not to be continuous; you have a better product if the smoking is uninterrupted.

When smoked, small fish may be wrapped separately and put in airtight containers in a cool, dry place.

The Roundup

Most of the procedures and recipes in this section involve materials that could, through not knowing or through affluence, be ignored. All the instructions are here because they didn't seem to fit easily anywhere else.

RENDERING LARD

Lard is in disrepute these days because of blanket indictments against animal fats as cholesterol-makers. This is a pity, because active, sensible eaters shouldn't automatically forgo the special flakiness and tenderness that good lard gives pastry and cakes—unless their doctor has advised them to do so.

Lard is fresh pork fat, rendered—i.e., melted—at no more than 255 F., and then congealed quickly and cold-stored for later use. The fine lard generally considered best by the purists comes from the "leaf" next to the bacon strip; backfat from along the loin and plate fat from the shoulder also are good (as in the photographs; and see also the labeled parts of a pig in "Salting Pork" in the Curing section). The caul fat (attached at the stomach) and the ruffle fat (around the intestines) usually make darker lard than the other parts do, and so are rendered separately.

A live 225-pound hog will yield slightly more than 25 pounds of all fats usable for lard; obviously only a small part of the total can come from the leaf (but it gives up a higher percentage of its weight in lard than the other sections do). So stop now to decide how you want to use the fat: to render the leaf separately; to combine leaf, loin, plate and trimmed fat; to combine caul; ruffle and trimmed fat, rendering them for soapmaking later.

Cut the fat in small pieces. Put a little of it in a large kettle over *low* heat and stir. When melting starts, add the rest of the fat gradually—but don't fill the kettle more than to 3 inches from the top, lest the fat boil over. Stir often and keep the heat low: the cracklings—bits of tissue—can stick and scorch.

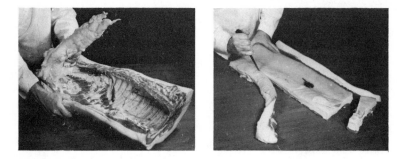

Main sources of lard: leaf fat, left above; trimming from bacon, right; plate fat from the shoulder, below left; back fat from the loin.

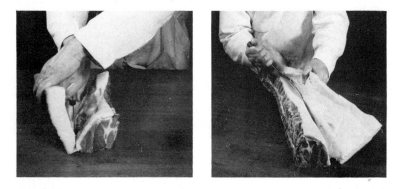

Cracklings that brown and float to the top will settle to the bottom later on when they lose fat and moisture. As the water in the tissues steams away, the temperature of the fat will rise slowly above 212 degrees Fahrenheit. Use a deep-frying thermometer to make sure the heat doesn't get above 255 F., which is the optimum temperature for thorough rendering.

Let the rendered lard cool a bit so all sediment and cracklings will settle to the bottom. Carefully dip the clear liquid from the top of the kettle into containers, filling them to the brim; cover tightly and seal. Label and store immediately at freezing or below to make a fine-grained product.

Strain the lard at the bottom of the kettle through several layers of cheesecloth to remove the settlings; pack and store as above.

Air and light make stored lard rancid, and spoil it irrevocably for cooking purposes. Thorough rendering (to 255 F.) eliminates the moisture that causes souring during storage.

320

SOAPMAKING

The Fundamental Rule

Never, *never, NEVER* make soap with young children around. Or pets.

Even a cold lye solution 1/6 as strong as the one below for soap-making may taste sweetish (much like a dose of baking soda in water to settle one's stomach) for a split second—but long enough for a child to swallow it; and then it burns painfully, with damage.

The heavy concentration of lye used in soap can strip off skin as easily as the peel is rubbed from a blanched peach.

Antidotes. Slosh eyes with cold water, follow immediately with cold boric-acid solution—which you'll do well to have handy by.

For hands, etc., wash immediately with cold water, followed by generous bathing with vinegar.

If taken internally, the sufferer should be made to drink salad oil (but don't pour a bit of it down the windpipe) AND TAKEN TO A DOCTOR AS FAST AS POSSIBLE.

Labels on containers give directions for other first-aid measures.

Lye can ruin a garbage disposal unit in the sink drain. Lye can raise Cain with the working of a septic tank.

Lye reacts violently with aluminum and is used in commercial drain-openers for just this reaction.

Equipment for Soapmaking

First-aid supplies—cold water, boric-acid solution, vinegar, salad oil

An enameled or granite kettle for warming the fat (in a small batch)

(A big iron kettle and/or a wooden tub for larger batches)

A sturdy enameled kettle for dissolving the lye in water

Floating or dairy thermometer

Wooden paddles or long-handled wooden spoons for stirring

A shallow wooden box, large enough to hold about 2½–3 quarts of liquid; soak the box to make it tight, and line it with clean wet muslin that's big enough to drape generously over all the sides

A board to cover the box

A dripping pan big enough to hold the wooden box

An expendable rug or blanket to keep the new soap warm for a while

Tough string or fine wire (for cutting the soap in bars)

Glass measuring cups

What Lye Is (and Does for Soap)

NOT THIS

Liquid or crystalline products that designate themselves as drain-openers contain nitrates, activating aids (like aluminum filings) and stabilizers. Such products are not remotely suitable for making soap.

O.K. COMMERCIAL LYES

The several crystalline preparations sold simply as "lye" are sodium hydroxide; these also can double as drain-openers, but they don't have the additives that make bad soap. They come in 13-ounce cans. If you handle the lye immediately after the can is opened you may use ounces in weight and ounces in volume interchangeably when faced with instructions that call for lye either in pounds or in less than 13 ounces. The stuff readily absorbs moisture from the air, expanding in the process, so work quickly to get reasonably accurate measurements. Cap any remainder the minute you're through measuring.

This usable type of lye is mixed with cold water—whereupon it reacts and heats the water, giving off fumes that make ammonia seem bland in comparison. When the solution stops acting, it begins to cool; but it's still frighteningly caustic.

When a solution of the right strength and temperature is poured into the right amount of clean warm fat at the right temperature, the fat saponifies—changes character and hardens.

OLD-TIME "POTASH WATER"

Another kind of lye can be made by leaching cold water through pure hardwood ashes.

Remove the head from a water-tight wooden barrel and set it, open end up, on trestles high enough to allow a wooden pail to be set under it. Bore a small hole in the barrel's bottom near the front; make a tight-fitting plug for it and drive it in. Put several bricks in the bottom of the barrel, arranged to hold a protecting board over the hole, plus a layer of straw: board and straw will prevent the ashes from packing too tightly on the bottom or fouling the hole.

Fill the barrel with firmly packed hardwood ashes. Make an opening in the center of the ashes, and in it pour all the cold water the barrel will hold. Cover the barrel and raise it at the rear so the liquid will run toward the front. Add more water the next day if the barrel will hold it.

After 3 weeks, remove the plug and draw off the lye into the wooden pail. The liquid will be, in the traditional saying, "strong enough to float an egg"—strong enough to make soap with. (Even if it's not, there's no worry: excess water can be boiled off when you make the soap.)

Fats Good for Soapmaking

Best for soap is tallow—rendered from beef or mutton fat as you rendered lard (q.v.); next best is lard, and a combination of lard and tallow; then comes olive oil, followed by other vegetable oils. Poultry fat doesn't do well alone. Mineral oil won't saponify at all.

All fats must be fresh, clean and salt-free to avoid disappointing results.

Master Recipe for Soap

Having the right temperature for both the lye solution and the fat is one way to ensure fine soap (the others are accurate measurement and fresh, clean, salt-free fat). Here are the temperatures:

Fresh, sweet lard at 80–85 F., lye solution at 70–75 F.

Half lard and half tallow at 100–110 F., with lye solution at 80–85 F.

All tallow at 120–130 F., with lye solution at 90–95 F.

Melt 6 pounds (*c.* 13½ cups) of clean rendered fat in a large enameled kettle until it's a clear liquid; cool it to the right temperature until it thickens; stir it occasionally to keep the fat from graining as it gets near room temperature.

Meanwhile, in a large enameled pot mix 1 just-opened can (13 ounces) of suitable crystalline household lye with 5 cups of cold water. Stir with a wooden paddle until it has dissolved—but stand clear of the fumes and avoid spatters of the caustic liquid: it will boil up like mad of its own accord. Let the solution cool to the proper temperature for the fat you're using.

When both fat and lye are the right heat, very carefully pour the warm lye into the fat in a *thin* steady stream, stirring the mixture very slowly and evenly (another pair of hands would be a great help here). If the combining temperatures are too cold or too hot, or if the fat and lye are combined too fast or stirred too hard, the soap will separate— and then you must boil the separated mixture with much extra water to make it get together again.

In 10 to 20 minutes of careful stirring the fat and lye will have blended thoroughly and become thick. Pour the saponified mixture at once into the soaked, cloth-lined box; set the box in the dripping pan to catch leaked soap. Lay the protecting board over the box and cover the whole shebang with a rug or blanket to hold the heat while the soap develops a good texture.

Don't disturb the soap for 24 hours. Then grasp the overhanging edges of the cloth liner and raise the soap block from the mold. Cut it by cinching strong twine or wire around the soap and pulling tight. Let the bars of young soap dry at room temperature in a draft-free place for 10 days or 2 weeks. Don't let the soap freeze during this time.

When the soap has conditioned, wrap each piece in paper and store it in a cool dry place. Aging improves soap.

Variations with Your Soap

Make floating soap by folding air into the thick saponified mixture before you pour it in the box-mold: pretend you're adding beaten egg whites to cake batter. A wire whisk works well here.

Scent the soap by wrapping it in natural blossoms or leaves; or by adding small amounts of concentrated homemade infusions while it's being stirred to saponify. Don't use commercial essences that have alcohol in them—alcohol can cause soap to separate.

Boost sudsing action by adding 2 tablespoons of borax to the 13-ounces-of-lye solution as it cools.

Make soap jelly by shaving 1 pound of soap into 1 gallon of fresh water; boil for 10 minutes; cool. Store in a closed container in a cool place. This is equally good for shampooing hair or for doing the kids' play-clothes in the washing machine.

Make your own soap flakes by gently shaving 3-day-old soap against the medium holes of a vegetable grater. Stir the shavings gently as they air-dry. Store in closed containers.

For more information write to Household Products Information, the Pennwalt Corporation, 3 Parkway, Philadelphia, Pennsylvania 19102.

FARMERS' SAUSAGE

Before you start, see instructions for canning pork sausage on pages 104—105, and freezing ground meat on page 170.

20 pounds of fresh pork trimmings—2/3 lean, 1/3 fat
½ cup pickling salt
6 tablespoons ground sage (omit if canning: it gets bitter)
3 tablespoons ground pepper
3 teaspoons ground ginger *or* ground nutmeg, if desired
2½ cups ice water (if you're freezing it in rolls like cookie dough)

Put the meat through the food grinder twice; add seasonings and put through a third time. Mix it all thoroughly on a large bread-board.

If you plan to freeze it—or just to refrigerate it—rolled in bulk, knead the ice water in gradually until the liquid is absorbed and the sausage is doughy. The water keeps the sausage from crumbling when it's sliced for frying.

BOLOGNA-STYLE SAUSAGE

This rule, which makes about 25 pounds of Bologna-style sausage, may be cut down to suit your fancy or your supply of meat. If canned, *it must be pressure-processed at 15 pounds* as described on page 105 (most other meats are processed at 10 pounds).

Prepare. Using the coarse knife of a food chopper, grind 20 pounds of lean beef and 5 pounds of lean pork; add seasonings, and re-grind with the fine knife. Usually ½ pound of salt and 2½ ounces (a standard small box) or less of pepper are enough. Garlic juice may be added, or finely minced garlic; also coriander or mace to suit your taste.

For this quantity of seasoned meat, add 3 to 4 pints of very cold water, and, using your hands, mix it all thoroughly until all the water is absorbed into the meat. Stuff tightly, without air pockets, into beef casings or rounds that have been soaked in cold water (such casings are available from butcher-supply houses). Use short casings; or tie long ones at intervals short enough to allow you to cut sections suitable for family use. Tie ends with stout string. Smoke the sausage for 2 to 3 hours at 60 to 70 degrees Fahrenheit (see Smoking).

Next, simmer the smoked bologna at about 200 F. until it floats. A full-size sausage will take a whale of a kettle; if you don't have a pot big enough, cut the thing in sections where you've tied it off, and cook it piecemeal, holding any extra pieces at 30 to 38 F. until they can go into the pot.

Storage. Store in the refrigerator any sausage you'll use quite soon.

Canning is best for longer-term storage at home (see above). Because of its fat content and seasonings, it doesn't hold flavor well when frozen.

FARM-WIFE'S PORK HEAD CHEESE

1 hog's head, thoroughly trimmed and then quartered
salt
pepper

Put the well-scrubbed quarters in a large kettle and cover with unsalted water. Simmer until meat falls from the bones—about 3 hours. Remove from heat and let cool until the meat can be handled, but don't let the broth get so cold that the fat congeals. Drain away the liquid, strain it well and return it to heat to reduce by 1/3 or 1/2.

Put the meat—which has been picked from the bones and gristle—in a wooden chopping bowl and chop it very fine. Add enough reduced broth to make a wet mixture and season all to taste with salt and pepper. Pack in several standard-size bread tins about ¾ full. Nest one pan on top of another with waxed paper in between and weight the top pan to press all the meat properly; if extra juice is pressed out it can be saved for stock if desired. Set the stack in the refrigerator over-night. In the morning slide each loaf from its pan and wrap it in moisture-vapor-resistant paper; freeze.

Of course you may add herb seasoning if you like; but do try this simple rule first before you jazz it up. This head cheese is nothing like the commercial product. It's grand in a sandwich; and served with slices of cold Liver Loaf and homemade Bologna Sausage (both q.v.) it makes the best platter of cold cuts ever.

PASTEURIZING MILK

When you count the tests and immunizations a milch cow must have before she's shown at even a small accredited fair or her milk is offered for public sale, you see why pasteurizing is a mandatory safeguard for our store-bought milk. And this doesn't guarantee that new spoilers can't attack it if it's handled carelessly once it's brought home.

For pasteurizing milk you need a dairy thermometer, a sterilized large spoon for stirring, and an out-size double boiler (rig one up by setting a large pot/kettle in an old-fashioned enameled dishpan).

Put milk in the inner pot, which you set in the outer one (the dishpan). Pour water in the outer container until it reaches the level of milk in the inside pot.

Put the whole thing on the stove and heat it until the hot water in the dishpan raises the temperature of the milk to 145 degrees F. Hold the milk there for 30 minutes, stirring to heat the milk evenly; check the thermometer in the milk pot to make sure you're maintaining a steady 145 F. Then take the milk from its hot-water bath and cool it by setting the milk pot in cold water. Get it down to 50 F. as soon as possible, then refrigerate.

COUNTRY-STYLE COTTAGE CHEESE

Cottage cheese is something you make at home only if you have considerable surplus fresh milk and more time than money. If you buy milk at supermarket prices to make cottage cheese, you'll be spending around 25 percent more for it per pound than you pay for the stuff ready made. However.

This type of cottage cheese has a small curd; it's well drained but not washed, so it's rather more soured-tasting than a cheese whose whey has been rinsed out; and the original rule has been translated from raw to pasteurized milk. The proportions are for 1 gallon of milk.

Bring the milk to 72 degrees F.—average room temperature in the kitchen anyway—and add 1/4 to 1/3 cup of fresh buttermilk. (Or add 1/8 to 1/4 cup of lactic "starter" made from rennet according to directions on the packet; and there's probably no reason why yogurt culture wouldn't work well too—experiment with proportions.)

Cover the kettle and keep the milk at 72 F. overnight—at least 16 hours, or until the milk has curdled into a jelly-like substance, rather firm, with some watery whey on top.

In the kettle, cut the curd in 1/4-inch pieces with a long-bladed knife. Slice the curd straight up and down in cuts about 1/4 inch apart; then give the kettle a 90-degree turn and cross-hatch another series of up-and-down slices. Now the trick is to cut these square little columns of curd into something like cubes, and you can do a fair job by cutting through the curd again at a 45-degree slant, considering the bottom of the kettle as the base of the angle, then giving the kettle a quarter-turn and making another series of angled slashes.

Set the pot of cut curd in a larger container of water, and *slowly*— so slowly that it takes 30 minutes to raise the milk from 72 to 100 F.—

heat the milk over hot water, stirring gently every 5 minutes or so to distribute the heat. When the curd has reached 100 F. you can raise its temperature more quickly to 115 F., and hold it there for about 15 minutes more. Test a curd: if it still breaks easily, bring the heat up to 120 F.; if it's firm but not tough, remove it from the hot water so it starts to cool. The higher the temperature, the tougher the curd is likely to be.

Dip off what whey you can, then pour the curd into a cloth-lined colander to drain for 5 minutes. The curd compacts if you let it drain a long time. People who want to wash the curd may do so now, by gathering the corners of the straining cloth to form a bag and dunking the bag of curd in fresh cold water, then letting it drain well.

Add salt if you want to counteract the sourish-acid taste of the unwashed curd, or if you simply like salted cottage cheese: 1 teaspoon of salt for 1 pound of cheese (1-gallon-of-milk worth) would be about right. Add 4 to 6 tablespoons of cream if you like.

Store in closed containers in the refrigerator.

If you're using safe raw milk you don't need buttermilk or a lactic starter to make the milk curdle: it will sour/clabber all by itself at room temperature. When it's satisfactorily curdled, cut the curd and proceed as for pasteurized curd above.

Cottage cheese made from raw milk is more likely to get a yeasty, sweetish, "off" taste than cheese from pasteurized milk does in cold storage, so don't let it hang around.

WATERGLASSING EGGS

Refrigeration is the best temporary storage for fresh eggs, with freezing (q.v.) recommended for longer holding. There are also old-fashioned methods for dealing with surplus eggs, the most feasible being bartering them for supplies at your neighborhood store; but there's also waterglassing.

Waterglass is sodium silicate, and you buy it from building-supply places nowadays, to seal concrete floors or to stick insulation around heating pipes. It's already dissolved, rather sirupy, and tastes like washing soda. It fills the pores of the eggshells, thus preventing moisture loss from the inside or air damage from the outside. It does well enough for a *maximum of 3 months* if the eggs are kept in cold storage.

Put fresh eggs—unwashed, but they may be wiped with a dry cloth— in a crock and cover them with several inches to spare with diluted waterglass, using 1 part waterglass to 11 parts of cooled, boiled water (1/3 cup waterglass to each 1 quart of water). Cover the crock and hold it under 40 F.

Remove eggs as needed for cooking and wash them before breaking. The whites will have lost a good deal of viscosity (they'll be worthless for meringue, for example), but the eggs are O.K. for cooked dishes calling for whole eggs. Examine each egg as it's broken (see Freezing Eggs) before adding it to the food mixture.

Note about fertile eggs. Farmers, who had plenty of experience with hens and their proclivities, would isolate the rooster from the flock for at least 1 month before putting any new-laid eggs down in waterglass.

DRYING PRODUCE IN A WOOD-STOVE OVEN

If you're familiar with the workings of an old wood-burning black iron cookstove, you know that the oven heats from the top: hot air from the firebox is routed by a series of drafts and baffles to travel over, down beside, and under the oven, to escape out the bottom of the flue at the rear of the stove. Therefore you keep food that's drying as much in the center of the oven as you can, and lower rather than higher.

Dry with an old, banked fire—air intake at the bottom of the firebox closed, drafts up through the stack closed. Feed the fire only when absolutely necessary, and then with very large hardwood, one billet at a time. You may even have to tilt the stove lids to cool the top of the oven; open the cross-draft regulator at the top of the firebox to keep the fire as low as you can.

Hang an oven thermometer on the upper rack of food to keep track of maximum temperature (the thermometer is near the lowest rack for electric or gas stoves). Do your drying with the oven door halfway or fully open, and put a chair in front of it so the door doesn't get closed inadvertently.

Control your stove's heat in these ways too if you're drying produce hung on racks above the cooking top.

Recipes

Bea Vaughan wrote down twice as many rules as there is room for here, so the cutting has had to emphasize ways to use food put by, and dishes not usually seen these days outside a collection of heirloom recipes like her own.

Many of her cookery books were handwritten, their pages of lovely and faded script blanket-stitched together by deep-country wives long ago. Others, formally printed and bound, contain the elliptical memoranda that were all that an expert home-maker needed for a new dish or a different method. For the most part, Mrs. Vaughan translated these "receipts" into modern usage—even to telling temperatures in Fahrenheit. But she left in such things as baking soda in tomato cream soup (to keep it from curdling, for who ever had heard of Vitamin C?), and lard in pastry (no dawn-to-dusk farmer knew about cholesterol, nor would he have given a hoot if he did), and white sugar (a luxury to be proud of, for the alternative was hunks of truly raw sugar, chipped from the barrel with a special hatchet and then crushed fine with a rolling pin).

Today's nutrient-minded cooks can always substitute in these and other cases. It will still, all of it, make good eating.

> Before tasting canned low-acid food, boil it hard for 15 minutes to destroy any hidden toxins (corn and greens require 20 minutes). If it looks spoiled or foams or has an off-odor during boiling, destroy it completely so it can't be eaten by people or animals.

Soups

Washday Soup

> 2 cups dried mixed beans, any kind
> ½ cup dried split peas
> 2 tablespoons rice
> 2 tablespoons barley
> 2 quarts cold water

(Continued on the next page)

2 large stalks celery, sliced
2 medium onions, peeled and sliced
2 medium potatoes, peeled and cubed
1 cup diced turnip
2 cups undrained canned tomatoes
1 teaspoon salt
¼ teaspoon pepper
ham bone (with some meat left on it)

Cover beans, peas, rice and barley with the cold water and let stand overnight. Bring to a boil in the same water, adding vegetables, salt and pepper. Simmer about 1 hour. Add ham bone and simmer about 1 hour longer. If water cooks away, add a bit more from time to time. Remove ham bone, pick off bits of meat and return them to soup. Serves 6 to 8.

Aunt Chat's Tomato Cream Soup

4 cups canned tomatoes, undrained
1 medium onion, peeled and chopped
2 stalks celery, chopped fine
4 cups scalded milk
about 1 tablespoon flour for thickening
pinch of baking soda (1/8 teaspoon)
1 tablespoon butter or margarine
salt and pepper to taste

Simmer tomatoes, onion and celery for 30 minutes. Thicken scalded milk with the flour, which has been mixed with a little cold water to make a paste. Stir over low heat until milk thickens slightly. Just before serving, add baking soda to the tomato mixture (to prevent curdling); as frothing subsides, pour all through a strainer into the hot milk, stirring constantly. Add butter and season to taste with salt and pepper. Serve at once. Serves 5 to 6.

The recipe may be doubled, but *never increase the amount of soda.*

Fish Chowder

about 1½ pounds haddock or cod, fresh or frozen
3 cups water
1 teaspoon salt
3 (¼-inch) slices fat salt pork, diced

(Continued on the next page)

3 medium potatoes, peeled and diced
2 medium onions, peeled and diced
4 cups milk
1 tablespoon butter or margarine
salt and pepper to taste

Put the fish in a kettle, add the water and salt. Poach slowly until the fish can be broken apart with a fork, but not long enough to get soft. Remove from the water—but *save the water to boil the potatoes in.* Boil the potatoes until tender. While potatoes are cooking, fry the salt pork in a small skillet until golden brown, add diced onions and cook slowly for 5 minutes longer. Remove skin and bones from fish (which is now cool enough to handle easily). To the kettle of undrained cooked potatoes, add the fish, then add pork and onions with the fat from the frying pan. Add milk. Let come just to boiling, add the butter, then pepper and salt to taste. Serve with pilot biscuit or common crackers. Makes 6 generous servings.

Salsify "Oyster" Stew

2 bunches salsify root (oyster plant)
½ teaspoon salt
water
about 5 cups hot milk
2 tablespoons butter or margarine
salt and pepper to taste

Wash and scrape salsify and cut in ½-inch slices. Barely cover with water, add ½ teaspoon salt, and simmer until very tender—about 25 minutes. Do not drain, but add the hot milk, butter, and salt and pepper to taste. Bring just to boiling and serve with oyster crackers. Serves 4 to 5.

The flavor improves if the stew is allowed to stand *without boiling* on low heat for 1 hour before serving.

Vegetable Dishes

Fried Pumpkin Blossoms

Gather the blossoms just before they are ready to open. Wash very gently and drain. Press blossoms flat with your fingers. Dip in beaten

(Continued on the next page)

egg, then in either cornmeal or fine cracker crumbs. Salt and pepper lightly, then fry in shallow hot fat until golden. Drain on paper and serve hot as you would a vegetable fritter to accompany meat. These are very delicate and will not stand long, so fry them just before serving.

Wild Fiddleheads

True fiddlehead greens, the young stalks of the Ostrich Fern (*Struthiopteris germanica*), appear in moist, fertile North Temperate woods in April and May, when American cowslips bloom in the marshes. Unlike most other ferns, they are *not* fuzzy. Rather, their characteristic is a paper-dry, parchment-like sheath that is scaling off. Gather them when they're about 4 inches above ground—3 inches of stalk, 1 inch of tight-curled "fiddlehead" tip. Before they have a chance to wilt, rub the dry scales from tips and stalks and wash well. Sprinkle lightly with salt and cook covered in a small amount of water until tender. Drain and serve with melted butter, with seasoned hot cream as a dressing, or on toast.

They're almost as good up to 6 inches or so: strip off the uncurled leaflets when scaling them, and be prepared to cook them a little longer.

Wild Cowslip Greens (Marsh marigold)

WARNING: NEVER EAT RAW COWSLIPS—THEY CONTAIN A
POISON THAT IS REMOVED BY REPEATED BOILING.

Gather young leaves of the American cowslip (marsh-marigold, *Caltha Palustris*), cutting them from the leafstalks without injuring the plant as it blooms in swampy areas in April-May. Cover the leaves with boiling water, bring again to a boil; drain. Cover again with fresh boiling water, bring to a boil, then drain. It is now safe to eat, so taste a leaf: if it seems a bit too pungent, repeat the fresh-boiling-water treatment. Drain, and cook in a small amount of water—salted if you like—until tender. Drain, chop coarsely, serve with butter, salt and pepper to taste, or season it with lemon or vinegar.

Stewed or Creamed Milkweed

Milkweed (*Asclepias syriaca*) comes along nearly a month after fiddleheads, and may be collected along any back-country road that's not been treated with chemical de-icers—(and get far enough off the road so
(Continued on the next page)

lead from car exhausts hasn't contaminated the vegetation). Gather the young stalks when they're about 5 inches high and the leaves are pressed closely together like praying hands. Rub the greens between your hands to remove the wool-like fuzz, then wash well. Because it is necessary to remove the bitter milk juice, several changes of cooking water are necessary. Cover milkweed with boiling water and boil five minutes; drain, boil for five minutes more in fresh water; repeat process again, this time adding salt to taste to the fresh water. Boil about 30 minutes in all—or until tender. Drain well and serve buttered and seasoned like fresh asparagus; or cover with hot seasoned cream or hot cream sauce and serve on toast as a main dish.

Plain Dandelion Greens

Early in the spring, even before the Ostrich Fern is producing its edible fiddleheads, come dandelion greens. Gather them when they are only a rosette of leaves without any blossom-stalk showing. Look for them in meadows, unkempt lawns, former barnyards that are growing up to grass, in pastures, and avoiding places frequented by dogs. Cut them off just below the surface of the soil—use a broad-bladed knife, or a piece of strap-iron with one end notched and the notch beveled to make a sharp cutting edge. Any tight little buds deep in the heart of the cluster are a dividend.

Wash well in deep water, and lift out, so grit and dirt sink to the bottom of the pan.

Handle like spinach for canning or freezing.

Only if you want to remove any bitter tang (delicious to many people) do you boil in two waters: cover with boiling water, cook 5 minutes, lift out greens and discard water; return greens to the pan with fresh water, salted, and cook until tender. Drain and serve hot, as is or garnished to taste.

Dandelion Greens, Potatoes and Cornmeal Dumplings

    3 pounds dandelion greens*
    1 teaspoon salt
    ¼-pound chunk of salt pork
    6 medium potatoes

Pick over and wash dandelions thoroughly in several changes of water. Place in a kettle, cover with unsalted boiling water and bring to boiling over medium heat. Cook 10 minutes, then drain to remove any lingering

(Continued on the next page)

grains of sand (this also will take away a little of the bitter tang, if desired). Drain dandelions and half cover with fresh boiling water, adding the salt. Slice the salt pork down to the rind so that it will still be in one piece and add it to the dandelions. Cover the kettle and simmer 1 hour. Add potatoes and cook 30 minutes longer. Make Cornmeal Dumplings and drop by small spoonfuls on top of boiling greens and potatoes. Cover tightly and cook 15 minutes. Remove dandelions, potatoes and dumplings to a serving platter; finish cutting the slices of pork so they can be arranged around greens. Serves 6.

* Fresh greens are best for this good old one-dish meal. You can use salted greens (q.v.) after they've freshened overnight in cold water. If you use canned or frozen greens, adjust the cleaning/cooking accordingly.

Cornmeal Dumplings

1 cup flour
1¼ teaspoons salt
2 teaspoons baking powder
1 cup cornmeal
1 beaten egg
about ¾ cup milk

Sift flour with salt and baking powder. Add the cornmeal and then the beaten egg, which has been combined with the milk. Stir well but do not beat. Drop by teaspoonfuls on top of boiling greens. Cover tightly and cook 15 minutes. Serve hot. Serves 6.

Four-Bean Salad

2 cups drained canned whole green beans
2 cups drained canned yellow wax beans
2 cups drained canned red kidney beans
2 cups drained canned garbanzos (chick peas)
2 medium onions, peeled
1 medium green pepper, seeded
3 medium stalks celery, trimmed
1 cup vinegar
½ cup water
1 cup sugar
½ cup salad oil
1 teaspoon salt

Cover drained green and yellow beans with cold water. Simmer 5 minutes; drain. Put drained kidney beans in colander and rinse with

(Continued on the next page)

fresh water; drain. Combine vinegar, water and sugar, and boil 2 minutes. Remove from heat and add oil and salt, mixing well. Combine all beans in a large bowl. Cut onions, pepper and celery in thin slices, then add to beans. Pour vinegar mixture over beans and mix in well. Cover and let stand in refrigerator several hours or overnight. The longer they stand, the better the flavor. Stir occasionally. Makes 8 to 10 servings.

Saturday Night Baked Beans

> 1 pound yellow-eye or pea beans
> ½ teaspoon baking soda (optional)
> 1 teaspoon salt
> ½ cup maple syrup*
> ½ teaspoon dry mustard
> ½ pound salt pork
> 1 small onion (optional)

Cover beans with cold water and let stand overnight. In the morning, drain and cover with fresh water. Add the soda. Cover and simmer until beans are just tender: *don't overcook.* (A good test is to spoon out several beans and blow on them; if the skin cracks, the beans are ready.) Drain and put beans in a pot or casserole. Add salt, maple syrup and mustard. Some people like the flavor of onion in their baked beans; if you do, tuck the whole peeled onion well down into the center. Add boiling water just to the top of the beans. Score the salt pork and place on the surface of the beans. Cover the pot and bake slowly in a 275 oven for at least 4 hours—you can scarcely bake beans too long, so don't worry about overcooking. But good baked beans should never be dry; inspect them occasionally and add a bit of boiling water if they appear dry. Six servings.

* Substitute ½ cup sorghum; or 1/3 cup raw sugar and 1/3 cup water; or 1/3 cup of corn syrup and 3 tablespoons molasses—or whatever combination of sweeteners you like, in the amount you like.

Maple-glazed Carrots and Onions

> 1 pint canned sliced carrots, drained
> 1 pint canned whole onions, drained
> ½ cup maple sirup
> ½ cup apple juice

Combine maple sirup and apple juice. Stir over low heat until mixture thickens and resembles caramel sirup. Add drained vegetables. Let stand over very low heat for about 30 minutes, stirring frequently to glaze evenly. Serve hot. Serves 6.

Quick Pickled Beets

    1 quart canned sliced beets, drained
    1 cup vinegar
    ¾ cup sugar
    ½ teaspoon salt
    2 teaspoons mustard seed
    ½ teaspoon celery seed
    1 large onion, peeled and thinly sliced

Drain beets, reserving 1 cup of the liquid. Combine liquid with the vinegar, sugar, salt and spices. Bring to boiling over moderate heat; add beets and onion slices. Bring again just to the boiling point. Remove from heat and cool. Cover and refrigerate for 24 hours for flavors to blend. Serve cold. Serves 12.

Succotash

    2 cups canned lima beans, drained
    2 cups canned whole-kernel corn, drained
    2 tablespoons butter or margarine
    small pinch of pepper
    1 teaspoon sugar
    ½ cup light cream
    salt to taste

Combine ingredients in order. Place over low heat and bring to just below boiling point: *do not boil.* Let stand over heat 10 minutes, then serve at once. Makes 4 to 6 servings.

Salsify "Oyster" Patties

    6 large salsify roots (2 cups mashed)
    1 egg, beaten
    ½ teaspoon salt
    pinch of pepper
    1 tablespoon butter, melted
    flour for dusting
    fat for frying

Wash and scrape salsify; slice and boil until tender—about 30 minutes.

337 (Continued on the next page)

Drain; mash well and mix with seasonings, beaten egg and melted butter. Shape in small cakes (about 2 tablespoonfuls to each cake), dust on both sides with flour, and fry in a small amount of hot fat, turning once, until brown. Serve hot. Serves 4.

Green Pea Cakes

      2 cups cooked green peas, drained
      1 tablespoon butter or margarine
      salt and pepper to taste
      2 eggs, beaten
      ¼ teaspoon salt
      ¼ teaspoon baking soda
      ½ teaspoon cream of tartar
      ½ cup sifted flour
      1 cup milk

Mash peas while hot, adding butter, salt and pepper to taste. Beat eggs well. Sift flour, salt, baking soda and cream of tartar; add to beaten eggs. Beat in the milk, then the mashed peas. Beat all well. Cook at once on a hot greased griddle as with any pancake. Serve at once. Makes 12 three-inch cakes.

Fresh or frozen peas are better than canned ones for these delicious fritter/pancakes.

Basic Vegetable Soufflé

      1 cup hot cream sauce
      1 cup minced, drained cooked vegetables (or canned)
      3 eggs, separated
      salt and pepper to taste

Combine hot cream sauce with the vegetables and heat to just below boiling point. Beat egg yolks until fluffy, then beat in the hot mixture. Season to taste with salt and pepper. Fold in stiffly beaten egg whites. Bake in a buttered 1½-quart casserole in a 325 oven for about 45 minutes. Serve hot. Serves 4.

Carrots, peas, cauliflower, asparagus, celery, eggplant, celery and onions may all be used in this way.

Corn Omelet

Mix 1 cup sweet corn kernels, cooked and cut from the cob, with 3

(Continued on the next page)

slightly beaten eggs, 2 tablespoons light cream, 1 teaspoon salt and a pinch of pepper. Cook as any omelet. Serves 3.

Cooked frozen corn may be used; so may canned whole-kernel corn, drained, but the omelet will not have as fine a flavor.

Eggernoggin

 2 tablespoons melted butter or margarine
 1 teaspoon salt
 pinch of pepper
 few grains cayenne pepper
 1 teaspoon grated onion
 1 cup undrained canned tomatoes
 1 teaspoon cornstarch
 1 teaspoon cold water
 6 eggs, slightly beaten
 1 teaspoon chopped fresh parsley (optional)

Melt butter in a heavy frying pan, add salt, pepper, cayenne and onion, and simmer 2 minutes. Add tomatoes and cook 10 minutes over low heat. Blend cornstarch with the cold water and add to tomato mixture, stirring and cooking 1 minute. Beat eggs just enough to break the yolks, and add them to the tomato mixture. Cook slowly, stirring as needed to prevent scorching. When thick as any scrambled eggs, remove from heat and serve at once. If desired, sprinkle chopped parsley over top. Serve either alone or on hot toast. Serves 4.

Baked Cabbage, Tomato and Cheese

 3 cups finely shredded cabbage
 1½ cups undrained canned tomatoes
 ¾ teaspoon salt
 1/8 teaspoon pepper
 1/8 teaspoon paprika
 2 teaspoons light brown sugar (raw)
 1 cup shredded sharp cheese (¼ pound)
 1 cup dry breadcrumbs
 2 tablespoons butter or margarine

Cook cabbage in boiling salted water for 5 minutes; drain. Combine tomatoes, salt, pepper, paprika and sugar. Bring just to boiling point. Arrange ½ of the tomato mixture in a buttered baking dish. Cover with ½ of the cabbage, then ½ the cheese and breadcrumbs. Repeat layers,

(Continued on the next page)

and dot the top with the butter. Bake in a 325 oven for about 30 minutes—or until browned. Serves 6.

Tomato-Corn Pudding

 2 cups canned cream-style corn
 1 cup canned tomatoes, undrained
 1 beaten egg
 ¼ cup saltine cracker crumbs
 ½ teaspoon seasoned salt
 pinch of pepper
 1 tablespoon minced onion
 1 tablespoon minced green pepper
 1 tablespoon melted butter or margarine

Combine all ingredients in order, then turn into a buttered 1½-quart baking dish. Bake uncovered in a 400 oven for about 30 minutes. Remove from oven and let stand 10 minutes before serving. Serves 6.

Garden Medley

 1/3 cup butter or margarine
 1 small onion, peeled and grated
 1/3 cup flour
 2 cups milk
 1 cup chicken broth
 1 teaspoon salt
 pinch of pepper
 1 (4-oz.) can sliced mushrooms, drained
 2 cups cooked asparagus (or canned)
 2 cups cooked green peas (or canned)
 2 cups cooked sliced carrots (or canned)
 1 beaten egg yolk

Melt butter, add onion and flour. Combine milk and chicken broth, then blend into butter mixture. Stir and cook over low heat until thickened and smooth. Season with the salt and pepper. Add the vegetables. Stir ¼ cup of the hot sauce into the beaten egg yolk, then add to mixture in skillet. Heat very hot *but don't boil.* Serve over hot toast, biscuits or rice. Serves 6.

Meat and Fish Dishes

Traditional Boiled Dinner

4 pounds corned beef
1 pound salt pork, unsliced
¼ cup brown (or raw) sugar*
1 large cabbage, quartered
10 large whole carrots, peeled
1 large turnip, peeled and cut in large chunks
8 large potatoes, peeled
8 parsnips, peeled
12 small beets, unpeeled

Simmer corned beef and salt pork for 1 hour in unsalted water to cover, to which you've added the ¼ cup of sugar. After an hour, add turnip, carrots and parsnips. Cook 1 more hour, then add potatoes and cabbage. Meanwhile cook beets separately in salted water until tender. When corned beef is very tender, remove to a platter with the salt pork. Drain vegetables and arrange around the meat. Drain beets, immerse briefly in cold water, and slip off skins; add to vegetables on platter. Serve at once. Serves 8.

* This boosts the flavor of corned beef, smoked shoulder or ham, but is not discernable in itself. Substitute 1/3 cup maple syrup or sorghum for the ¼ cup brown/raw sugar.

Red Flannel Hash

4 cups corned beef (leftovers of Boiled Dinner)
4 cups cooked potatoes
other leftover vegetables from Boiled Dinner
salt to taste
bacon fat for browning

The amounts given here are intended to show proportions rather than actual amounts, since leftovers seldom come out evenly. The rule-of-thumb is to have equal amounts of corned beef and potatoes, and enough beets to make the hash dark red. Put corned beef, potatoes and other vegetables through the meat grinder, using a coarse knife. Season to taste with salt and pepper, and brown in melted bacon fat in a large frying pan. Put on a low rack under the broiler for a few minutes to brown the top.

Hearty Vegetable-Beef Stew

    about 2 pounds stewing beef, cubed
    1½ quarts water
    1 bay leaf
    ½ cup diced celery
    ¼ cup diced green pepper
    4 medium carrots, peeled and sliced
    1 large onion, peeled and diced
    1 teaspoon salt
    ¼ teaspoon pepper
    4 medium potatoes, peeled and cubed
    2 cups undrained canned tomatoes
    ¼ cup tomato catsup
    1 cup canned tomato juice
    ¼ medium head of cabbage
    1 teaspoon sugar

Combine first nine ingredients. Cover and simmer 2 hours. Add remaining ingredients and simmer 1 hour longer. Add additional salt and pepper, if needed. Serves 8.

Roast Venison

In her classic *The Venison Book—How To Dress, Cut up and Cook Your Deer,* Audrey Alley Gorton points out that deer meat that has been properly dressed, skinned, trimmed and chilled should be treated like a prime cut of beef except for one difference. Which is: because venison fat is strong-tasting and acts like mutton fat, it must be trimmed away, and therefore the roast must be cooked with added lard, salt pork or bacon to prevent dryness. Otherwise, season it and cook it by your favorite method for roast beef, including degree of doneness.

    However, if you have doubts about the flavor of your venison, marinate and cook it as follows:

    5-pound haunch roast
    ¼ pound salt pork, cut in strips
    1 teaspoon salt
    1/8 teaspoon pepper
    8 cups buttermilk
    4 medium onions, peeled and chopped
    3 bay leaves

Add bay leaves, onions and salt to the buttermilk to make a marinade.

(Continued on the next page)

Marinate the venison refrigerated for 48 hours, turning it night and morning. Discard marinade and lard venison well with the strips of salt pork tucked into deep slits cut in the meat. Place in a roasting pan and roast uncovered in a 350 oven until tender, allowing 20 minutes to the pound.

Baked Liver Loaf

1½ pounds beef liver, cut in strips
½ cup dry breadcrumbs
1 large onion, ground
¾ pound sausage
1 teaspoon salt
pinch of pepper
pinch each of marjoram, rosemary and basil
¼ teaspoon sage
1 egg, slightly beaten
1/3 cup light cream
4 large strips of bacon

Dredge liver strips in the breadcrumbs, then put them through the medium knife of a food grinder, with the onion. Mix with sausage and seasonings. Add cream to the egg and mix thoroughly in with the meat mixture. Pack firmly into a standard-size bread tin. Cut each bacon strip in half and lay it across the top, forming a solid layer of bacon. Bake in a 375 oven for about 1 hour. Serves 6 to 8.

This tasty loaf is also good sliced cold, like a portion of pâté, or served cold with potato salad.

Liver Cutlets

1 pound beef liver
½ cup finely chopped suet*
1/3 cup dry breadcrumbs
1¼ teaspoons salt
pinch of pepper
pinch of nutmeg
pinch of mace
few grains of cayenne pepper
2 eggs, beaten
melted fat for frying

Barely cover the liver with water and simmer until tender. Drain. Put it

 (Continued on the next page)

through the food grinder, using a medium knife, then combine with the suet. Add breadcrumbs and seasonings, then the eggs, mixing all thoroughly. Form in small balls or flat cakes and pan-fry in a small amount of melted fat until browned. Serves 6.

* Suet compensates for the total lack of fat in the meat, thereby keeping the patties juicy and preventing their sticking to the pan. *And* it cooks out, adding to the fat in the pan; so just drain the patties on paper for a few seconds before serving.

Boiled Beef Tongue

    1 fresh (or frozen) beef tongue
    2 tablespoons vinegar
    1 tablespoon salt
    4 whole cloves
    3 bay leaves

Soak the tongue in cold water for several hours and scrub it thoroughly. Put it in a deep covered kettle with fresh water to come two inches above the tongue; add vinegar, salt and spices, and bring to a boil uncovered. Skim well, put on the cover tightly, reduce heat and simmer until fork-tender through the thickest part—about 3 or 3½ hours. Remove tongue, dip it in cold water and slip off the skin; trim any fat or gristle from the underside. Serve hot slices with a sharp condiment like horseradish; or let it cool whole in its liquor, drain and slice, and serve cold with salad. Serves 4 to 6.

Baked Stuffed Heart

    1 large beef heart
    8 cups cold water
    1 cup vinegar
    1 teaspoon salt
    2 cups Sausage Stuffing (about ½ batch)
    ½ cup water

Soak the heart for 1 hour or longer in the cold water, to which the vinegar has been added. Drain and cut away fat and tubes. Parboil for 1 hour in fresh water to which the 1 teaspoon of salt has been added. Remove and drain well. Stuff the heart with Breadcrumb Sausage Stuffing (q.v.) and sew it together at the top. Place in a heavy baking pan that has a lid, add the ½ cup fresh water. Cover and bake in a 350 oven until tender—about 2 or 3 hours. Serves 6.

(Continued on the next page)

Two veal or pork hearts may be used for the same yield. If the smaller hearts are used, parboiling may be omitted and the salt added to the ½ cup of water in the pan for baking.

Breadcrumb Sausage Stuffing

3 cups coarse dry breadcrumbs
2 teaspoons sage or poultry seasoning
1 teaspoon salt
1/8 teaspoon pepper
½ pound sausage meat
¼ cup melted sausage fat
½ cup hot water

Add seasonings to breadcrumbs. Fry sausage meat gently for about 10 minutes, but do *not* let it get crisp and brown. Remove meat and drain, reserving ¼ cup of the fat. Add fat to breadcrumbs and seasonings, then add sausage meat. Stir in the hot water. Mix well but do not beat. Let cool before stuffing a bird; do not pack tightly, or it will be soggy. About 4½ cups.

Hamburger and Onion Shortcake

1 tablespoon melted butter or margarine
4 medium onions, sliced thin
½ pound lean hamburger
1 teaspoon salt
¼ teaspoon pepper
2 eggs, beaten
1 cup sour cream
paprika
½ batch Buttermilk Biscuits (1 cup flour)

Simmer butter and onions over low heat for about 10 minutes—until tender but not brown. Add hamburger, crumbling with a fork, and cook it for about 5 minutes until meat loses its red color. Beat eggs, sour cream and seasonings well, and combine with meat mixture. Make half the rule for Buttermilk Biscuits (q.v.), roll out on a floured board to about ¼ inch thick. Press the pastry into a lightly greased 9-inch pie tin. Pour the meat mixture over the biscuit pastry, sprinkle with paprika, and bake in a 375 oven for about 35 minutes. Serve hot, cut in wedges. Four hearty servings for hungry people.

Chili Con Carne

    2 tablespoons melted fat
    1 medium onion, peeled and chopped
    1 pound ground beef
    2½ cups undrained canned tomatoes
    4 cups cooked (or canned) kidney beans
    1 tablespoon chili powder
    1 teaspoon salt

Simmer fat and onions for 5 minutes. Add meat, breaking it apart with fork, and cook until red color has disappeared. Add tomatoes, beans, chili powder and salt. Cover and cook very slowly for 1 hour, tasting after the first 15 minutes to see if you want more chili powder or salt. Serve hot in bowls. Serves 10 to 12.

Frizzled Dried Beef

    2 tablespoons butter or margarine
    ¼ pound dried beef, shredded
    3 tablespoons flour
    2 cups milk
    tiny dash of pepper

Melt butter in a frying pan, then add the beef. Stir over moderate heat until the beef begins to look crisp at the edges. Blend in the flour and stir for 3 minutes. Add the milk. Cook and stir until mixture just comes to boiling. Season to taste with the pepper—no salt will be needed. Serve hot over toast, hot biscuits or with boiled potatoes. Serves 4.

Ham and Dried Apples with Egg Dumplings

(This fine old Pennsylvania Dutch rule is based on using uncooked home-cured ham and dried apples: there's nothing "instant" about it, and it's wonderful eating.)

    end of ham with bone, about 3 pounds
    2 cups dried apples
    2 tablespoons light brown sugar (or raw)

Soak dried apples for several hours (or overnight if they're quite
(Continued on the next page)

leathery) until they've softened a bit and begun to plump. Meanwhile cover ham with cold water and bring to a boil, covered. Simmer about 2 hours, then add drained apples; simmer about 1 hour longer. Remove ham to a platter, lift apples from the pot with a slotted spoon, and place them around the ham; keep all hot while the dumplings are cooking. Serves 6.

Egg Dumplings

1½ cups sifted flour
3 teaspoons baking powder
½ teaspoon salt
1 tablespoon butter or margarine
about ¼ cup milk
1 beaten egg

Sift flour with baking powder and salt. Rub in the butter with your fingertips and stir in enough milk to make a soft dough. Stir in the beaten egg. Drop from a spoon into the boiling ham broth. Cover tightly and simmer about 12 minutes. Arrange dumplings on the platter around the ham and apples, and serve.

Fried Salt Pork and Gravy

½ pound salt pork, sliced very thin
flour and cornmeal for dredging
2 tablespoons flour for thickening gravy
2 cups milk (or sour cream)

Cover pork slices with boiling water and let stand 3 minutes: *do not allow to cook.* Remove slices and drain well. In a mixture of equal amounts of flour and cornmeal, dredge the slices. Fry in a heavy frying pan in their own fat until crisp and golden brown. Remove slices and drain on a paper towel: keep hot. Pour off enough fat from the pan to leave only 2 tablespoonfuls. Return the pan to heat and blend the flour into the fat. Add the milk. Stir and cook over low heat until smooth and thickened, making a creamy gravy speckled with tiny crumbs of pork. Serve pork slices with boiled potatoes, the gravy in a bowl on the side. Serves 4 to 5.

Olden cooks sometimes made the gravy with sour cream and omitted the flour, since the cream needs no additional thickening. The sour-cream gravy has an unusual and good flavor.

Sausage Yorkshire Pudding

1 pound sausage (bulk or link)
1 cup milk
2 eggs, very well beaten
1 cup sifted flour
½ teaspoon salt

Make small patties of sausage and arrange them in the bottom of a 9-inch-square cake pan. (If link sausage is used, prick each link several times with a fork, and arrange in the pan.) Bake for 15 minutes in a 425 oven. Meanwhile beat milk into eggs, slowly add flour sifted with salt, and continue beating until big bubbles rise from the bottom of the batter. Take sausage from the oven, and drain off enough fat to leave about 1/8 inch of fat covering the bottom of the pan. Quickly pour batter onto hot sausage and fat and return to the oven. Bake 30 minutes more at 425—or until puffed high with brown peaks but not too crisp. Serve at once, cut in squares. Serves 4 to 6.

Fish Hash

2 cups flaked cooked fish
2 cups diced cooked potatoes, cooled
2 tablespoons melted bacon fat
1 small onion, peeled and minced
2 hard-cooked eggs, peeled and chopped fine
1 teaspoon salt
pinch of pepper
1 teaspoon Worcestershire sauce (optional)
2/3 cup milk

Sauté onion in the melted fat until light golden—about 5 minutes. Meanwhile stir gently together the fish, potatoes, chopped eggs, seasonings and milk. Mix lightly, then turn into the skillet with the onion and fat. Cover and cook over moderate heat until the bottom is crusty and brown (lift an edge to see). With a pancake turner, fold half the hash over the other half, as with a puffed omelet, and serve at once. Serves 5.

Codfish Gravy

Allow 1 cup hot unsalted cream sauce to each 1 cup of freshened salt codfish. Freshen fish in cold water overnight, then drain. Cover with

(Continued on the next page)

fresh water and simmer 5 minutes. Drain well and add to cream sauce. Serve hot with boiled potatoes.

"Picked" Fish Dinner

    2 pounds salt codfish fillets
    8 medium potatoes, peeled
    1 pint sliced canned beets (6 medium if fresh)
    ½ pound salt pork, diced
    4 tablespoons flour
    2 cups milk
    salt and pepper to taste

Freshen codfish overnight in cold water to cover. Drain, cover with fresh water; bring just to boiling, and simmer gently until tender but not mushy. Remove to a hot platter when done, and pull out any bones without breaking up the fish; keep hot. Meanwhile boil the potatoes in salted water; separately, heat the beets (boil, skin and slice them if they're fresh). While vegetables are cooking, gently fry the diced salt pork until just golden; remove from pan and keep hot, leaving 4 table-spoons fat in the skillet. Stir in the flour, then the milk, and stir and cook until smooth and thickened; season with salt and pepper. To serve, cover the hot fish with cooked pork bits and arrange potatoes and sliced beets around the fish. Serve gravy separately. Six hearty big helpings.

Codfish Balls

    1 cup shredded salt codfish
    6 medium potatoes, peeled
    1 tablespoon butter or margarine
    1/8 teaspoon pepper
    1 beaten egg
    fat for frying

Soak codfish in cold water for 1 hour. Drain and cover with boiling water to cover well. Add potatoes and cook until tender. Drain well. Mash with a fork and add butter and pepper. Stir in beaten egg. Mix lightly but well. Shape into balls and fry in deep fat, or brown in shallow fat in skillet until browned on both sides. Makes about 8 good-sized balls, or 4 hearty servings.

Breads, Cakes and Cookies

Quick Pumpkin Bread

    1½ cups sugar
    ½ cup vegetable oil
    2 eggs
    1 2/3 cups flour
    ¼ teaspoon baking powder
    1 teaspoon baking soda
    ¾ teaspoon salt
    ¼ teaspoon cinnamon
    ½ teaspoon cloves
    ½ teaspoon nutmeg
    1 cup strained canned pumpkin
    ½ cup chopped nuts
    1 cup raisins

Thoroughly mix together the first three ingredients. Sift together the dry ingredients and add to the sugar mixture. Mix well. Add pumpkin, nuts and raisins. Pour into two greased 8½ x 4½ x 2½-inch bread pans and bake in a 350 oven for 1½ hours. Remove from pans and cool on a rack.

Apple Bran Bread

    2 cups bran
    2 teaspoons salt
    ½ cup sugar
    2 tablespoons melted butter or margarine
    1½ cups sweetened applesauce
    1½ cups boiling water
    1 yeast cake (or envelope dry yeast)
    1/3 cup lukewarm water
    about 8 cups sifted flour

Combine the first five ingredients, then stir in the boiling water. Let stand until lukewarm. Soften yeast in the lukewarm water and add to the first mixture when it has cooled to lukewarm. Add flour to make a smooth, easily handled dough. Knead slightly on a floured board, place in a large bowl; cover and let rise in a warm place until doubled. Knead again until smooth, then shape in 2 loaves. Place in lightly greased bread tins and cover with a towel; let rise until doubled. Bake in a 350 oven for about 50 minutes or until bread tests done. Turn out on a wire rack and cool thoroughly before slicing.

Country Buttermilk Biscuits

2 cups flour
1 teaspoon salt
1 teaspoon any baking powder
½ teaspoon baking soda
4 tablespoons lard (or vegetable shortening)
about ¾ cup buttermilk

Sift flour with baking powder, salt and soda. Quickly rub in lard, then add enough buttermilk to make a soft dough that yet can be handled. Turn out on a floured board and knead lightly a few strokes, then gently roll out to about ¾ inch thick. Cut in rounds, bake on a greased sheet in a 425 oven for 15 minutes. Makes about 15 biscuits.

Substitute shortening: An equal amount of any solid vegetable shortening may be used instead of the lard. So may oil—but it does not give the same lightness and texture that solid shortening does.

Mincemeat Fruit Cake

1 cup firmly packed light brown sugar (or raw)
½ cup softened shortening
2 eggs, separated
2 cups canned mincemeat
2 cups sifted flour
1 teaspoon baking soda
1 teaspoon salt
1 cup chopped pitted dates
1 cup chopped nuts
¼ cup rum or brandy (optional)

Cream sugar with the shortening, then beat in the egg yolks. Beat well, then stir in mincemeat. Sift flour with the baking soda and salt. Combine with dates and nuts, then add to batter. Mix well and fold in stiffly beaten egg whites. Turn into a large bread tin which has been greased and lined with waxed paper. Bake in a 300 oven for about 1½ hours. Turn out on a wire rack and cool thoroughly before slicing. Serves 8 to 10. Or will keep for several weeks if well wrapped from air.

Two small loaves instead of one large "spend better," as the country housewives used to say. Reduce baking time by 20 to 30 minutes.

This dark and moist cake may also be served instead of the traditional plum pudding (for which see also Steamed Carrot Pudding): just warm the slices in the top of a double boiler and serve with fruity sauce.

Dried Apple Fruit Cake

3 cups dried apples
3 cups light molasses (right: there's no other sweetening)
1 cup seeded raisins
3 cups flour
1 cup softened shortening
3 eggs, beaten
1 teaspoon baking soda
1 teaspoon salt
1 teaspoon cinnamon
½ teaspoon nutmeg
¼ teaspoon cloves

Soak apples overnight in just enough water to cover. In the morning cut apples quite fine, add molasses, and cook until apples are very tender. Add raisins and cook 5 minutes more. Remove from heat; cool. Add shortening and eggs. Sift dry ingredients together and add. Blend well, then pour into 2 standard-size bread tins lined with waxed paper. Bake in a 350 oven for 1 hour—or until a toothpick poked in the center comes out clean. Cool on a rack, remove from pans and peel off the paper. Wrap and store.

The bits of apple in this very old cake taste like citron.

Applesauce Cake with Praline Topping

2¾ cups sifted flour
1 1/3 cups sugar
2 teaspoons baking powder
¼ teaspoon baking soda
½ teaspoon salt
1½ teaspoons ground cinnamon
½ teaspoon ground cloves
½ cup softened shortening
2 cups canned smooth applesauce
2 eggs, to be beaten in
1½ cups seedless raisins

Sift flour with sugar, baking powder, baking soda, salt, cinnamon and cloves. Add shortening and applesauce. Beat with electric beater until blended, about 2 minutes. Add eggs and beat 1 minute longer. Stir in raisins. Bake in a greased 13 x 9 cake pan in a 350 oven for about 35 minutes—or until cake tests done. Spread cake with Praline Topping

(Continued on the next page)

and place under broiler on the lowest rack for 5 minutes. Topping should be golden brown and bubbling when done. Cool cake in the pan set on wire rack. Serve slightly warm or cold. Makes 20 servings.

Praline Topping

½ cup softened butter or margarine
¾ cup firmly packed light brown (raw) sugar
¼ cup undiluted evaporated milk
¾ cup shopped nuts
2/3 cup flaked coconut

Blend butter and sugar, then beat in evaporated milk. Blend thoroughly, stir in nuts and coconut. Spread on cake, broil as directed.

Carrot-Orange Cookies

1 cup mashed carrots (2 cups canned sliced, drained)
1 cup sugar
1 cup softened shortening
1 tablespoon grated orange rind
½ teaspoon vanilla
1 egg
2 cups sifted flour
2 teaspoons baking powder
½ teaspoon salt

Combine carrots, sugar, shortening, grated orange rind, vanilla and the egg and beat hard until thoroughly mixed. Sift flour with the baking powder and salt; stir into the batter. Mix well. Drop by heaping teaspoonfuls onto a greased cookie pan. Bake in a 375 oven for about 20 minutes. Cool on a wire rack. Makes 4 dozen.

Pumpkin Cookies

1/3 cup shortening
1 cup sugar
2 eggs
1 teaspoon vanilla
1 teaspoon lemon extract
1 cup mashed cooked pumpkin (or canned)
2½ cups flour
4 teaspoons baking powder
¼ teaspoon salt
½ teaspoon ginger

(Continued on the next page)

½ teaspoon nutmeg
1 cup seeded raisins
½ cup chopped nuts

Cream shortening and sugar, beat eggs in well. Stir in the vanilla and lemon extract. Put pumpkin through a sieve and add, mixing well. Sift dry ingredients and add with the raisins and nuts. Mix thoroughly. Drop by the teaspoonful onto a greased cookie pan and bake about 15 minutes in a 375 oven. Makes 4 dozen.

Puddings and Pies

Old Settler Indian Pudding

5 tablespoons yellow cornmeal
4 cups milk, scalded
2 tablespoons butter
1 cup maple sirup*
2 eggs, beaten
1 teaspoon cinnamon
¾ teaspoon ginger
1 teaspoon salt
1 cup cold milk

Add cornmeal to hot milk, and cook over low heat until thickened, stirring constantly. Remove from heat, add butter, maple sirup, beaten eggs, spices and salt. Mix well and pour into a buttered baking dish. Bake in a 300 oven for about 1 hour. Stir and add the 1 cup of cold milk and continue baking for 1 more hour. Serve warm with plain or whipped cream, even vanilla ice cream. Serves 8 to 10.

    * ½ to 2/3 cup brown (raw) sugar and ¼ cup molasses may be substituted. Experiment.

Basic Rule for Fruit Cobblers

around ¾ cup sugar
1 tablespoon cornstarch
1 cup boiling water
3 cups prepared fresh fruit
1 tablespoon butter or margarine
¼ teaspoon cinnamon (optional)
1/8 teaspoon nutmeg (optional)

(Continued on the next page)

Topping

1 cup sifted flour
1 tablespoon sugar
1½ teaspoons baking powder
½ teaspoon salt
¼ cup shortening
½ cup milk

Prepare fruit by washing, stemming, peeling and slicing as necessary. Combine sugar and cornstarch, blend with boiling water. Stir over moderate heat until it boils, then cook 1 minute more. Add prepared fruit, and pour all into a buttered 10 x 6-inch baking dish and dot with butter. Sprinkle with spices, if desired (cinnamon is especially good with fresh blueberries and blackberries). Put the dish in a 400 oven to keep hot while you make the topping. Combine sifted flour, sugar, baking powder and salt; sift together. Rub in shortening and stir in milk to make a soft dough. Drop by spoonfuls on to surface of the hot fruit. Bake at 400 for 30 minutes. Serve warm with plain cream. Serves 6.

Be sure the fruit mixture is bubbling hot when you add the dough, otherwise the topping will have raw spots underneath.

Adjust the amount of sugar according to tartness of the fruit used.

Canned Fruit Cobblers

Following Basic Cobbler recipe, use 1 quart of Open-Kettle Canned fruit *but omit* the boiling water, and *cut down* the sugar to ½ cup, or to taste.

Betsy Pudding

½ cup firm jam
1 egg
2 tablespoons sugar
small pinch of salt
¼ teaspoon nutmeg
1 tablespoon melted butter or margarine
2 cups scalded milk
1 cup coarse dry breadcrumbs
1 teaspoon vanilla

Spread jam over the bottom of a buttered small casserole. Beat the egg with sugar, salt, spice and melted butter, then beat in the hot milk. Stir

(Continued on the next page)

355

in the breadcrumbs and vanilla. Mix well, then pour it over the jam. Bake in a 350 oven for about 40 minutes—or until puffed and brown. Serve warm or cold. Serves 4 to 6.

Steamed Carrot Pudding

    1 cup grated raw carrots (about 3 medium)
    1 cup grated raw potatoes (about 2 medium)
    1 teaspoon baking soda
    ½ cup butter or margarine, melted
    1 cup brown (raw) sugar
    1½ cups flour
    1 teaspoon salt
    1 teaspoon ground cinnamon
    ½ teaspoon ground nutmeg
    ½ teaspoon ground cloves
    1 cup seeded raisins
    1 cup heavy cream for whipping

Dissolve soda in combined grated potatoes and carrots. Stir in melted butter and sugar. Sift flour with salt and spices and add to first mixture. Stir in raisins. Steam 3 hours in a tightly covered, greased pudding mold. Serve hot with the whipped cream, sweetened to taste. Serves 6 to 8.

Steaming

Round tins (1-pound coffee cans are fine) with tight-fitting covers do well if you have no pudding mold. Heavy waxed paper or foil held firmly in place with a rubber band will serve as a cover in a pinch.

Fill the well-greased mold about 2/3 full of batter. Cover it, and put it on a trivet or rack in a pan of boiling water that comes halfway up the sides of the mold. If the mold tries to float, put a weight on it.

If water level drops, add more boiling water, and do *not* let the water stop boiling.

Pie Pastry (2 crusts)

    2 cups flour
    1 teaspoon salt
    2/3 cup lard (or other solid shortening)
    about 1/3 cup ice water

Sift flour and salt and cut in the lard—using knives, pastry blender or

(Continued on the next page)

rubbing it in lightly with the fingertips—until the mixture has a coarse, mealy appearance. Moisten gently with the very cold water, using just enough to hold the dough together and let you gather it lightly in to a ball. Divide in two equal parts. Roll each on a floured board to about 1/8 inch thick, making each round about 2 inches more in diameter than the size of your pie pan (11 inches for a 9-inch pan). Fold and lift from the board, unfolding and easing to line the pan—be careful not to stretch it; trim. Fill. Fold, lift and fit top crust over the filling: trim, leaving 1 inch extra all around, and fold it under the edge of the bottom crust, pressing to seal. Vent the top with slits or pricked holes. Bake according to directions for specific pies.

For 1 crust: Halve the recipe; roll out, fit without stretching, trim with 1½ inches extra all around. Fold overlapping edge back on itself and flute with your fingertips to make a standing rim. Fill and bake.

Baked pie shell: Halve the basic recipe; roll out; trim to 1½ inches extra all around. Fit extra carefully into the pie pan: if it's stretched, the pastry will sag and shrink during baking; flute the stand-up rim, but *don't press* it against the edge of the pan. Prick many small holes on sides and bottom (to prevent steam bubbles in the cooked pastry). Bake about 15 minutes in a 450 oven. Cool before filling.

Leftover pastry: Cut in rounds or squares; put a dab of jam or jelly on each, fold over in half, seal the edges, prick to vent, and bake on a cookie sheet in a hot oven (425–450) for 10 or 15 minutes. Or roll out in two equal pieces; put grated natural Cheddar cheese on one, press the other on top of it; cut in small squares and bake in a hot oven until done.

Basic Berry Pie

> 3 cups fresh berries
> about 1 cup sugar
> ¼ cup sifted flour
> small dash of salt
> 2 tablespoons margarine or butter
> ¼ cup cold water
> pastry for 2-crust pie

Turn the berries into a bowl. Sift sugar, flour and salt together and gently mix with the berries. Turn into a pastry-lined 9-inch pie pan. Dot with the margarine, then pour the cold water over all. Cover with the

(Continued on the next page)

top crust, seal and crimp the edges and cut a vent in the top as usual. Bake in a 450 oven for 10 minutes; reduce heat to 375 and bake about 30 minutes longer. Cool before serving. Serves 8.

Unsweetened, whole frozen berries can be used in this good old rule; so may Cold-Water Canned blueberries, drained. Blackberries and blueberries take kindly to ¼ teaspoon of cinnamon and 1 tablespoon of lemon juice. The amount of sugar depends on the tartness of the berries.

Cranberry Pie

> 3 cups chopped cranberries
> 1½ cups sugar
> 1 tablespoon flour
> pinch of salt
> ¼ cup molasses
> ¼ cup hot water
> pastry for 2-crust pie

Cranberries may be coarsely chopped or simply cut in half. Add sugar, flour and salt. Add molasses to the hot water, then mix with cranberries. Bake in two crusts (top crust vented) in a 450 oven for 10 minutes; reduce heat to 350 and bake about 35 minutes longer. Cool before serving. Serves 8.

Either fresh or Cold-Water Canned berries may be used. This is an old-time favorite in New Jersey, Massachusetts and Wisconsin, where in the fall the ground looks like an old Paisley shawl with the russets and browns of the cranberry bushes.

Rhubarb Pie

> 3 cups sliced uncooked rhubarb
> 1 cup sugar
> 2 tablespoons flour
> few grains salt
> 1 beaten egg
> pastry for 2-crust, 9-inch pie

Combine first five ingredients. Put the mixture in a pastry-lined pie pan. Cover with the top crust, seal around the edge and cut or prick vents in the center. Bake in a 400 oven for about 50 minutes. Cool before cutting. Serves 8.

Maple Pumpkin Pie

    2 eggs
    3 tablespoons sugar
    ½ teaspoon ground ginger
    ¾ teaspoon cinnamon
    pinch of salt
    ¾ cup maple sirup
    1 cup undiluted evaporated milk
    2 cups canned pumpkin
    pastry for 9-inch bottom crust

Beat eggs well, then beat in sugar, spices and salt. Add the maple sirup, evaporated milk and pumpkin, beating all with a rotary beater. Pour into the pastry-lined pan and bake in a 450 oven for 10 minutes; reduce heat to 350 and bake about 40 minutes longer—or until a knife blade comes out clean when inserted near center. Serve cold or slightly warm with an honest natural Cheddar store cheese.

Applesauce Custard Pie

    1 cup sweetened applesauce, very smooth
    1 cup milk
    2 beaten eggs
    pinch of salt
    ¼ teaspoon ground nutmeg
    pie pastry for 1 crust

Beat eggs well, and combine with applesauce, milk and seasoning. Continue beating together until thoroughly blended, then pour into a pastry-lined, 9-inch pie pan and bake in a 425 oven for 10 minutes; reduce heat to 350 and continue baking for 25 minutes longer—or until the custard filling is set. (Test by inserting a table-knife blade near the center of the filling: if it comes out clean, the custard is done.) Cool. Serves 6 to 8.

Mince Pie: Use 3 cups Mincemeat or Green Tomato Mincemeat (in Preserves) and the basic 2-crust rule for a generous 9-inch pie. Bake 10 minutes at 425, reduce to 350 and bake 25 minutes more. Serve with natural Cheddar. Serves 8.

Oddments

Hay-time Switchel

    1 cup light brown sugar (raw)
    1 cup apple cider vinegar
    ½ cup light molasses
    1 tablespoon ground ginger
    1 quart cold water

Combine and stir well. Makes about 6 seven-ounce glasses.

    This can be refrigerated, but old-timers made it with cold, cold spring water, and said nothing quenched a thirst or cooled a dusty throat in haying time so well as this homey drink. (It's a good energy-restorer without promoting "cotton mouth" in athletes; cross-country skiers or snowshoers should drink it during a tour race with the chill off, though.)

Rhubarb Punch

    8 cups diced uncooked rhubarb, not peeled
    5 cups water
    about 2 cups honey or sugar
    6 oranges
    3 lemons
    a few drops of red food coloring, if needed
    1 quart pale dry ginger ale, chilled

Simmer the rhubarb in the water until it's quite mushy. Strain (use a muslin jelly bag if you want it really clear), and measure the liquid into an enameled kettle. Add 1/3 cup sugar or honey for each 1 cup of rhubarb juice, stirring over low heat until the sweetening has dissolved. Cool. Add strained juice of oranges and lemons plus food coloring; chill. Just before serving, add ginger ale carefully. Serve over ice cubes. Makes about 3½ quarts of punch before icing.

    In olden days, variations of this very good cooler were made for hill-country weddings where oranges and lemons were rare and ginger ale was virtually unheard of.

Index